Anglo-Americans in
Spanish Archives

ANGLO-AMERICANS
IN
SPANISH ARCHIVES

Lists of Anglo-American Settlers in
the Spanish Colonies of America

A Finding Aid

By
Lawrence H. Feldman

To

Miranda Buttimore

a friend

Table of Contents

5

1. Introduction

Spain and the Anglo-Americans

When Spain took over the French territory of Louisiana in 1766 she imposed a system of name taking that was already more than two centuries old. From the earliest days of her New World empire censuses were taken of colonists, of subjects, of soldiers, and most importantly, of taxpayers. A head tax was almost universal among her tribute-paying subjects, and it depended upon standard and regular censuses. Among these subjects eventually came to be included the Anglo-Americans entering her territory from the east. The foreigners coming into Spanish territory were required to pledge allegiance to the Spanish Crown. Their militia was inscribed on muster rolls. And, of course, censuses were taken of the new settlers noting their religion, family (if any), livestock, and slaves.

At first most of these English speakers became Spanish subjects thanks to the conquests of war. When Spain allied itself with the American colonists in their war for independence, its armies recaptured its old territories and some former French possessions in the Floridas. The frontier fort of Manchak, and the settlements at Baton Rouge and Natchez, fell in 1779. Pensacola was captured in 1781 and St. Augustine was ceded to Spain in 1784. During the two decades that these territories had been under British rule new colonists had come to settle its lands and develop its resources. Many, especially along the Gulf Coast and along the Mississippi, stayed after the territory reverted to Spanish control (Davis 1971; Tebeau 1971).

It was after the success of the American Revolution, and the open invitation of a Spanish government eager to fill the sparsely settled lands, that a second wave of aliens appeared in great numbers. Some were Tories fleeing republican government. Others were adventurers looking for excitement on the farthest frontier. Many were seeking unclaimed lands. With the consent and agreement of the Spanish government, entire new settlements were established, one of the best known of these being New Madrid. Others (e.g. Natchez), thanks to the huge influx of Anglo-Americans, might well be considered new towns.

7

Eventually all these lands would be lost to Spain. In 1798, after an aborted uprising of American settlers and under pressure from the United States government which claimed these lands as its own, Natchez and the fort of Nogales (at the site of Vicksburg, Mississippi) were evacuated by Spanish troops. Tombecbé, Alabama was abandoned the following year (1799) and New Orleans was sold by the French to the Americans in 1803. In 1810, eastern Louisiana (i.e. Baton Rouge) declared its independence from Spain and was promptly annexed by the Americans. In 1813 the port of Mobile was annexed by the United States, and finally in 1821 the remainder of Spanish Florida was transferred to American possession.

When early in the nineteenth century Louisiana and the Floridas came under United States rule, the records of the Hispanic administration went with the departing bureaucrats to the closest Spanish territory. Given their contents, which often contained papers of a rather private nature (e.g. reports from spies), it is no wonder that they were removed to Havana, Cuba.[1] As part of a process intended to bring all obsolete colonial files to a single repository, most were again moved, this time to Seville, Spain. In Seville, the investigator can still find letters, reports and census documents for the lands that eventually became the states of Missouri, Arkansas, Louisiana, Alabama, Mississippi and Florida in the Archivo General de Indias. This volume is intended to be an aid for those seeking information on family history in this and other archives of Spain.

---

[1]The official in charge of one of these archives, in response to an inquiry by a secret agent of the Spanish Crown, wrote "I believe that you are already well convinced that I have acted in a manner befitting a faithful servant of the honorable Spanish Monarchy and that I have fulfilled sincerely the duties which friendship imposes upon me. I have even done more, since I have sent to the Archives of Havana all that pertains to the previous history; feeling sure that before the United States shall be in a position to conquer that capital, you and I, Jefferson, Madison, with all the secretaries of the different departments . . . will have made many days' journeys on the voyage to the other world" (Hill 1916:xvii-xix).

2. The Archives of Spain

Working in Spanish Archives

"You . . . need to approach the Spanish archives with the proper mental spirit. They are archives, not libraries and even less genealogical society libraries. The vast majority of the papers are cataloged only by bundles of inclusive dates within general categories reflecting the administrative structure of the empire. There are very few card files listing individuals. . . . Nor are the archives staffed so that they can answer general inquiries by mail or do research for you, although they will supply copies of documents (if they have the equipment) if you can give an exact or very nearly exact citation. . .

"To illustrate my point, let me tell you about a poor fellow I met at Simancas in 1970. He was a beginning graduate student who had decided to use his 21-day European vacation for something more than just sightseeing. His topic was an obscure double agent from the late 16th century. In London the staff of the British Museum had been able to find his man in a file they had of the rather limited manuscript collections of that institution. When our student turned up in Simancas, he could not speak the language, nor read the script, and was terribly angered to find that the archive did not possess a card file (with typed cards, of course!) in which he might look up his man so that he could arrange to photocopy the relevant documents and be on his way to Lisbon. He left frustrated and angry at Spaniards" (Hoffman 1980).

One must also check the calendar. In the summer the Archivo General de Indias is closed on Saturdays from July 1st to October 1st. Most archives in central or southern Spain are closed in August. Local and national holidays will close all archives several times a year. Military archives close on days special for the armed forces. The months most likely to find archives open every working day are February and October.

9

Those who have not previously used Spanish archives should come prepared with letters of introduction from the nearest Spanish consul or appropriate United States institutions (e.g. universities). These, plus two or more small photographs (the kind one gets from the automat picture machines found in many of the major cities of Spain) will get you A Tarjeta de Investigator. This identity card, issued by the national archives administered by the Ministry of Education, will provide entry into most other public archives. Archives of the other ministries (e.g. military) require their own ID. A letter of introduction from the cultural attaché at the United States Embassy may be required for these other archives.

Archivo General de Indias

For those who search for information on family history, the Papeles de Cuba, in the Archivo General de Indias in Seville is the most rewarding. The Hill (1916) catalogue offers a useful point of departure to the contents of 928 of its boxes of documents (or legajos). Hill abstracts the contents of each Louisiana box. The present work, with its tabulations of names and commentary, is intended to provide more details on individuals than provided by Hill but it by no means exhausts all available data.

Surprises lurk in unlikely documents. Thus the Inventario del Archivo del Ouachita (AGI Cuba 137a), a listing of municipal manuscripts in a town of largely French beginnings, notes under "Contracts de Marriages" a marriage in 1794 between a British couple named John Davis and Nancy Harman. Documents are often sorted into files (or expedientes) for the different settlements, but one should not be misled by the apparent order of the boxes. A systematic search of all material from the appropriate years would be wise. Data on most topics can be found anywhere in a box; hence there is no substitute for a page-by-page survey of the documents.

Be prepared to find material in three languages-- English, French and Spanish. Those lacking a knowledge of French would be wise to bring a small dictionary for that language. In some boxes texts in French are more abundant than material in either Spanish or English.

Generally, the text is easy to read, and an expert familiar with the documents and the languages can scan an average of five boxes per day. "The greatest problems one has are the occasional carry-overs of gothic letters and the highly original and phonetic spellings and abbreviations. For example: December -- Diciembre in Spanish -- is sometimes rendered as "Xbre." "En" and "es" which begin words may be special signs while "n" is often omitted as a letter but supplied as a mark which appears to be a line over the preceding vowel. It is not hard to learn the more common abbreviations. . . A technique which also helps, when you find a letter or sign you cannot make out, is to look back into the text to see if a similar form appears in a word where you could understand it. . ." (Hoffman 1980).

There are sometimes problems arising from the condition of the documents themselves. The paper used often was not of the best quality and some documents listed in the Hill (1916) catalogue have been removed "for restoration" (Table 1). These are not available for study by the investigator. Other manuscripts may lack words once written on missing portions.

Table 1. Documents in Restoration

Location	Date	Source
Mobile AL	1788-07-05	Cuba 2361
Mobile AL	1789	Cuba 0202
Natchez MS	1788/12/31	Cuba 2361
New Orleans LA	1778	Cuba 0191
Opelousas LA	1788	Cuba 23
St. Louis MO	1795	Cuba 2364:70

The "Papeles de Cuba" are the provincial archives of the Spanish administration in Louisiana and West Florida. Documents sent to Spain when these lands still were Spanish colonies were often deposited in what became the papers of the "Audiencia de Santo Domingo" of the Archivo General de Indias. Pena y Camara et al (1968) provides a useful catalogue of their contents.[2] Less likely to have details on local individuals, this

---

[2]Loyola University (New Orleans) has microfilm copies of the Santo Domingo and Cuban papers for Louisiana (Hoffman 1980).

section is not as useful for studies of individual families.[3] The same may be said for the papers in section 9 (Estado) of the AGI. The documents noted here (Bermúdez Plaza 1949) are for events more likely to have an international dimension (e.g. arrests of foreign sailors).[4]

North America wasn't the only place where Anglo-American colonists intruded on Spanish territory. Belize, in Central America, was established as an autonomous British enclave under Spanish jurisdiction in the 1780s.[5] Reports of Spanish inspectors and British superintendents appear in the correspondence of the governors of Yucatan. They, like notes on earlier illegal British settlers, may be found in the papers of the Yucatan governors of the Audiencia de Mexico.[6] Other sections of the AGI (e.g. Audiencia de Santo Domingo) also contain manuscripts pertaining to Belize.

There is another source of information on northern Europeans that provides data not restricted to the former Spanish possessions in North America. Beginning with the era of the War for American Independence, and extending until the loss of the last American colonies at the end of the nineteenth century, colonial Hispanic ports were visited by ships flying the United States flag. There are many references to this shipping, often including the names of crew members, at the AGI. The last years of the eighteenth century and the first decade of the nineteenth are the most likely to yield information.

A quick means of locating information on these voyages is through the letters and reports of the governors of the different provinces (cf. Audiencia de Mexico, Audiencia de Guatemala, Audiencia de Santa Fe, etc.). The boxes containing eighteenth/nineteenth century "inventarios" of this correspondence can be very helpful in finding data. Most of these documents will be in very good condition, and very easy to read.

---

[3]Documents poorly preserved in the Papeles de Cuba, thanks to years of storage in a tropical climate, are sometimes duplicated in the Audiencia de Santo Domingo. Papers of the Audiencia de Santo Domingo are generally in very good condition.

[4]The Archivo Historico Nacional (Madrid) has an equivalent section (also called Estado) among its holdings (Gomez Canedo 1961). Other Louisiana manuscripts (1767-1792) may be found in the Biblioteca Nacional (Madrid) (Gomez Canedo 1961).

[5]The former name of this territory was British Honduras.

[6]The section of Estado, in the Archivo Historico Nacional, also contains papers on Belize, as does the AGS.

Also in the letters and reports of the governors may be found reports of foreign shipwrecks. Thus a 1729 document reports on the discovery of forty survivors, "among them men, children and women", on the southwest coast of Puerto Rico. Their ship, en route from Londonderry, Ireland for Philadelphia with Irish colonists for Pennsylvania, had been lost in a storm (AGI Santo Domingo 546). Another mishap, in 1649, deposited 133 Swedish colonists on the shores of the same island (Santo Domingo 156). This document provides the earliest listing of northern European names in the present work.

The AGI is open to the researcher from 8 AM to 2.45 PM Monday through Friday. When open on Saturdays the hours are 9 AM to 1.45 PM. Copy services are reliable but slow. It usually takes at least three weeks to fill an order.

Archivo General de Simancas

The Archivo General de Indias is the most important of Spanish colonial archives but it is by no means the only source of information on northern Europeans and Anglo-Americans who came into Spanish territory or service. The files at Simancas (near Valladolid) are the European counterpart of the Archivo de General de Indias. Established in 1545, they are the major repository for Spanish documents of the sixteenth, seventeenth and eighteenth centuries. Anglo-Americans who came to the attention of Spanish authorities under their European nationality would appear in these papers. But there are also colonial military records in Simancas. Twenty manuscript boxes (Secretaria de Guerra XII, legajos 6912-6932) document affairs in the Floridas and Louisiana between 1779 and 1807. They include details on the conquest of the Gulf Coast from the English and information on the American rebellion at Natchez. Also containing service records of soldiers from Florida and Louisiana Territory (legajos 7291-7292) and other military records from the same area dating from 1787 to 1800 (legajos 7299-7300), the AGS is the most important Spanish repository for Louisiana Territory outside of the Archivo General de Indias (Plaza Bores 1986).[7] Entrance requirements for the AGS are the

---

[7]The service records are for the Louisiana regiment (years 1787, 1791, 1792, 1794-97), the Mississippi volunteer infantry (years 1792, 1796, 1797), Mississippi militia (1792, 1796, 1797), New Orleans militia (1792, 1796, 1797). See Magdaleno (1958) for the names of the servicemen.

same as for the AGI. Hours open to the public tend to be fewer in the winter.

Archivo General Militar, Segovia

There are two sections that are of potential interest here. Section 1 (Personal) contains the service records of military officers and professional soldiers, beginning at the end of the sixteenth century. There are 55,250 boxes of documents in this section.   A published nine-volume index (Anonymous 1959-1963) for this material is available in the larger libraries of the United States and Europe. Section 9 (Justicia), the repository for army legal records (criminal cases, wills, etc.) since the eighteenth century, contains 5,010 boxes. The army archives at Segovia allow one to trace the careers of professional army officers, many of whom were northern European in origin. It is not the place to obtain data on part-time militia. For this, Simancas and the Papeles de Cuba in Seville will be far more useful.

The archive is open only from 9 to 1.30 Monday through Friday. It is closed on all military holidays. Investigators can not obtain permission to use the facilities in Segovia. They must first obtain an identification card at the Servicio Histórico Militar on Calle Mártires de Alcalá 9, Madrid. Using the manuscript number in the published catalogue, it is said to be possible to obtain a photocopy of a sought-after record by mail. The address of this archive is: Archivo General Militar, Alcázar de Segovia, Distrito Postal 40071, Segovia.

Archivo General de Marina "Don Alvaro de Bazan", Viso del Marques

This is the naval archive of Spain. Among the many sections into which its documentation is divided, that known as "Corso y Presas" has a special interest for North Americans. There are 108 boxes (2079-2187) with details on American ships and crews seized by the Spanish government between 1797 and 1831 (Guillén y Tato 1953; Vigón Sánchez 1985). In addition to published catalogues, there are computer printout listings at the Museo Naval (Montalban 2, Madrid) with further details on the holdings at Viso del Marques. An identification card, and an appointment to use the very limited facilities, should first be obtained at the Museo Naval before going out to Viso del Marques. One should also note that the Museo Naval archives (in Madrid), while not large, are very well organized and contain

14

material on all parts of the world. The extensive card files allow one to search for information on particular individuals.

Other Spanish Repositories

The national archives of Spain are divided into three broad groups. There are the so-called "Archivos Administrativos," of which there are eighty-seven. There are also the two "Archivos Intermedios," or temporary repositories (Archivo General de la Administración in Alcala de Henares and the Depósito Regional in Cervera), and the fifty-seven Archivos Históricos (Anonymous 1979). Beyond these there are the manuscript collections of the public libraries, to be found in almost every town of any size in Spain, and the various archives associated with the Catholic Church. For families of northern European origin, only a few of these will have any importance.

Most trade with the New World prior to the nineteenth century went through Seville or Cadiz. The Canary Islands (Tenerife and Gran Canaria) were ports of call well known to foreign shipping. Burgos, the headquarters of the wool trade, and the ports of the north (especially Corona, Santander, Bilbao, and San Sebastian) were always important for trade with northern Europe. All these communities are the most likely to have useful data in their local archives.

Archivos Históricos Provinciales usually hold the local notarial records (wills, sales of property, debt instruments, partnerships, powers of attorney, etc.). The huge collection of notarial records in Seville (21,678 books), dating from the fifteenth century, has its own repository. Currently (1990) this material is closed to the public while the archive undergoes renovations. In Cadiz the AHP, now in the Casa de Las Cadenas (c/Cristobal Colon 12), has notarial records (dating from the sixteenth century) from Cadiz (5,951 boxes), Puerto de Santa María (1,401 boxes), and other towns in this province. Unique among archives of this type, there is a card file for the years 1741 to 1775, and computer generated indices that give details on the contents of the notarial records. Work is continuing in expanding the years included in these files.

There are 4,138 boxes of notarial records (years 1505-1884) in the AHP of Tenerife and 2,754 (years 1509-1884) in the AHP of Las Palmas, Gran Canaria. Further detail on the Tenerife holdings may be found in Gonzalez Yanes (1984). The Consulado de Burgos, combining the functions of a guild and mercantile court, managed the wool trade with the north.

Its archives extend from 1462 to 1829. They may be found in the Archivo Diputacion Provincial (Palacio de la Diputación, Burgos). The Santander AHP, in addition to the usual notarial records (1540-1800s) has correspondence of the foreign consuls in that port with local officials (1791-1826).[8] A large collection of notarial records (1519-1862) exists in Coruna (Lopez Gomez 1988).[9] Details on other provincial archives are given in Hoffman (1980).

3. Using the Tabulations of Names

This work abstracts the essence of the genealogical data, the names of individuals and, where possible, other family data in a tabulated format. A survey of AGI manuscripts produced the ninety-three entries listed in Table 2. Of these, close to one-third pertain to settlements in Missouri (31%), Mississippi (27%) and Louisiana (26%), with the remainder of entries pertaining to Alabama (7%), Florida (5%), Belize in Central America (3%), and colonists intending to settle in what would become Delaware (1%).[10] This division is somewhat misleading, for the colonial administrative district of Natchez, which makes up the largest part of the Mississippi entries, included communities in what are now Louisiana and Alabama. Most Missouri entries are for the community of New Madrid.

Table 2. References: Location, Date, Source, Content

Alabama

Mobile AL	1781	Cuba 2359:415	surrender list
Mobile AL	1785	Cuba 0198b:984-985	allegiance oath
Mobile AL	1786/01/01	Cuba 2360:467on	census
Mobile AL	1795/12/31	Cuba 0212b:616-616r	slave owners
Tombecbé AL	1781	Cuba 2359:417-418	surrender list
Tombecbé AL	1791	Cuba 0052:1121	new arrivals

---

[8]For further details on the AHP Santander see Vaquerito Gil et al. (1980).

[9]These are part of the holdings of Archivo del Reino de Galicia. Further details on this archive may be found in Gil Merino (1976).

[10]These last were, of course, Swedes. Many of the other "Anglo" colonists were German in origin. Being that most members of these groups quickly assimilated into the Anglo culture, they are considered Anglos for the purposes of the present work.

Belize

Belize	1787/07/23	Sto Domingo 2687	inhabitants
Belize	1787/08/04	Sto Domingo 2687	inhabitants
Belize	1792	Mexico 3025:#48	land owners

Delaware

New Sweden DE 1649/09		Sto Domingo 0156	colonists

Florida

Pensacola FL	1781/05	Cuba 0200:916	census
Pensacola FL	1784	Cuba 2360:443-453	census
Pensacola FL	1820/07/25	Cuba 1944	census
Saint Augustine FL	1799	Cuba 0426	contributors
Saint Augustine FL	1797-1811	Cuba 0426	allegiance oath

Louisiana

Atakapas LA	1785	Cuba 2360:454-458r	census
Baton Rouge LA	1782	Cuba 0192:327	census
Baton Rouge LA	1786	Cuba 0192:328	census
Baton Rouge LA	1795	Cuba 0034:272	census
Baton Rouge LA	1799/04/24	Cuba 0106	contributors
Baton Rouge LA	1804/07/21	Cuba 0106	rebels
Baton Rouge LA	1805	Cuba 0106	petition
Bayou Sarah LA	1792	Cuba 2353:645-648	census
Bayou Sarah LA	1799/04/24	Cuba 0106	contributors
Galveztown LA	1796/01/28	Cuba 0212b:270	slave owners
Manchak LA	1791	Cuba 2362:432	census
Manchak LA	1795	Cuba 0034:273	census
New Feliciana LA	1793	Cuba 0208a:353	census
New Feliciana LA	1799/04/24	Cuba 0106	contributors
New Feliciana LA	1808	Cuba 0106	allegiance oath
New Orleans LA	1797-1803	Cuba 0548:536-579	allegiance oath
Opelousas LA	1785	Cuba 2360:458r-465	census
Opelousas LA	1794/11/10	Cuba 211a:717-717r	census
Rapids LA	1781/06/01	Cuba 0194:152-154r	surrender list
Rapids LA	1797a	Cuba 0208a:438	petition
Rapids LA	1797b	Cuba 0212b:554-555	petition
Tensa LA	1781	Cuba 2359:416	surrender list
Tensa LA	1785/01/12	Cuba 0198b:984-985	allegiance oath
Tensa LA	1787/01/04	Cuba 0200:773	allegiance oath

17

Mississippi

Natchez MS	1781/06/01	Cuba 0194:152-154r	surrender list
Natchez MS	1782/05/06	Cuba 0193a:519-524	census
Natchez MS	1783	Cuba 0261:116-119	allegiance oath
Natchez MS	1784	Cuba 0116:515-521	census
Natchez MS	1786	Cuba 0261:120-144	allegiance oath
Natchez MS	1787a	Cuba 0200:596-599	census
Natchez MS	1787b	Cuba 0013:28,75-85	allegiance oath
Natchez MS	1788	Cuba 0014:229-317a	militia rolls
Natchez MS	1788a	Cuba 0261:164-182	allegiance oath
Natchez MS	1788a	Cuba 2361:55-76	allegiance oath
Natchez MS	1788b	Cuba 0014	allegiance oath
Natchez MS	1789a	Cuba 0015:68a-429	allegiance oath
Natchez MS	1789a	Cuba 0261:184-188	allegiance oath
Natchez MS	1789b	Cuba 16:220-225	tobacco growers
Natchez MS	1790a	Cuba 2362:37on	allegiance oath
Natchez MS	1790a	Cuba 0016:248	new arrivals
Natchez MS	1790b	Cuba 2362:320-322	petition
Natchez MS	1792	Cuba 2353:645-648	census
Natchez MS	1795	Cuba 0188c	allegiance oath
Natchez MS	1796	Cuba 0212b:369-370	letter of thanks
Natchez MS	1799/04/24	Cuba 0106	contributors
Nogales MS	1793	Cuba 0047	new arrivals
Nogales MS	1794	Cuba 0047	new arrivals
Nogales MS	1795	Cuba 0127	new arrivals
Nogales MS	1795	Cuba 0048:581-589	new arrivals

Missouri

New Bourbon MO	1797	Cuba 2365:345	census
New Madrid MO	1790/04/15	Cuba 0016:367	allegiance oath
New Madrid MO	1789/04/22	Sto Domingo 2553:489	land owners
New Madrid MO	1789/11/30	Cuba 2361:318	allegiance oath
New Madrid MO	1790/01/27	Sto Domingo 2554	land owners
New Madrid MO	1790/10/25	Cuba 0121:599	allegiance oath
New Madrid MO	1790/12/31	Cuba 0121:600	allegiance oath
New Madrid MO	1790/12/31	Cuba 0017:f.62	census
New Madrid MO	1791/04/30	Cuba 2362:67-67r	new arrivals
New Madrid MO	1791/04/31	Cuba 0122a:416-427	allegiance oath
New Madrid MO	1791/07/25	Cuba 0122a:416-427	allegiance oath
New Madrid MO	1791/08/10	Cuba 0122a:416-427	allegiance oath
New Madrid MO	1791/08/19	Cuba 0122a:416-427	allegiance oath
New Madrid MO	1791/12/19	Cuba 0122a:416-427	allegiance oath
New Madrid MO	1792-1794	Cuba 0122b:926-947	allegiance oath
New Madrid MO	1793/11/20	Cuba 2363:315-316r	census
New Madrid MO	1793/03/31	Cuba 2363:313-314r	census
New Madrid MO	1793-1795	Cuba 2363:293-310	allegiance oath
New Madrid MO	1794	Cuba 0686:757-800	militia rolls
New Madrid MO	1794/12/02	Cuba 2363:317-319	census
New Madrid MO	1795/08/08	Cuba 0022:f.1031	new arrivals
New Madrid MO	1795/11/20	Cuba 2364:351-354	census

New Madrid MO	1796/07/1	Cuba 2365:334-339	census
New Madrid MO	1796/12/21	Cuba 2364:355-359	census
New Madrid MO	1796-1797	Cuba 0131:777-778	allegiance oath
New Madrid MO	1797/12/01	Cuba 2365:341-344	census
Saint Genevieve MO	1787-1789	Cuba 0016:216	new arrivals
Saint Louis MO	1782	Cuba 2360:210-213r	militia rolls
Saint Louis MO	1787-1789	Cuba 0016:216	new arrivals

An attempt was made to inspect all census documents for Louisiana Territory and the Floridas mentioned in Hill (1916). Those that contained numerous Anglo-American names were abstracted for this volume. Other censuses were predominantly French, especially those from Arkansas and western Louisiana (Table 3). Some merely provided a summary total of the number of inhabitants (Table 4). Neither of these last two categories have been copied for this volume.

Table 3. Listings of French Surnames[11]

Arkansas	1794/10/28	Cuba 2364:345-346r	census
Arkansas	1796/12/31	Cuba 2364:349-350r	census
Arkansas	1798/12/31	Cuba 2365:364-366	census
Atakapas LA	1799	Cuba 0216a:386	census
Avoyelles LA	1795	Cuba 198a:282-283	census
Avoyelles LA	1796	Cuba 212a:402	census
Costa Alemanes LA	1778	Cuba 0191	census
Mobile AL	1780	Cuba 193	census
Natchitoches LA	1781	Cuba 212a	census
Natchitoches LA	1795	Cuba 0211a:700-703	census
Natchitoches LA	1799	Cuba 0216a:606/607	census
New Orleans LA	1795	Cuba 0211a:56-66	census
New Orleans LA	1795/1798	Cuba 0212a	census
New Orleans LA	1796/11/14	Cuba 02212b:134-137r	census
Opelousas LA	1796	Cuba 2364	census
Ouachita (Fort Miro) LA	1795	Cuba 2364	census
Punta Cortada LA	1796/05/31	Cuba 0212b:506-509	census
San Juan del Bayu LA	1799	Cuba 0216a:869	census

Table 4. Summary Total Population Data

Baton Rouge LA	1805	Cuba 0142b	census
Mobile AL	1788	Cuba 1425a:90	census
Mobile AL	1805	Cuba 0142b	census
Natchez MS	1793/04/27	Cuba 2353:644	census

---

[11] Other Arkansas census documents cited in Hill (1916) but not seen by the author of this volume are those for 1777 (AGI Cuba 190), 1791 (AGI Cuba 204) and 1793 (AGI Cuba 123).

Natchez MS	1794	Cuba 0031	census
New Orleans LA	1799	Cuba 0216a:61	census
Pensacola FL	1788	Cuba 1425a:90	census
Pensacola FL	1802	Cuba 0059:948	census
Pensacola FL	1819	Cuba 1876b	census

The other category of documents systematically inspected for this work consists of oaths of allegiance to the Spanish Crown. Of the entries in Table 2, close to one-third are allegiance oaths and an equal amount are census manuscripts (for a total of 59% of the sample). Actually this under counts the total of allegiance oaths. Series of such documents, all from the same legajo and from the same or adjacent years, were placed under one entry in Table 2. Associated with them, and also grouped into a limited number of entries, were the reports of new arrivals.[12] These often were the same people who appeared in Allegiance Oaths.[13] Many of them arrived in Spanish territory floating downstream, on the Ohio and Mississippi rivers, from Pennsylvania, Kentucky and other portions of American territory. Most entries were recorded at the military post of Nogales (Vicksburg) or Natchez. No attempt was made to copy out the many documents in the Papeles de Cuba containing the names of emigrants arriving by sea at New Orleans or other ocean ports.

Other types of manuscripts represent accidental discoveries. Further work would doubtless reveal additional material. In this category are the lists of rebels, slave owners, landowners (in Belize), British settlers reporting their presence to the Spanish authorities after the capture of the British military posts (surrender lists), militia rolls, tobacco growers, voluntary contributors of funds (contributors), and signers of petitions and letters. Further search, especially in the papers of the Audiencia de Santo Domingo papers for Cuba, should reveal additional documents on foreigners who turned up in Hispanic territory due to shipwrecks.

Those seeking information on particular individuals should use the tabulations of names presented here to locate when and where that individual was active. Then, having located the person in time and space, they should use the published catalogues (and unpublished indices or

---

[12]Two manuscripts, Cuba 2362:37 (allegiance oaths) and Cuba 0016:248 (new arrivals) have been combined for purposes of reference under Natchez MS 1790a. Many of the entries may be found in both documents.

[13]Of these last, only a sample of those returning to the United States was copied for this volume.

inventarios in the archives) to identify the boxes that must be read to obtain further information. Only in this manner, by an actual reading of the documents, can one learn all that one can about individuals of the past.

4. The Settlements and the Names of Their Inhabitants

Systems of Reference and Procedures of Compilation

Each tabulated name comes from a primary source-- an original Spanish archival manuscript. For those who wish to examine a name in that document the citations are given in each Table. Please note that the citation is always in the abridged form of Location/Date (e.g. Mobile 1781). To get the manuscript section name and box number one must look under Location/Date in Table 2 (References). It should be noted that the numbers given after those of the box (e.g. Cuba 2359:415 with 2359 being the box number) are folio rather than page numbers. A folio is a sheet of paper on both sides of which there may be writing (the reverse indicated by "r"). Hence "616-616r" indicates that the document cited includes both sides of a single sheet of paper.

Where alternative forms of the same name are given, the form used here is always that normal for the native language of the speaker. Thus given "Jorge" and "George", or "Guillermo" and "William", these tables will use the English form for a native speaker of English. In other words if a man named John Smith is listed using only the Spanish form of his name (i.e. Juan Smith), that is the way he will appear in the text. But if he is listed as both Juan and John, then he will appear in the text only as John. Names which are illegible have been omitted from the listings. Quite frequently additional data (e.g. number of livestock per family) may be found in the original documents. All such associated data, of only marginal interest for genealogical studies, have been omitted from these listings.

Alabama

Mobile was established by the French in 1711. After little less than twenty years under English control, it was captured by Spanish forces on March 14, 1780. In the tabulations of Mobile names the nationality (N) of the inhabitants is indicated by "f" (French) or "a" (American). In a document of the Audiencia de Santo Domingo (1436), dated May 20, 1791, is another, partial, listing of the inhabitants of Mobile (Coker and Inglis 1980:54). This manuscript, the results of an inspection of Friar Cirilo de Barcelona, has not been examined for this present work. As noted elsewhere, Mobile was annexed by the United States on 15 April 1813.

Although San Esteban de Tombecbé (modern St. Stephan) began as a Spanish fort in 1789, English settlers had previously occupied these lands. A 1781 tabulation of their names is given here. Totals of male children (MC) or female children (FC) may be seen in the Tombecbé listing. Tombecbé lost its garrison with the evacuation of the Spanish on the 5th of February 1799. Indian nations held land independently of the European powers. Their inhabitants, particularly those noted in these lists, often included European settlers who were being governed according to Indian laws. Those nations providing immigrants were the Choctaw ("Chacta"), Chickasaw ("Chicacha"), and Cherokee ("Chevaquis").

Table 5. Mobile Names

	Names	Wife	Origin	Date	N
1	Alby, Juan			1795-12-31	
2	Alexandre, Francisco	single		1786-01-01	f
3	Alexandre, Juan Bautista	widow		1786-01-01	f
4	Arnot, Juan	x		1786-01-01	f
5	Baker, Jean			1785	
6	Baker, Jean	widow		1786-01-01	a
7	Barrom, Rubin	widow		1786-01-01	a
8	Barrow, Richard			1785	
9	Batt, Joseph La	x		1786-01-01	f
10	Battes, Ephrem	x		1786-01-01	a
11	Battes, Joseph	x		1786-01-01	a
12	Battes, Thomas	x		1786-01-01	a
13	Bautista, Pedro	x		1786-01-01	f
14	Bercachea, Josef		Cherokee	1781	
15	Bette, Thomas			1785	
16	Blackwell, Nathaniel	single		1786-01-01	a
17	Blocue, Maria.	widow		1786-01-01	f
18	Bodin, Luis	x		1786-01-01	f
19	Bodin, Monluis	x		1786-01-01	f
20	Bodro, Ma.	widow		1786-01-01	f
21	Bourguiynon, Maria	widow		1786-01-01	f
22	Bourie, Comette	single		1786-01-01	f
23	Bouzare, Joseph	x		1786-01-01	f
24	Bowkoz, Anthony			1785	
25	Brouillet, Juan	x		1786-01-01	f
26	Broutin, Naciso	x		1786-01-01	f
27	Brownin, Ben	x		1786-01-01	a
28	Cacaup, Nicolas	x		1786-01-01	f
29	Chastry, Juan	single		1786-01-01	f
30	Cheney, Belly	x		1786-01-01	a
31	Colin, Juan Baptista			1795-12-31	
32	Colins, Honore			1795-12-31	
33	Colman, Richard	x		1786-01-01	a
34	Colomb, Joseph	widow		1786-01-01	f
35	Conneway, Carlos	x		1786-01-01	a
36	Cooper, Henry		North Carolina	1781	
37	Cooper, William		North Carolina	1781	
38	Copengen, John			1781	
39	Coppingens, Jean	single		1786-01-01	a

		Names	Wife	Origin	Date	N
40	Corriere, Francisco	x		1786-01-01	f
41	Courege, Juan	single		1786-01-01	f
42	Cristian, Nicolas	x		1786-01-01	f
43	Dandley, James			1786-01-01	a
44	Davis, John	single		1786-01-01	a
45	Denuy, Carlos	x		1786-01-01	f
46	Dolain, Thomas			1785	
47	Doliye, Dom.	x		1786-01-01	f
48	Dubuisson, Francisco	x		1786-01-01	f
49	Duglese, Jean			1785	
50	Duiett, Luis	single		1786-01-01	f
51	Ellis, Carlos	x		1786-01-01	f
52	Fasre, Bautista	x		1786-01-01	f
53	Faure, Ma.	widow		1786-01-01	f
54	Folks, Jean	single		1786-01-01	a
55	Frasery, Alex		Choctaw nation	1781	
56	Gargaret, Maria	widow		1786-01-01	f
57	Geniez, Santiago	single		1786-01-01	f
58	Giroud, David		Choctaw nation	1781	
59	Hardrige, Joseph	single		1786-01-01	a
60	Helveson, Godefroy	x		1786-01-01	a
61	Hiteliliny, John		North Carolina	1781	
62	Hollinger, Adam	single		1786-01-01	a
63	Hudson, Thomas	single		1786-01-01	a
64	Hunney, Jean	x		1786-01-01	a
65	James, Benjamin		Choctaw nation	1781	
66	Johnson, Daniel	single		1786-01-01	a
67	Johnston, John	x		1786-01-01	a
68	Joyce, Juan	single		1786-01-01	f
69	Juran, Pedro	widow		1786-01-01	f
70	Kaller, Hennrique			1795-12-31	
71	Killcreass, Robert	x		1786-01-01	a
72	Kreis, Joseph	x		1786-01-01	f
73	Kreps, Agustin	x		1786-01-01	f
74	Kreps, Augustin			1795-12-31	
75	Kreps, Francisco	x		1786-01-01	f
76	Kreps, Francisco			1795-12-31	
77	Kreps, Hugo	x		1786-01-01	f
78	Kreps, Josef			1795-12-31	

	Names	Wife	Origin	Date	N
79	Kreps, Ma.	widow		1786-01-01	f
80	Kreps, Pedro	widow		1786-01-01	f
81	Kreps, Pedro			1795-12-31	
82	Kurtan, Cornelius	x		1786-01-01	f
83	Labon Cooper, Henry		North Carolina	1781	
84	Ladner, Mathurin	widow		1786-01-01	f
85	Ladvier, Santiago	x		1786-01-01	f
86	Lancette, Juan Bautista La	x		1786-01-01	f
87	Lancette, Luis	x		1786-01-01	f
88	Lancette, Pedro La			1786-01-01	f
89	Langerin, Pedro	single		1786-01-01	f
90	Lawrence, Jean	widow		1786-01-01	a
91	Lawrence, John			1785	
92	Lawrence, Joseph	widow		1786-01-01	a
93	Linder, Juan (the father)	x		1786-01-01	a
94	Linder, Juan (the son)	x		1786-01-01	a
95	Lorandiny, Juan Bautista	x		1786-01-01	f
96	Louisbourg	x		1786-01-01	f
97	Loysons, Guillermo	single		1786-01-01	a
98	Lusser, Luis	single		1786-01-01	f
99	Magee, Malcom		Chickasaw nation	1781	
100	Marcelin, Maria	widow		1786-01-01	f
101	Mazurier, Ma.	widow		1786-01-01	f
102	McCluer, Walter		North Carolina	1781	
103	McCoy, Donald			1785	
104	McGrew, James	x		1786-01-01	a
105	McGrew, John	x		1786-01-01	a
106	McNamie, Pedro	x		1786-01-01	a
107	McNanuer, Peter		North Carolina	1781	
108	Merrey, Francisco	single		1786-01-01	a
109	Merrey, Samuel	x		1786-01-01	a
110	Michel, Ma.	widow		1786-01-01	f
111	Miller, Robert	single		1786-01-01	a
112	Mims, Samuel	single		1786-01-01	a
113	Mincy, Shadrick	single		1786-01-01	a
114	Miny, Samuel			1781	
115	Mioux, Carlos	single		1786-01-01	f
116	Mitchell, Guillermo			1795-12-31	
117	Moreau, Joseph	single		1786-01-01	f

	Names	Wife	Origin	Date	N
118	Morin, Jose	x		1786-01-01	f
119	Moro, Agn.	x		1786-01-01	f
120	Narbonne, Antonio	x		1786-01-01	f
121	Nicolas, Antoine	x		1786-01-01	f
122	Odel, Juan		Cherokee	1781	
123	Ollbay, John		Tombecbe	1781	
124	Philipes, George	single		1786-01-01	a
125	Phillups, George	x		1786-01-01	a
126	Piburn, Jacob			1785	
127	Prouet, Besley	x		1786-01-01	a
128	Prowell, William	x		1786-01-01	a
129	Pyburn, Jacob	x		1786-01-01	a
130	Randon, John	x		1786-01-01	a
131	Rane, Cornellius	x		1786-01-01	a
132	Riddle, William			1781	
133	Rochan, Maria	widow		1786-01-01	f
134	Rolins, Ben	x		1786-01-01	a
135	Rubroce, Valentin	x		1786-01-01	f
136	Saucier, Cretien	x		1786-01-01	f
137	Saussaye, Santiago de la	x		1786-01-01	f
138	Skipper, Michel	single		1786-01-01	a
139	Smith, George			1781	
140	Snell, Henrique	single		1786-01-01	a
141	Snoddy, Wiliam		North Carolina	1781	
142	Steddam, Moyse	x		1786-01-01	a
143	Swafford, Thomas	single		1786-01-01	a
144	Swillevant, Patrick	single		1786-01-01	a
145	Tang, Joseph Chas	x		1786-01-01	f
146	Teflo, Mathias	x		1786-01-01	f
147	Tervin, Richard	single		1786-01-01	a
148	Texton, Askin		Choctaw nation	1781	
149	Trouittes, Pedro	x		1786-01-01	f
150	Walker, Abraham	x		1786-01-01	a
151	Watter, Thomas			1781	
152	Weckley, George	x		1786-01-01	a
153	Weekley, George			1781	
154	Wells, Edward			1785	
155	Wells, Edward	x		1786-01-01	a
156	Wheat, Thomas	x		1786-01-01	a

	Names	Wife	Origin	Date	N
157	Whitehead, Guillermo	single		1786-01-01	a
158	William, Ezechiel	x		1786-01-01	a
159	William, Guillermo	x		1786-01-01	a
160	Wimberley, John	widow		1786-01-01	a
161	Word, Daniel	single		1786-01-01	f
162	Yong, Henrique	single		1786-01-01	a

Table 6. Tombecbé Names

	Names	1781	1791	Wife	MC	FC
1	Abrams, Robert	x				
2	Alby, John	x				
3	Allen, Charles	x				
4	Alloy, John	x				
5	Atkinson, Thomas	x				
6	Azbel, John	x				
7	Azbill, John	x				
8	Bailey, Richard	x				
9	Baily, Thomas	x				
10	Baird, John	x				
11	Baley, Thomas	x				
12	Banks, Sutton	x				
13	Banks, Sutton	x				
14	Barette, Thomas		x	x		1
15	Barker, Yfren		x	x	4	3
16	Baskett, Thomas	x				
17	Bassett, Thomas	x				
18	Bastat, Thomas	x				
19	Bastian, John	x				
20	Billings, Ichebod	x				
21	Bird, Abraham	x				
22	Bird, Abraham	x				
23	Biskett, Thomas	x				
24	Bisson, Peter	x				
25	Booth, John	x				
26	Braday, John	x				
27	Bradley, Henry	x				
28	Bradley, Henry	x				
29	Brady, John	x				
30	Brazeal, Eliza	x				
31	Brown, James	x				
32	Brown, John	x				
33	Brown, John	x				
34	Brown, Thomas	x				
35	Brown, Thomas	x				
36	Bruner, Guillermo		x	x		
37	Bruner, Jorge		x	x		
38	Bruner, Juan		x	x	1	5
39	Buciguin, Francisco		x	x	1	3

	Names	1781	1791	Wife	MC	FC
40	Burnet, Daniel	x				
41	Burnet, William	x				
42	Burnett, William	x				
43	Carbank, Stephen	x				
44	Chauet, Richard	x				
45	Chiny, Guillermo		x	x	4	3
46	Chrote, Richard	x				
47	Clark, John	x				
48	Clark, John	x				
49	Collins, William	x				
50	Collins, William	x				
51	Cooper, Jack	x				
52	Cooper, James	x				
53	Cooper, Samuel	x				
54	Cooper, Samuel	x				
55	Cordrey	x				
56	Corek, Richard	x				
57	Cowan	x				
58	Cowen, Robert	x				
59	Craig, Thomas	x				
60	Creay, John	x				
61	Dawson, John	x				
62	Dawson, John	x				
63	Deforge	x				
64	Deforge, John	x				
65	Deforge, Peter	x				
66	Dyer, John	x				
67	Dyson, Leonard	x				
68	English, John	x				
69	Evans, John	x				
70	Farley, John	x				
71	Farmar, Robert	x				
72	Farrow, Alexander	x				
73	Farrow, Alexander	x				
74	Flood, Walter	x				
75	Foget, John	x				
76	Follon, Daniel	x				
77	Fooy, Benjamin	x				
78	Fordice, James	x				

	Names	1781	1791	Wife	MC	FC
79	Fullet, Mordicai	X				
80	Fulsom, Israel	X				
81	Fulson, Ebinezer	X				
82	Gallehan, Patrick	X				
83	Garner, John	X				
84	Georgius, Philip	X				
85	Gilchrist, John	X				
86	Gilcrist, Jesse	X				
87	Gilehart, Nimrod	X				
88	Gilliss, David	X				
89	Giroud, David	X				
90	Gon, Alexander	X				
91	Gone, Alexander	X				
92	Gordon, William	X				
93	Gordon, William	X				
94	Graige, Robert	X				
95	Gretion, John	X				
96	Grey, James	X				
97	Grey, James	X				
98	Grey, Robert	X				
99	Grotim, John	X				
100	Guity, Paty		X	widow	3	
101	Hackman, John	X				
102	Halede, Juan		X			
103	Hall, Henry	X				
104	Hall, Henry	X				
105	Hancock, John	X				
106	Hancock, John	X				
107	Hancock, William	X				
108	Hancock, William	X				
109	Hanon, Vartan		X	X		2
110	Harnest, John	X				
111	Harrel, Jacob	X				
112	Harrison, Peter	X				
113	Hat, Benllun		X	X	4	1
114	Hickman, John	X				
115	Highebottom, James	X				
116	Higinbottom, Samuel	X				
117	Hoggatt, James	X				

	Names	1781	1791	Wife	MC	FC
118	Holmes, Thomas	x				
119	Hood, Walter	x				
120	Hooper, Absalom	x				
121	Hoplon, Abner	x				
122	Horne, Benjamin	x				
123	Hubbard, Stephen	x				
124	Hull, Daniel	x				
125	Ironmonger, Joseph	x				
126	Jackson, James	x				
127	Jackson, John	x				
128	Jackson, Joseph	x				
129	Jackson, William	x				
130	Johnston, John	x				
131	Jones, Russel	x				
132	Joyner, William	x				
133	Keil, George	x				
134	Kemp, William	x				
135	Keston, Thomas	x				
136	Lemonan, Gilbert	x				
137	Littell, Abraham	x				
138	Little, Abraham	x				
139	Little, Thomas	x				
140	Llewellyn, Abedneys	x				
141	Lord, Gersham	x				
142	Lord, Graham	x				
143	Lott, Absalom	x				
144	Lott, John	x				
145	Lott, John	x				
146	Love, Thomas	x				
147	Loyd, Samuel	x				
148	Madier, Alexander	x				
149	Man, George	x				
150	Man, George	x				
151	Marcelas, Peter	x				
152	Marseles, Peter	x				
153	Mather, Alexander	x				
154	Mathews, Andrew	x				
155	Mathews, Andrew	x				
156	Mathews, John	x				

	Names	1781	1791	Wife	MC	FC
157	Matteair, Ezehel	X				
158	Mayes, Abraham	X				
159	McClendon, Joel	X				
160	McCurtin, Cornelius	X				
161	McCurtin, Cornelius	X				
162	McGilivray, Fendly	X				
163	McGillivray, Fineley	X				
164	McGillivray, James	X				
165	McGlaccon, Edmond	X				
166	McGlaccon, James	X				
167	McGlaughlin, John	X				
168	McGrew, John	X				
169	McIntire, John	X				
170	McIntosh, John	X				
171	McIntyre, Peter	X				
172	McMullen, James	X				
173	MCullogh, John	X				
174	Medows, Edward	X				
175	Megochan, John	X				
176	Mgillivray, James	X				
177	Mgillivray, Lachlin	X				
178	Mgillivray, Laughlin	X				
179	Mitchel, James	X				
180	Moatimer, Daniel	X				
181	Moore, Arthur	X				
182	Moore, Roger	X				
183	Morais, John	X				
184	Munford, James	X				
185	Muray, John	X				
186	Murray, John	X				
187	Nell, Jesse	X				
188	Nobles, Joshua	X				
189	Oats, Jeremiah	X				
190	Oats, William	X				
191	Oats, William	X				
192	Philips, Guillermo		X		2	3
193	Pieare, Thomas	X				
194	Pigg, John	X				
195	Poor, Patrick	X				

	Names	1781	1791	Wife	MC	FC
196	Poplin, James	x				
197	Powers, James	x				
198	Quithe, Benjamin	x				
199	Ratleff, William	x				
200	Raunsford, John	x				
201	Read, Hardy	x				
202	Reah, Frances	x				
203	Rees, Huberd	x				
204	Reese	x				
205	Reston, Thomas	x				
206	Rice, John	x				
207	Rims, Tobauyes		x	x	1	3
208	Routh, Benjamin	x				
209	Ruth, Benjamin	x				
210	Ruth, Francis	x				
211	Safold, Isham	x				
212	Safold, Joshua	x				
213	Satts, Henry	x				
214	Sawer, Ephraim	x				
215	Setodel, Simon		x	x	1	1
216	Simon, Gilbert	x				
217	Smith, John	x				
218	Smith, John	x				
219	Smith, Thomas	x				
220	Snell, Christopher	x				
221	Solomon, Hyam	x				
222	Speirs, William	x				
223	Stacy, Joshua	x				
224	Steel, John	x				
225	Stephens, William	x				
226	Stevens, William	x				
227	Stone, Simon		x	x	2	1
228	Strachan, Patrick	x				
229	Strachan, Patrick	x				
230	Stuart, Charles	x				
231	Stuart, Charles	x				
232	Sulivan, Cornelius	x				
233	Tavis, Joseph	x				
234	Taylor, Thomas	x				

	Names	1781	1791	Wife	MC	FC
235	Taylor, Thomas	x				
236	Tividale, William	x				
237	Tivodale, William	x				
238	Tompson, Laichy		x	x		
239	Troup, George	x				
240	Troup, George	x				
241	Tucker, Charles	x				
242	Turnbull, John	x				
243	Turnbull, Walter	x				
244	Turnbull, Walter	x				
245	Vansant, George	x				
246	Vanzant, Stephen	x				
247	Walker, Joel	x				
248	Walker, Joel	x				
249	Wall, Jesse	x				
250	Ward, Daniel	x				
251	Ward, Daniel	x				
252	Whitehead, Amos	x				
253	Whitehead, John	x				
254	Whitehead, John	x				
255	Williams, John	x				
256	Williams, Thomas	x				
257	Wino, Joseph	x				
258	Wynn, John	x				
259	Zoty, Juan		x	x	2	1

For the period prior to the official establishment of British settlements in Belize there are several manuscript sources mentioning individual settlers. One of the earliest is Morales (1714). Asterisks in Table 7 (Belize Names) indicate individuals whose land grants, if any, were not confirmed by the Spanish authorities.[14]

---

[14]Relacion de varios sugetos de los establecimientos yngles ... no es posible al senior Capitan General librarles licencias, 3 Septiembre 1792 (AGI Mexico 3025).

Table 7. Belize Names

	Name	Area	Date
1	Alder, Charles	*	1792
2	Antoiny, Scipio	*	1792
3	Armstrong, Charles	*	1792
4	Balentine, James	Valis*	1792
5	Banantine, James	*	1792
6	Bannaty		1787/07/23
7	Bard, Jon.		1787/08/04
8	Barrett, Mary	Valis	1792
9	Beatty, William		1787/07/23
10	Beatty, William		1787/08/04
11	Belisle, Marcus	Valis	1792
12	Bennantine, James	Sibun*	1792
13	Bennet, William	Valis	1792
14	Bennett, Marskal	islet in Bight lagoon, Valis	1792
15	Bess, Mary	Valis	1792
16	Blanford, Susana	Valis	1792
17	Blith, Peggy	Valis	1792
18	Blyth, John	*	1792
19	Bonner, George	Valis	1792
20	Boon, Tomas	Valis	1792
21	Bourke, Thomas		1787/07/23
22	Bourneau, Anth.	Valis	1792
23	Braken, Mary	Valis	1792
24	Bramwell		1787/08/04
25	Bramwell, Tomas	*	1792
26	Briggs, William	Valis	1792
27	Brislow, J.		1787/08/04
28	Briston, John		1787/07/23
29	Brohier, Robert	North River	1792
30	Brohun, G. B.		1787/07/23
31	Bule, Absolum		1787/07/23
32	Bull, Absolam	*	1792
33	Burd, Sutton	Valis	1792
34	Burell, Tomas	Valis	1792
35	Burke, Mary	Valis	1792
36	Burrell, Nelly	North River	1792
37	Burton, Jera.		1787/07/23
38	Cale, Nehemiah	Rio Nuevo	1792
39	Campbell, Archibald	Rio Nuevo	1792

	Name	Area	Date
40	Campbell, Colin		1787/07/23
41	Campbell, Graham	Bealerdam Creek*	1792
42	Cand, Jonathan	Valis	1792
43	Card, Jack	Valis	1792
44	Card, Jonathan	Valis*	1792
45	Catto, Thomas		1787/07/23
46	Catto, Thomas		1787/08/04
47	Catto, Tomas	Roaring Creek	1792
48	Clapper, John	Valis*	1792
49	Clark, Tomas	*	1792
50	Clarke, Thomas		1787/07/23
51	Costen, Isaac		1787/07/23
52	Crafts, Nicolas	Valis	1792
53	Crawford, George	*	1792
54	Crofts, William	Valis	1792
55	Cuningham, A.		1787/08/04
56	Cunningham, Andrew	Valis	1792
57	Cunningham, James	Valis	1792
58	Curry, John		1787/07/23
59	Dalton, Honera	Valis	1792
60	Davis, David	Valis	1792
61	Davis, Thomas		1787/07/23
62	Davis, Thomas		1787/08/04
63	Davis, Tomas	Valis	1792
64	Dawson, Nicholas	*	1792
65	Dean, John		1787/07/23
66	Dean, John		1787/08/04
67	Derison, Abraham	Valis	1792
68	Devalt		1787/07/23
69	Devalt		1787/08/04
70	Dodd, Geo.		1787/08/04
71	Dodd, George		1787/07/23
72	Dodd, George	Spanish Creek*	1792
73	Dondak, C. C.		1787/08/04
74	Dondele, C.C.		1787/07/23
75	Douglas, Rob		1787/07/23
76	Douglas, Robert	Valis	1792
77	Dulendue, Solas	*	1792
78	English, Robert	Valis	1792

	Name	Area	Date
79	Ernest, Catherine	*	1792
80	Euins, David	Valis	1792
81	Evans, David		1787/07/23
82	Evans, David		1787/08/04
83	Farell, Benjamin	Valis	1792
84	Fitzgibbon, Gerard		1787/08/04
85	Flowers, William	*	1792
86	Fowler, Sarah	Valis	1792
87	Gabourel, Joshua	North River	1792
88	Gale, Matias	Rio Nuevo, Valis	1792
89	Garbutt, John	Valis	1792
90	Garnet, Ben		1787/08/04
91	Garnett, Benjamin		1787/07/23
92	Gautier, Ed.		1787/08/04
93	Geddis, Molly	Valis	1792
94	Gelmour, Simeon	Valis	1792
95	Gladina, Nancy	Valis	1792
96	Golson, John	Valis	1792
97	Gordon and Potts	Valis	1792
98	Gordon, James	Rio Nuevo	1792
99	Gordon, John		1787/07/23
100	Grace, Ann	Rio Nuevo	1792
101	Graham, Thomas		1787/07/23
102	Grant, James	Valis*	1792
103	Green, Rodolphus	Valis	1792
104	Greenhill, Josiah		1787/07/23
105	Hamilton, L.		1787/08/04
106	Hamilton, Lehas		1787/07/23
107	Hamilton, Murray	*	1792
108	Harris, Lewis	Valis	1792
109	Hayes, Malachy		1787/07/23
110	Haylock, Elenor	Valis	1792
111	Hayluck, Francis	Valis	1792
112	Hecky, Francis	Valis*	1792
113	Hekey, Francis	*	1792
114	Hemming, Nancy	Valis	1792
115	Henry, Peter		1787/07/23
116	Henry, Peter		1787/08/04
117	Henry, Peter	*	1792

	Name	Area	Date
118	Hernon, Eduard	Valis	1792
119	Hewlete, Daniel	*	1792
120	Hewlett, George	*	1792
121	Hewm, James	Valis	1792
122	Hill, E. F.		1787/07/23
123	Hill, E. F.		1787/08/04
124	Hill, Edward Felix	Valis*	1792
125	Hoare, Richard		1787/07/23
126	Hoare, Richard	Rio Nuevo	1792
127	Hodge, Eleanor Maria	*	1792
128	Hodskinson, Robert	Spanish Creek	1792
129	Holmes Smith, John	Rio Nuevo	1792
130	Holmes, Frank	*	1792
131	Hones, Enry	Rio Nuevo	1792
132	Hoover, Jacob	Valis*	1792
133	Hughes, Ediward	Spanish Creek	1792
134	Hume, James		1787/07/23
135	Hume, James		1787/08/04
136	Humphries, Liv		1787/07/23
137	Humpreys, Garnet	Valis	1792
138	Inasey, Eml		1787/07/23
139	Jackson, Thomas		1787/07/23
140	Jackson, Thomas		1787/08/04
141	Jackson, Thomas 2nd		1787/07/23
142	Jackson, William	Sibun	1792
143	Jefferies, Henrrieta	Rio Nuevo	1792
144	Jefferies, Mrs.	Valis	1792
145	Jones, Basil		1787/07/23
146	Jones, Edivard	Rio Nuevo	1792
147	Jones, Henri	Rio Nuevo	1792
148	Jones, Joare	*	1792
149	Jones, John	Valis	1792
150	Jones, Joshua	Valis	1792
151	Kaye, Robert	*	1792
152	Kier, William	*	1792
153	Kirkpatrick, Allan		1787/08/04
154	LaCorie, J. P.		1787/07/23
155	Lamb, David	Valis	1792
156	Lanless, John		1787/08/04

	Name	Area	Date
157	Lawless, John	Valis	1792
158	Leck, John		1787/07/23
159	Love, William	Valis*	1792
160	Lovell, George	Valis	1792
161	Markalls, Henry	Valis	1792
162	Marton, Abner	Valis	1792
163	Maskall, Henry		1787/07/23
164	Maskall, Henry	Valis	1792
165	Massen, Edmund	Valis*	1792
166	Mauger, George		1787/08/04
167	Mauger, George	*	1792
168	Mayer, L.		1787/08/04
169	McAuley Bartlet, Nda	Spanish Creek	1792
170	McElhanny, William		1787/07/23
171	McKensie, Frederick	Rio Nuevo*	1792
172	McLan, A		1787/08/04
173	Meighan, Edmund	Valis	1792
174	Meighan, Edward		1787/07/23
175	Meighan, Lau.		1787/07/23
176	Meighan, Laurence	Bealerdam Creek*	1792
177	Mercer		1787/07/23
178	Meyer, Levis		1787/07/23
179	Mivelt, John	Valis	1792
180	Moodie, Geo.		1787/07/23
181	Moodie, George	Valis	1792
182	Moodie, Henry		1787/08/04
183	Mucklehany, William	Valis	1792
184	Mucklehenny, William		1787/08/04
185	Nauger, Geor		1787/07/23
186	Neal, John		1787/07/23
187	Neal, John		1787/08/04
188	Neal, John	Valis	1792
189	Obrien, R. F.		1787/08/04
190	Obrien, R. J.		1787/07/23
191	Obrien, Richard H.	Rio Nuevo	1792
192	Park, Tomas	*	1792
193	Parker		1787/07/23
194	Parker, Phineas	*	1792
195	Parslon, Thomas		1787/07/23

	Name	Area	Date
196	Paslow, Tomas	Valis	1792
197	Pattenett, Ann	Valis	1792
198	Penn, William	Valis	1792
199	Penn, William	Valis*	1792
200	Perez, Clarinda	Valis	1792
201	Perez, Maria	Valis	1792
202	Perry, Robert		1787/07/23
203	Pingadery, William	Sibun*	1792
204	Pitt, Charles	Valis*	1792
205	Pitt, William	*	1792
206	Plyapper, G.		1787/07/23
207	Potts, John		1787/07/23
208	Potts, John	Rio Nuevo	1792
209	Potts, Thomas & Ann Grace	Rio Nuevo	1792
210	Potts, Tomas	Rio Nuevo	1792
211	Price, Samuel	Valis	1792
212	Purnell, William		1787/07/23
213	Rayburn, George	Valis	1792
214	Remington, Thomas		1787/07/23
215	Remington, Thomas		1787/08/04
216	Remington, Tomas	*	1792
217	Remington, Tomas Arnold	Valis	1792
218	Rennalls, Mr.	*	1792
219	Robertson, Tomas	Valis	1792
220	Robinson, Josias	*	1792
221	Robinson, Thomas		1787/07/23
222	Sandwich, R. B.		1787/08/04
223	Sebastian, Daniel	Valis	1792
224	Sebastian, William	Valis	1792
225	Seddon, James		1787/07/23
226	Seddon, James		1787/08/04
227	Seddon, James	*	1792
228	Sharp, Robert	Sibun	1792
229	Shaw, James	Valis	1792
230	Siwasey, Emanuel	Rio Nuevo	1792
231	Slusher, John Jacob	Sibun*	1792
232	Smith, Clarisa	Valis	1792
233	Smith, Dury	Valis	1792
234	Smith, J. A.		1787/07/23

	Name	Area	Date
235	Smith, John H.		1787/08/04
236	Smith, Tomas	*	1792
237	Snelling, Richard	Valis*	1792
238	Southerland, William	Valis	1792
239	Stan, Steven	Valis	1792
240	Stenner, Henry	Valis	1792
241	Sullivan, Jakson	Valis	1792
242	Tampson, George	*	1792
243	Taylor, Grace	Valis	1792
244	Taylor, Joe	*	1792
245	Teeling, Luve		1787/07/23
246	Tellet, William	Valis	1792
247	Thomson		1787/07/23
248	Thomson, J. L.		1787/08/04
249	Tiving, John	Valis	1792
250	Tizon, William	Valis	1792
251	Tonoston, Lidya	Valis	1792
252	Tood, Noel	Valis	1792
253	Trapp, Jean	Valis	1792
254	Troy, Mrs.	Valis	1792
255	Tucker, Betty,	Valis	1792
256	Tucker, William		1787/07/23
257	Tucker, William		1787/08/04
258	Tucker, William	Barton Creek, Valis	1792
259	Tyler, Elisha	Valis	1792
260	Usher, William		1787/07/23
261	Usher, William		1787/08/04
262	Usher, William	Valis	1792
263	Usher, William	Valis*	1792
264	Valentine, Jas.		1787/08/04
265	Vernon, Noel	Little Salt Creek	1792
266	Victory, Mary	Valis	1792
267	Von Horn, Charles	Valis	1792
268	Wagner, John	*	1792
269	Wagner, Mary	Valis	1792
270	Wall, Ester	Rio Nuevo	1792
271	Watkins, W.		1787/08/04
272	Watkins, Walter		1787/07/23
273	White, Mary	Valis	1792

	Name	Area	Date
274	White, William	Valis	1792
275	Williams, Elizabeth	Valis	1792
276	Willson, John		1787/08/04
277	Wilson, Hugh		1787/07/23
278	Wilson, Hugh	Rio Nuevo	1792
279	Winter, Steven	Valis	1792
280	Witter, John		1787/07/23
281	Worgal, Benjamin	Rio Nuevo*	1792
282	Wright, Samuel	Rio Nuevo*	1792
283	Yarborough, J. D.		1787/07/23
284	Yarborough, James	Sibun	1792
285	Young, Aaron	Sibun	1792
286	Younger, John	Valis	1792

Delaware

On the eighth of September 1649, the governor of Puerto Rico received notice of a ship anchored between the two adjacent islets of Vieques and Palominos. The governor sent two frigates to investigate, shortly after which the wind blew the foreign ship into the shallow water adjacent to Palominos islet where it was lost. The frigates brought back to San Juan "the 133 persons, men and women of the Kingdom of Sweden who were going to a settlement of theirs on the coast of Florida, as can be seen in their dispatches a copy of which has been sent to Your Majesty".[15] Salvaged by divers from the Swedish ship (the Rooster of Sweden) "were 18 pieces of artillery, 14 of iron of 8 and 6 pounds of caliber and 4 small ones of bronze which served as pedreros, 2 cables, one anchor, and the very badly treated sails. One of the men on the ship was the intended named Governor of the said populations".[16]

Prisoners were sent to Seville and thence back to Sweden, thirty individuals arriving in Stockholm on the 8th of February 1651. Others were still on Puerto Rico as late as the 14th of August 1654. Further details on the baggage of individual colonists and crewmen may be seen in the text (AGI Santo Domingo 156) in both the letter of the Puerto Rican governor and the lawsuit instigated by the Swedes to recover property stolen by the Spaniards. Unfortunately there are only eighteen names. Possibly other individuals may be named in the papers of the governors of Cuba and the Audiencia de Santo Domingo. Prisoners would have traveled through these jurisdictions on their way back to Spain. Papers of the Casa de Contratacion, the normal repository for foreign prisoners remitted from the Indies, and those of the Secretariat handling foreign affairs (Secretaria de Estado), might contain further information. The former are in a separate section of the Archivo de Indias while the second may be seen at the Archivo de Simancas.

---

[15]The colonists were headed for the colony of New Sweden, lands today within the modern state of Delaware. Reference is from AGI Santo Domingo 156.

[16]Pedreros, as the term is used here, are small bore cannon capable of using stones as ammunition.

Table 8. Swedish Names, 1649

	Names	position
1	Amondson, Hans	gobernador
2	Benson, Mons	el M. jeto
3	Burgis, Engiber	
4	Cleanp, Hans	furriero
5	Hans, Engri	
6	Jonson, Daniel	sto. mayor
7	Jonson, Juan	Buchovn
8	Jonson, Lars	scribe
9	Laus, Brita	
10	Lucque, Jochin	
11	Nels, Margarita	
12	Nertunes, Matias	el predicant
13	Nilson, Anderi	contestable
14	Olius, Brita	
15	Olius, Segri	
16	Parson, Jans	Sturkex
17	Peri, Catalina	
18	Ysa, Ana	

47

Florida

Unlike most of the areas covered in this volume, there is an excellent genealogical guide to the Spanish censuses of western Florida (Coker and Inglis 1980). It provides a very careful and complete reproduction of the material available in the AGI Papeles de Cuba. Therefore, with one exception, the purpose of the tabulations provided here is merely to assist the researcher in checking for individuals who subsequently, or previously, moved to another part of the Spanish colonial empire. The exception is a census for 1781 Pensacola that was somehow overlooked by Coker and Inglis. In Table 9 (Pensacola Names) MS refers to marital status (m= married, w= widowed, s= single), MC is male children and FC female children. The date and references of the entries in Table 10 (Pensacola Occupation and Origins) may be determined by searching for the same names in Table 9.

Most of the eastern Florida papers, particularly those for Saint Augustine, were never sent to Spain. "The archive of the office of the governor of East Florida was turned over in its entirety to the United States government, and consequently no papers from that office were found among the Papeles de Cuba. This archive was placed in charge of the United States Land Office and suffered many years of neglect. Finally in 1905 these papers were discovered by the Librarian of Congress, and arrangements were made to have them deposited in the Library of Congress, where they are now to be found" (Hill 1916:xxiii).

Table 9. Pensacola Names

	Name	MS	Age	MC	FC	Date
1	Acosta, Dolores	m	33			1784-06-20
2	Acosta, Domingo	m	21		1	1784-06-20
3	Acosta, Francisca	m	29			1784-06-20
4	Acosta, Josefa Maria	m				1784-06-20
5	Acosta, Pedro	m	35		2	1784-06-20
6	Acostra, Andres	m	30			1784-06-20
7	Aguila y Madrid, Maria	m	30			1784-06-20
8	Aguilar, Juan	m	47	2	2	1784-06-20
9	Alba, Pedro		22			1784-06-20
10	Alvarado, Francisco	m	24	1		1784-06-20
11	Amer, John					1781-05
12	Amos, James					1781-05
13	Armas, Jose Luis	m	45	4	4	1784-06-20
14	Armas, Rosa de	m	28			1784-06-20
15	Arnold, Mathew					1781-05
16	Arou, Paula	w	38			1820-05-25
17	Artiles, Cecila	m	34			1784-06-20
18	Ballester, Juan	s	31			1784-06-20
19	Balls, Cenon	s	27			1784-06-20
20	Banoz, Carlos	m	58	1	3	1820-05-25
21	Bario, Manuel	m	34		2	1820-05-25
22	Bay, Elihu Hall					1781-05
23	Bell, Mrs.					1781-05
24	Benitez, Josefa	m	42			1784-06-20
25	Besley, Barth W.					1781-05
26	Betancour, Margarita	m	35			1784-06-20
27	Bichs, Luci	w	39		1	1784-06-20
28	Bird, Julia	w	40			1820-05-25
29	Bolona, Antonio	m	56		1	1784-06-20
30	Bonet, Francisco					1784-06-20
31	Botello, Lazaro	m	27	1		1784-06-20
32	Brashier, Jesse					1781-05
33	Bronnahan, Juan	m	35			1820-05-25
34	Bruce, James					1781-05
35	Buciere, Miguel	m	41	2	2	1784-06-20
36	Burns					1781-05
37	Burns, William					1781-05
38	Cablar, Juan	s	48			1784-06-20
39	Cabral, Matias	m	31	1		1784-06-20

	Name	MS	Age	MC	FC	Date
40	Cabrera, Baltazar	m	26	1	1	1784-06-20
41	Cabrera, Josefa	m	46			1784-06-20
42	Calder, Maria	m	16			1784-06-20
43	Carballo, Julian	s				1784-06-20
44	Carmen Rodriquez, Maria	m	21			1784-06-20
45	Carol, Richard					1781-05
46	Carranza, Jose Antonio	s	31			1784-06-20
47	Castejon, Leon	m	26			1784-06-20
48	Castilleja, Alonso	s	28			1784-06-20
49	Castillo, Antonio	m	49		2	1784-06-20
50	Castillo, Juan	m	26	1	1	1784-06-20
51	Chrystil					1781-05
52	Cisesc, Ricardo	s	33			1784-06-20
53	Clifton, William					1781-05
54	Colino, Nicolas	w	45			1784-06-20
55	Colomin, Antonio	s	26			1784-06-20
56	Comins, Tomas	m	30	2	1	1784-06-20
57	Constant, Jacobo	s	50			1784-06-20
58	Cooper, Guillermo	w	67			1820-05-25
59	Corona, Vicent					1781-05
60	Coruna, Jose Antonio	m	30	1	1	1784-06-20
61	Coruna, Josefa	m	30			1784-06-20
62	Crozer, Mary					1784-06-20
63	Crozer, Mary					1781-05
64	Danes, Luisa	m	48			1820-05-25
65	Delfin, Francisco	m	50			1784-06-20
66	Dobf, Isabel		23			1784-06-20
67	Domingo, Jose		42	1	1	1784-06-20
68	Donald, Robert					1781-05
69	Duncan, William					1781-05
70	Duran, Bartolome		30			1784-06-20
71	Espino, Ana	w	48	1		1784-06-20
72	Espino, Rosalia	w	41	2		1784-06-20
73	Fairlie, James					1781-05
74	Falcon, Jose	m	50	1	2	1784-06-20
75	Falconer, John					1781-05
76	Fardif, Constancio		40			1784-06-20
77	Farmer, Mrs					1781-05
78	Felipa, Antonia	m	38			1784-06-20

	Name	MS	Age	MC	FC	Date
79	Fernandez, Juan	m	60			1820-05-25
80	Ferrea, Antonio	s	22			1784-06-20
81	Fiallo, Maria	m	50			1784-06-20
82	Filibert, Pedro	m	60			1820-05-25
83	Finley, John					1781-05
84	Forneret, Luis		49			1784-06-20
85	Fuente, Rosalia de la	w	48	1		1784-06-20
86	Galan, Rita	m	42			1784-06-20
87	Gallegos, Juan	m	26			1784-06-20
88	Gane, Luis	m	28			1784-06-20
89	Garcia, Francisco		31			1784-06-20
90	Garden, William					1781-05
91	Garzon, Antonio	w	56	2		1784-06-20
92	Gauld, George					1781-05
93	Gil, Miguel	w	48			1784-06-20
94	Glover, John					1781-05
95	Gonzalez, Andrea	m	41			1784-06-20
96	Gonzalez, Bernardo	m	33	3	1	1784-06-20
97	Gonzalez, Gabriel	s	24			1784-06-20
98	Gonzalez, Maria	m	30			1784-06-20
99	Gorman, Nancy	s	47			1820-05-25
100	Griest, James					1781-05
101	Grinud, Maria	w	40			1820-05-25
102	Guerir, Maria Ignacia		20	1	1	1784-06-20
103	Guerra, Salvador	m	50	3	3	1784-06-20
104	Gutierrez Arroyo, Francisco	s	21			1784-06-20
105	Halley, David					1781-05
106	Hannay, John					1781-05
107	Heardford, Maria	s	33			1820-05-25
108	Hernandez, Catalina	w	48			1784-06-20
109	Hernandez, Manuel	m	41	1	1	1784-06-20
110	Herr, Luisa	m	22			1784-06-20
111	Hidalgo, Isabel	m	40			1784-06-20
112	Hodge, David					1781-05
113	Irving, James					1781-05
114	Johnson, William					1781-05
115	Johnstone, Captain					1781-05
116	Kirk, James					1781-05
117	Kirton, Thomas					1781-05

	Name	MS	Age	MC	FC	Date
118	Labalet, Felicitas	m	19			1784-06-20
119	Labalet, Mariana	m	18			1784-06-20
120	Lacombe, Vicente	s	45			1784-06-20
121	Lacosta, Juan	s	26			1784-06-20
122	LaFont, Maria	m	26			1784-06-20
123	LaRua, Francisco					1784-06-20
124	Legg, Henry					1781-05
125	Lengro, Mariana		26	1		1784-06-20
126	Lincken, Cristina	s	30			1784-06-20
127	Lorimer, John					1781-05
128	Macario, Maria	m	16			1784-06-20
129	Macullagh, Alex					1781-05
130	Marin, Gabriel	m	42	2	1	1784-06-20
131	Marreno, Julian	m	30		3	1784-06-20
132	Marshall, William					1781-05
133	Martin, Allen					1781-05
134	Martin, Domingo	m	39		1	1784-06-20
135	Martin, Juana	m	40			1784-06-20
136	Martinez, Josefa	m	19			1820-05-25
137	Mauricio, Antonio	s	34			1784-06-20
138	Melos, Ysabel		32	3	1	1784-06-20
139	Mendez, Francisca	m	22			1784-06-20
140	Mesa, Gabriel	m	22	1	1	1784-06-20
141	Mesias, Maria		38			1784-06-20
142	Mitchell, John					1781-05
143	Molina, Hermenegildo	s	25			1784-06-20
144	Molna, Bernardo	s	23			1784-06-20
145	Moore, Alexander					1781-05
146	Moore, John					1781-05
147	Mora, Alonso	o	12			1784-06-20
148	Mora, Antonia	o	12			1784-06-20
149	Morales, Jose Pablo	m	42	2		1784-06-20
150	Morel, Jose	s	11			1820-05-25
151	Morel, Maria	m	21			1820-05-25
152	Morel, Rebeca	w	40			1820-05-25
153	Moreno, Maria	m	16			1784-06-20
154	Murray, James					1781-05
155	Negas, Diego	m	39	1	1	1784-06-20
156	Negri, Josefa	m	22			1784-06-20

	Name	MS	Age	MC	FC	Date
157	Neil, Arthur					1781-05
158	Nieves, Petronila de las	m	32			1784-06-20
159	Nitsenger, Mariana	w	40	4	4	1784-06-20
160	Noriega, Jose		26			1784-06-20
161	Olsa, Francisca	m	24			1784-06-20
162	Oneil, Arturo					1784-06-20
163	Oneil, James					1781-05
164	Orgalles, Pablo	m	20			1784-06-20
165	Ortega, Joaquin	m	30	1		1784-06-20
166	Ortiz, Manuel	w	25			1784-06-20
167	Paden					1781-05
168	Paines, Francisco	m	41	1	1	1784-06-20
169	Palmes, Maria	m	17			1784-06-20
170	Pashley, Thomas					1781-05
171	Patricio, Domingo	s	34			1784-06-20
172	Patricio, Maria	m	33			1784-06-20
173	Paz, Paula de la	m	44			1784-06-20
174	Perauas, Joaquin		50			1784-06-20
175	Perera, Catalina	m	63	1		1784-06-20
176	Perez, Maria	m	49			1784-06-20
177	Peston, Bobe	s	50			1820-05-25
178	Pichol, Ysabel	m	60	1	2	1784-06-20
179	Pino, Manuel	m	28		2	1784-06-20
180	Porter					1781-05
181	Preta, Ysabel	m	37			1784-06-20
182	Publico, Jose	m	36		2	1784-06-20
183	Puente, Pedro de la	s	34			1784-06-20
184	Purcell, Joseph					1781-05
185	Quintana, Miguel	m	35	3	1	1784-06-20
186	Rainsford, Captain					1781-05
187	Ramos, Melchora	m	46			1784-06-20
188	Ramsey					1781-05
189	Rendon, Juana	m	61			1820-05-25
190	Reyes, Jose de los	w				1784-06-20
191	Ribas, Gabriel	m	28			1784-06-20
192	Richardson, Barnd.					1781-05
193	Rivera, Jayme		60			1784-06-20
194	Roche, Enrique	m	26		1	1784-06-20
195	Rodriguez, Juan		25			1784-06-20

	Name	MS	Age	MC	FC	Date
196	Rodriguez, Sebastiana	m	29			1784-06-20
197	Rodriquez, Dorotea	m	40			1784-06-20
198	Rodriquez, Jacobina	w	42		1	1784-06-20
199	Rodriquez, Juan	m	50	3	2	1784-06-20
200	Roxas, Jose	m	40	4	1	1784-06-20
201	Roxas, Maria	m	27			1784-06-20
202	Ruby, Juan Roberts		55			1784-06-20
203	Ruiz, Juan	m	24			1784-06-20
204	Safold, Ysham					1781-05
205	Sage, Ramon	s	32			1784-06-20
206	Samacona, Juan	s	35			1784-06-20
207	Sanabria, Jose	s	46			1784-06-20
208	Sanchez, Carlos	m	26			1784-06-20
209	Sanchez, Jose	m	24	2	1	1784-06-20
210	Sanchez, Maria Isabel	m	23			1784-06-20
211	Sans, Julio	s	19			1820-05-25
212	Sardina, Angela	m	25			1784-06-20
213	Sardina, Josefa	m	18			1784-06-20
214	Sardina, Manuel	m	62			1784-06-20
215	Sawsaloni, Geronimo		30			1784-06-20
216	Seamark, Richard					1781-05
217	Shakespear, Stephen					1781-05
218	Simpson, John					1781-05
219	Smit, Guillermo	m	40			1784-06-20
220	Smit, Maria	m	40			1784-06-20
221	Sola, Jose	s	29			1784-06-20
222	Soto, Maria Josefa	m	19			1784-06-20
223	Stephens, Phenix					1781-05
224	Stephenson, John					1781-05
225	Stequet, Judit	w	33	1		1784-06-20
226	Stokes, John					1781-05
227	Strachan, Patrick					1781-05
228	Strother, Arthur					1781-05
229	Suarez Vera, Antonio	m	46	1		1784-06-20
230	Suarez, Antonio	m	40	2		1784-06-20
231	Suarez, Catalina	m	33			1784-06-20
232	Suarez, Josefa	m	25			1784-06-20
233	Suarez, Juan	m	40	3		1784-06-20
234	Suarez, Pedro	m	37	2	1	1784-06-20

	Name	MS	Age	MC	FC	Date
235	Sucie, Beltran	s	30			1784-06-20
236	Swanson, Peter					1781-05
237	Tait, Robert					1781-05
238	Toral, Matias	s				1784-06-20
239	Travis, James					1781-05
240	Tresgel, Jose	s	71			1784-06-20
241	Underwood, Thomas					1781-05
242	Vega, Estevan	m	39	2	1	1784-06-20
243	Velet, Pedro de					1784-06-20
244	Vera, Francisca de	m	40			1784-06-20
245	Wadman					1781-05
246	Walters, William					1781-05
247	Watson, George					1781-05
248	Wegg, Edmund Rush					1781-05
249	Wesner, Leonard					1781-05
250	White, Isaac					1781-05
251	White, John					1781-05
252	Whiteside, William					1781-05
253	Williams, Isabel	s	30			1820-05-25
254	Wilton, William					1781-05
255	Wirare, Maria	m	36			1820-05-25
256	Wisner, Leonard					1781-05
257	Ymeson, Juan		29			1784-06-20
258	Ynernanity, Juan	m	34			1820-05-25
259	Ynzer, Juan Francisco	s	60			1820-05-25
260	Ysla, Gaspar	s	22			1784-06-20

Table 10. Pensacola Occupations and Origins

	Name	Occupation or Status	Origin
1	Acosta, Francisca	wife Domingo Martin	
2	Acosta, Josefa Maria	wife Baltazar Cabrera	
3	Aguila y Madrid, Maria	wife Diego Negas	
4	Amer, John	ordnance	
5	Amos, James	ordnance officer	
6	Armas, Rosa de	wife Jose Pablo Morales	
7	Arnold, Mathew	bricklayer	
8	Arou, Paula	dressmaker, white	Virgina
9	Artiles, Cecila	wife Pedro Acosta	
10	Banoz, Carlos	shopkeeper, white	Normandy
11	Bario, Manuel	shepherd ("merino"), white	Virginia
12	Bay, Elihu Hall	provisional Secretary	
13	Bell, Mrs.	widow	
14	Benitez, Josefa	wife Josefa Benitez	
15	Besley, Barth W.	carpenter	
16	Betancour, Margarita	wife Bernardo Gonzalez	
17	Bird, Julia	farmer, white	Carolina
18	Brashier, Jesse	yeoman	
19	Bronnahan, Juan	medical doctor, white	England
20	Bruce, James	"Counsellor"	
21	Buciere, Miguel		England
22	Burns	military housekeeper	
23	Burns, William	pilot	
24	Carmen Rodriquez, Maria	wife Francisco Alvarado	
25	Carol, Richard	planter	
26	Chrystil	military housekeeper	
27	Clifton, William	Chief Justice	
28	Cooper, Guillermo	farmer, white	Carolina
29	Corona, Vicent	liquor retailer	
30	Coruna, Josefa	wife Jose Antonio Coruna	
31	Crozer, Mary		England
32	Crozer, Mary	widow	
33	Danes, Luisa	wife Pedro Filibert	Luisiana
34	Donald, Robert	merchant	
35	Duncan, William	court cryer	
36	Fairlie, James	merchant	
37	Falconer, John	merchant	
38	Farmer, Mrs	widow	
39	Felipa, Antonia	wife Jose Roxas	

	Name	Occupation or Status	Origin
40	Fernandez, Juan	retired sergeant	Seville
41	Filibert, Pedro	farmer, white	Germany
42	Finley, John	schoolmaster	
43	Galan, Rita	wife Antonio Bolona	
44	Garden, William	commisary	
45	Gauld, George	magistrate	
46	Glover, John	carpenter, master	
47	Gorman, Nancy	laundress, mulatto	Baltimore
48	Griest, James	pilot	
49	Grinud, Maria	white	England
50	Halley, David	military housekeeper	
51	Hannay, John	tailor	
52	Heardford, Maria	dressmaker, mulatto	Virginia
53	Herr, Luisa	wife Enrique Roche	
54	Hodge, David	"counsellor"	
55	Irving, James	carpenter	
56	Johnson, William	pilot	
57	Johnstone, Captain	military gentleman	
58	Kirk, James	planter	
59	Kirton, Thomas	gaoler	
60	LaFont, Maria	wife Tomas Comins	
61	Legg, Henry	carpenter	
62	Lorimer, John	magistrate	
63	Macario, Maria	wife Carlos Sanchez	
64	Macullagh, Alex	provisional Marshal	
65	Marshall, William	magistrate	
66	Martin, Allen	Comptroller	
67	Martinez, Josefa	wife Juan Bronnahan, white	Pensacola
68	Melos, Ysabel		England
69	Mendez, Francisca	wife Domingo Acosta	
70	Mitchell, John	magistrate	
71	Moore, Alexander	planter	
72	Moore, John	barman	
73	Morel, Jose	son Rebeca Morel, white	Mobile
74	Morel, Maria	wife Manuel Bario, white	Virginia
75	Morel, Rebeca	white	Virginia
76	Murray, James	general clerk	
77	Negri, Josefa	wife Juan Castillo	
78	Neil, Arthur	ordnance officer	

	Name	Occupation or Status	Origin
79	Oneil, James	shopkeeper	
80	Paden	military housekeeper	
81	Pashley, Thomas	tailor	
82	Patricio, Maria	wife Juan Rodriquez	
83	Paz, Paula de la	wife Antonio Suarez V.	
84	Perera, Catalina	wife Manuel Sardina	
85	Peston, Bobe	carpenter, black	Charleston
86	Pichol, Ysabel	wife Francisco Delfin	
87	Porter	military housekeeper	
88	Preta, Ysabel	wife Miguel Buciere	
89	Purcell, Joseph	surveyor general	
90	Rainsford, Captain	military gentleman	
91	Ramsey	military housekeeper	
92	Rendon, Juana	wife Juan Fernandez	Ireland
93	Richardson, Barnd.	carpenter	
94	Rodriguez, Sebastiana	wife Matial Cabral	
95	Rodriquez, Dorotea	wife Antonio Suarez	
96	Roxas, Maria	wife Miguel Quintana	
97	Safold, Ysham	deputy surveyor	
98	Sans, Julio	laundress, mulatto	Georgia
99	Sardina, Angela	wife Gabriel Mesa	
100	Seamark, Richard	shopkeeper	
101	Shakespear, Stephen	shopkeeper	
102	Simpson, John	tavern keeper	
103	Smit, Guillermo		England
104	Smit, Maria	wife Guillermo Smit	
105	Stephens, Phenix	constable	
106	Stephenson, John	"counsellor"	
107	Stokes, John	baker	
108	Strachan, Patrick	planter	
109	Strother, Arthur	magistrate	
110	Suarez, Catalina	wife Estevan Vega	
111	Suarez, Josefa	wife Manuel Pino	
112	Swanson, Peter	merchant	
113	Tait, Robert	magistrate	
114	Travis, James	carpenter	
115	Underwood, Thomas	house keeper	
116	Velet, Pedro de	priest	
117	Wadman	military housekeeper	

	Name	Occupation or Status	Origin
118	Walters, William	yeoman	
119	Watson, George	ship carpenter	
120	Wegg, Edmund Rush	Attorney General	
121	Wesner, Leonard	blacksmith	
122	White, Isaac	tailor	
123	White, John	carpenter	
124	Whiteside, William	blacksmith	
125	Williams, Isabel	laundress, mulatto	Carolina
126	Wilton, William	ordnance officer	
127	Wirare, Maria	wife Carlos Banoz	Philadelphia
128	Wisner, Leonard	blacksmith	
129	Ynernanity, Juan	trader, white	Scotland
130	Ynzer, Juan Francisco	barber, white	Germany

Table 11. Saint Augustine Names

	Name	Date	Origin
1	Abadia, Juan	1797 (1797/1811)	France
2	Abadie, Juan	1797 (1797/1811)	France
3	Addison, Juan	1803 (1797/1811)	Ireland
4	Aguilar, Diego	1799	
5	Aguirre, Felipe	1799	
6	Aguirre, Tomas	1799	
7	Alkin, David	1799	
8	Albarez, Geronimo	1799	
9	Allinbill, Avery	1802 (1797/1811)	
10	Alvarez, Jose	1811 (1797/1811)	Portugal
11	Andrews, Roberto	1799	
12	Artheley, Federico	1799	
13	Atkinson, Andres	1799	
14	Avery, Duley	1802 (1797/1811)	
15	Ayreault, Juan	1798 (1797/1811)	
16	Bacon, Jose	1804 (1797/1811)	Massachusetts
17	Baker, Woothbon	1803 (1797/1811)	Americano
18	Bayer, Adam	1805 (1797/1811)	United States
19	Beespuner, Guillermo	1803 (1797/1811)	Americano
20	Belnap, Asa	1803 (1797/1811)	Americano
21	Bendicho, Manuel Fernandez	1799	
22	Berta, Antonio	1799	
23	Bethune, Fanguhan	1803 (1797/1811)	England
24	Bettes, Samuel	1803 (1797/1811)	Americano
25	Bird, Bartolome	1811 (1797/1811)	Ireland
26	Blunt, Reddin	1799	
27	Bonmaison, Juan	1803 (1797/1811)	France
28	Bousguet, Juan Jose	1799	
29	Boutemps, Francisco	1797 (1797/1811)	France
30	Brachelos, Juan	1799	
31	Brenan, Jayme	1803 (1797/1811)	Ireland
32	Brosua, Pedro	1798 (1797/1811)	France
33	Brown, Ephrain	1803 (1797/1811)	Americano
34	Bugley, Francisco	1799	
35	Bungo, Jose Pero	1799	
36	Bushnell, Eusebio	1799	
37	Butman, Estevan	1800 (1797/1811)	Americano
38	Cain, Guillermo	1799	
39	Capo, Antonio	1799	

	Name	Date	Origin
40	Capo, Lorenzo	1799	
41	Carns, Ricardo	1803 (1797/1811)	Americano
42	Carter, Tomas	1799	
43	Carter, Ysaac	1799	
44	Cashen, Santiago	1799 (1797/1811)	
45	Castro y Fenner, Bartolome	1799	
46	Chapman, Roberto	1803 (1797/1811)	Americano
47	Clarke, Juan	1803 (1797/1811)	United States
48	Collier, Thomas	1804 (1797/1811)	England
49	Connor, Bryan	1806 (1797/1811)	Charleston
50	Cook, Guillermo	1797 (1797/1811)	Virginia
51	Cook, Jorge	1799	
52	Cooper, Juan	1806 (1797/1811)	Virginia
53	Coplan, Jonatas	1803 (1797/1811)	Scotland
54	Corifario, Pedro	1799	
55	Cortes, Dimas	1799	
56	Costa, Benito	1797 (1797/1811)	France
57	Cowen, Robert	1799	
58	Craig, Guillermo	1799 (1797/1811)	United States
59	Crambert, Agustin	1797 (1797/1811)	France
60	Creighthon, Alexandro	1799	
61	Creswell, Simeon	1803 (1797/1811)	Prussia
62	Crosbi, Miguel	1799	
63	Cuarse, Enrique	1805 (1797/1811)	Philadelphia
64	Daniel, William	1805 (1797/1811)	Philadelphia
65	Davis, Juan	1803 (1797/1811)	Americano
66	Davis, Samuel	1803 (1797/1811)	Americano
67	Dean, Patricio	1804 (1797/1811)	
68	Delany, Juan Guillermo	1799 (1797/1811)	Denmark
69	Diaz Bernix, Pedro	1799	
70	Diaz, Rafael	1799	
71	Druon, Pedro	1797 (1797/1811)	France
72	Drysdale, Alexandro	1803 (1797/1811)	Scotland
73	Dubarny, Estevan	1798 (1797/1811)	France
74	Duncan, Santiago	1811 (1797/1811)	Scotland
75	Duprat, Alexandro	1808 (1797/1811)	
76	Easton, Guillermo	1802 (1797/1811)	Americano
77	Edwards, Juan	1799	
78	Ellis, Mateo	1803 (1797/1811)	Americano

	Name	Date	Origin
79	Elsworth, Guillermo	1802 (1797/1811)	
80	Entzalgo, Juan Antonio	1799	
81	Ewing, Adam	1802 (1797/1811)	
82	Facio, Francisco Felipe	1799	
83	Faune, Francisco	1797 (1797/1811)	France
84	Fay, Carlos	1802 (1797/1811)	France
85	Ferguson, Anselmo	1803 (1797/1811)	Americano
86	Fernandez, Jose	1799	
87	Fitz Patrick, Guillermo	1799	
88	Fitz, Guillermo	1797 (1797/1811)	Ireland
89	Fitz-Gerald, Gulillermo	1799	
90	Fitzpatrick, Balentin	1799	
91	Fleming, Jorge	1799	
92	Fleuny, Juan	1797 (1797/1811)	France
93	Florian, Martin	1798 (1797/1811)	France
94	Flotard, Juan	1801 (1797/1811)	France
95	Foley, Juan	1803 (1797/1811)	Ireland
96	Fontune, Miguel	1799 (1797/1811)	USA
97	Frost, Yese	1799	
98	Fuentes, Ramon	1799	
99	Gallup, Paleg	1802 (1797/1811)	
100	Garvan, David	1800 (1797/1811)	
101	Geigor, Juan	1805 (1797/1811)	Pennsylvania
102	Gigante, Miguel	1797 (1797/1811)	France
103	Gilbert, Robert (son)	1799	
104	Gilbert, Roberto (son)	1799	
105	Gomez, Jose Maria	1799	
106	Gonzalez, Santiago	1799	
107	Gould, Patricio	1803 (1797/1811)	
108	Green, Pedro Wilkes	1804 (1797/1811)	Americano
109	Green, Samuel	1805 (1797/1811)	Isle of Providence
110	Griffin, Christobal	1805 (1797/1811)	England
111	Guadarrama, Matheo	1799	
112	Guilland, Rene	1797 (1797/1811)	France
113	Guillet, Miguel	1798 (1797/1811)	
114	Hall, Jayme	1799	
115	Hall, Nataniel	1799	
116	Hand, Oren	1804 (1797/1811)	Americano
117	Hardy, Carlos	1804 (1797/1811)	

	Name	Date	Origin
118	Harrison, Samuel	1799	
119	Hening, Sorge	1803 (1797/1811)	Americano
120	Henricks, Ysaac	1799	
121	Henry, Juan Lazaro	1800 (1797/1811)	United States
122	Hernandez, Gaspar	1802 (1797/1811)	
123	Hernandez, Martin	1799	
124	Hibberson, Jose	1809 (1797/1811)	England
125	Hogan, Ruben	1799	
126	Holderpok, Jorge	1803 (1797/1811)	Americano
127	Holmes, Jaime M.	1799 (1797/1811)	
128	Hoopen, Juan	1802 (1797/1811)	Maryland
129	Hosnur, Youngs	1806 (1797/1811)	Charleston
130	Hoyt, Moses	1802 (1797/1811)	Americano
131	Huestas, Antonio	1799	
132	Huet, Gregorio Jose	1799	
133	Hull, Abiather	1802 (1797/1811)	
134	Hull, Ambrocio	1801 (1797/1811)	Americano
135	Hunt, Jose	1803 (1797/1811)	Americano
136	Hurlbert, Daniel	1803 (1797/1811)	Americano
137	Hutchinson, Santiago	1803 (1797/1811)	Americano
138	Israel, Jose	1803 (1797/1811)	Americano
139	Jaksson, Montague	1803 (1797/1811)	
140	Keen, Jayme	1803 (1797/1811)	Ireland
141	Kelly, Pedro	1802 (1797/1811)	United States
142	Kelsall, Juan	1803 (1797/1811)	England
143	Key, Felipe	1802 (1797/1811)	Maryland
144	King, Sara	1799	
145	King, Silas Saul	1799 (1797/1811)	
146	Kingsley, Zefanias	1803 (1797/1811)	Louisiana
147	L'Henry, Morris	1803 (1797/1811)	
148	Lacey, Antonio	1799	
149	LaFont, Guillermo	1798 (1797/1811)	France
150	Lamb, Tomas	1799	
151	Land, Guillermo	1803 (1797/1811)	Americano
152	Lasagna, Mariano	1799	
153	Laurence, Guillermo	1802 (1797/1811)	Scotland
154	Lavallete, Antonio	1797 (1797/1811)	France
155	Leslie, Juan	1799 (1797/1811)	Scotland
156	Letphens, Manuel	1803 (1797/1811)	England

	Name	Date	Origin
157	Loftin, Juan	1799	
158	Long, Jorge (son)	1802 (1797/1811)	Americano
159	Loomis, Guillermo R.	1805 (1797/1811)	
160	Lorente, Jose	1799	
161	Lorenzo, Juan	1798 (1797/1811)	France
162	Lynch, Miguel	1803 (1797/1811)	Ireland
163	Macqueen, Juan	1799	
164	Main, Jacobo	1803 (1797/1811)	
165	Mancier, Antonio	1802 (1797/1811)	United States
166	Mañe, Juan	1799	
167	Marcos, Samuel Menden	1802 (1797/1811)	
168	Marshall, George	1804 (1797/1811)	England
169	Martin, Enrique Burill	1802 (1797/1811)	United States
170	Martinez, Martin	1799	
171	Matair, Luis	1799	
172	Matanza, Antonio	1799	
173	Maudsley, Pedro	1803 (1797/1811)	England
174	Mauran, Juan R.	1804 (1797/1811)	Halle, Saxony
175	Maxey, Roberto	1799	
176	Maza, Fernando de la	1799	
177	McCleery, Juan	1800 (1797/1811)	
178	McCormick, David	1803 (1797/1811)	Ireland
179	McDowell, Donald	1800 (1797/1811)	Scotland
180	McEnery, Jayme	1801 (1797/1811)	
181	Mcenery, Juan	1801 (1797/1811)	Ireland
182	McFee, Constancia	1804 (1797/1811)	Georgia
183	McHandy, Robert	1803 (1797/1811)	Scotland
184	McIntosh, Juan H.	1803 (1797/1811)	Georgia
185	McLean, Juan	1804 (1797/1811)	Americano
186	McNeil, Orniel	1803 (1797/1811)	
187	McQueen, Santiago	1803 (1797/1811)	Scotland
188	Meers, Samuel	1799 (1797/1811)	
189	Meigs, Daniel	1804 (1797/1811)	Americano
190	Mercer, Heyland	1804 (1797/1811)	Americano
191	Migal, Jose	1798 (1797/1811)	France
192	Miles, Samuel	1804 (1797/1811)	Americano
193	Mills, Urias	1803 (1797/1811)	Americano
194	Moore, Davis	1799	
195	Moreno, Juan Bautista	1797 (1797/1811)	France

	Name	Date	Origin
196	Morris, Ricardo	1799	
197	Morrison, David	1799 (1797/1811)	
198	Morrison, Jorge	1804 (1797/1811)	Virginia
199	Mudey, Pedro Francisco	1803 (1797/1811)	Scotland
200	Munro, Santiago	1803 (1797/1811)	Scotland
201	Murray, George	1802 (1797/1811)	Scotland
202	Nadar, Andres	1798 (1797/1811)	France
203	Nagin, Jose	1799	
204	Nazaret, Nicolas	1799	
205	Nelson, Ambrosio	1799	
206	Nichols, Silas	1803 (1797/1811)	Americano
207	Northrop, Guillermo	1802 (1797/1811)	United States
208	Noyues, Gregorio	1799	
209	Oak, Pedro	1803 (1797/1811)	Sweden
210	Oleary, Daniel	1801 (1797/1811)	United States
211	Oneylly, Margarita	1799	
212	OReylly, Miguel	1799	
213	Ormond, Santiago	1803 (1797/1811)	Scotland
214	Ortega Diaz, Jose	1799	
215	Otis, Thomas	1803 (1797/1811)	Americano
216	Papi, Gaspar	1799	
217	Parker, Jacobo	1801 (1797/1811)	United States
218	Parker, Jose	1803 (1797/1811)	United States
219	Parraig, Guillermo	1797 (1797/1811)	France
220	Paulsen, Jorge	1803 (1797/1811)	Americano
221	Pearson, Juan	1803 (1797/1811)	Americano
222	Peirce, Phinihas	1804 (1797/1811)	Americano
223	Pelot, Jayme	1799	
224	Pemblaut, Juan	1797 (1797/1811)	France
225	Pengree, Rebeca	1799	
226	Perez, Francisco	1799	
227	Pinto, Miguel	1808 (1797/1811)	Bordeaux
228	Ponce de Leon, Jose	1799	
229	Ponell, Antonio	1799	
230	Pons, Ana	1799	
231	Pons, Mathias	1799	
232	Potter, Obadiah	1805 (1797/1811)	
233	Poupan, Rene	1798 (1797/1811)	France
234	Pratt, Juan	1804 (1797/1811)	Americano

	Name	Date	Origin
235	Prichard, Roberto	1799	
236	Reed, Ezra	1807 (1797/1811)	Charleston
237	Reed, Lebbeus	1805 (1797/1811)	New York
238	Regger, Juan	1802 (1797/1811)	United States
239	Reyes, Domingo	1799	
240	Roberto, Carlos	1803 (1797/1811)	Paris
241	Robinson, Samuel	1802 (1797/1811)	Americano
242	Rodriguez Caler, Pedro	1799	
243	Rodriguez, Lorenzo	1799	
244	Rodriquez, Santos	1799	
245	Ross, Roberto	1800 (1797/1811)	Americano
246	Rovina, Francisco	1799	
247	Roza, Jose	1800 (1797/1811)	
248	Ruiz del Campo, Antonio	1799	
249	Ruiz del Canto, Francisco	1799	
250	Ruvell, Samuel	1799	
251	Samson, Santiago	1804 (1797/1811)	Ireland
252	Samuel, Juan	1803 (1797/1811)	England
253	Sanchez, Francisco	1799	
254	Sanchez, Juan	1799	
255	Sanchez, Miranda	1799	
256	Sargent, Samuel	1804 (1797/1811)	
257	Saunderson, Alexandro	1803 (1797/1811)	Ireland
258	Senet, Mariana	1804 (1797/1811)	Santo Domingo
259	Sharp, Juan	1811 (1797/1811)	England
260	Sheredan, Dionisio	1803 (1797/1811)	Ireland
261	Sheridan, Owen	1799 (1797/1811)	
262	Sherman, Smauel	1803 (1797/1811)	Americano
263	Sibbald, Jorge	1804 (1797/1811)	Americano
264	Simpson, Walter	1804 (1797/1811)	Americano
265	Smith, Esequias	1805 (1797/1811)	United States
266	Spicer, Cristopher	1799	
267	Strepha, Jaime	1803 (1797/1811)	Ireland
268	Sturge, Thomas	1803 (1797/1811)	
269	Suarez, Gregorio	1799	
270	Tate, Eduard	1799	
271	Taylor, Jorge	1803 (1797/1811)	Americano
272	Teasdale, Isaac	1802 (1797/1811)	England
273	Tening, Pedro	1799	

	Name	Date	Origin
274	Tianopoly, Juan	1799	
275	Todd, Londsay	1803 (1797/1811)	Scotland
276	Tomas, Francisco	1803 (1797/1811)	Americano
277	Tompson, Ysom	1799	
278	Toole, Jayme	1803 (1797/1811)	Ireland
279	Tornells, Pedro	1799	
280	Torp, Juan	1799	
281	Trasuer, Federico	1802 (1797/1811)	Americano
282	Travers, Guillermo	1799	
283	Travers, Thomas	1799	
284	Trenor, Patricio	1803 (1797/1811)	Ireland
285	Trunbull, Juan	1803 (1797/1811)	
286	Turdue, Guillermo	1799	
287	Ulmen, Guillermo	1804 (1797/1811)	Americano
288	Underwood, Jehu	1804 (1797/1811)	
289	Utley, Elisha	1802 (1797/1811)	United States
290	Vaughan, Daniel	1799	
291	Velazaluce, Sebastian	1799	
292	Vermonnet, Juan	1804 (1797/1811)	France
293	Vernier, Felipe Francisco	1808 (1797/1811)	
294	Villalonga, Juan	1799	
295	Waldegrove, Eduardo	1811 (1797/1811)	England
296	Wales, Santiago	1804 (1797/1811)	South Carolina
297	Wall, Andres Leon	1797 (1797/1811)	France
298	Waterman, Eliza	1803 (1797/1811)	Americano
299	Way, Jose	1805 (1797/1811)	Pennsylvania
300	Webb, Jose	1803 (1797/1811)	Americano
301	Webbey, Jorge	1802 (1797/1811)	Americano
302	Weir, Francisco	1809 (1797/1811)	Smyrna in Greece
303	Wheeler, Eleph	1804 (1797/1811)	
304	White, Enrique	1799	
305	White, Juan Philip	1804 (1797/1811)	Americano
306	Whity, Constancio	1803 (1797/1811)	
307	Williams, Burton	1800 (1797/1811)	
308	Williams, Guillermo	1803 (1797/1811)	Americano
309	Williams, Samuel	1803 (1797/1811)	Americano
310	Williams, Samuel	1803 (1797/1811)	Americano
311	Willson, Jose	1797 (1797/1811)	
312	Workman, Santiago	1803 (1797/1811)	Ireland

	Name	Date	Origin
313	Yguiniz, Jose Antonio	1799	
314	Ynneraril, Juan	1802 (1797/1811)	Scotland
315	Youngblood, Jose	1799	
316	Younge, Enrique	1803 (1797/1811)	Americano
317	Zamorano, Gonzalo	1799	
318	Zouve, Jorge	1803 (1797/1811)	England
319	Zuvizanueta, Jose	1799	

Louisiana

Several of the settlements noted here have changed their name or otherwise vanished from the map. Atakapas is now St. Martinsville and Rapids is Pineville. Galveztown was established between 1777 and 1779 by American fugitives from the battles of the American Revolution. It had vanished by 1816, the last entry in the local church records being 1807 (Montero de Pedro 1979). Bayou Sarah (adjacent to the modern St. Francisville) was in the District of Feliciana while Manchak (Fort Butte) was south of Baton Rouge (cf. Davis 1971). Bayou Sarah, administered for a time from Natchez, is also noted with the entries for that town (see Table 14, Natchez Districts).

Table 12. Baton Rouge Names

	Names	1782	1786	1795	1799	1804	1805
1	Abrams, Bazilio					x	
2	Adam, Emmerick				x		
3	Addison, Guillermo			x			
4	Air, Robert						x
5	Alexandre, Henry		x	x			
6	Allain, Pablo			x			
7	Allain, Pedro			x			
8	Allain, Simon			x			
9	Amiot, Juan Baptista			x			
10	Andry, Pedro			x			
11	Arbour, Juan			x			
12	Arbur, Francisco			x			
13	Avelioly, James						x
14	Ayer, widow			x			
15	Babin, Gregorio			x			
16	Babin, Joseph			x			
17	Babin, Pablo			x			
18	Babin, Pedro			x			
19	Babins, Simon			x			
20	Balinger, Balentin			x			
21	Banoud, Robert						x
22	Barba, Jose Maria de			x			
23	Barley, Michael M.						x
24	Beck, David				x		
25	Belange, Nicolas			x			
26	Bell, Jacobo				x		
27	Bergel, Gregorio				x		
28	Bermojo, Cirso				x		
29	Betancur, Miguel			x			
30	Bienville, Juan Baptista			x	x		
31	Birch, Marie	x					
32	Blanchard, Santiago			x			
33	Bostes, Enrique			x			
34	Boudro, Juan			x			
35	Boulo, Jacques	x					
36	Bousel, Juan Baptista			x			
37	Boyd, Adam			x	x		
38	Bradford, Abelard						x
39	Bradford, David						x

	Names	1782	1786	1795	1799	1804	1805
40	Bradford, Enrique (son)					x	
41	Bradford, Leonardo					x	
42	Bradford, Nathan					x	
43	Bro, Jose			x			
44	Brosard, Francisco			x			
45	Brotte			x			
46	Buck, John						x
47	Burch, Jacques		x				
48	Burch, Santiago			x			
49	Campbell, Jean	x					
50	Carney, Thomas						x
51	Caten, Alexandro				x		
52	Cavanaugh, Jacobo					x	
53	Chaney, Baley						x
54	Chaney, James J.						x
55	Chaney, William Jones						x
56	Charp, Jose				x		
57	Clark, Jonathan					x	
58	Clarke, Daniel			x			
59	Clempiter, Jorge				x		
60	Clempiter, Jose				x		
61	Clempiter, Juan				x		
62	Cobb, Arthuro					x	
63	Cobb, Federico				x		
64	Cobb, Guillermo					x	
65	Cochran, Robert						x
66	Colin, Henry			x	x		
67	Comos, Juan Baptista			x			
68	Cooper, Juan						x
69	Curtin, Thomas	x	x	x	x		
70	Dalton, Thomas						x
71	Daniel, Patrick M.						x
72	Davis, Daniel	x					
73	Davis, Marie	x					
74	Davison, James						x
75	Delate, Claudio			x			
76	Desalles, Pedro				x		
77	Descautel, Antonio			x			
78	Deuset, Francisco			x			

	Names	1782	1786	1795	1799	1804	1805
79	Devall, Richard				x		x
80	Devis, Richard				x		
81	Dilbig, Thomas						x
82	Doan, Anne	x					
83	Dorch, Guillermo				x		
84	Douleth, Matheo					x	
85	Droughan, John				x		
86	Dubal, Mordama			x			
87	Dubal, Ricardo			x			
88	Dubal, Ricardo			x			
89	Dugas, Jucin			x			
90	Dunbar, Guillaume	x	x	x			
91	Duplantier, Arman			x			
92	Duplantier, Armand			x	x		x
93	Endergil, Juan				x		
94	Engelhurt, Philip				x		
95	Errick, Juan					x	
96	Ervehen, John						x
97	Escott, Anne	x					
98	Espinar, Domingo				x		
99	Fanna, (dead)			x			
100	Farell, Jose				x		
101	Flower, James						x
102	Flower, Richard						x
103	Foultis, Estevan					x	
104	Fridge, Alexander						x
105	Fridge, Catherine	x					
106	Fridge, John	x	x	x	x		x
107	Fuelier, widow			x			
108	Gairy, Jorge			x			
109	Gale, John						x
110	Gally, Juan				x		
111	Garcia, Juan			x	x		
112	Garnhart, Enrique					x	
113	Garnhart, Jorge					x	
114	Glasgot, Nimen				x		
115	Gordon, Jean	x					
116	Grange, Jose			x			
117	Gray, Phil						x

	Names	1782	1786	1795	1799	1804	1805
118	Griffith, Llewellyn C.						X
119	Heber, Francisco			X			
120	Hebert, Bautista				X		
121	Hebert, Belony				X		
122	Hebert, Carlos				X		
123	Hebert, Francisco				X		
124	Henry, Juan Baptista			X			
125	Henry, Mairi milicano			X			
126	Heu, Samuel		X				
127	Heuall, John						X
128	Hickly, David				X		
129	Hicky, Daniel			X			X
130	Hicky, Philip						X
131	Higgins, Barney				X		X
132	Hilling, Helene	X					
133	Hilling, Jaques	X					
134	Hins, James				X		
135	Hogg					X	
136	Hubauset, Pablo			X			
137	Hughes					X	
138	Hwier, widow			X			
139	Jennings, Jean	X					
140	Kavanagh, George					X	
141	Kelcay, Jeremie		X				
142	Kelisy, Geremias			X			
143	Kelisy, Geremias			X			
144	Kelly					X	
145	Kemper, Nathan					X	
146	Kemper, Samuel					X	
147	Kimball, Benjamin				X		
148	Kimball, Federico				X		
149	Kirkland, Jesse					X	
150	Kirkland, Samuel					X	
151	Labaube, Pedro			X			
152	Labaube, Ysidoro			X			
153	Landay, Herman				X		
154	Landay, Maturin			X			
155	Landry, Fermin			X			
156	Lebane, Oliver				X		

	Names	1782	1786	1795	1799	1804	1805
157	Leblanc, Pedro			X			
158	Lejeune, Francisco			X			
159	Lejeune, Gregorio			X			
160	Lejeune, Juan Baptista			X			
161	Lelly, Thomas			X			
162	Lewis, Asahel	X					
163	Longepee, Javir				X		
164	Lothrop, Isaac				X		
165	Lovo, Ysidoro				X		
166	Maffret, Juan			X			
167	Mahier, Miguel			X			
168	Main, Juan			X			
169	Malet, Juan Baptista				X		
170	Malet, widow			X			
171	Marie, Anne	X					
172	Marion, Luis			X			
173	Marshall, William		X	X	X		
174	McColler, David				X		
175	McIntosh, Jaques	X					
176	Miler, Jacob			X			
177	Mills, John						X
178	Mobichau, Carlos			X			
179	Moleson, Santiago			X			
180	Moore, David S.					X	
181	Moore, Juan					X	
182	Morgan, Miguel					X	
183	Morrison, Guillermo					X	
184	Moss, David			X			
185	Murdock, John						X
186	Muss, Hisak			X			
187	Nash, Isabelle	X					
188	Nash, Jacob	X	X				
189	Nash, widow			X			
190	Nichols, George	X					
191	Nillin, Santiago			X			
192	Northin, Zacharius				X		
193	Obrien, Mary				X		
194	Obrien, Noel			X			
195	Obrien, Veuve		X				

	Names	1782	1786	1795	1799	1804	1805
196	Obrien, widow			X			
197	Oconnor, John				X		X
198	Oneal, Juan					X	
199	Palio, Pedro			X			
200	Passau, George						X
201	Patin, Alexandro			X			
202	Pedesclaus, Pedro			X			
203	Perry, Samuel					X	
204	Pirrie, James						X
205	Podras, Julian			X			
206	Poret, Jeau						X
207	Poussett, Francis	X	X		X		
208	Proffitt, George	X	X				
209	Profit, (dead)			X			
210	Profit, Carlos			X			
211	Rapali, Garred				X		
212	Rapalie, Garza	X	X				
213	Ross, David		X				
214	Rowel, Huberto			X			
215	Rowill, Hubert			X	X		
216	Ruis, Ebache			X			
217	Russ, Abaza	X					
218	Russ, Abigalia				X		
219	Russ, Catherine	X					
220	Russ, Ezechias	X					
221	Russ, Guillaume	X					
222	Schallion, Nicholas		X				
223	Sequen, Francisco			X			
224	Sharp, Ysaac					X	
225	Sholar, Levi					X	
226	Smis, Juan			X			
227	Smith, Benjamin	X	X				
228	Smith, Jacques	X					
229	Smith, Madama			X			
230	Smith, Santiago			X			
231	Steen, Samuel				X		
232	Sters, Samuel			X			
233	Stirling, Alice						X
234	Stirling, Lewis						X

	Names	1782	1786	1795	1799	1804	1805
235	Tenio, widow			X			
236	Terio, Eusebio			X			
237	Thomas, Enrique			X			
238	Thomas, widow				X		
239	Tiboderno, Enrique				X		
240	Tibodo, Pedro			X			
241	Tilly, Tomas				X		
242	Trahan, Juan Baptista				X		
243	Trahan, Juan Maria			X			
244	Trahan, Juan Pablo			X			
245	Tullie, Jean Charles				X		
246	Turnbull, Juan			X			
247	Vahamonde, Joseph Vazquez			X			
248	Vikener, David			X			
249	Villeret, Abraham				X		
250	Wall, Jean	X					
251	Wall, Santiago			X			
252	West, Credo				X		
253	Westbury, Guillermo					X	
254	White, David						X
255	Williams, David	X	X				
256	Williams, Guillaume	X					
257	Willin, Jacques		X				
258	Ybruard, Antonio				X		
259	Young, James				X		
260	Young, Moses					X	

Table 13. Other Louisiana Names

	Name	Place/Date	Origin
1	Abcher, Jn.	Atakapas 1785	
2	Abrey, Phil	New Feliciana 1808	
3	Acosta, Jose	Manchak 1791	
4	Adam, Emmoricus	Manchak 1791	
5	Adams, Thomas	New Orleans 1797	Anglo Americano
6	Adan, Enrique	Manchak 1795	
7	Airon, Thomas	New Feliciana 1793	
8	Albeziz	Opelousas 1785	
9	Ale, Juana (widow Degle)	Manchak 1791	
10	Alman, Juan	Galveztown 1796	
11	Alston, John	Bayou Sarah 1799	
12	Alston, Solomon	Bayou Sarah 1799	
13	Alston, William	Bayou Sarah 1799	
14	Anderson, Benjamin	Rapids 1781 ?	
15	Anderson, Jacques	Rapids 1781 ?	
16	Anderson, Joseph	Rapids 1781 ?	
17	Anderson, Salomon	Rapids 1781 ?	
18	Andrews, Jh.	Opelousas 1794	
19	Andrus, B.	Atakapas 1785	
20	Angelar, Phe.	Manchak 1795	
21	Anselaim	Opelousas 1785	
22	Aquen, Richard	New Feliciana 1793	
23	Asbill, John	Tensa 1781	
24	Aucoin, Baptista	Manchak 1795	
25	Aucoin, Pedro	Manchak 1795	
26	Audibeu	Opelousas 1785	
27	Aurel, Bd.	Opelousas 1785	
28	Austin, John	New Feliciana 1808	
29	Auwin, Gregoire	New Feliciana 1793	
30	Babin, Gregorio	Manchak 1791	
31	Babin, Gregorio	Manchak 1795	
32	Babin, Jose	Manchak 1791	
33	Babin, Pedro	Manchak 1791	
34	Babin, Yh.	Atakapas 1785	
35	Babino	Atakapas 1785	
36	Babino, Ve	Atakapas 1785	
37	Bailly, Laurent	Opelousas 1785	
38	Bailly, Laurent	Opelousas 1794	
39	Baily, Richard	Tensa 1781	

	Name	Place/Date	Origin
40	Bain, Juan	New Orleans 1797	Anglo Americano
41	Baker	New Feliciana 1808	
42	Baker, John	Bayou Sarah 1799	
43	Baleingre, Balentin	Manchak 1791	
44	Balthazard, B.	Opelousas 1785	
45	Bapill, William	Tensa 1781	
46	Bara, Ruln	Opelousas 1794	
47	Bara, Ve	Atakapas 1785	
48	Barber, Anthoine	New Feliciana 1793	
49	Barhile, John	New Feliciana 1799	
50	Barker, B.	New Feliciana 1808	
51	Barker, Richard	Tensa 1781	
52	Barns, Saml	New Feliciana 1808	
53	Barre	Opelousas 1785	
54	Batin	Opelousas 1785	
55	Bauregar, Widow	Manchak 1795	
56	Beard, Thomas	Rapids 1781 ?	
57	Beaulieu, Jb.	Opelousas 1785	
58	Beaulieuaine	Opelousas 1785	
59	Beausoleil, Yh.	Atakapas 1785	
60	Beauzel	Atakapas 1785	
61	Belair, Augustin	Opelousas 1794	
62	Belard, Ant	Opelousas 1785	
63	Bello, Donato	Opelousas 1785	
64	Belveune, Richard	New Feliciana 1793	
65	Benet, Antoine	Rapids 1781 ?	
66	Benois, Daniel	Manchak 1795	
67	Benoiz, J. B.	Atakapas 1785	
68	Benoiz, Ol.	Opelousas 1785	
69	Benuoa, Daniel	Manchak 1791	
70	Berard, Yn	Atakapas 1785	
71	Bernard, Felix	New Feliciana 1793	
72	Bernard, Jr	Atakapas 1785	
73	Bernard, Me	Atakapas 1785	
74	Bernard, Salomon	Rapids 1781 ?	
75	Bernehille, Jean	New Feliciana 1793	
76	Berwick, Thomas	Opelousas 1794	
77	Bewick, Thomas	Rapids 1781 ?	
78	Bichaire, Jean	New Feliciana 1793	

	Name	Place/Date	Origin
79	Bichers, Samuel	New Feliciana 1799	
80	Biggs, Caleb	Bayou Sarah 1799	
81	Bihm, Jb.	Opelousas 1785	
82	Bingley, A.	New Feliciana 1808	
83	Birgo, Luis	Rapids 1797a	
84	Blak, Guillermo	Galveztown 1796	
85	Blanchard	Opelousas 1785	
86	Blanchard, Anselme	New Feliciana 1793	
87	Blanchard, Isidoro	Manchak 1791	
88	Blanchard, Jacque	New Feliciana 1793	
89	Blanchard, Victor	Manchak 1791	
90	Boisdore	Opelousas 1785	
91	Boisdoré pere	Opelousas 1794	
92	Boisdore, J.	Opelousas 1794	
93	Bok, Joseph	New Feliciana 1793	
94	Bolard, Geor	Opelousas 1785	
95	Bolris	Atakapas 1785	
96	Bonder, Guillaume	Rapids 1781 ?	
97	Bonnain, Ant.	Atakapas 1785	
98	Bonnain, Jn. Ls.	Atakapas 1785	
99	Bonnain, Paul	Atakapas 1785	
100	Bonnain, Ve.	Atakapas 1785	
101	Booth, John	Tensa 1781	
102	Borch, John	New Feliciana 1808	
103	Borda, Ve	Atakapas 1785	
104	Borde, La	Opelousas 1785	
105	Bosker, Raphael	Rapids 1781 ?	
106	Boteler, Jose	Manchak 1791	
107	Boudrau, Frois	Atakapas 1785	
108	Boudreau, Augin	Atakapas 1785	
109	Bouillion, Juan	Manchak 1795	
110	Bouillon	Atakapas 1785	
111	Bouillon	Opelousas 1785	
112	Bouley	Opelousas 1785	
113	Bourg, Charle	New Feliciana 1793	
114	Bourg, Jean	New Feliciana 1793	
115	Bourg, Jh.	Opelousas 1794	
116	Bourg, Yh.	Opelousas 1785	
117	Bourrassa, Ch.	Opelousas 1785	

	Name	Place/Date	Origin
118	Boutin, Paul	Opelousas 1785	
119	Boutin, Th.	Opelousas 1794	
120	Bouzassa, Chs.	Opelousas 1794	
121	Bradee, Carlos	New Orleans 1798	Anglo Americano
122	Bradford, David	New Feliciana 1799	
123	Bradley, Richard	Rapids 1797a	
124	Brahan, Santiago	New Feliciana 1799	
125	Brandon	Opelousas 1785	
126	Branton, Jean	Rapids 1781 ?	
127	Brasseue, Blse.	Opelousas 1785	
128	Brau, Firmin	Atakapas 1785	
129	Braveler, John	New Feliciana 1808	
130	Brenton, John	Opelousas 1794	
131	Brigate, Adam	Rapids 1781 ?	
132	Brignac, Ve	Opelousas 1785	
133	Brodemigue, Richard	New Feliciana 1793	
134	Broderick, Guillermo	Bayou Sarah 1799	
135	Bronen, Jum	New Feliciana 1793	
136	Brosard, Pedro	Manchak 1795	
137	Brosset	Opelousas 1785	
138	Broussard, Amt	Atakapas 1785	
139	Broussard, Crugin.	Atakapas 1785	
140	Broussard, Fr.	Atakapas 1785	
141	Broussard, J. B.	Atakapas 1785	
142	Broussard, Ls.	Opelousas 1785	
143	Broussard, Pre	Atakapas 1785	
144	Broussard, Rene	Atakapas 1785	
145	Broussard, S.	Atakapas 1785	
146	Broussard, Silvn.	Atakapas 1785	
147	Broussard, Thre	Atakapas 1785	
148	Broussard, Yh	Atakapas 1785	
149	Brown	Opelousas 1785	
150	Brown, David	New Orleans 1799	Anglo Americano
151	Brown, Guillermo	Bayou Sarah 1792	
152	Brown, J. S.	Opelousas 1794	
153	Brown, James	Rapids 1797a	
154	Brown, John	New Feliciana 1808	
155	Brudhomme	Opelousas 1785	
156	Brumberry, William	New Feliciana 1808	

	Name	Place/Date	Origin
157	Brumfield	New Feliciana 1808	
158	Brunel	Opelousas 1785	
159	Bste., Ja.	Opelousas 1794	
160	Buda, Pablo Dominic	Manchak 1791	
161	Bugeoz	Atakapas 1785	
162	Buinay, John	Rapids 1797a	
163	Bullon, Juan	Manchak 1791	
164	Bun, Jacob	Opelousas 1794	
165	Burch, Jeremias	New Orleans 1797	Anglo Americano
166	Bureau, John	Opelousas 1794	
167	Burke, Carlos	Manchak 1795	
168	Burnett, Benjamin	New Feliciana 1799	
169	Burnett, D.	Tensa 1781	
170	Byarad, John	Rapids 1797b	
171	Cabshar, Jean	Rapids 1781 ?	
172	Calleghan, Pañ.	Opelousas 1785	
173	Came	Atakapas 1785	
174	Camel, James	Opelousas 1794	
175	Camotée, De.	Opelousas 1785	
176	Campo	Opelousas 1785	
177	Caratch, J.	Opelousas 1785	
178	Carelin, Jacques	Rapids 1781 ?	
179	Carene, Ebenezer	Rapids 1781 ?	
180	Carier, Michel	Opelousas 1794	
181	Carlin	Atakapas 1785	
182	Carnes, Thomas	New Feliciana 1799	
183	Carney, Thomas	New Feliciana 1808	
184	Caron	Opelousas 1785	
185	Carr, Joseph	Rapids 1781 ?	
186	Carriere	Opelousas 1785	
187	Case, La	Opelousas 1785	
188	Castille, Ve	Atakapas 1785	
189	Cathegan, Thomas	New Feliciana 1793	
190	Cazieze, Pu.	Opelousas 1794	
191	Champagne	Atakapas 1785	
192	Champin, Nicholas	Tensa 1781	
193	Charles	Opelousas 1785	
194	Charp, Jose	Manchak 1791	
195	Charp, Santiago	Manchak 1791	

	Name	Place/Date	Origin
196	Charpe, Jacobo	Manchak 1795	
197	Charpe, Jose	Manchak 1795	
198	Chretien	Opelousas 1785	
199	Clark	Opelousas 1785	
200	Clark, Jonathan	New Feliciana 1799	
201	Clayton	Opelousas 1785	
202	Clec, Charles	Tensa 1781	
203	Clermon	Atakapas 1785	
204	Cloctinet, Louia	New Feliciana 1793	
205	Clusso, J. B.	Opelousas 1785	
206	Cobite, Ve	Atakapas 1785	
207	Codrey, Thomas (son)	Tensa 1781	
208	Coffin, Jorge	New Orleans 1799	Anglo Americano
209	Coffins Fils	Opelousas 1785	
210	Coffins Pere	Opelousas 1785	
211	Coleman, John Raford	Bayou Sarah 1799	
212	Colette	Atakapas 1785	
213	Colino, Luk	Opelousas 1794	
214	Colins filo	Opelousas 1794	
215	Colins pere	Opelousas 1794	
216	Colins, Guillermo	Bayou Sarah 1799	
217	Collignood	Opelousas 1785	
218	Colline, Luc (father)	Rapids 1781 ?	
219	Collingrood, Robert	Rapids 1781 ?	
220	Collins, Guillaume	Rapids 1781 ?	
221	Collins, Luc (son)	Rapids 1781 ?	
222	Collins, Theophilus	Rapids 1781 ?	
223	Comau, Chs.	Opelousas 1785	
224	Comeau, Simon	New Feliciana 1793	
225	Comon	Opelousas 1785	
226	Coneau, Chs.	Opelousas 1794	
227	Cordery, Thomas (father)	Tensa 1781	
228	Cormier, Jn. Bte.	Atakapas 1785	
229	Corprel, Gabriel Martin	Rapids 1797a	
230	Coskain, Antoine	Rapids 1781 ?	
231	Coter	Opelousas 1785	
232	Coujlon, Robert M.	New Feliciana 1808	
233	Cowen, Robert	Tensa 1781	
234	Creigy, Guillermo	New Orleans 1798	Anglo Americano

	Name	Place/Date	Origin
235	Crichine	Atakapas 1785	
236	Crook, Yas	Opelousas 1785	
237	Culp, G.	New Feliciana 1808	
238	Cuny, Ve	Opelousas 1785	
239	Cuts, John	Rapids 1797a	
240	Daigle, Alexandro	Manchak 1795	
241	Daigle, Luis	Manchak 1795	
242	Daigre, Baptista	Manchak 1795	
243	Daigre, Francisco	Manchak 1795	
244	Daigre, Pablo	Manchak 1795	
245	Dalphen, Francois	Tensa 1781	
246	Daltesse	Atakapas 1785	
247	Darby	Atakapas 1785	
248	Darby, St. Marc	Atakapas 1785	
249	Daves, Thomas	Rapids 1797a	
250	De Populas	Opelousas 1785	
251	Declouez, Cher.	Atakapas 1785	
252	Decuir, Fois	Atakapas 1785	
253	Decuir, J. Pre	Atakapas 1785	
254	Dée, Le	Atakapas 1785	
255	Degle, Francisco	Manchak 1791	
256	Degle, Francisco Alex.	Manchak 1791	
257	Degle, Juan Baptista	Manchak 1791	
258	Degle, Luis	Manchak 1791	
259	Degle, Pablo	Manchak 1791	
260	Degle, Simon	Manchak 1791	
261	Degle, Simon Pedro	Manchak 1791	
262	Delainé, Mathieu	New Feliciana 1793	
263	Delamorandier	Opelousas 1785	
264	Delgado, Jn.	Opelousas 1785	
265	Delhodmme	Atakapas 1785	
266	Deloignon	Atakapas 1785	
267	Demarets, Ve	Opelousas 1785	
268	Derbanne, J. B.	Opelousas 1785	
269	Derçon, Guillaume	Rapids 1781 ?	
270	Dermett, Bryan M.	New Feliciana 1808	
271	Derovien	Atakapas 1785	
272	Desholels, Nas.	Opelousas 1785	
273	Deverneys, Antonio	New Orleans 1798	

	Name	Place/Date	Origin
274	Devidrine	Opelousas 1785	
275	Dial, John	Rapids 1797a	
276	Dicouel	Opelousas 1785	
277	Dixon, Joseph	New Orleans 1798	Anglo Americano
278	Dobroy, John B.	Rapids 1797a	
279	Doiron, Widow	Manchak 1795	
280	Doiron, Ysak	Manchak 1795	
281	Donlevey, Tamauge	Rapids 1797a	
282	Dorée	Atakapas 1785	
283	Dortch, John	New Feliciana 1799	
284	Dotche, Guillaume	New Feliciana 1793	
285	Doucez, Ma	Atakapas 1785	
286	Doucez, Yh	Atakapas 1785	
287	Doyle, Joshua	New Feliciana 1808	
288	Duaron, Alexandro	Manchak 1791	
289	Duaron, Hissak	Manchak 1791	
290	Duaron, Juan Bauptista	Manchak 1791	
291	Ducresz	Atakapas 1785	
292	Dugas, Amt.	Atakapas 1785	
293	Dugas, Chs.	Atakapas 1785	
294	Dugas, Jn	Atakapas 1785	
295	Dugas, Pre	Atakapas 1785	
296	Duhon, B.	Atakapas 1785	
297	Duhon, Ch.	Atakapas 1785	
298	Duhon, Claude	Atakapas 1785	
299	Dulisne	Opelousas 1785	
300	Dunman, John	Opelousas 1794	
301	Dunman, Reuben	Bayou Sarah 1792	
302	Duplantier, Arman	Manchak 1795	
303	Dupuia, Charle	New Feliciana 1793	
304	Dupuid, Ambroin	New Feliciana 1793	
305	Dupuy, Carlos	Manchak 1795	
306	Duralde	Opelousas 1785	
307	Durbin, Joseph	Tensa 1781	
308	Duval, Jean	Atakapas 1785	
309	Eleson	Tensa 1781	
310	Elliott, Thomas	New Feliciana 1799	
311	Ellis, Hardi	Opelousas 1785	
312	Eneson Carenton, Juan	New Feliciana 1799	

	Name	Place/Date	Origin
313	Engelard, Felipe	Manchak 1791	
314	Erls, Richard	Rapids 1797a	
315	Escouffié	Opelousas 1785	
316	Eskildsen, Pedro	New Orleans 1798	Denmark
317	Eubanks, Stephen	Tensa 1781	
318	Eveille, L'	Atakapas 1785	
319	Fample, Margarita	Manchak 1791	
320	Faoullar, Jobile	Rapids 1797a	
321	Fauger, F. S.	Opelousas 1794	
322	Faustin, Ys.	Atakapas 1785	
323	Favul, Jeouque	New Feliciana 1793	
324	Fermier	Opelousas 1785	
325	Figuron	Opelousas 1785	
326	Fitz, Benjamin	Rapids 1781 ?	
327	Fitzpatrik, Juan	Manchak 1791	
328	Fleury, Joseph	New Orleans 1803	San Maloen France
329	Flowers, Samuel	New Feliciana 1799	
330	Fohe, Jean	Rapids 1781 ?	
331	Fontenau	Opelousas 1785	
332	Fontenau, B.	Opelousas 1785	
333	Fontenau, Bair	Opelousas 1785	
334	Fontenau, La Rose	Opelousas 1785	
335	Fontenau, Pre	Opelousas 1785	
336	Fontenau, Tomas	Opelousas 1794	
337	Fontenau, Y.Ls	Opelousas 1785	
338	Fontenau, Yas.	Opelousas 1785	
339	Fonteneau, Simon	Opelousas 1794	
340	Fonteneu, Jacques	Opelousas 1794	
341	Fontenu, Henri	Opelousas 1785	
342	Fonton, Juan	New Orleans 1797	Anglo Americano
343	Forc, Jn	Atakapas 1785	
344	Fore, Simon	Manchak 1795	
345	Forget, Peter de	Tensa 1781	
346	Foriet, Florentin	Opelousas 1794	
347	Forman, Ed.	Opelousas 1785	
348	Fosite, Robero	New Feliciana 1793	
349	Foster, James	New Feliciana 1799	
350	Fourman, Edouard	Opelousas 1794	
351	Foutchec	Atakapas 1785	

	Name	Place/Date	Origin
352	Frahan, Juan Bautista	Manchak 1791	
353	Frahan, Remon	Manchak 1791	
354	Frannel, Augusto	New Orleans 1803	Wervicq Flanders
355	Frederie	Opelousas 1785	
356	Frines	Opelousas 1785	
357	Frugé, Pu.	Opelousas 1794	
358	Fruge, Ve.	Opelousas 1785	
359	Fruland, Isaac	New Feliciana 1808	
360	Fry, Than.	Opelousas 1785	
361	Fulford, Guillermo Gibson	New Orleans 1797	Anglo Americano
362	Fuller, Mortacea	Tensa 1781	
363	Fullie, Isidoro	Manchak 1791	
364	Fullie, Juan Carlos	Manchak 1791	
365	Fulton, Alex	Rapids 1797b	
366	Fulton, Alex.	Rapids 1797a	
367	Gaille, Jean	New Feliciana 1793	
368	Gallehon, Patrick	Tensa 1781	
369	Gallien, Ve	Opelousas 1785	
370	Gardnhart, Michal	Bayou Sarah 1799	
371	Garner, John	Tensa 1781	
372	Garrette	Opelousas 1785	
373	Gartles, John W.	New Feliciana 1799	
374	Gilchrisl	Opelousas 1785	
375	Gilks, Bukins	New Feliciana 1799	
376	Giroid, Firmin	Atakapas 1785	
377	Godeau	Opelousas 1785	
378	Gomeo, Jacques	Opelousas 1794	
379	Gomez, Ys.	Opelousas 1785	
380	Gonssoulin	Atakapas 1785	
381	Gordon, David	New Feliciana 1793	
382	Gorman, Simon	Rapids 1797a	
383	Gormon, Joseph	Rapids 1797a	
384	Gradenigo	Opelousas 1785	
385	Grange, Ana (widow Frahan)	Manchak 1791	
386	Grange, Bap.	Opelousas 1785	
387	Grange, Baptiste	Opelousas 1794	
388	Grangé, Yh.	Opelousas 1785	
389	Gray, Robert	Tensa 1781	
390	Gray, William	Tensa 1781	

	Name	Place/Date	Origin
391	Green, John	Bayou Sarah 1792	
392	Grelol, Pre	Atakapas 1785	
393	Grévenbesiz, J. B.	Atakapas 1785	
394	Grevenbesiz, Ls.	Atakapas 1785	
395	Grevenbeu, Barmy	Atakapas 1785	
396	Grevenbeu, Fois	Atakapas 1785	
397	Grews, Richard	Bayou Sarah 1799	
398	Griffith, Llwellyn	New Feliciana 1808	
399	Grubb, Benj	Rapids 1797a	
400	Guenard	Opelousas 1785	
401	Guenard, Jean	New Feliciana 1793	
402	Guenne, Ambroise	New Feliciana 1793	
403	Guiday, Ana (widow)	Manchak 1791	
404	Guiday, Joseph	Manchak 1795	
405	Guiday, Juan	Manchak 1795	
406	Guiday, Pedro	Manchak 1795	
407	Guidrie, Jh	Atakapas 1785	
408	Guidrie, Pre	Opelousas 1785	
409	Guidry, Francisco	Manchak 1795	
410	Guidry, Jose	Manchak 1791	
411	Guidry, Malau	Manchak 1795	
412	Guidry, Pedro (1st)	Manchak 1791	
413	Guidry, Pedro (2nd)	Manchak 1791	
414	Guidry, Pedro (2nd)	Manchak 1795	
415	Guidry, Soulier	Manchak 1795	
416	Guillaume	Atakapas 1785	
417	Guillaume, Guillaume	New Feliciana 1793	
418	Guillebeau, Chs	Atakapas 1785	
419	Guillebeau, F	Atakapas 1785	
420	Guillebeau, Yn.	Atakapas 1785	
421	Guillory, Cde	Opelousas 1785	
422	Guillory, Jh.	Opelousas 1785	
423	Guillory, Thomas	Opelousas 1794	
424	Guilory, B.	Opelousas 1785	
425	Haise, Guillaume	New Feliciana 1793	
426	Haise, Malzejuis	Rapids 1781 ?	
427	Halonde	Atakapas 1785	
428	Haltement, David	New Feliciana 1793	
429	Hamy, James H.	New Feliciana 1808	

	Name	Place/Date	Origin
430	Hanchet	Opelousas 1794	
431	Hanchett	Opelousas 1785	
432	Hanley, Richard	Rapids 1797a	
433	Harang, Tomas	New Feliciana 1799	
434	Harbaur, John	New Feliciana 1808	
435	Harbour, Sam	New Feliciana 1808	
436	Harbour, Thomas	Bayou Sarah 1799	
437	Hargrove, Benjin.	Atakapas 1785	
438	Harn, Moses	New Feliciana 1808	
439	Harshaw, Archibald	New Orleans 1798	Anglo Americano
440	Hays, Bosman	Opelousas 1794	
441	Hays, John	Opelousas 1794	
442	Hays, William	Opelousas 1794	
443	Haysse	Opelousas 1785	
444	Hebe, Alesey	Manchak 1795	
445	Hebe, Belony	Manchak 1795	
446	Hebe, Juan Carlos	Manchak 1795	
447	Heber, Carlos	Manchak 1795	
448	Heber, Juan Baptista	Manchak 1795	
449	Heber, Juan Pedro	Manchak 1795	
450	Hebers, J.	Atakapas 1785	
451	Hebers, Jh.	Atakapas 1785	
452	Hebers, Jn	Atakapas 1785	
453	Hebers, Min	Atakapas 1785	
454	Hebeu, Pierre	New Feliciana 1793	
455	Henderson, John	Rapids 1797a	
456	Henson, Widow	Manchak 1795	
457	Here, Andres	Bayou Sarah 1792	
458	Hergeroder	Opelousas 1785	
459	Herling, Alexan	New Feliciana 1793	
460	Herman, Jacob	Opelousas 1794	
461	Herman, Jacob	Rapids 1781 ?	
462	Herman, Jb.	Opelousas 1785	
463	Hetty, Ps.	Opelousas 1794	
464	Heury, Pierre	New Feliciana 1793	
465	Hicky, Daniel	Manchak 1795	
466	Higui, Daniel	Manchak 1791	
467	Hjollies	Opelousas 1785	
468	Hogarty, Peter	Rapids 1797a	

	Name	Place/Date	Origin
469	Holden, Thomas	New Orleans 1797	Anglo Americano
470	Holftur, King	Rapids 1797b	
471	Hollaway, John	Rapids 1797b	
472	Holmes, Joseph	Rapids 1797a	
473	Holmes, Joseph	Rapids 1797b	
474	Hooten, Phillip	Rapids 1797a	
475	Hopkins, Ebenezer	New Orleans 1798	Anglo Americano
476	Hortin, Abraham	Bayou Sarah 1792	
477	Houssaye, La	Atakapas 1785	
478	Houvre	Atakapas 1785	
479	Howard, Philipe	Rapids 1781 ?	
480	Howpock, Michel	Rapids 1781 ?	
481	Hubart, Stephen	Tensa 1781	
482	Hulain, L.	Atakapas 1785	
483	Hull, Dow	Rapids 1797a	
484	Hull, John	Rapids 1797a	
485	Hutch, Louis	Rapids 1797a	
486	Hutchinson, Samuel	Bayou Sarah 1799	
487	Iguin, Jacque	New Feliciana 1793	
488	Ingram, Joseph	Rapids 1781 ?	
489	Isabelle	Atakapas 1785	
490	Jackson, Harvis	Tensa 1781	
491	Jackson, Joseph	Tensa 1781	
492	James, Samuel	New Orleans 1797	Anglo Americano
493	Jeansonne, Chs.	Opelousas 1785	
494	Jeansonne, Jh.	Opelousas 1785	
495	Jeansonne, Yn.	Opelousas 1785	
496	Jeun, Bse le	Opelousas 1785	
497	Jeune, Le	Opelousas 1785	
498	Johnson, Isaac	New Feliciana 1808	
499	Johnson, John	New Feliciana 1808	
500	Johnston, Isaac	Opelousas 1794	
501	Jones, Michael	New Feliciana 1799	
502	Jonston, George	Tensa 1781	
503	Kare, Marc	New Feliciana 1793	
504	Karic, Mark	New Feliciana 1799	
505	Kemplin, Nicholas	New Feliciana 1799	
506	Kenny, Yn	Opelousas 1785	
507	Kimball, Benjamin	New Feliciana 1808	

	Name	Place/Date	Origin
508	King, George	Rapids 1781 ?	
509	Kirkland, William	New Feliciana 1799	
510	Klein Peter, Jorge	Manchak 1795	
511	Klein Peter, Joseph	Manchak 1795	
512	Klempeter, Juan Baptista	Manchak 1795	
513	Kreger, Godfrey	Opelousas 1794	
514	L'Allemand, Jean	Opelousas 1785	
515	Labastier	Opelousas 1785	
516	Labaube, Pedro	Manchak 1795	
517	Labaube, Ysidro	Manchak 1795	
518	Labauve, B.	Atakapas 1785	
519	Labbé	Atakapas 1785	
520	Lablancherie, Jose	New Orleans 1803	Bordeaux France
521	LaFleur, Baptista	Opelousas 1794	
522	LaFleur, Jacques	Opelousas 1794	
523	Laitets, Nathan	New Feliciana 1793	
524	Lalonde, Gulilone	Atakapas 1785	
525	Lamirande fils	Opelousas 1785	
526	Lamirande, Jh.	Opelousas 1785	
527	Landon, Jacque	New Feliciana 1793	
528	Landre, Amani	Atakapas 1785	
529	Landri, Basile	Atakapas 1785	
530	Landri, Firmin	Atakapas 1785	
531	Landri, Jh.	Atakapas 1785	
532	Landri, Opes	Atakapas 1785	
533	Langebourg	Opelousas 1785	
534	Langevin	Atakapas 1785	
535	Langevin, Chs.	Opelousas 1794	
536	Langlois, Ant.	Opelousas 1785	
537	Langlois, Antne.	Opelousas 1794	
538	Langrois	Opelousas 1785	
539	Larche, Jean	New Feliciana 1793	
540	Larche, Santiago	Manchak 1795	
541	Lark, John	Opelousas 1794	
542	Latiolais	Opelousas 1785	
543	Launier, Silin.	Opelousas 1785	
544	Láutreparz, de	Atakapas 1785	
545	Lavergne, Ls.	Opelousas 1785	
546	Le Blanc, Com.	Atakapas 1785	

	Name	Place/Date	Origin
547	Le Blanc, Josine	Atakapas 1785	
548	le Blanc, Rene	Atakapas 1785	
549	Leblan, Pedro	Manchak 1791	
550	LeBlanc, Simon	Atakapas 1785	
551	LeBlé, Bmi	Opelousas 1785	
552	Lebrau, Margarita (widow)	Manchak 1791	
553	Lechandre, Juan Bautista	Manchak 1791	
554	Ledoux	Opelousas 1785	
555	Ledoux, F.	Opelousas 1794	
556	Ledoux, Mc	Opelousas 1794	
557	LeFleur, Ys.	Opelousas 1785	
558	Leger, Jean	Rapids 1781 ?	
559	Leimelle	Opelousas 1785	
560	Lejeuare, David	New Feliciana 1799	
561	Lejeune, Andre	New Feliciana 1793	
562	Leleu	Atakapas 1785	
563	Leonard, Yn.	Opelousas 1785	
564	Levans, Nicholas	Rapids 1797a	
565	Lever, Juan Carlos	Manchak 1791	
566	Lever, Juan Pedro	Manchak 1791	
567	Levi Wels, Samuel	Opelousas 1794	
568	Levi Wels, Stephen	Opelousas 1794	
569	Lewellyn, Complan G.	New Feliciana 1808	
570	Linescom, Bazil	Opelousas 1794	
571	Lirasune, Isaac	Rapids 1797a	
572	Lisette	Atakapas 1785	
573	Liver, Jean	Rapids 1781 ?	
574	Loileau, Augte.	Opelousas 1794	
575	Loisel	Atakapas 1785	
576	Lopes, Andres	Manchak 1791	
577	Lopez, Andres	Manchak 1795	
578	Louis, Grand	Opelousas 1794	
579	Louviere, S.	Atakapas 1785	
580	Lulalford, Thomas	Rapids 1797a	
581	Lum, John	New Feliciana 1799	
582	Lyson, Jean	Rapids 1781 ?	
583	Lytle, Nathan	New Feliciana 1799	
584	Mahiou, Francoia	New Feliciana 1793	
585	Maiale, Patrice	Rapids 1781 ?	

	Name	Place/Date	Origin
586	Maille, Andre	Opelousas 1785	
587	Makolei, Pak.	Opelousas 1785	
588	Malgros, Benjamin	Rapids 1781 ?	
589	Malgros, William	Rapids 1781 ?	
590	Malrot	Opelousas 1794	
591	Malvol	Opelousas 1785	
592	Manadue, Henry	Bayou Sarah 1799	
593	Manne	Opelousas 1785	
594	Manuel, Pre	Opelousas 1785	
595	Marcantel	Opelousas 1785	
596	Marcantel, De.	Opelousas 1785	
597	Marchall	Opelousas 1785	
598	Marianne, John	Opelousas 1794	
599	Marie, Andre	Opelousas 1785	
600	Martin, Andres	Manchak 1795	
601	Martin, Claude	Atakapas 1785	
602	Martin, Gab.	Opelousas 1785	
603	Martin, Gabriel	Rapids 1781 ?	
604	Martin, Yh.	Atakapas 1785	
605	Martin, Zacie	Opelousas 1785	
606	Martini, Ant	Atakapas 1785	
607	Mathe, Madam	Galveztown 1796	
608	Mau, Ve	Atakapas 1785	
609	Maureau, Ve	Opelousas 1785	
610	Maureau, Ve	Opelousas 1785	
611	Maurice, Ve	Opelousas 1785	
612	Mauriceau	Opelousas 1785	
613	Mayes, Stephen	Bayou Sarah 1799	
614	Maze, John	New Feliciana 1808	
615	Mc. Jeannis	Opelousas 1785	
616	McCormier	Opelousas 1785	
617	McDanel	Opelousas 1785	
618	McDaniel, John	Opelousas 1794	
619	McFarten, John	New Feliciana 1799	
620	McLanen, Js.	Opelousas 1794	
621	Meco, Juan	Galveztown 1796	
622	Meders, Edward	Tensa 1781	
623	Melançon, Bto	Atakapas 1785	
624	Melançon, Jh	Atakapas 1785	

	Name	Place/Date	Origin
625	Melone, John	Tensa 1781	
626	Meolloh, Guillaume	Rapids 1781 ?	
627	Mersten, John	Tensa 1781	
628	Meullion	Opelousas 1785	
629	Migue, Jean	Opelousas 1785	
630	Milan, Pb.e	Opelousas 1785	
631	Mill, Evan	Rapids 1781 ?	
632	Miller, G.	Opelousas 1785	
633	Miller, Yb.	Opelousas 1785	
634	Mills, Gilbert	New Feliciana 1799	
635	Mills, John	New Feliciana 1799	
636	Milward, Juan	New Orleans 1798	Anglo Americano
637	Mix, Joseph	Manchak 1791	
638	Mlik, Reuben	Rapids 1797a	
639	Monk, Jorge	New Orleans 1798	Anglo Americano
640	Monrroy, La subcere.	Bayou Sarah 1792	
641	Moor, Ruben	Bayou Sarah 1799	
642	Morales, Juan	Manchak 1795	
643	Morel, Yh	Opelousas 1785	
644	Morton, John	New Feliciana 1808	
645	Mouton, Chapeau	Atakapas 1785	
646	Mouton, Min	Atakapas 1785	
647	Mouton, Mre	Atakapas 1785	
648	Mur, Simon	Atakapas 1785	
649	Murphey, James	Tensa 1781	
650	Murphy, John	Tensa 1781	
651	Nair, Jean	Rapids 1781 ?	
652	Nelson, Christian	Bayou Sarah 1799	
653	Nero, Andrí	Opelousas 1794	
654	Normand, Maria	Atakapas 1785	
655	Norton, Zacaria	Manchak 1791	
656	Nouvre, Jacobo	Manchak 1795	
657	Nugens, Ed.	Opelousas 1785	
658	Nugent, Edmund	Rapids 1781 ?	
659	Nugent, Mathew	Rapids 1797a	
660	Nugent, Mathieu (father)	Rapids 1781 ?	
661	Nugent, Thomas	Rapids 1797a	
662	Oats, William	Tensa 1781	
663	Obrien, Juan	New Orleans 1799	Anglo Americano

	Name	Place/Date	Origin
664	Oconor, Juan	Bayou Sarah 1792	
665	Odum, Abraham	Rapids 1781 ?	
666	Ofallon, Mathew	New Feliciana 1799	
667	Olibie, Anselmo	Manchak 1795	
668	Olivie Blanchar, Anselmo	Manchak 1791	
669	Olivier, M.	Opelousas 1785	
670	Ory, Luis	Manchak 1791	
671	Ouad, Francoise	New Feliciana 1793	
672	Owins, Calib	Manchak 1795	
673	Ozenne	Atakapas 1785	
674	Palin	Atakapas 1785	
675	Panel, Jacob	Rapids 1797a	
676	Paoly, Jose	Galveztown 1796	
677	Paper, Roberd	New Feliciana 1793	
678	Par, Thomas	Rapids 1781 ?	
679	Pau, Manuel	Opelousas 1794	
680	Paul, Gary	Rapids 1797b	
681	Paulset, Francisco	Bayou Sarah 1792	
682	Peare, Ezeckeal, W.	Tensa 1781	
683	Pellerin, Ve.	Atakapas 1785	
684	Penfield, Nathaniel	New Orleans 1798	Anglo Americano
685	Penueres, Guillaume	New Feliciana 1793	
686	Pere, Prejon	Atakapas 1785	
687	Perey	Opelousas 1785	
688	Piburn, Jacob	Tensa 1785/01/12	
689	Picard	Atakapas 1785	
690	Pike, Juan	New Orleans 1798	Anglo Americano
691	Pin	Opelousas 1785	
692	Piper, John	New Feliciana 1808	
693	Piper, Robert	New Feliciana 1799	
694	Pipes, Gill	Bayou Sarah 1799	
695	Pitipier, Jorge	Manchak 1791	
696	Pitipier, Joseph	Manchak 1791	
697	Pitipier, Juan	Manchak 1791	
698	Pitre	Opelousas 1785	
699	Pointe, Pae La	Atakapas 1785	
700	Poirel, Flin	Opelousas 1785	
701	Poirez, Ches	Opelousas 1785	
702	Pollock, Jorge	New Orleans 1802	Neverry, Ireland

	Name	Place/Date	Origin
703	Pornel, Manke	Rapids 1797b	
704	Pradier	Atakapas 1785	
705	Prater, William	Opelousas 1794	
706	Prejean, Chs.	Atakapas 1785	
707	Prejean, Marin	Atakapas 1785	
708	Prevol, Ve	Atakapas 1785	
709	Prince, Yh.	Atakapas 1785	
710	Prisman, Than	Opelousas 1785	
711	Prosper, Juan	Manchak 1791	
712	Prospero, Juan	Manchak 1795	
713	Provange, Daniel	Manchak 1795	
714	Querkil	Opelousas 1785	
715	Quinelty	Opelousas 1785	
716	Quinisime	Opelousas 1785	
717	Raitre, Me.	Opelousas 1785	
718	Ramard, Rd.	Opelousas 1785	
719	Ransford, John	Tensa 1781	
720	Ratliff, D.	New Feliciana 1808	
721	Reed	Opelousas 1785	
722	Reide, William	Opelousas 1794	
723	Relyn, Juan	Manchak 1791	
724	Rhodes, Etienne	Rapids 1781 ?	
725	Ribas, Francisco	Manchak 1795	
726	Ribas, Francisco	Manchak 1795	
727	Rice, Emanuel	Rapids 1797a	
728	Rice, Emanuel	Rapids 1797b	
729	Richar, Jose	Manchak 1791	
730	Richard, Fab.	Opelousas 1785	
731	Richard, Joseph	Manchak 1795	
732	Richard, Mln	Opelousas 1785	
733	Richard, Pre	Opelousas 1785	
734	Richard, Victor	Opelousas 1785	
735	Richardson, Henry	New Feliciana 1799	
736	Ridde, Yn.	Atakapas 1785	
737	Ride, John	Rapids 1781 ?	
738	Ridou	Opelousas 1785	
739	Rill, Tha.	Opelousas 1785	
740	Riter, Mt.	Opelousas 1785	
741	Rivard, Ve	Opelousas 1785	

	Name	Place/Date	Origin
742	Rivas, Francisco	Galveztown 1796	
743	Roberz, Biny	Opelousas 1785	
744	Robichar, Eusebio	Manchak 1795	
745	Robin	Opelousas 1785	
746	Robin, Fs.	Opelousas 1794	
747	Robissay, F.	Atakapas 1785	
748	Roger, Louis	Atakapas 1785	
749	Rols, David	Bayou Sarah 1792	
750	Romain, Lç.	Opelousas 1785	
751	Roman	Opelousas 1785	
752	Roquigny	Atakapas 1785	
753	Roulille, La	Opelousas 1785	
754	Rousseau	Atakapas 1785	
755	Routlé	Atakapas 1785	
756	Roy, Jh.	Opelousas 1785	
757	Roy, Joel	Opelousas 1785	
758	Roy, Joseph	Opelousas 1794	
759	Ruth, Benjamin	Rapids 1781 ?	
760	Ruth, François	Rapids 1781 ?	
761	Ruth, Zaiken	Rapids 1781 ?	
762	Ryland, James	Bayou Sarah 1792	
763	Sabol	Opelousas 1785	
764	Safold, Jahem	Tensa 1781	
765	Sainteler	Opelousas 1785	
766	Samuiel, Silvain	Opelousas 1794	
767	Saunier, Yh.	Opelousas 1785	
768	Savire, Pre	Opelousas 1785	
769	Savoye, Ve	Atakapas 1785	
770	Scott, Alexander	New Feliciana 1808	
771	Sem	Atakapas 1785	
772	Semer	Atakapas 1785	
773	Sewkles, Adam	Bayou Sarah 1799	
774	Shadwell, John	New Feliciana 1808	
775	Sibley, Joseph	New Orleans 1797	Anglo Americano
776	Silvestre, Yh	Opelousas 1785	
777	Simes, Jean	New Feliciana 1793	
778	Single, Adam	New Feliciana 1793	
779	Smith, Lutheo	New Feliciana 1808	
780	Smith, Thomas	Tensa 1781	

	Name	Place/Date	Origin
781	Smith, William	Tensa 1781	
782	Snell, Christian	Tensa 1781	
783	Snow, Isaac	New Orleans 1799	Anglo Americano
784	Snow, Isaiah	New Orleans 1798	Anglo Americano
785	Soileau, Aug.	Atakapas 1785	
786	Soileau, J. B.	Opelousas 1785	
787	Soileau, Noel	Opelousas 1785	
788	Sorel	Atakapas 1785	
789	Soto, Don M. de	Opelousas 1785	
790	Souderis	Atakapas 1785	
791	Soulie, Juan Luis	Manchak 1795	
792	Spericot, Mathieu	New Feliciana 1793	
793	St Louis	Opelousas 1785	
794	Stachey, Joshua	Tensa 1781	
795	Stanley, Robert	New Orleans 1798	United States
796	Stark, Robert	Bayou Sarah 1792	
797	Stelly, Bap.	Opelousas 1785	
798	Stelly, Fr.	Opelousas 1785	
799	Stelly, Y. G.	Opelousas 1785	
800	Stelly, Yn.	Opelousas 1785	
801	Stephens, John	Bayou Sarah 1799	
802	Stewart, John	New Feliciana 1808	
803	Sthoutes, Ve	Opelousas 1785	
804	Stirling, Alexander	New Feliciana 1799	
805	Stirling, Luvis	New Feliciana 1808	
806	Stix	Atakapas 1785	
807	Storup, George P.	Bayou Sarah 1799	
808	Stout, Belly	Opelousas 1794	
809	Stout, Michel	Opelousas 1794	
810	Strachan, Patrick	Tensa 1781	
811	Stuart, Abraham	Rapids 1781 ?	
812	Sturges, Bourlow	New Orleans 1798	Anglo Americano
813	Suisse, Js.	Opelousas 1785	
814	Sulavant, Cornelius	Tensa 1781	
815	Sulier, Juan Moris	Manchak 1791	
816	Swayze, Stephen	Bayou Sarah 1799	
817	Tabor, Ysaac	New Feliciana 1799	
818	Tamus	Atakapas 1785	
819	Taylor, Pedro	New Feliciana 1799	

	Name	Place/Date	Origin
820	Taylor, William	New Feliciana 1799	
821	Teahan, Memon	Manchak 1795	
822	Teal	Opelousas 1785	
823	Temer, Robert	Tensa 1781	
824	Templete, Juan	Manchak 1795	
825	Terbonnes, Ve	Opelousas 1785	
826	Terbonnesairy	Opelousas 1785	
827	Terrioz, Paul	Atakapas 1785	
828	Tesson	Opelousas 1785	
829	Testa, Pedro de	New Orleans 1801	Dieppe, Normandy
830	Theriau, Marie	New Feliciana 1793	
831	Theuy	Opelousas 1785	
832	Thibaudol, Pre	Opelousas 1785	
833	Thibaudoz, Ans.	Atakapas 1785	
834	Thibaudoz, Ant.	Atakapas 1785	
835	Thibaudoz, Ofr.	Atakapas 1785	
836	Thibaudoz, There	Atakapas 1785	
837	Thilluerp, Robert	Tensa 1781	
838	Thomas, Enrriche	Manchak 1791	
839	Thomier, John	Rapids 1797a	
840	Thornson, Juan	New Orleans 1799	Anglo Americano
841	Thorp, Robert	Bayou Sarah 1799	
842	Todd, Adam	New Orleans 1797	Anglo Americano
843	Togeal, John	Tensa 1781	
844	Tormelle, Efraime	Rapids 1781 ?	
845	Toubesu	Opelousas 1785	
846	Tracy, Isaac	New Orleans 1799	New London USA
847	Trahan, Ats.	Atakapas 1785	
848	Trahan, Hoñ.	Opelousas 1785	
849	Trahan, J. B.	Atakapas 1785	
850	Trahan, Joseph	Manchak 1795	
851	Trahan, Juan	Manchak 1795	
852	Trahan, Paul	Atakapas 1785	
853	Trahan, Pre	Opelousas 1785	
854	Trahan, Rene	Atakapas 1785	
855	Trahan, Ve	Atakapas 1785	
856	Trahan, Ve	Atakapas 1785	
857	Trahan, Yn.	Atakapas 1785	
858	Trahan, Yoh	Atakapas 1785	

	Name	Place/Date	Origin
859	Triste, Widow	Manchak 1795	
860	Tullier, Juan	Manchak 1795	
861	Tullier, Ysidoro	Manchak 1795	
862	Tulter, Charles	Tensa 1781	
863	Ussé, Pedro	Manchak 1791	
864	Vassaur, Le	Opelousas 1785	
865	Veillon, Francisco	Opelousas 1794	
866	Veillon, Ls.	Opelousas 1785	
867	Vellan, Mathew	New Feliciana 1808	
868	Verrel, Ph.	Atakapas 1785	
869	Verres, F.	Atakapas 1785	
870	Vicks, John	Rapids 1797a	
871	Victor, BPd.	Atakapas 1785	
872	Viger, Ch.	Opelousas 1785	
873	Vighan, Jean	Rapids 1781 ?	
874	Villiers, De	Opelousas 1785	
875	Vingant, George	Tensa 1781	
876	Vingant, Stephan	Tensa 1781	
877	Violetta, La	Opelousas 1785	
878	Wabb, Michel	Opelousas 1794	
879	Waglen, Thomas	New Feliciana 1799	
880	Wahates, Jean	New Feliciana 1793	
881	Walker, Joseph	Rapids 1797b	
882	Walkers, Abram	Tensa 1781	
883	Walks, Joseph	Rapids 1797a	
884	Wall, Juan	Bayou Sarah 1792	
885	Wallace, Josúe	Rapids 1781 ?	
886	Wallée, Jn.	Opelousas 1785	
887	Walles	Opelousas 1785	
888	Wayble, Jah	Opelousas 1785	
889	Wayble, Mc.	Opelousas 1785	
890	Weed, Joel	Bayou Sarah 1799	
891	Welch, Jacobo	Opelousas 1794	
892	Wells, Samuel	Opelousas 1785	
893	Wells, Samuel	Opelousas 1794	
894	Wells, Samuel	Rapids 1781 ?	
895	Wells, Willing	Rapids 1797a	
896	Welton, Juan	Bayou Sarah 1792	
897	Welton, Patience	Bayou Sarah 1799	

	Name	Place/Date	Origin
898	Wep, William	Galveztown 1796	
899	Wesl, Roger	Opelousas 1785	
900	West, Nathaniel	Opelousas 1794	
901	White, David	New Feliciana 1799	
902	White, James	Rapids 1797b	
903	White, Reuben	Rapids 1797b	
904	Wiggins, Daniel	Rapids 1797b	
905	Wikle, Jorge	Galveztown 1796	
906	Wikoff	Opelousas 1785	
907	Wikoff, Guillaume	Rapids 1781 ?	
908	Wiks, Guilhume	New Feliciana 1793	
909	Williams, William	New Feliciana 1799	
910	Willson, Robert	Rapids 1797a	
911	Wils, Willing	Opelousas 1794	
912	Wisse	Atakapas 1785	
913	Yarbres, James	Rapids 1781 ?	
914	Yarbres, Thomas	Rapids 1781 ?	
915	Yasbres, Miguel	Rapids 1781 ?	
916	Young, John	Rapids 1797a	
917	Young, Robert	New Feliciana 1808	
918	Ysak, Naughten	Manchak 1795	
919	Zeringue, Pre	Atakapas 1785	

Mississippi

The only breakdown of the region governed from Natchez is by district (Table 14, Natchez Districts). In 1787 there were four: Santa Catalina, Second Creek, Coles Creek, and Bayou Pierre. By 1792 there were seven: Second and Sandy Creek, Buffalo Creek, Homochito, Villa Gayoso (Coles Creek), Bayou Pierre, Rio Black and Bayou Sarah.

In the "Date" column of Table 20 (Natchez Origins), the symbol "a" stands for 1788 and earlier while "b" indicates 1789 or later. Most arrivals (91%) came from Kentucky (54%), Pennsylvania (14%), North Carolina (12%), Cumberland (8%) or Virginia (3%)[17]. North Carolina provided the largest number of emigrants arriving before 1789 (11%).

In Table 15 (Natchez Militia) the ranks are corporal (cabo), sergeant (sargento), second lieutenant (subteniente), lieutenant (teniente) and captain. The term "private" is here used to indicate all other individuals identified in the manuscripts without a rank.

---

[17]Cumberland is now eastern Tennessee and the western edge of North Carolina. A few settlers came from Kaskakia, a settlement in what would eventually become the state of Illinois.

	Name	1787	1792	1795
1	Abrams, Robert		Second & Sandy Creek	
2	Adams, Charles		Santa Catalina	
3	Adams, Guillermo		Villa Gayoso	
4	Adams, Jacobo		Second & Sandy Creek	
5	Adams, Richard	Santa Catalina	Santa Catalina	
6	Adams, Tomas		Villa Gayoso	
7	Alcheson, Guillermo		Second & Sandy Creek	
8	Aldrige, Jorge		Second & Sandy Creek	
9	Alexander, Isaac	Second Creek	Second & Sandy Creek	
10	Alexander, Reuben	Second Creek		
11	Alston, John		Buffalo Creek	
12	Alston, Phelipe Luis		Buffalo Creek	
13	Alston, William		Buffalo Creek	
14	Alva, Stephan		Villa Gayoso	
15	Ambrose, Estevan		Homochito	
16	Andelton, Juan		Villa Gayoso	
17	Anderson, Darius		Second & Sandy Creek	
18	Anderson, Francisco		Santa Catalina	
19	Anderson, Juan		Villa Gayoso	
20	Andrews, Ishamar		Santa Catalina	
21	Andrews, Whamore	Santa Catalina		
22	Arden, Juan		Villa Gayoso	
23	Armstreet, John	Second Creek	Second & Sandy Creek	
24	Armstrong, Moses		Bayou Pierre	
25	Bailey, George	Second Creek	Second & Sandy Creek	
26	Baindo, Jose		Villa Gayoso	
27	Bajsel, Guillermo		Bayou Pierre	
28	Baker, Daniel	Santa Catalina		
29	Baker, Guillermo		Santa Catalina	
30	Bankes, Sutton	Santa Catalina	Santa Catalina	
31	Baptista, Juan		Santa Catalina	
32	Bard, Joel	Santa Catalina		
33	Barket, Asina		Second & Sandy Creek	
34	Barland, William		Santa Catalina	
35	Barrows, Ebenezer		Second & Sandy Creek	
36	Bartley, Juan		Buffalo Creek	
37	Bates, Ephraim	Second Creek	Second & Sandy Creek	
38	Bayley, George	Santa Catalina		
39	Bayly, Tarpley		Villa Gayoso	

	Name	1787	1792	1795
40	Beakly, Adam		Villa Gayoso	
41	Beams, Tomas		Bayou Pierre	
42	Beanden, Jesua		Santa Catalina	
43	Beardman, Guillermo		Villa Gayoso	
44	Bell, Andres		Santa Catalina	
45	Bell, Benjamin	Santa Catalina		
46	Bell, Hugh		Villa Gayoso	
47	Bell, Richard	Santa Catalina	Santa Catalina	
48	Bell, Richard	Second Creek		
49	Belt, Benjamin		Santa Catalina	
50	Benoit, Gabriel		Santa Catalina	
51	Bernard, Joseph		Santa Catalina	
52	Bickley, Adam	Santa Catalina		
53	Bingaman, Christian	Santa Catalina		
54	Bingaman, Christian (son)	Santa Catalina		
55	Bingman, Adam	Santa Catalina	Santa Catalina	
56	Bingman, Christopher		Santa Catalina	
57	Bishop, William		Villa Gayoso	
58	Bisland, Juan		Santa Catalina	
59	Boardman, Carlos		Santa Catalina	
60	Bodio, Juan		Second & Sandy Creek	
61	Bolls, Juan		Santa Catalina	
62	Bonill, Elias		Second & Sandy Creek	
63	Bonner, James		Santa Catalina	
64	Bonner, Joseph	Santa Catalina		
65	Bonner, Moses (father)	Santa Catalina	Santa Catalina	
66	Bonner, Moses (son)	Santa Catalina	Santa Catalina	
67	Bonner, Will (William)		Santa Catalina	
68	Bonnet, Jose		Santa Catalina	
69	Booth, John		Bayou Pierre	
70	Bovards, William		Villa Gayoso	
71	Brasbean, Benjamin		Bayou Pierre	
72	Brashcart, Tobias		Big Black	
73	Brashears, Benjamin	Santa Catalina		
74	Brocas, William		Bayou Pierre	
75	Brocus, William	Santa Catalina		
76	Brown, Guillermo		Bayou Sarah	
77	Brown, Jacob			
78	Brown, Nathaniel		Villa Gayoso	

	Name	1787	1792	1795
79	Brown, Obediah	Santa Catalina	Homochito	
80	Brown, William	Bayou Pierre	Bayou Pierre	
81	Bruin, Pedro		Bayou Pierre	
82	Brunel, Elias	Santa Catalina		
83	Bryan, Jeremiah	Santa Catalina		
84	Bryan, Jeremias (wife)		Santa Catalina	
85	Bullen, John	Santa Catalina	Santa Catalina	
86	Bullock, Benjamin		Second & Sandy Creek	
87	Burch, Guillermo		Villa Gayoso	
88	Burling, Tomas		Second & Sandy Creek	
89	Burnet, Daniel		Bayou Pierre	
90	Burnet, John		Bayou Pierre	
91	Butler, Nataniel		Second & Sandy Creek	
92	Cable, Jacob	Coles Creek	Villa Gayoso	
93	Calender, Alexander	Santa Catalina		
94	Calot, John	Santa Catalina		
95	Calvet, the Widow		Santa Catalina	
96	Calvet, William		Second & Sandy Creek	
97	Calvit, Frederick	Santa Catalina		
98	Calvit, Joseph		Santa Catalina	
99	Calvit, Thomas	Coles Creek	Villa Gayoso	
100	Calvit, William	Santa Catalina		
101	Campbell, Robert		Big Black	
102	Camus, Pedro		Santa Catalina	
103	Carel, Benjamin	Santa Catalina		
104	Carpenter, the Widow		Santa Catalina	
105	Carradine, Parker	Coles Creek	Villa Gayoso	
106	Carrell, Benjamin		Homochito	
107	Carter, Charles		Santa Catalina	
108	Carter, Jesse	Santa Catalina	Second & Sandy Creek	
109	Carter, Nehemiah	Second Creek	Second & Sandy Creek	
110	Carter, Richard	Santa Catalina		
111	Carter, Roberto	Santa Catalina	Santa Catalina	
112	Case, William	Second Creek		
113	Cason, Charles	Second Creek	Santa Catalina	
114	Catton, Roberto		Santa Catalina	
115	Cembrely, Estevan		Bayou Pierre	
116	Chambers, Daniel		Bayou Pierre	
117	Chambers, John		Homochito	

	Name	1787	1792	1795
118	Chambers, William		Second & Sandy Creek	
119	Charboneau, Louis	Second Creek		
120	Cheney, Guillermo		Big Black	
121	Cilond, Adam		Villa Gayoso	
122	Clark, Daniel		Buffalo Creek	Buffalo
123	Clark, Gibson	Bayou Pierre	Bayou Pierre	
124	Clark, Gibson	Santa Catalina		
125	Clark, Jaime		Villa Gayoso	
126	Clark, Lucia		Villa Gayoso	
127	Clark, William		Villa Gayoso	
128	Cleary, Jorge		Villa Gayoso	
129	Cobb, Arthur	Second Creek	Second & Sandy Creek	
130	Cobin, Jacob		Bayou Pierre	
131	Cobin, Samuel		Bayou Pierre	
132	Coburn, Jacob	Santa Catalina		
133	Cochran, Roberto		Santa Catalina	
134	Cogan, Patricio		Bayou Pierre	
135	Coil, Marcos		Villa Gayoso	
136	Colbertson, The Widow		Santa Catalina	
137	Cole, Guillermo		Villa Gayoso	
138	Cole, James (father)	Santa Catalina	Villa Gayoso	
139	Cole, James (son)	Santa Catalina	Villa Gayoso	
140	Cole, Mark	Santa Catalina		
141	Cole, Salomon		Villa Gayoso	
142	Coleman, Ephraim		Villa Gayoso	
143	Coleman, Israel		Santa Catalina	
144	Coleman, Jeremiah		Santa Catalina	
145	Coles, James	Coles Creek		
146	Collender, Alexandro		Villa Gayoso	
147	Collerman, Guillermo		Buffalo Creek	
148	Collins, Carlos		Villa Gayoso	
149	Collins, Denis		Villa Gayoso	
150	Collins, J.			Buffalo
151	Collins, Josua		Villa Gayoso	
152	Collins, William		Buffalo Creek	
153	Conely, Redman		Villa Gayoso	
154	Conner, Juan		Santa Catalina	
155	Cooper, Henry	Second Creek	Second & Sandy Creek	
156	Cooper, Henry (son)	Second Creek		

	Name	1787	1792	1795
157	Cooper, Jaime		Second & Sandy Creek	
158	Cooper, Samuel		Second & Sandy Creek	
159	Cooper, Samuel	Second Creek	Second & Sandy Creek	
160	Cooper, William	Second Creek	Second & Sandy Creek	
161	Correl, Juan		Santa Catalina	
162	Correl, Juan		Bayou Pierre	
163	Corry, Jeremiah		Homochito	
164	Corry, Job	Santa Catalina	Homochito	
165	Cory, Ricardo		Homochito	
166	Cott, Estevan		Villa Gayoso	
167	Cott, Juan		Villa Gayoso	
168	Courtney, John	Coles Creek	Villa Gayoso	
169	Cowel, Juan		Second & Sandy Creek	
170	Coyleman, Jacobo		Bayou Pierre	
171	Coyles, Hugh		Santa Catalina	
172	Crane, Mrs.	Santa Catalina		
173	Crane, Waterman	Santa Catalina	Bayou Pierre	
174	Cravin, John		Second & Sandy Creek	
175	Crayton, Roberto		Villa Gayoso	
176	Crumhott, Jacobo		Villa Gayoso	
177	Crutheirs, Juan		Villa Gayoso	
178	Cruzert, William	Second Creek		
179	Culbertson, Samuel	Second Creek		
180	Cummins, Thomas		Homochito	
181	Cunninghan, Catalina		Second & Sandy Creek	
182	Curtis, Benjamin		Villa Gayoso	
183	Curtis, M.		Santa Catalina	
184	Curtis, Richard	Santa Catalina	Villa Gayoso	
185	Curtis, William	Coles Creek	Villa Gayoso	
186	Danah, Tomas		Santa Catalina	
187	Daniel, William	Santa Catalina		
188	Daniels, Thomas		Villa Gayoso	
189	Daugherty, Antonio		Buffalo Creek	
190	Davenport, Jaime		Bayou Pierre	
191	Davis, Guillermo		Santa Catalina	
192	Davis, Samuel	Coles Creek	Villa Gayoso	
193	Davis, Samuel	Santa Catalina		
194	Dayton, Ebenezer		Santa Catalina	
195	De Brady, Juan		Santa Catalina	

	Name	1787	1792	1795
196	Denham, Reuben	Second Creek		
197	Dervin, Elizabet		Bayou Pierre	
198	Devall, Richard	Coles Creek		
199	Divet, Ezekiel		Santa Catalina	
200	Dix, Juan		Santa Catalina	
201	Dixon, Roger		Villa Gayoso	
202	Domange, Jorge		Villa Gayoso	
203	Donaldson, Juan		Villa Gayoso	
204	Doren, Miguel		Santa Catalina	
205	Douglas, Ana		Villa Gayoso	
206	Douglas, Archival		Villa Gayoso	
207	Douglas, Daniel		Villa Gayoso	
208	Douglas, David		Villa Gayoso	
209	Douglas, Earl	Coles Creek		
210	Douglas, Estevan		Villa Gayoso	
211	Dow, Jose		Homochito	
212	Duesbery, Juan		Second & Sandy Creek	
213	Dumbar, Guillermo		Second & Sandy Creek	
214	Dun, Richard		Santa Catalina	
215	Dunavan, John	Santa Catalina		
216	Dunbar, Robert		Santa Catalina	
217	Duncan, Joseph	Santa Catalina	Santa Catalina	
218	Dunman, Reuben		Bayou Sarah	
219	Durch, Guillermo		Villa Gayoso	
220	Dwet, Jese		Bayou Pierre	
221	Dyson, Clement	Coles Creek	Villa Gayoso	
222	Dyson, Joseph		Villa Gayoso	
223	Dyson, Thomas	Coles Creek	Villa Gayoso	
224	Earheart, Jacobo		Second & Sandy Creek	
225	Eastman, Abel		Villa Gayoso	
226	Edward, Jaime		Villa Gayoso	
227	Eldergill, John	Santa Catalina		
228	Elliot, Guillermo		Santa Catalina	
229	Elliot, James	Coles Creek		
230	Ellis, Abraham		Homochito	
231	Ellis, John (father)		Second & Sandy Creek	
232	Ellis, John (son)		Second & Sandy Creek	
233	Ellis, Ricardo		Santa Catalina	
234	Ellis, Ricardo		Second & Sandy Creek	

	Name	1787	1792	1795
235	Ellis, Richard	Second Creek	Second Creek	
236	Elmore, Juan		Santa Catalina	
237	Ervin, James	Second Creek	Second & Sandy Creek	
238	Ervin, Juan		Second & Sandy Creek	
239	Erwin, William		Villa Gayoso	
240	Fairbanks, William	Coles Creek	Villa Gayoso	
241	Falconer, Guillermo		Villa Gayoso	
242	Farquhar, John	Santa Catalina		
243	Farroco, Alexandro		Second & Sandy Creek	
244	Ferguson, Juan		Santa Catalina	
245	Ferguson, William	Coles Creek	Villa Gayoso	
246	Fillis, Jacob	Second Creek		
247	Finn, Jaime		Bayou Pierre	
248	Fitzgerald, George		Santa Catalina	
249	Fitzgerald, Jaime		Santa Catalina	
250	Five, Isaac		Bayou Pierre	
251	Fletcher, Benjamin		Second & Sandy Creek	
252	Fletcher, William	Santa Catalina	Second & Sandy Creek	
253	Flowers, Elijah	Santa Catalina	Bayou Pierre	
254	Flowers, Josiah	Santa Catalina		
255	Flowers, Samuel	Santa Catalina	Santa Catalina	
256	Foard, Juan		Second & Sandy Creek	
257	Foard, Tomas		Second & Sandy Creek	
258	Foley, Patricio		Homochito	
259	Fooy, Benjamin		Bayou Pierre	
260	Ford, John	Santa Catalina		
261	Forman, Ezekiel		Santa Catalina	
262	Forman, Ismy		Villa Gayoso	
263	Forman, Jorge		Villa Gayoso	
264	Forster, James		Santa Catalina	
265	Foster, James	Santa Catalina	Santa Catalina	
266	Foster, John	Santa Catalina	Santa Catalina	
267	Foster, Mary	Santa Catalina	Santa Catalina	
268	Foster, Thomas	Santa Catalina	Santa Catalina	
269	Foster, William		Santa Catalina	
270	Fowler, Jose		Villa Gayoso	
271	Frail, Eduardo		Bayou Pierre	
272	Gaillard, Ann	Second Creek		
273	Gaillard, Ysac		Homochito	

	Name	1787	1792	1795
274	Gallimore, David		Second & Sandy Creek	
275	Garet, Juan		Villa Gayoso	
276	Garkind, Juan		Villa Gayoso	
277	Gibson, Gil	Santa Catalina	Santa Catalina	
278	Gibson, Reuben	Santa Catalina	Santa Catalina	
279	Gibson, Robert	Coles Creek		
280	Gibson, Samuel	Santa Catalina	Santa Catalina	
281	Gibson, Samuel		Bayou Pierre	
282	Gilbert, Cristobal		Second & Sandy Creek	
283	Gilbert, William		Santa Catalina	
284	Gillaspie, Guillermo		Santa Catalina	
285	Glascock, William		Second & Sandy Creek	
286	Glascok, Jaime		Santa Catalina	
287	Glason, Abraam		Villa Gayoso	
288	Godwin, Richard		Bayou Pierre	
289	Goodwind, Pheby		Bayou Pierre	
290	Grafton, Daniel		Santa Catalina	
291	Grant, Alexandro		Villa Gayoso	
292	Gras, Antonio		Santa Catalina	
293	Gredy, Juan		Villa Gayoso	
294	Green, Abner	Coles Creek	Second & Sandy Creek	
295	Green, Abraam		Villa Gayoso	
296	Green, Henry		Villa Gayoso	
297	Green, John		Bayou Sarah	
298	Green, Joseph	Coles Creek	Villa Gayoso	
299	Green, Nathan		Villa Gayoso	
300	Green, Thomas Masten	Coles Creek	Villa Gayoso	
301	Greenfield, Jesse		Second & Sandy Creek	
302	Greenleaf, David		Villa Gayoso	
303	Greffin, Juan		Villa Gayoso	
304	Grey, Buflin		Homochito	
305	Griffin, Gabriel		Villa Gayoso	
306	Griffin, John	Santa Catalina		
307	Griffin, Thomas	Santa Catalina		
308	Grims, Ricardo		Bayou Pierre	
309	Guise, Michael	Santa Catalina	Villa Gayoso	
310	Gunnels, Federico		Big Black	
311	Hackett, Jonathan	Santa Catalina		
312	Hains, John		Santa Catalina	

	Name	1787	1792	1795
313	Hains, Stephen		Santa Catalina	
314	Hamberlin, William		Villa Gayoso	
315	Hamberling, Juan		Villa Gayoso	
316	Hamilton, Jesse	Second Creek	Villa Gayoso	
317	Hansfeld, Guillermo		Buffalo Creek	
318	Harkins, Guillermo		Bayou Pierre	
319	Harman, Cristian		Santa Catalina	
320	Harman, James		Bayou Pierre	
321	Harmon, James	Santa Catalina		
322	Harrigal, Daniel		Second & Sandy Creek	
323	Harrison, Joseph	Santa Catalina	Santa Catalina	
324	Harrison, Richard	Santa Catalina	Villa Gayoso	
325	Hartley, Jacob		Bayou Pierre	
326	Harvard, Carlos		Santa Catalina	
327	Hawkins, Peter	Coles Creek		
328	Haybraker, John	Coles Creek		
329	Hayes, James	Second Creek		
330	Heady, Samuel	Second Creek	Second & Sandy Creek	
331	Helen, James	Santa Catalina		
332	Hellbrand, David		Villa Gayoso	
333	Hemell, Carlos		Bayou Pierre	
334	Henderson, Alexander		Santa Catalina	
335	Henderson, William	Santa Catalina	Santa Catalina	
336	Here, Andres		Bayou Sarah	
337	Higdon, Jepthah	Santa Catalina	Santa Catalina	
338	Higgins, Barney		Homochito	
339	Higginson, Stuart		Villa Gayoso	
340	Hill, Pedro		Villa Gayoso	
341	Hiller, Margarita		Second & Sandy Creek	
342	Hilonds, Jaime		Villa Gayoso	
343	History, Ephraim		Bayou Pierre	
344	Hoard, Joseph	Santa Catalina		
345	Hoard, Robert	Second Creek		
346	Hobbard, Tomas		Bayou Pierre	
347	Holladay, Juan		Second & Sandy Creek	
348	Holland, John	Santa Catalina		
349	Holland, Jorge		Second & Sandy Creek	
350	Holmes, Benjamin		Second & Sandy Creek	
351	Holmes, Sarah	Second Creek	Second & Sandy Creek	

	Name	1787	1792	1795
352	Holt, David	Coles Creek	Villa Gayoso	
353	Holt, Dibial (Sibdal)	Coles Creek	Villa Gayoso	
354	Holt, Elizabeth	Coles Creek		
355	Holt, John	Coles Creek		
356	Hortin, Abraham		Bayou Sarah	
357	Hortley, John	Second Creek		
358	Howard, Charles	Coles Creek		
359	Howard, Joshua		Second & Sandy Creek	
360	Howe, William		Bayou Pierre	
361	Hudsalt, Jemima	Second Creek		
362	Hufman, Jacobo		Villa Gayoso	
363	Huggs, Tomas		Santa Catalina	
364	Huittler, Daniel		Santa Catalina	
365	Hulbert, William	Santa Catalina		
366	Humphrey, Ana		Bayou Pierre	
367	Humphrey, Jorge		Bayou Pierre	
368	Humphries, Eustice	Coles Creek	Villa Gayoso	
369	Hunter, Enrique		Villa Gayoso	
370	Hunter, Narcisco		Villa Gayoso	
371	Hush, Little Beay		Villa Gayoso	
372	Hutchins, Anthony	Second Creek	Second & Sandy Creek	
373	Igdom, Maria		Santa Catalina	
374	Isenhood, Barnet	Santa Catalina		
375	Isenhoot, Bernabe		Villa Gayoso	
376	Ivers, Juan		Bayou Pierre	
377	Jacken, Tomas		Santa Catalina	
378	John, George		Villa Gayoso	
379	John, James		Santa Catalina	
380	Johns, Carlos		Santa Catalina	
381	Johns, David		Buffalo Creek	
382	Johnson, Edmund		Villa Gayoso	
383	Johnston, Issac	Second Creek	Second & Sandy Creek	
384	Jones, David			Buffalo
385	Jones, David (son)			Buffalo
386	Jones, James			Buffalo
387	Jones, John	Coles Creek	Villa Gayoso	
388	Jones, Mateo		Second & Sandy Creek	
389	Jourdan, Stephen	Santa Catalina		
390	Jourdan, Thomas	Santa Catalina	Santa Catalina	

	Name	1787	1792	1795
391	Kannady, David		Second & Sandy Creek	
392	Karr, Samuel		Villa Gayoso	
393	Kelly, James		Second & Sandy Creek	
394	Kelly, Thomas		Santa Catalina	
395	Kennard, Sarah	Second Creek		
396	Kennson, Nataniel		Villa Gayoso	
397	Kenty, Jaime		Villa Gayoso	
398	Kid, Robert	Santa Catalina		
399	Killian, George	Santa Catalina	Santa Catalina	
400	Kincade, John	Santa Catalina		
401	King, Caleb	Santa Catalina	Homochito	
402	King, Charles		Santa Catalina	
403	King, Joseph	Santa Catalina		
404	King, Juan		Villa Gayoso	
405	King, Justo		Villa Gayoso	
406	King, Justus (or Justice)	Santa Catalina		
407	King, Prosper		Villa Gayoso	
408	King, Ricardo		Villa Gayoso	
409	King, Richard	Santa Catalina		
410	Kinrick, Juan		Santa Catalina	
411	Kirk, James		Homochito	
412	Kirkland, Guillermo		Villa Gayoso	
413	Kirkland, Samuel		Villa Gayoso	
414	Laforce, Joseph	Santa Catalina		
415	Lambert, David	Santa Catalina		
416	Lambert, David		Homochito	
417	Lambert, David	Second Creek		
418	Landon, Davis		Homochito	
419	Landphier, Tomas		Second & Sandy Creek	
420	Laneer, Benjamin		Second & Sandy Creek	
421	Lanhart, Adam		Villa Gayoso	
422	Leanheart, Adam	Second Creek	Second Creek	
423	Lee, John Hill	Santa Catalina		
424	Lee, William	Second Creek	Second & Sandy Creek	
425	Leonard, Israel		Santa Catalina	
426	Lewis, Isaac		Santa Catalina	
427	Leyeune, David		Buffalo Creek	
428	Leyeune, Salomon		Santa Catalina	
429	Lintot, Bernard	Santa Catalina	Santa Catalina	

	Name	1787	1792	1795
430	Lobdell, James		Bayou Pierre	
431	Lobellas, Eduardo		Buffalo Creek	
432	Lobellas, Juan		Buffalo Creek	
433	Lobellas, Tomas		Buffalo Creek	
434	Lord, Richard		Bayou Pierre	
435	Lovelace, Edward			Buffalo
436	Lovelace, George			Buffalo
437	Lovelace, John (father)	Second Creek		Buffalo
438	Lovelace, John (son)			Buffalo
439	Lovelace, Richard			Buffalo
440	Lovelace, Thomas			Buffalo
441	Lovelace, William			Buffalo
442	Lum, Guillermo		Villa Gayoso	
443	Lum, John		Santa Catalina	
444	Lusk, John		Homochito	
445	Lyaton, Jaime		Bayou Pierre	
446	Lyons, Jermas		Buffalo Creek	
447	Madden, Manuel (Emaniel)	Santa Catalina	Santa Catalina	
448	Maggot, Daniel	Santa Catalina		
449	Maggot, Roswell (Rosel)	Santa Catalina		
450	Man, Frederick		Santa Catalina	
451	Manadne, Enrrique		Santa Catalina	
452	Manadne, Enrrique (son)		Santa Catalina	
453	Manedeau, Henry	Santa Catalina		
454	Mansco, Federico		Villa Gayoso	
455	Marbel, Earl		Villa Gayoso	
456	Martin, John	Santa Catalina		
457	Martin, Juan		Villa Gayoso	
458	Martin, Thomas		Second & Sandy Creek	
459	Martin, Thomas		Second & Sandy Creek	
460	Marvill, Abner		Villa Gayoso	
461	Masters, Jonathan		Second & Sandy Creek	
462	Mather, Guillermo		Villa Gayoso	
463	Mather, Jaime		Bayou Pierre	
464	Mays, Abraham		Villa Gayoso	
465	Mays, Stephen	Santa Catalina	Santa Catalina	
466	Mayson, Richard	Coles Creek		
467	McCabe, Edward		Santa Catalina	
468	McCoy, Donald		Homochito	

113

	Name	1787	1792	1795
469	McCullock, Mateo		Homochito	
470	McDermot, Patricio		Villa Gayoso	
471	McDougle, Guillermo		Second & Sandy Creek	
472	McDuffey, Arch		Second & Sandy Creek	
473	McFarland, David		Bayou Pierre	
474	McFee, Juan		Second & Sandy Creek	
475	McGill, Daniel		Second & Sandy Creek	
476	McHeath, Patricio		Bayou Pierre	
477	McIntoche, Guillermo		Santa Catalina	
478	McIntosh, Eunice	Santa Catalina	Santa Catalina	
479	McIntyre, James		Santa Catalina	
480	Milburn, Enrrique		Villa Gayoso	
481	Miller, Daniel		Bayou Pierre	
482	Miller, Jacobo		Second & Sandy Creek	
483	Miller, Jose		Homochito	
484	Miller, Richard	Santa Catalina	Santa Catalina	
485	Miller, Robert		Homochito	
486	Miller, William		Bayou Pierre	
487	Minor, Estevan		Second & Sandy Creek	
488	Minorby, Miguel		Second & Sandy Creek	
489	Mitchel, David	Second Creek	Second & Sandy Creek	
490	Monrroy, La subcere.		Bayou Sarah	
491	Monsanto, Benjamin		Santa Catalina	
492	Monson, Jesse		Villa Gayoso	
493	Monson, Roberto		Villa Gayoso	
494	Moore, Alexandro		Santa Catalina	
495	Moore, Tomas		Santa Catalina	
496	Moran, William	Santa Catalina		
497	Morgan, Guillermo		Second & Sandy Creek	
498	Morgan, Thomas	Second Creek	Second & Sandy Creek	
499	Morning, Guillermo		Santa Catalina	
500	Mulhollon, the Widow		Santa Catalina	
501	Mulkey, David	Santa Catalina	Santa Catalina	
502	Muris, Groves		Villa Gayoso	
503	Murray, Guillermo		Villa Gayoso	
504	Murray, Jorge		Villa Gayoso	
505	Murray, Tomas		Homochito	
506	Myer, Federico		Big Black	
507	Mygatt, Margarita		Santa Catalina	

	Name	1787	1792	1795
508	Naylor, Francisco		Bayou Pierre	
509	Naylor, Juan		Bayou Pierre	
510	Nelson, Peter	Second Creek	Second & Sandy Creek	
511	Newman, Ezekiel		Villa Gayoso	
512	Newman, Ysac		Villa Gayoso	
513	Newton, John	Second Creek	Second & Sandy Creek	
514	Nichols, Thomas	Santa Catalina		
515	Nichols, Tomas		Second & Sandy Creek	
516	Nicholson, Enrrique		Homochito	
517	Nicholson, James		Homochito	
518	Noling, William	Coles Creek		
519	Norton, Abraham		Santa Catalina	
520	Norton, Abraham	Santa Catalina		
521	Noskins, Ezekiel		Bayou Pierre	
522	Novres, Jorge		Big Black	
523	Oconnor, Mary	Santa Catalina		
524	Oconor, Juan		Bayou Sarah	
525	Odum, David	Coles Creek	Villa Gayoso	
526	Odum, John	Santa Catalina	Santa Catalina	
527	Ogden, Daniel	Santa Catalina	Buffalo Creek	Buffalo
528	Ogden, Isaac			Buffalo
529	Ogden, Richard			Buffalo
530	Ogden, William			Buffalo
531	Oglesby, James	Second Creek	Second & Sandy Creek	
532	Oiler, Mark	Santa Catalina		
533	Oiler, the Widow		Santa Catalina	
534	Ophil, Eliza		Santa Catalina	
535	Orange		Buffalo Creek	
536	Owings, William	Santa Catalina	Santa Catalina	
537	Oxbury, John		Santa Catalina	
538	Palmer, Archibald	Second Creek	Homochito	
539	Parmer, Archibald	Santa Catalina		
540	Paterson, Guillermo		Villa Gayoso	
541	Patterson, John	Second Creek	Second & Sandy Creek	
542	Paulset, Francisco		Bayou Sarah	
543	Percey, Jacobo		Santa Catalina	
544	Percy, Charles Luke		Buffalo Creek	Buffalo
545	Percy, Thomas G.			Buffalo
546	Perkins, John		Santa Catalina	

	Name	1787	1792	1795
547	Perkins, Jonathan		Santa Catalina	
548	Perkins, Joseph		Santa Catalina	
549	Perry, Daniel	Second Creek	Villa Gayoso	
550	Perry, Maydelen		Villa Gayoso	
551	Phipps, Henry	Second Creek		
552	Phipps, Samuel		Second & Sandy Creek	
553	Phips, Henry		Homochito	
554	Pipes, Windsor		Santa Catalina	
555	Pips, Abner		Santa Catalina	
556	Pittman, Bukner		Bayou Pierre	
557	Platner, Henry		Villa Gayoso	
558	Porter, Samuel		Villa Gayoso	
559	Potter, Ebenezer		Buffalo Creek	
560	Pountney, William	Santa Catalina		
561	Pourchous, Antonio		Santa Catalina	
562	Presley, Pedro		Second & Sandy Creek	
563	Preston, Guillermo		Second & Sandy Creek	
564	Price, Leonardo		Bayou Pierre	
565	Pritchards, Job		Santa Catalina	
566	Proctor, Reuben		Bayou Pierre	
567	Pruit, Beesley	Second Creek	Second & Sandy Creek	
568	Pyatte, Jacobo		Bayou Pierre	
569	Raby, Cader	Santa Catalina	Santa Catalina	
570	Ramer, Miguel		Santa Catalina	
571	Randell, Tensa		Bayou Pierre	
572	Ranner, Samuel		Santa Catalina	
573	Rapalise, Juana		Second & Sandy Creek	
574	Rapalye, Garet		Big Black	
575	Rapalye, Isaac		Big Black	
576	Rapalye, Santiago		Big Black	
577	Ratcliffe, John	Second Creek	Second & Sandy Creek	
578	Ratcliffe, William	Second Creek	Second & Sandy Creek	
579	Reed, Thomas		Santa Catalina	
580	Reilly, Tomas		Santa Catalina	
581	Rice, Manuel		Bayou Pierre	
582	Rice, Reuben		Bayou Pierre	
583	Rich, Jorge		Santa Catalina	
584	Rich, Juan		Villa Gayoso	
585	Richards, Estevan		Bayou Pierre	

	Name	1787	1792	1795
586	Richards, Mordica		Homochito	
587	Richardson, George	Second Creek		
588	Richardson, Henry	Second Creek		
589	Richardson, James		Second & Sandy Creek	
590	Roach, William			Buffalo
591	Roach, Henry	Santa Catalina	Buffalo Creek	Buffalo
592	Roach, John			Buffalo
593	Rob, Nicolas		Second & Sandy Creek	
594	Rob, Nicolas (son)		Second & Sandy Creek	
595	Roberts, John		Villa Gayoso	
596	Robeson, Tomas		Villa Gayoso	
597	Robinson, Archivald		Villa Gayoso	
598	Roddy, Augustus		Homochito	
599	Roddy, Ricardo		Villa Gayoso	
600	Rols, David		Bayou Sarah	
601	Routh, Elias		Villa Gayoso	
602	Routh, Jeremiah		Villa Gayoso	
603	Routh, Job		Villa Gayoso	
604	Routh, Margaret	Coles Creek	Villa Gayoso	
605	Row, Margarita		Buffalo Creek	
606	Ruker, Jonathan		Villa Gayoso	
607	Rule, Thomas	Santa Catalina	Santa Catalina	
608	Rundell, Seth		Bayou Pierre	
609	Ryan, William	Second Creek	Santa Catalina	
610	Ryland, James		Bayou Sarah	
611	Sanders, James		Second & Sandy Creek	
612	Savage, Ana	Second Creek	Homochito	
613	Scandling, Andreu		Santa Catalina	
614	Schophel, Joseph	Santa Catalina		
615	Scoggins, Juan		Santa Catalina	
616	Scophil, Jose		Villa Gayoso	
617	Scriber, Estevan		Villa Gayoso	
618	Serlot, Pedro		Bayou Pierre	
619	Shaw, Cornelio		Santa Catalina	
620	Shepman, Maria		Villa Gayoso	
621	Shilling, Jacob		Villa Gayoso	
622	Shilling, Palser	Santa Catalina	Santa Catalina	
623	Shonaner, Juan		Santa Catalina	
624	Silkreg, Guillermo		Santa Catalina	

	Name	1787	1792	1795
625	Simmons, Charles	Coles Creek	Villa Gayoso	
626	Sinclair, Gaspar Mitchel	Coles Creek	Villa Gayoso	
627	Sivesay, David		Homochito	
628	Sivezay, Gabriel		Homochito	
629	Slater, Hugh		Second & Sandy Creek	
630	Slater, Joseph		Second & Sandy Creek	
631	Sloan, Archibel		Santa Catalina	
632	Sluter, Juan		Bayou Pierre	
633	Smiley, Thomas	Coles Creek	Villa Gayoso	
634	Smith, Adolphfus [sic], F.			Buffalo
635	Smith, Calvin		Second & Sandy Creek	
636	Smith, Catalina		Santa Catalina	
637	Smith, David		Villa Gayoso	
638	Smith, Ebenezer		Bayou Pierre	
639	Smith, Elias		Bayou Pierre	
640	Smith, James		Buffalo Creek	
641	Smith, John	Coles Creek	Villa Gayoso	
642	Smith, John		Bayou Pierre	
643	Smith, John Moses			Buffalo
644	Smith, Lucins		Bayou Pierre	
645	Smith, Martin	Santa Catalina		
646	Smith, Pedro		Buffalo Creek	
647	Smith, Philander		Second & Sandy Creek	
648	Smith, Philetus	Second Creek		
649	Smith, Philinu		Santa Catalina	
650	Smith, Philitus		Santa Catalina	
651	Smith, Tere		Bayou Pierre	
652	Smith, the Widow		Santa Catalina	
653	Smith, Thomas		Bayou Pierre	
654	Smith, William		Santa Catalina	
655	Smith, William			Buffalo
656	Smith, William	Bayou Pierre		
657	Smith, William		Santa Catalina	
658	Smith, Zachariah	Santa Catalina		
659	Smith, Zachariah (father)		Buffalo Creek	Buffalo
660	Smith, Zachariah (son)		Buffalo Creek	Buffalo
661	Solivester		Santa Catalina	
662	Spain, Francis	Coles Creek	Villa Gayoso	
663	Spain, Jaime		Villa Gayoso	

	Name	1787	1792	1795
664	Spires, Juan		Second & Sandy Creek	
665	Splun, Tomas		Villa Gayoso	
666	Stampley, George	Coles Creek	Villa Gayoso	
667	Stampley, Henry	Coles Creek		
668	Stampley, Jacob		Villa Gayoso	
669	Stampley, John	Coles Creek	Villa Gayoso	
670	Stampley, Margarita		Villa Gayoso	
671	Stark, Robert		Bayou Sarah	
672	Steel, John	Second Creek		
673	Stephenson, Stephen	Second Creek	Second & Sandy Creek	
674	Sterns, Stephen	Santa Catalina		
675	Stewart, James		Second & Sandy Creek	
676	Still, Benjamin		Villa Gayoso	
677	Stock, Guillermo		Santa Catalina	
678	Stockstill, Jose		Second & Sandy Creek	
679	Stoddard, James	Santa Catalina		
680	Stokman, Federico		Bayou Pierre	
681	Stoop, Jacobo		Santa Catalina	
682	Stout, Juan		Second & Sandy Creek	
683	Stowars, Juan		Big Black	
684	Stowars, Juan		Santa Catalina	
685	Straddler, Edward	Santa Catalina		
686	Strawbraker, John		Villa Gayoso	
687	Strong, Juan Conrad		Santa Catalina	
688	Sullivan, Daniel		Santa Catalina	
689	Sullivan, Patricio		Buffalo Creek	
690	Sullivan, Patricio		Villa Gayoso	
691	Surget, Pedro		Second & Sandy Creek	
692	Swasey, Elija	Santa Catalina		
693	Swazey, Gabriel	Santa Catalina		
694	Swazey, John	Santa Catalina		
695	Swazey, Nathan	Second Creek	Second Creek	
696	Swazey, Richard	Santa Catalina	Santa Catalina	
697	Swazey, Samuel	Santa Catalina	Santa Catalina	
698	Tabor, Isaac	Santa Catalina	Santa Catalina	
699	Tabor, William	Bayou Pierre	Bayou Pierre	
700	Take, Juan		Villa Gayoso	
701	Take, Miguel		Villa Gayoso	
702	Tanner, David	Santa Catalina		

	Name	1787	1792	1795
703	Tarinton, Tomas		Bayou Pierre	
704	Tavely, James	Coles Creek		
705	Taylor, Isac		Villa Gayoso	
706	Terry, Jaime		Santa Catalina	
707	Terry, John	Coles Creek	Villa Gayoso	
708	Texada, Manuel	Coles Creek		
709	Thomas, William	Coles Creek	Villa Gayoso	
710	Throckmorton, Roberto		Villa Gayoso	
711	Todd, Roberto		Santa Catalina	
712	Tomas, Juan		Santa Catalina	
713	Tomlinston, Nathaniel	Santa Catalina	Santa Catalina	
714	Tomlston, Nataniel		Second & Sandy Creek	
715	Tomlston, Nataniel		Homochito	
716	Tooy, Isaac		Bayou Pierre	
717	Trasher, Juan		Bayou Pierre	
718	Trevillon, Richard	Second Creek		
719	Trockmorton, Mordica		Villa Gayoso	
720	Troop, Jorge		Santa Catalina	
721	Truely, Benet	Santa Catalina	Villa Gayoso	
722	Truely, James		Villa Gayoso	
723	Turpin, Philip Pleasant	Santa Catalina		
724	Twely, Nataniel		Santa Catalina	
725	Twins, Tomas		Bayou Pierre	
726	Vancheret, Jose		Santa Catalina	
727	Vancheret, Juan		Santa Catalina	
728	Vilaret, Luis		Santa Catalina	
729	Voice, Tomas		Bayou Pierre	
730	Vousdan, Guillermo		Santa Catalina	
731	Vousdan, William	Second Creek		
732	Wade, James		Santa Catalina	
733	Wadkins, Andres		Villa Gayoso	
734	Walker, Gideon	Santa Catalina		
735	Wall, John		Bayou Sarah	Buffalo
736	Waltman, David	Santa Catalina		
737	Warren, Thomas	Santa Catalina		
738	Waths, Roberto		Villa Gayoso	
739	Weasner, Jorge		Santa Catalina	
740	Weed, Joel		Second & Sandy Creek	
741	Weeks, William		Santa Catalina	

	Name	1787	1792	1795
742	Welch, Sarah	Second Creek		
743	Welton, John	Santa Catalina		
744	Welton, Juan		Bayou Sarah	
745	West, Cato	Coles Creek	Villa Gayoso	
746	West, Little Berry		Second & Sandy Creek	
747	West, William	Santa Catalina	Second & Sandy Creek	
748	Wethers, Jese		Santa Catalina	
749	Whitaker, Daniel	Santa Catalina		
750	White, Lily		Buffalo Creek	
751	White, Mateo		Second & Sandy Creek	
752	White, Mathew	Santa Catalina		
753	White, Reuben	Santa Catalina		
754	White, Reuben	Bayou Pierre		
755	Whitman, John	Santa Catalina		
756	Wicks, William	Santa Catalina		
757	Wiley, John		Santa Catalina	
758	Wilkerson, Juan		Bayou Pierre	
759	Willey, James		Santa Catalina	
760	Williams, David		Santa Catalina	
761	Williams, Hezekiah	Second Creek		
762	Williams, John		Villa Gayoso	
763	Williams, Miguel		Second & Sandy Creek	
764	Willson, William		Buffalo Creek	
765	Wilson, Juan		Santa Catalina	
766	Withers, Jesse	Second Creek		
767	Withers, Mary	Second Creek		
768	Withers, Robert		Second & Sandy Creek	
769	Witley, Salomon		Bayou Pierre	
770	Woolley, Melling		Bayou Pierre	
771	Young, Elizabet		Villa Gayoso	
772	Young, Guillermo		Bayou Pierre	
773	Young, Juan		Villa Gayoso	
774	Zeines, Juan		Villa Gayoso	

Table 15. Natchez Militia

	Name	Rank
1	Abrams, Roberto	private
2	Adams, Jacob	cabo
3	Adams, Richard	private
4	Alexander, Isaac	private
5	Alva, Estevan	private
6	Armstreet, John	private
7	Armstrong, Moises	private
8	Azevedo, Pedro	private
9	Bacon, William	private
10	Bailey, George	private
11	Bales, Sphzam	private
12	Bankes, Sutton	teniente
13	Barland, William	cabo
14	Baya, William	private
15	Beid, Joel	private
16	Bell, Richard	private
17	Belt, Benjamin	sargento
18	Benel, Elias	private
19	Bernard, Joseph	private
20	Bingaman, Adam	captain
21	Bingaman, Christian	private
22	Bingaman, Luis	private
23	Bolls, Juan	cabo
24	Bonner, James	private
25	Bonner, Joseph	private
26	Bonner, Moses	private
27	Borne, Squire	private
28	Bowas, Tomas	private
29	Bozeland, John	private
30	Brandon, Gerard	cabo
31	Breen, Joseph	private
32	Brocus, William	private
33	Brody, Juan	private
34	Brown, Obediah	private
35	Brown, Thomas	private
36	Brown, William	private
37	Bryan, Jeremiah	sargento
38	Bullen, John	private
39	Bullock, Jorge	private

	Name	Rank
40	Burnet, Daniel	private
41	Burnet, John	private
42	Burvel, Juan	private
43	Cable, Jacob	private
44	Calvit, Frederick	private
45	Calvit, John	private
46	Calvit, Joseph	private
47	Calvit, Thomas	private
48	Calvit, William	private
49	Campbell, Robert	private
50	Camus, Pedro	private
51	Carr, John	sargento
52	Carradine, Parker	private
53	Carrell, Benjamin	private
54	Carter, Carlos	private
55	Carter, Charles	private
56	Carter, Joseph	private
57	Carter, Nehemiah	private
58	Carter, Roberto	private
59	Case, William	private
60	Cason, Charles	private
61	Chacheret, Luis	private
62	Chaffe, Abner	private
63	Chambers, John	private
64	Charboneau, Louis	private
65	Clark, Gibson	private
66	Clark, John	private
67	Clark, William	private
68	Cobb, Arthur	private
69	Cobb, William	private
70	Cole, Estevan	private
71	Cole, James	private
72	Cole, Mark	private
73	Coleman, Toumerk	private
74	Coles, James	private
75	Colle, Marcos	private
76	Collins, William	cabo
77	Comparg, Francisco	private
78	Cooper, Henry	cabo

	Name	Rank
79	Cooper, Samuel	private
80	Cooper, Samuel	private
81	Cooper, William	cabo
82	Corry, Job	private
83	Courtney, John	private
84	Crane, Waterman	cabo
85	Culbertson, Samuel	private
86	Curtis, Benjamin	private
87	Curtis, Jonathan	private
88	Curtis, William	private
89	Daniel, William	private
90	Davis, Juan	private
91	Davis, Landon	private
92	Davis, Samuel	private
93	Dayton, Ebenezer	private
94	Dejoy, Jacque	private
95	Devall, Richard	subteniente
96	Divet, Ezekiel	sargento
97	Drake, Benjamin	private
98	Druel, Bovly	private
99	Dun, Richard	cabo
100	Dunbar, Robert	sargento
101	Dunnam, Ruben	private
102	Dyson, Clement	private
103	Elliot, James	private
104	Ellis, Abram	teniente
105	Ellis, Juan	captain
106	Ellis, Juan	private
107	Ellis, Ricardo	subteniente
108	Ellis, Richard	private
109	Erwin, William	private
110	Esllins, Taushn	private
111	Fage, Juan	private
112	Fairbanks, William	private
113	Ferguson, Juan	cabo
114	Ferguson, William	private
115	Filizger, Jorge	private
116	Flower, Josiah	cabo
117	Flowers, Elijah	private

	Name	Rank
118	Ford, Robert	private
119	Foster, John	cabo
120	Foster, Thomas	private
121	Foster, William	private
122	Gaillard, Isaac	cabo
123	Gibson, Reuben	private
124	Gibson, Samuel	subteniente
125	Gilbert, William	private
126	Glascock, William	private
127	Gockey, Juan	private
128	Gooding, Ricardo	private
129	Grafton, Daniel	private
130	Gras, Antonio	private
131	Green, Abner	private
132	Green, Henry	private
133	Green, Thomas Masten	private
134	Greffin, Juan	private
135	Griffin, Gabriel	private
136	Grubson, Grubion	private
137	Guise, Michael	cabo
138	Hamberlin, William	private
139	Hannan, Archebal	private
140	Harman, Cristian	cabo
141	Harmon, Hezikiah	private
142	Harrison, Joseph	private
143	Harrison, Joseph	cabo
144	Harrison, Richard	captain
145	Hartley, John	private
146	Hawid, Charles	private
147	Hawkins, Peter	private
148	Hayes, James	private
149	Henderson, Juan	private
150	Henderson, William	private
151	Herdy, Samuel	private
152	Herwin, James	private
153	Higdon, Jesse (Jepthah)	private
154	Hodel, David	private
155	Holladay, Juan	private
156	Holmes, Benjamin	private

	Name	Rank
157	Holmes, Joseph	private
158	Holmes, Simon	private
159	Holt, John	private
160	Homes, Benjamin	private
161	Horten, Estevan	private
162	Hulbert, Tomas	private
163	Hult, James	private
164	Humphreys, Eustachio	private
165	Hutchins, Samuel	subteniente
166	Jones, John	private
167	Jones, Mateo	private
168	Jourdan, Thomas	sargento
169	Kelly, Juan	cabo
170	Kid, Robert	private
171	Killian, George	cabo
172	King, Caleb	private
173	King, Charles	private
174	King, Prosper	private
175	King, Richard	sargento
176	Kirk, James	private
177	Kook, Jorge	private
178	Labady, Joaquin	private
179	Laforce, Joseph	private
180	Lambert, David	private
181	Landock, Pedro	private
182	Laprint, Juan	private
183	Lapuente, Juan Baptista	private
184	Lavis, Ysaac	private
185	Leanheart, Adam	cabo
186	Leapheart, Jacob	private
187	Lee, William	private
188	Lintot Juan	private
189	Lintot, William	private
190	Lord, Tomas	private
191	Lum, John	cabo
192	Lusk, John	private
193	Madden, Manuel (Emaniel)	private
194	Maggot, Daniel	private
195	Maggot, Roswell (Rosel)	sargento

	Name	Rank
196	Manedeau, Henry	private
197	Martin, John	cabo
198	Maurace, Pedro	private
199	Mays, Abraham	private
200	Mays, Stephen	private
201	McHanlos, Guillermo	private
202	McIntosh, Samuel	teniente
203	McIntyre, James	private
204	Mcor, Samuel	private
205	Miguel, David	private
206	Miller, Joseph	private
207	Miller, Richard	private
208	Monard, Joseph	private
209	Montgomery, John	private
210	Morgan, Thomas	private
211	Mouvas, Gales	private
212	Mulkey, David	private
213	Nask, Thomas	private
214	Nelson, Peter	private
215	Newton, John	private
216	Noling, William	private
217	Odum, David	cabo
218	Odum, John	private
219	Ogden, Daniel	private
220	Oglesby, James	private
221	Owings, William	private
222	Oxbury, John	private
223	Pepes, Wenson	private
224	Pera, Juan	private
225	Perkins, Joseph	private
226	Philips, John	private
227	Phipps, Henry	private
228	Phipps, Samuel	private
229	Povus, Daniel (son)	private
230	Powel, Marke	private
231	Pruit, Beesley	private
232	Quirk, Edmond	private
233	Quirk, William	private
234	Rab, Nicolas	private

	Name	Rank
235	Raby, Cader	cabo
236	Raines, Samuel	private
237	Rallis, Juan	private
238	Ratcliffe (Rattef), William	private
239	Richardson, George	private
240	Richardson, Henry	private
241	Richardson, James	private
242	Richey, Juan	private
243	Robeson, Thomas	private
244	Roulk, Soumiak	private
245	Roull, Toumlak	private
246	Routh, Job	private
247	Rule, Thomas	private
248	Sanders, James	private
249	Sankley, Gaspar	private
250	Sect, William	private
251	Seoggins, Jonas	private
252	Shilling, Palser	private
253	Shunk, John	private
254	Simmons, Charles	private
255	Smily, Thomas	private
256	Smith, Benjamin	sargento
257	Smith, David	private
258	Smith, Ebenezer	private
259	Smith, Israel	private
260	Smith, James	private
261	Smith, John	sargento
262	Smith, Jorge	private
263	Smith, Peter	private
264	Smith, Philander	private
265	Smith, Samuel	private
266	Smith, William	private
267	Solidet, Samuel	private
268	Spain, Francis	private
269	Spires, Juan	private
270	Stampley, George	private
271	Stampley, Henry	private
272	Stampley, John	sargento
273	Stephenson, Stephen	private

	Name	Rank
274	Stowars, Juan	cabo
275	Strawbraker, John	cabo
276	Stroder, James	sargento
277	Stul, Juan	private
278	Suzget, Carlos	private
279	Swasey, Elija	private
280	Swazey, John	private
281	Swazey, Nathan	cabo
282	Swazey, Richard	private
283	Swazey, Samuel	private
284	Tabor, Isaac	private
285	Tabor, William	private
286	Tanner, David	private
287	Texada, Manuel	private
288	Thomas, William	private
289	Thukston, Abraam	private
290	Tifes, Ysaak	private
291	Tomlinston, Nathaniel	private
292	Tonshon, Ysaac	captain
293	Touman, Jorge	private
294	Trudey, Baptista	private
295	Truely, Benet	cabo
296	Truely, James	sargento
297	Truman, Tomas	private
298	Tsenhood, Barney	private
299	Turfey, Patricio	private
300	Turpin, Philip Pleasant	private
301	Tuvey, John	private
302	Tuy, Nataniel	private
303	Ury, Roberto	private
304	Vancheret, Jose	private
305	Vaude, Thomas	private
306	Wade, James	private
307	Walker, Pedro	private
308	Wallmon, David	private
309	Walter, Samuel	private
310	Weathus, Jose	private
311	Wently, Ricardo	private
312	West, Cato	private

	Name	Rank
313	West, William	private
314	Whete, Carlos	private
315	Whitaker, Daniel	cabo
316	White, John	private
317	White, Reuben	private
318	Whitman, John	private
319	Whular, Jose	private
320	Wilkins, Tomas	private
321	Williams, Hezekiah	private
322	Wilson, William	private
323	Woods, John	private
324	Wousdan, William	private
325	Wuaks, William	private

Table 16. Natchez Names 1781/1786

	Name	1781	1782	1783	1784	1786
1	Abadden, Emanuel		X			
2	Abamey, John		X			
3	Abore, John		X			
4	Aborris, Grove		X			
5	Aby, Cader		X		X	
6	Adams, Charles		X		X	
7	Adams, Manuel					X
8	Adams, Richard		X			
9	Albertson, Jeremiah				X	
10	Alexander, Isaac		X			
11	Alexander, Mary				X	
12	Alexander, Reuben		X		X	
13	Allen, John		X			
14	Allen, Nathan		X			
15	Alston, James (son)		X			
16	Alston, John		X			
17	Alston, William		X			
18	Alva, Estevan				X	
19	Alvarez, Julian			X		
20	Andrew, Thomas		X			
21	Aradley, Edward			X		
22	Armstreet, John		X		X	
23	Armstrong, James				X	
24	Ashbraner				X	
25	Athom, Philip		X			
26	Aveezey, Elija				X	
27	Bailey, George		X			
28	Bairfield, James				X	
29	Baker, Daniel		X			
30	Baker, Thomas			X		
31	Balk, Benjamin		X			
32	Ban, John					X
33	Bankes, Sutton				X	
34	Barland, William				X	
35	Basset, William				X	
36	Baylugh, James		X			
37	Bays, Bosman		X			
38	Beabron, Anthony		X			
39	Beater, Hall		X			

	Name	1781	1782	1783	1784	1786
40	Bedeil, Jonathan					x
41	Bedell, Elias					x
42	Bell, Samuel	x				
43	Berrent, David		x			
44	Bingaman, Adam				x	
45	Bingaman, Christian				x	
46	Bingaman, Christopher		x		x	
47	Blommant, Jean		x			
48	Boain, Adam			x		
49	Bolt, David		x			
50	Bolt, John		x			
51	Bonner, James		x			
52	Bonner, Moses		x		x	
53	Bonner, Moses (son)		x			
54	Bouls, John				x	
55	Boyd, Thomas		x			
56	Boyde, Thomas		x			
57	Brandon, Gerard	x				
58	Brasfield, Joshua			x		
59	Brassell, Robert				x	
60	Brocus, William		x		x	
61	Brown, Guillermo		x			
62	Brown, Jacob					x
63	Brown, Jediah				x	
64	Brown, John			x		
65	Brown, John			x		
66	Brown, John			x		
67	Brown, Nathaniel		x			
68	Brown, Obediah		x			
69	Brown, William			x	x	
70	Bryan, Jeremiah				x	
71	Bullock, John				x	
72	Burner, Soloman				x	
73	Burnet, John				x	
74	Burney, Simon					x
75	Burns, Patrick		x			
76	Burrel, Curtis		x			
77	Cable, Jacob				x	
78	Cafe, Guilliaum		x			

	Name	1781	1782	1783	1784	1786
79	Calender, Alexander		x		x	
80	Caler, Joseph					x
81	Calvert, Thomas		x			
82	Calvet, William			x		
83	Calvit, Frederick			x	x	
84	Calvit, John					x
85	Calvit, Joseph				x	
86	Calvit, Thomas				x	
87	Calvit, William				x	
88	Cameron, Evan		x			
89	Campbell, Robert		x			
90	Carradine, Parker		x		x	
91	Carrel, Talbort				x	
92	Carrell, Benjamin				x	
93	Carron, Walter		x			
94	Carter, Charles				x	
95	Carter, Jesse		x			
96	Carter, Jesse		x			
97	Carter, Nehemiah		x		x	
98	Carter, Nehemiah		x			
99	Carter, Robert				x	
100	Carter, Thomas		x			
101	Case, William					x
102	Cason, Charles				x	
103	Cautherine, Elizabeth				x	
104	Chambort, John		x			
105	Charboneau, Louis				x	
106	Chatten, Thomas		x			
107	Choate, John				x	
108	Christian, Jacob					x
109	Clark, Gibson				x	
110	Clark, John		x			
111	Cleamom, Pat		x			
112	Clermon		x			
113	Cobb, Arthur			x	x	
114	Cobb, Jacob		x			
115	Coburn, Jacob		x			
116	Colbert, Thomas			x		
117	Coleman, Jeremiah		x			

133

	Name	1781	1782	1783	1784	1786
118	Coleman, Nicolas					X
119	Collell, Francisco			X		
120	Collins, Jean	X				
121	Colman, John		X			
122	Conticle		X			
123	Cooper, Samuel		X			
124	Cora, James (father)		X			
125	Cora, John		X			
126	Corry, Job				X	
127	Courtney, John				X	
128	Craig, Silas (father)		X			
129	Crain, Silas		X		X	
130	Cravin, John				X	
131	Crider, Michael		X			
132	Croso, David				X	
133	Crow, David			X	X	
134	Cruely, Bennet		X			
135	Curtis, Benjamin				X	
136	Curtis, Benjamin				X	
137	Curtis, John		X			
138	Curtis, Richard		X		X	
139	Curtis, Richard (son)		X			
140	Curtis, William		X		X	
141	Daniel, Robert				X	
142	Davis, Daniel		X			
143	Davis, Samuel		X		X	
144	Dawney, Guillermo					X
145	Dawson, John		X			
146	Day, Benjamin		X			
147	Day, Nayor		X			
148	Deajon, Clem		X			
149	Delaina, John			X		
150	Delbe, Stephen		X			
151	Demanch, Nicolas (father)					X
152	Demaus, George					X
153	Devall, Richard				X	
154	Dickson, Lewis			X		
155	Donnan, Rubin					X
156	Donne, John				X	

	Name	1781	1782	1783	1784	1786
157	Douglas, Earl		x		x	
158	Dowd, Rodger				x	
159	Dowlin, William				x	
160	Dromgold, James		x			
161	Drynns, Thomas					x
162	Dugan, Tomas					x
163	Duit, William				x	
164	Dun, George		x			
165	Dun, James				x	
166	Dun, Richard		x			
167	Dunbar, Robert		x		x	
168	Dunbarr, Robert		x			
169	Dunesson, John				x	
170	Dunn, John		x			
171	Dureght		x			
172	Duvall, Richard		x			
173	Dwight, Sixins		x			
174	Dyson		x			
175	Dyson, Elimon				x	
176	Dyson, Joseph		x		x	
177	Dyson, Thomas				x	
178	Eason, Charles			x		
179	Eldergill, John			x		
180	Ellis, John	x	x			
181	Ellis, John (father)				x	
182	Ellis, John (son)				x	
183	Ellis, Richard	x	x		x	x
184	Erwall, James			x		
185	Erwin, William		x		x	
186	Evans, Thomas				x	
187	Evin, John		x			
188	Ewiner, Jean		x			
189	Fairbanks, William	x			x	
190	Farquhar, John				x	
191	Farra, Alexander				x	
192	Farrell, Thomas				x	
193	Ferguson, William				x	
194	Fife, Isaac				x	
195	Finly, James				x	

135

	Name	1781	1782	1783	1784	1786
196	Flanigan, Thomas		X			
197	Flannelly, Carl					X
198	Fleet, James				X	
199	Fletcher, William					X
200	Flowers, Elijah				X	
201	Flowers, John		X			
202	Flowers, Joseph				X	
203	Flowers, Josiah		X			
204	Ford, Joseph				X	
205	Ford, Robert		X		X	
206	Forester, Joseph				X	
207	Foster, James		X		X	
208	Foster, John		X		X	
209	Foster, Mary				X	
210	Foster, Sarah				X	
211	Foster, Thomas		X			
212	Foster, William		X			
213	Frank, French		X			
214	Freed, John					X
215	Freeman, Thomas				X	
216	Fulsom, Israel				X	
217	Fulton, David		X		X	
218	Gallimore, David				X	
219	Garrino, Thomas		X			
220	Gibson, Gibion		X		X	
221	Gibson, Reuben		X		X	
222	Gibson, Samuel		X		X	
223	Gillard, Tacitus				X	
224	Goble, Emphium		X			
225	Godwin, Richard				X	
226	Goth, Jacob		X			
227	Grafton, Daniel		X		X	
228	Graham, David			X		
229	Graven, Jack		X			
230	Green, Abner				X	
231	Green, Joseph				X	
232	Green, Rodolph		X			
233	Green, Thomas				X	
234	Griffin, Gabriel		X		X	

	Name	1781	1782	1783	1784	1786
235	Griffin, John		X		X	
236	Griffin, Thomas				X	
237	Grigson, James		X			
238	Grimes, Hattvi		X			
239	Grun, Joseph		X			
240	Guise, John		X			
241	Guise, Michael		X		X	
242	Gwins, William				X	
243	Hain, Francis		X			
244	Hall, Juan					X
245	Hamberlin, William				X	
246	Hambleton, Jesse		X			
247	Hamboilin, Anthony		X			
248	Hammand, Caphas		X			
249	Hana, Lewis			X		
250	Hansburey, Calel		X			
251	Harmbroy, Jacob		X			
252	Harmon, Joseph		X			
253	Harmon, Samuel		X			
254	Harmon, Stephen		X			
255	Harmon, Thomas		X			
256	Harrison		X			
257	Harrison, Richard				X	
258	Hartin, John		X			
259	Hartley, John				X	
260	Hawkins, Peter		X		X	
261	Hayward, Charles				X	
262	Heady, Samuel		X			
263	Henderson, William				X	
264	Hids, John		X			
265	Higdon, Jesse (Jepthah)			X	X	
266	Hill, Jeremiah				X	
267	Holden, Joseph		X			
268	Holloway, George				X	
269	Holloway, John		X			
270	Holmes, Benjamin		X			
271	Holmes, Joseph		X			
272	Holmes, Sarah				X	
273	Holmes, Simon		X			

	Name	1781	1782	1783	1784	1786
274	Holsten, Stephen		X		X	
275	Holsten, Stephen (father)		X			
276	Holston, John		X			
277	Holt, Debral				X	
278	Hortin, Abraham		X			
279	Housdan, William				X	
280	Hovington, John		X			
281	Hovington, Peter		X			
282	Hovington, Peter (father)		X			
283	Howland, Guillaium		X			
284	Hubbert, William				X	
285	Hudsel, Gemema				X	
286	Hughs, Samuel		X			
287	Hulbert, William				X	
288	Hulbost, William		X			
289	Humphrey, Ostrip		X			
290	Humphries, Eustice				X	
291	Hutchings, Anthony		X			
292	Hutchins, Ann				X	
293	Irwin, James				X	
294	Isenhood, Barnet			X		
295	Ivey, Nathaniel		X		X	
296	Jackson, James		X		X	
297	James, Thomas		X			
298	Jenkin		X			
299	Johnson, Daniel		X			
300	Johnson, Elijah		X			
301	Johnson, Nathaniel		X			
302	Johnston, Issac		X		X	
303	Jones, Charles			X		
304	Jones, Guillermo					X
305	Jones, Henry			X		
306	Jones, John		X			
307	Jones, John		X		X	
308	Jones, Robert			X		
309	Jones, Russell				X	
310	Jourdan, Stephen				X	
311	Jourdan, Thomas		X		X	
312	Karnis, Richard			X		

	Name	1781	1782	1783	1784	1786
313	Kelly, James		x		x	
314	Kenfre, Benjamin		x			
315	Kennard, Sarah				x	
316	Kennedy, John		x			
317	Kid, Robert		x		x	
318	Killian, George			x	x	
319	Kinam, James				x	
320	King, Cable		x			
321	King, Cable		x			
322	King, Charles				x	
323	King, Joseph		x			
324	King, Justice		x			
325	King, Justus (or Justice)		x		x	
326	King, Richard		x			
327	Knap, Abraham		x			
328	Kogves, Robert		x			
329	Kohan, Joseph		x			
330	Kulca, Thomas		x			
331	Lafleur, Magret				x	
332	Lambert, Daniel				x	
333	Lavel, Francis		x			
334	Leanheart, Adam		x		x	
335	Leapheart, Jacob		x		x	
336	Lefleure, Henry		x			
337	Leonard, Alexandre		x			
338	Lewis, Isaac				x	
339	Lightholer, Christopher		x			
340	Lindsay, Thomas					x
341	Lion, Jacob		x			
342	Lobdel, Abraham					x
343	Lobdell, James					x
344	Logger, Thomas					x
345	Lord, Richard					x
346	Lott, Thomas		x			
347	Lousll, John					x
348	Love, Robert		x			
349	Lovelace, John		x			
350	Lovelace, Thomas		x			
351	Lovell, James					x

	Name	1781	1782	1783	1784	1786
352	Lum, John		X		X	
353	Lusk, John		X		X	
354	Luting, James				X	
355	Lyman, Captain		X			
356	Lyman, Jean		X			
357	Mackin, James					X
358	Madden, Manuel (Emaniel)				X	
359	Maggot, Daniel		X		X	
360	Maggot, Roswell (Rosel)		X		X	
361	Manadiac, Henry			X		
362	Manedeau, Henry				X	
363	Manier, William				X	
364	Marn, Martin			X		
365	Martin, Jacque		X			
366	Martin, James		X			
367	Martin, John				X	
368	Martin, Nehemiah		X		X	
369	Mathus, Isariel		X			
370	Mavor, Christopher		X			
371	Mayers, Richard				X	
372	Mays, Abraham				X	
373	Mays, Stephen				X	
374	McCaland, David					X
375	McDuffey, Arch		X			
376	McFarland, James					X
377	McFarland, John				X	
378	McGill, James				X	
379	McGill, Thomas			X		
380	Mchan, Moses				X	
381	McIntosh, Eunice				X	
382	McIntosh, James					X
383	McKan, Moses		X			
384	McMean, Patrick		X			
385	McMullin, Jayme					X
386	McMurray, John				X	
387	Menzies, Archibald					X
388	Migal, Daniel		X			
389	Miller, Daniel			X		
390	Minor, Estevan			X		X

	Name	1781	1782	1783	1784	1786
313	Kelly, James		x		x	
314	Kenfre, Benjamin		x			
315	Kennard, Sarah				x	
316	Kennedy, John		x			
317	Kid, Robert		x		x	
318	Killian, George			x	x	
319	Kinam, James				x	
320	King, Cable		x			
321	King, Cable		x			
322	King, Charles				x	
323	King, Joseph		x			
324	King, Justice		x			
325	King, Justus (or Justice)		x		x	
326	King, Richard		x			
327	Knap, Abraham		x			
328	Kogves, Robert		x			
329	Kohan, Joseph		x			
330	Kulca, Thomas		x			
331	Lafleur, Magret				x	
332	Lambert, Daniel				x	
333	Lavel, Francis		x			
334	Leanheart, Adam		x		x	
335	Leapheart, Jacob		x		x	
336	Lefleure, Henry		x			
337	Leonard, Alexandre		x			
338	Lewis, Isaac				x	
339	Lightholer, Christopher		x			
340	Lindsay, Thomas					x
341	Lion, Jacob		x			
342	Lobdel, Abraham					x
343	Lobdell, James					x
344	Logger, Thomas					x
345	Lord, Richard					x
346	Lott, Thomas		x			
347	Lousll, John					x
348	Love, Robert		x			
349	Lovelace, John		x			
350	Lovelace, Thomas		x			
351	Lovell, James					x

	Name	1781	1782	1783	1784	1786
430	Peters, John		X			
431	Phipps, Elijah				X	
432	Phipps, Henry		X			
433	Phipps, Samuel		X		X	
434	Pichins, David			X		
435	Pichins, John			X		
436	Piernas, Pedro			X		
437	Pipes, Ebenezer		X			
438	Pipes, Windsor		X		X	
439	Pittman, Noah			X		
440	Plannet, Charliy					X
441	Platner, Henry				X	
442	Pollock, Thomas				X	
443	Porborn, Jacob				X	
444	Potten, Guilliano		X			
445	Pradon, Alexandre		X			
446	Prock, Mathias		X		X	
447	Pulson, Captain		X			
448	Quirk, Edmond					X
449	Rab, Nicolas (father)					X
450	Rab, Nicolas (son)					X
451	Rahos, William			X		
452	Raily, George				X	
453	Random, Andrew		X			
454	Rap, Nicolas					X
455	Ratcliffe (Rattef), William				X	
456	Ray, Archibel			X		
457	Real, William					X
458	Richardson, George			X	X	
459	Richardson, Henry				X	
460	Richardson, James			X		
461	Roach, Henry		X		X	
462	Roads, John		X			
463	Roberts, Rotvih		X			
464	Rogers, Benjamin		X		X	
465	Rogers, Patrick		X			
466	Ross, Daniel		X			
467	Routh				X	
468	Routh, Jeremiah		X		X	

	Name	1781	1782	1783	1784	1786
469	Ryan, William				X	
470	Ryland, James					X
471	Sample, Joseph		X			
472	Sanders, John		X			
473	Savage, Ann				X	
474	Sephley, Conrad					X
475	Sham, Francois				X	
476	Shaver		X			
477	Shell, Horling		X			
478	Shever, Leval			X		
479	Shoals, Christopher			X		
480	Shote, John		X			
481	Shunk, John		X		X	
482	Silkreg, Guillermo		X			
483	Simmons, Charles		X		X	
484	Simmons, James		X		X	
485	Sinclair, Gaspar Mitchel				X	
486	Slater, Joseph				X	
487	Sloan, Archibel			X		
488	Smily, Thomas				X	
489	Smith, David				X	
490	Smith, Israel		X		X	
491	Smith, James		X			X
492	Smith, John		X		X	
493	Smith, John		X		X	
494	Smith, Philander				X	
495	Smith, Randolph				X	
496	Smith, Richard		X	X	X	
497	Smith, Samuel					X
498	Smith, William		X			
499	Smith, William				X	
500	Smith, William		X			
501	Smith, William Benjamin				X	
502	Smith, Zachariah				X	
503	Stampley, George		X		X	
504	Stampley, Henry		X		X	
505	Stampley, Jacob		X			
506	Stampley, John		X		X	
507	Stampley, Peter		X			

	Name	1781	1782	1783	1784	1786
508	Standley, Benjamin		x			
509	Standley, Joseph		x		x	
510	Steel, John					x
511	Stephenson, Joseph		x			
512	Stephenson, Stephen		x		x	
513	Still-Lee, John				x	
514	Strawbraker, John		x		x	
515	Swasey, Elija		x		x	
516	Swazey, Elija		x			
517	Swazey, Gabriel		x		x	
518	Swazey, Nathan		x		x	
519	Swazey, Richard		x		x	
520	Swazey, Samuel		x			
521	Swazey, Sarah				x	
522	Sweezey, Samuel		x			
523	Tabor, William				x	
524	Taylor, Abraham				x	
525	Tell, Stephen			x		
526	Terney, George				x	
527	Terry, John				x	
528	Thomas, Heinrich					x
529	Thsaison, Richard		x			
530	Tomlinston, Nathaniel				x	
531	Towhan, Stephen		x			
532	Townshead, John		x			
533	Townson, John				x	
534	Trevillon, Richard				x	
535	Trijo, Charles				x	
536	Truely, James		x		x	
537	Tsenhood, Barney				x	
538	Turney, George		x			
539	Turpin, Philip Pleasant		x		x	
540	Tuvey, John		x			
541	Usher, Joseph				x	
542	Wade, James				x	
543	Walk, Pat		x			
544	Walker, Samuel					x
545	Waltman, Daniel		x		x	
546	Watkins, John		x			

	Name	1781	1782	1783	1784	1786
547	Weathers, Zebulon			x	x	
548	Weed, Joel		x		x	
549	Weeks, William		x			
550	Welch, Andrew		x			
551	Welch, Sarah				x	
552	Wenton, John		x			
553	West, Cato				x	
554	West, Quille		x			
555	West, William		x		x	
556	Wettles, Elijah		x			
557	White, Amory		x			
558	White, Jerushe				x	
559	White, John				x	
560	White, Mathew				x	
561	Whitefield		x			
562	Wiggins, Israil		x			
563	Wighlands, Jacobo					x
564	Will, Wicked		x			
565	William, Edevard					x
566	Williams, Guilliams		x			
567	Williams, John		x			
568	Willson, James		x		x	
569	Wilson, William			x	x	
570	Winfre, Jacob		x			
571	Woods, John			x		
572	Woods, Margret				x	
573	Yreno, Cunter		x			

Table 17.   Natchez Names 1787/1788

	Name	1787a	1787b	1788a	1788b
1	Abrams, Roberto		x		
2	Adams, Charles		x		
3	Adams, Jacob		x		
4	Adams, Richard	x	x		
5	Alexander, Isaac	x	x		
6	Alexander, Reuben	x	x		
7	Andrews, Whamore	x			
8	Aquelon, Michel		x		
9	Armstreet, John	x			
10	Arrigel, Daniel H.			x	
11	Asbel, Isaac		x		
12	Bailey, George	x			
13	Baker, Daniel	x			
14	Bander, George		x		
15	Bankes, Sutton	x			
16	Bard, Joel	x			
17	Barland, William		x		
18	Barlud, Tomas			x	
19	Barney, Hugh			x	
20	Barofield, James		x		
21	Baron, Richard		x		
22	Basset, William				x
23	Bates, Ephraim	x	x		
24	Baxter, Reubin		x		
25	Bayler, Rubin		x		
26	Bayley, George	x			
27	Bayly, Tarpley			x	
28	Beatley, William			x	
29	Bell, Benjamin	x	x		
30	Bell, Richard	x			
31	Bell, Richard	x	x		
32	Bell, William		x		
33	Belly, George		x		
34	Beset, William			x	
35	Bevel, Esaic		x		
36	Bickley, Adam	x	x	x	
37	Bifelin, John		x		
38	Bile, Abner				x
39	Bingaman, Adam	x	x		

146

	Name	1787a	1787b	1788a	1788b
40	Bingaman, Christian	X			
41	Bingaman, Christian (father	X	X		
42	Bingaman, Christian (son)		X		
43	Bingaman, Luis		X		
44	Bird, Towel		X		
45	Bohaman, James			X	X
46	Bonner, James		X		
47	Bonner, Joseph	X	X		
48	Bonner, Moses		X		
49	Bonner, Moses		X		
50	Bonner, Moses (father)	X			
51	Bonner, Moses (son)	X			
52	Bonney, Hugh				X
53	Boolins, John		X		
54	Booweas, Thomas		X		
55	Boyd, William		X		
56	Boyds, Alexandre		X		
57	Brabeson, Nicolas		X		
58	Brandon, Christopher		X		
59	Brandon, Gerard		X		
60	Brashears, Benjamin	X	X		
61	Bresino, Francisco		X		
62	Brobston, Nicolas		X		
63	Brocus, William	X	X		
64	Brown, Jacob	X			
65	Brown, Nathaniel		X		
66	Brown, Obediah	X	X		
67	Brown, William	X	X		
68	Bruin, Pedro Brian			X	
69	Brunel, Elias	X			
70	Brunt, James		X		
71	Bryan, Jeremiah	X	X		
72	Buker, Anthony		X		
73	Bukly, Adam			X	
74	Bullen, John	X			
75	Bullock, Benjamin		X		
76	Burel, Benjamin		X		
77	Burel, George		X		
78	Burner, John		X		

	Name	1787a	1787b	1788a	1788b
79	Burnet, John	X			
80	Burney, Simon			X	
81	Cable, Jacob	X	X		
82	Caison Cuper, Henry		X		
83	Caldaucle, Ysaac			X	
84	Calender, Alexander	X	X		
85	Calot, John	X			
86	Calvit, Frederick	X	X		
87	Calvit, John		X	X	
88	Calvit, John		X	X	
89	Calvit, Joseph		X		
90	Calvit, Thomas	X	X		
91	Calvit, William	X	X		
92	Care, Samuel		X		
93	Carel, Benjamin	X	X		
94	Carr, John		X		
95	Carradine, Parker	X	X		
96	Carter, Charles		X		
97	Carter, Jesse	X	X		
98	Carter, Nehemiah	X	X		
99	Carter, Richard	X			
100	Carter, Roberto	X	X		
101	Case, William	X	X		
102	Casebord, Robert		X		
103	Cason, Charles	X			
104	Chacheret, Luis		X		
105	Chaffe, Abner			X	X
106	Chambers, John			X	X
107	Chambers, Silas			X	X
108	Chambre, Daniel		X		
109	Champin, John			X	
110	Charboneau, Louis	X	X		
111	Charles, Ricardo			X	
112	Chiine, Thomas		X		
113	Christian, Jacob		X	X	
114	Clark, Gibson	X	X		
115	Clark, John		X	X	
116	Clarke, Gibson	X			
117	Cleson, David		X		

	Name	1787a	1787b	1788a	1788b
118	Cobb, Arthur	x	x		
119	Cobdel, Abraam		x		
120	Coburn, Jacob	x	x		
121	Cochran, Robert			x	x
122	Cohoran, George		x		
123	Cohoran, Peter		x		
124	Cole, James (father)	x			
125	Cole, James (son)	x			
126	Cole, Mark	x	x		
127	Coleman, Jeremiah		x		
128	Coles, James	x	x		
129	Colins, Josua		x		
130	Colins, William		x		
131	Collins, John			x	
132	Collins, William			x	
133	Colman, Ephraim		x		
134	Colman, John		x		
135	Cols, James		x		
136	Cols, Salomon		x		
137	Cols, Steven		x		
138	Comins, Thomas		x		
139	Cook, George			x	
140	Cooper, Henry	x			
141	Cooper, Henry (father)		x		
142	Cooper, Henry (son)	x			
143	Cooper, Samuel		x		
144	Cooper, Samuel	x	x		
145	Cooper, William	x	x		
146	Core, Job		x		
147	Core, Richard		x		
148	Coreles, John		x		
149	Corry, Job	x			
150	Courtney, John	x	x		
151	Coyles, Hugh			x	
152	Crane, Hibon		x		
153	Crane, Mrs.	x			
154	Crane, Waterman		x		
155	Crane, Waterman	x			
156	Cravin, John		x		

	Name	1787a	1787b	1788a	1788b
157	Cruzert, William	X			
158	Culbertson, Samuel	X	X		
159	Curtis, Benjamin		X		
160	Curtis, Jonathan		X		
161	Curtis, Richard	X	X		
162	Curtis, William	X	X		
163	Daniel, William	X	X		
164	Darix, John		X		
165	Davis, Samuel	X	X		
166	Davis, Samuel	X			
167	Davis, Tomas			X	X
168	Dayton, Ebenezer			X	
169	Deetz, Henry			X	
170	Denham, Reuben	X			
171	Devall, Richard	X			
172	Dill, James		X		
173	Diuly, Amen		X		
174	Done, John		X		
175	Done, Richard		X		
176	Donnan, Rubin		X		
177	Douglas, Earl	X	X		
178	Dove, Joseph		X		
179	Dowd, Rodger		X		
180	Drake, Benjamin			X	
181	Duls, Henry				X
182	Dumon, George		X		
183	Dunavan, John	X			
184	Duncan, Joseph	X			
185	Durcan, Joseph		X		
186	Duvall, Richard		X		
187	Dwet, Israel		X		
188	Dyon, William		X		
189	Dyson, Clement	X	X		
190	Dyson, John		X		
191	Dyson, Joseph		X		
192	Dyson, Thomas	X	X		
193	Eastman, Abel			X	X
194	Eldergill, John	X			
195	Elherington, John			X	X

	Name	1787a	1787b	1788a	1788b
196	Elliot, James	x	x		
197	Ellis, Abram		x		
198	Ellis, John		x		
199	Ellis, John		x		
200	Ellis, John (father)	x			
201	Ellis, John (son)	x			
202	Ellis, Ricardo		x		
203	Ellis, Richard	x	x		
204	Ellis, Richard (son)		x		
205	Emphris, Justus		x		
206	Eneyohton, Roberto			x	
207	Erdelgil, John		x		
208	Ervin, James	x			
209	Ervin, Juan			x	
210	Erwin, John				x
211	Fague, Michel		x		
212	Fairbanks, William	x	x		
213	Fak, John		x		
214	Farel, Thomas		x		
215	Faro, Alexandre		x		
216	Farquhar, John	x	x		
217	Feim, James				x
218	Ferguson, Juan		x		
219	Ferguson, William	x	x		
220	Fife, Isaac		x		
221	Fiflyd, Yoriek		x		
222	Fillis, Jacob	x			
223	Fine, Jesse		x		
224	Finn, James		x		
225	Fitzgerald, George		x		
226	Fleet, James		x		
227	Fletcher, Benjamin			x	
228	Fletcher, William	x	x		
229	Fliz, John			x	
230	Flowers, Elagiha		x		
231	Flowers, Elijah	x	x		
232	Flowers, Josiah	x	x		
233	Flowers, Samuel	x	x		
234	Foley, Patrick		x	x	

	Name	1787a	1787b	1788a	1788b
235	Fondais, James		X		
236	Fontener, William		X		
237	Fooy, Benjamin			X	X
238	Foozeman, George		X		
239	Ford, John	X	X		
240	Ford, Joseph		X		
241	Ford, Robert		X		
242	Fordais, James		X		
243	Forester, Joseph		X		
244	Foster, James	X	X		
245	Foster, John	X	X		
246	Foster, Mary	X			
247	Foster, Thomas	X	X		
248	Foster, William		X		
249	Freeman, Thomas		X		
250	Furny, George		X		
251	Gaillard, Ann	X			
252	Gaillard, Isaac		X		
253	Gamble, William			X	
254	Gaskin, John			X	X
255	Gasland, James		X		
256	Gelesbie, William		X		
257	Genis, Robert M.		X		
258	Gibson, David		X		
259	Gibson, Gibion		X		
260	Gibson, Gil	X			
261	Gibson, Randolf		X		
262	Gibson, Reuben	X	X		
263	Gibson, Robert	X	X		
264	Gibson, Samuel	X	X		
265	Gilbert, Cristi		X		
266	Gilbert, John		X		
267	Gilbert, William		X		
268	Glasscork, James				X
269	Gleson, David		X		
270	Godwin, Richard	X	X		
271	Grace, John		X		
272	Grafton, Daniel		X		
273	Grant, Alexandre		X		

	Name	1787a	1787b	1788a	1788b
274	Grayseock, James			x	
275	Greek, Henry			x	
276	Green, Abner	x	x		
277	Green, John			x	
278	Green, Joseph	x	x		
279	Green, Thomas	x	x		
280	Green, Thomas Masten	x	x		
281	Greepy, Thomas		x		
282	Griffin, Gabriel		x		
283	Griffin, John	x			
284	Griffin, Thomas	x			
285	Gris, Michel		x		
286	Grufin, John		x		
287	Guise, Michael	x			
288	Hackett, Jonathan	x			
289	Hackpale, John			x	
290	Hadey, Samuel		x		
291	Hakuet, Jonathan		x		
292	Halten, Roberto			x	
293	Hamberlin, William		x		
294	Hamilton, Jesse	x			
295	Hamlet, John				x
296	Hamtel, John			x	
297	Haris, Charles		x		
298	Harman, Azechiel		x		
299	Harman, James	x	x		
300	Harmon, Hezikiah		x		
301	Harmon, James	x			
302	Harrigal, Daniel				x
303	Harrison, Joseph	x	x		
304	Harrison, Richard	x	x		
305	Hartley, John		x		
306	Harton, Abraam		x		
307	Haskinson, Ezekiel			x	
308	Hatten, Robert				x
309	Haukins, Peter		x		
310	Hawers, John		x		
311	Hawid, Charles		x		
312	Hawkins, Peter	x			

	Name	1787a	1787b	1788a	1788b
313	Hay, Archibal		x		
314	Haybraker, John	x	x		
315	Hayeesard, Joshua			x	
316	Hayes, James	x			
317	Hayward, Stephen			x	
318	Hayward, Toucha				x
319	Heady, Samuel	x			
320	Helchen, Benjamin				x
321	Helen, James	x			
322	Henderson, William	x	x		
323	Herhart, Jacob		x		
324	Herickland, Dan			x	
325	Herovin, James		x		
326	Herowins, William		x		
327	Hesse, James		x		
328	Higdon, Jesse (Jepthah)	x	x		
329	Hitleel, John		x		
330	Hivens, Thomas		x		
331	Hoard, Joseph	x			
332	Hoard, Robert	x			
333	Hocktit, Josua		x		
334	Hogdon, Daniel		x		
335	Holand, John		x		
336	Holland, John	x			
337	Holmes, Sarah	x			
338	Hols, David		x		
339	Holsten, George			x	x
340	Holsten, Stephen		x		
341	Holston, King		x		
342	Holt, David	x			
343	Holt, Debdall		x		
344	Holt, Dibial	x			
345	Holt, Elizabeth	x			
346	Holt, John	x	x		
347	Homes, Benjamin		x		
348	Homes, Joseph		x		
349	Homes, Simson		x		
350	Homes, Thomas		x		
351	Hooens, Benjamin		x		

	Name	1787a	1787b	1788a	1788b
352	Hookus, Henry		X		
353	Horeless, Edouard		X		
354	Horflein, George			X	
355	Hortley, John	X			
356	Hoskins, Joseph		X		
357	Howard, Charles	X			
358	Howard, Joshua			X	
359	Hudsalt, Jemima	X			
360	Hulbert, William	X	X		
361	Humphries, Eustice	X			
362	Hunter, Enrique		X		
363	Hutchins, Anthony	X	X		
364	Hutchins, Samuel		X		
365	Iller, Mark		X		
366	Isenhood, Barnet	X	X		
367	Johnson, Robert		X		
368	Johnson, Thomas		X		
369	Johnston, Issac	X	X		
370	Jonas, Matheus		X		
371	Jones, John	X	X		
372	Jordain, James		X		
373	Jourdan, Stephen	X	X		
374	Jourdan, Thomas	X	X		
375	Kelkood, William		X		
376	Kelly, Juan		X		
377	Kennard, Sarah	X			
378	Kid, Robert	X	X		
379	Killian, George	X	X		
380	Kincade, John	X			
381	King, Caleb	X	X		
382	King, Charles		X		
383	King, Joseph	X	X		
384	King, Justus (or Justice)	X	X		
385	King, Prosper		X		
386	King, Richard	X	X		
387	Kinkead, John		X		
388	Kuritz, Headman		X		
389	Lael, William		X		
390	Laforce, Joseph	X			

	Name	1787a	1787b	1788a	1788b
391	Lambert, David	x	x		
392	Lambert, David	x			
393	Land, John			x	x
394	Lanord, Israel		x		
395	Leanheart, Adam	x	x		
396	Lee, John Hill	x			
397	Lee, William	x			
398	Leeton, James		x		
399	Leonard, Alexandre		x		
400	Lintot, Bernard	x	x		
401	Lipeheart, Jacob		x		
402	Liveing, Lovis				x
403	Lobdell, James		x		
404	Lord, Richard		x		
405	Lord, Tomas			x	x
406	Loreless, Edouard		x		
407	Lorkins, Joseph		x		
408	Louvden, Tomas			x	
409	Lovelace, John	x			
410	Lovelace, Thomas		x		
411	Lovelad, John		x		
412	Loving, Louis			x	
413	Lucas, Charles		x		
414	Lum, John		x		
415	Lusk, John		x		
416	Madars, Manuel		x		
417	Madden, Manuel (Emaniel)	x			
418	Maggot, Daniel	x	x		
419	Maggot, Roswell (Rosel)	x	x		
420	Magoune, Hugh			x	
421	Makefaik, Roger		x		
422	Manedeau, Henry	x	x		
423	Marbal, Ezra			x	x
424	Marbel, Abner			x	x
425	Marney, John			x	x
426	Martin, John	x	x		
427	Martin, Nehemiah		x		
428	Mathieu, John Allen		x		
429	Mays, Abraham		x		

	Name	1787a	1787b	1788a	1788b
430	Mays, Stephen	x	x		
431	Mayses, Richard		x		
432	Mayson, Richard	x			
433	McCable, Edouard		x		
434	McDugall, William			x	x
435	McFarland, John		x		
436	McGovebick, Rubin			x	x
437	McGovebick, Rubin			x	x
438	McGuore, Hugh				x
439	McIntoche, William		x		
440	McIntosh, Eunice	x			
441	Michel, David		x		
442	Miller, Daniel		x		
443	Miller, Richard	x	x		
444	Miller, William			x	x
445	Mils, Joseph		x		
446	Minor, John			x	
447	Mitchel, David	x			
448	Montgomery, John		x		
449	Moore, Alexander (son)		x		
450	Moore, Alexandro		x		
451	Moran, William	x			
452	Mordock, John			x	x
453	Morgan, David				x
454	Morgan, Thomas	x	x		
455	Moring, William		x		
456	Mulkey, David	x	x		
457	Murray, Edouard		x		
458	Murry, Samuel			x	
459	Muson, James		x		
460	Nagle, George		x		
461	Nask, Thomas		x		
462	Nayne, Samuel		x		
463	Nelson, Peter	x	x		
464	Nenthan, Martin			x	
465	Newgent, Mathieu		x		
466	Newgent, Thomas Headman		x		
467	Newman, Benjamin			x	
468	Newman, Ezekiel			x	

	Name	1787a	1787b	1788a	1788b
469	Newton, John	X	X		
470	Nichols, Thomas	X			
471	Noling, William	X	X		
472	Norton, Abraham	X			
473	Nukles, Thomas		X		
474	Oamel, Robert		X		
475	Oconnor, Mary	X			
476	Odum, David	X	X		
477	Odum, John	X	X		
478	Ogden, Daniel	X			
479	Oglesby, James	X	X		
480	Oiler, Mark	X			
481	Olery, Cornelius			X	
482	Ormsleyton, John			X	
483	Owings, William	X			
484	Owins, William		X		
485	Oxbury, John	X			
486	Palmer, Archibald	X	X		
487	Parmer, Archibald	X			
488	Patterson, John	X	X		
489	Paul, George		X		
490	Paul, Jacob		X		
491	Pawal, Marek		X		
492	Peray, John		X		
493	Perkins, John		X		
494	Perkins, Joseph		X		
495	Perry, Daniel	X	X		
496	Perry, Daniel (son)		X		
497	Pert, Sebastian			X	
498	Philips, John		X		
499	Philis, Jacob		X		
500	Phipps, Elijah		X		
501	Phipps, Henry	X	X		
502	Phipps, Samuel		X		
503	Pipes, Windsor		X		
504	Platner, Henry		X		
505	Pountney, William	X			
506	Proctor, Reuben			X	
507	Provoit, Poisely		X		

	Name	1787a	1787b	1788a	1788b
508	Pruit, Beesley	x			
509	Quirk, Edmond		x		
510	Raby, Cader	x	x		
511	Randolf, Henry		x		
512	Ratcliffe (Rattef), William	x	x		
513	Ratcliffe, John	x	x		
514	Rayner, Daniel		x		
515	Raysals, Thomas		x		
516	Reed, Thomas			x	
517	Richards, Stephen			x	x
518	Richardson, George	x	x		
519	Richardson, Henry	x	x		
520	Richardson, James		x		
521	Ride, John		x		
522	Rinread, John		x		
523	Roach, Henry	x	x		
524	Robeson, Thomas		x		
525	Rockler, Rubin				x
526	Roker, Jonathan		x		
527	Routh, Margaret	x			
528	Rud, Thomas			x	x
529	Rule, Thomas	x	x		
530	Rule, Thomas	x	x		
531	Rundell, Josiah			x	x
532	Rundell, Seth			x	x
533	Ruvik, Headman		x		
534	Ryan, William	x			
535	Sanders, James		x		
536	Sanders, John			x	
537	Savage, Ann	x			
538	Savage, John			x	
539	Schophel, Joseph	x	x		
540	Selden, George			x	x
541	Sherot, Henry		x		
542	Shilling, Palser	x			
543	Shilling, Polsen		x		
544	Short, John		x		
545	Short, William			x	x
546	Shunk, John		x		

	Name	1787a	1787b	1788a	1788b
547	Sile, Abner			x	
548	Silkezag, William		x		
549	Simmons, Charles		x		
550	Simmons, James	x			
551	Simpson, Henry		x		
552	Simpson, Henry		x		
553	Simpson, John		x		
554	Sinclair, Gaspar Mitchel	x			
555	Smily, Thomas	x	x		
556	Smith, David		x		
557	Smith, Ebenezer		x		
558	Smith, James		x		
559	Smith, John	x	x		
560	Smith, Joseph		x		
561	Smith, Lucius		x		
562	Smith, Martin	x	x		
563	Smith, Peter		x		
564	Smith, Philander		x		
565	Smith, Philetus	x			
566	Smith, Phitalus		x		
567	Smith, Thomas		x		
568	Smith, William	x	x		
569	Smith, William	x			
570	Smith, William	x			
571	Smith, William Benjamin		x		
572	Smith, Zachariah	x	x		
573	Sneer, Tomas			x	
574	Snikler, Gaspar		x		
575	Solivan, William		x		
576	Spain, Francis	x	x		
577	Spalding, James			x	x
578	Spires, Juan		x		
579	Staiter, Joseph		x		
580	Stampley, George	x	x		
581	Stampley, Henry	x	x		
582	Stampley, John	x	x		
583	Steel, John	x			
584	Stephenson, Stephen	x	x		
585	Sterns, Stephen	x			

	Name	1787a	1787b	1788a	1788b
586	Sthounton, John			X	
587	Stil, John		X		
588	Stoddard, James	X			
589	Stone, Micael		X		
590	Straddler, Edward	X			
591	Stricklin, Daniel				X
592	Stroder, James		X		
593	Sutton Baulis, Richard		X		
594	Swasey, Elija	X	X		
595	Swazey, Elija		X		
596	Swazey, Gabriel	X	X		
597	Swazey, John	X	X		
598	Swazey, Nathan	X	X		
599	Swazey, Richard	X	X		
600	Swazey, Samuel	X	X		
601	Tabor, Isaac	X	X		
602	Tabor, William	X	X		
603	Tanner, David	X	X		
604	Tats, John			X	
605	Tavely, James	X			
606	Taylor, Abraham		X		
607	Taylor, Isaac			X	X
608	Terry, John	X	X		
609	Texada, Manuel	X			
610	Thomas, William	X			
611	Thompson, Cristobal				X
612	Tisen, Jon			X	
613	Tomlinston, Nathaniel	X	X		
614	Tompson, John		X		
615	Tomson, John		X		
616	Townsend, John		X		
617	Trenthan, Martin				X
618	Treplot, George			X	
619	Trevillon, Richard	X	X		
620	Truely, Benet	X	X		
621	Truely, James		X		
622	Turner, Matheo			X	
623	Turpin, Philip Pleasant	X	X		
624	Vahan, John		X		

	Name	1787a	1787b	1788a	1788b
625	Vausdan, William		X		
626	Vause, Thomas		X		
627	Vousdan, William	X	X		
628	Vzie, Robert		X		
629	Wade, James		X		
630	Waden, Thomas		X		
631	Waker, Gidion		X		
632	Walker, Andreu			X	X
633	Walker, Gideon	X			
634	Walker, Samuel		X		
635	Walteman, David		X		
636	Walter, Andreu			X	
637	Waltman, David	X	X		
638	Waltman, David	X	X		
639	Walton, John		X		
640	Warren, Thomas	X			
641	Wausdan, William		X		
642	Weegle, George		X		
643	Weeks, William		X		
644	Weetman, John		X		
645	Welch, Sarah	X			
646	Welton, John	X			
647	West, Berry		X		
648	West, Cato	X	X		
649	West, John			X	X
650	West, William	X	X		
651	Westy, Richard			X	
652	Whitaker, Daniel	X	X		
653	Whitaker, Daniel	X	X		
654	White, David		X		
655	White, Henry		X		
656	White, James		X		
657	White, Mathew	X	X		
658	White, Reuben	X	X		
659	Whitman, John	X			
660	Wicks, William	X			
661	Wide, Joel		X		
662	Wiel, Thomas		X		
663	Williams, Hezekiah	X			

	Name	1787a	1787b	1788a	1788b
664	Williams, Israel		x		
665	Wilson, John		x		
666	Wilson, William		x		
667	Wise, Robert		x		
668	Withers, Jesse	x	x		
669	Withers, Mary	x			
670	Woods, John		x		
671	Woolley, Melling			x	
672	Young, Conrad		x		

Table 18. Natchez Names 1789/1792

	Name	1789a	1789b	1790a	1790b	1792
1	Abrams, Robert		X			X
2	Adam, David		X			
3	Adams, Charles					X
4	Adams, Guillermo					X
5	Adams, Jacobo					X
6	Adams, Richard					X
7	Adams, Tomas					X
8	Addeson, William	X				
9	Aherans, John	X				
10	Alabram, John	X				
11	Alcheson, Guillermo					X
12	Aldrige, Jorge					X
13	Alexander, Isaac		X			X
14	Allen, Thomas	X				
15	Almstrong, William			X		
16	Alston, James		X			
17	Alston, John					X
18	Alston, John		X			
19	Alston, Phelipe Luis					X
20	Alston, William					X
21	Alva, Stephan		X		X	X
22	Ambrose, Estevan		X			X
23	Andelton, Juan					X
24	Anderson, Darius					X
25	Anderson, Francisco					X
26	Anderson, Juan					X
27	Anderson, Thomas		X	X		
28	Andrews, Ishamar					X
29	Apliquet, John			X		
30	Arden, John			X		
31	Arden, Juan					X
32	Armstreet, John		X		X	X
33	Armstrong, Moses		X		X	X
34	Armstrong, Robert			X		
35	Arver, Juan				X	
36	Ash, Thomas				X	
37	Axeltilas, Daniel			X		
38	Ayas, Jose	X				
39	Bacon, Richard		X			

	Name	1789a	1789b	1790a	1790b	1792
40	Bager, Thomas	x				
41	Bailey, George					x
42	Baindo, Jose					x
43	Baird, William	x				
44	Bajsel, Guillermo					x
45	Baken, Juan Baptista	x				
46	Baker, Guillermo					x
47	Baker, Juan Baptista	x				
48	Bakers, William	x				
49	Balde, Benjamin				x	
50	Baley, George		x			
51	Ball, Andreu	x				
52	Ball, John	x				
53	Ballard, Tulding	x				
54	Ballow, Thomas		x			
55	Balmer, William	x				
56	Bankes, Sutton					x
57	Baptista, Juan					x
58	Barket, Asina					x
59	Barland, William				x	x
60	Barnard, Joseph		x			
61	Barnet, William	x				
62	Barris, James	x				
63	Barrows, Ebenezer					x
64	Bartle, Andrea	x				
65	Bartle, Jacobo	x				
66	Bartley, Juan					x
67	Barton, Juan	x				
68	Bater, Juan Baptista	x				
69	Bates, Ephraim		x			x
70	Bates, Jese			x		
71	Baur, John	x				
72	Bayley, George				x	
73	Bayly, Tarpley					x
74	Beakly, Adam					x
75	Beal, Benjamin			x		
76	Beall, Andres	x				
77	Beall, Andrew		x			
78	Bealles, James			x		

	Name	1789a	1789b	1790a	1790b	1792
79	Beams, Tomas					x
80	Beanden, Jesua					x
81	Beardman, Guillermo					x
82	Beattery, James			x		
83	Beck, Jacobo	x				
84	Beggers, James	x				
85	Bell, Andres					x
86	Bell, Guillermo				x	
87	Bell, Hugh					x
88	Bell, John	x			x	
89	Bell, Richard				x	x
90	Bell, Samuel		x		x	
91	Bell, William		x			
92	Bellu, William	x				
93	Beloo, Dage			x		
94	Belt, Benjamin		x			x
95	Bennell, Elias		x			
96	Benoit, Gabriel		x			x
97	Berkley, Eduardo	x				
98	Bernard, Joseph					x
99	Beship, Guillermo			x		
100	Bingman, Adam		x			x
101	Bingman, Christopher		x			x
102	Biothe, John	x				
103	Biovey, Little			x		
104	Bishand, John		x			
105	Bishop, William			x		x
106	Bisland, Juan					x
107	Biwig, Peter Louis	x				
108	Blaine, James	x				
109	Bley, Tarpay				x	
110	Blockly, John	x				
111	Boardman, Carlos					x
112	Bodio, Juan					x
113	Boggs, Juan				x	
114	Boland, Simeon				x	
115	Bolling, Christian	x			x	
116	Bolls, Juan				x	x
117	Boner, Moses		x			

	Name	1789a	1789b	1790a	1790b	1792
118	Bonill, Elias					x
119	Bonner, James		x		x	x
120	Bonner, Joseph		x			
121	Bonner, Moses (father)				x	x
122	Bonner, Moses (son)				x	x
123	Bonner, Will (William)	x			x	x
124	Bonnersen, Moses		x			
125	Bonnet, Jose					x
126	Boone, Joseph	x				
127	Booth, John		x		x	x
128	Boro, Philip			x		
129	Borruy, David			x		
130	Bosely, John	x				
131	Boulig, Simon			x		
132	Bovards, William	x				x
133	Bowls, John		x			
134	Bowner, Edward			x		
135	Boyers, Enrique			x		
136	Boyle, John			x		
137	Boyo, Alexandro				x	
138	Brachflor,Christopher	x				
139	Brand, John	x			x	
140	Brandon, Gerard		x		x	
141	Brasbean, Benjamin					x
142	Brashars, Tobias	x				
143	Brashcart, Tobias					x
144	Brashear, Job	x				
145	Brawn, Tomas	x				
146	Brenan, James	x				
147	Brian, Jeremias(wife)					x
148	Bridis, John	x				
149	Brinly, John	x				
150	Brinly, John	x				
151	Brocas, William		x			x
152	Brockham, William	x				
153	Brockway, Jesse			x		
154	Broconte, George	x				
155	Brocus, William				x	
156	Broder, Guillermo			x		

167

	Name	1789a	1789b	1790a	1790b	1792
157	Brooke, Juan				x	
158	Brough, Richard			x		
159	Brown, Guillermo			x		x
160	Brown, James			x		
161	Brown, John	x				
162	Brown, Nathaniel					x
163	Brown, Obediah				x	
164	Brown, Obediah		x		x	x
165	Brown, Thomas	x				
166	Brown, William	x		x		
167	Bruin, Pedro					x
168	Bruin, Peter B.		x			
169	Buckholls, Peter	x				
170	Bueralter, George			x		
171	Bull, John			x		
172	Bullen, John		x		x	x
173	Bullen, Joseph	x				
174	Bullert, Perminus	x				
175	Bullock, Benjamin		x		x	x
176	Bungo, William	x				
177	Burch, Guillermo				x	x
178	Burch, Juan				x	
179	Burgde, William	x				
180	Buriens, Jame	x				
181	Burk, John	x				
182	Burling, Tomas					x
183	Burman, Luvlhy	x				
184	Burnet, Daniel				x	x
185	Burnet, John				x	x
186	Burnett, John		x			
187	Burns, Samuel	x				
188	Burns, Thomas	x				
189	Bushnell, Eusebio			x		
190	Busk, Reubin	x				
191	Buskirk, Thomas	x				
192	Bussh, Samuel	x				
193	Buter, Joseph	x				
194	Butler, Nataniel					x
195	Butler, Thomas	x				

	Name	1789a	1789b	1790a	1790b	1792
196	Cable, Jacob		x			x
197	Cacan Cooper, Enrique				x	
198	Cacenhot, Jacob	x				
199	Cacerey, John		x			
200	Cagel, John	x				
201	Calender, Alexander				x	
202	Calhoon, James	x				
203	Callaghan, Daniel	x				
204	Calvet, the Widow					x
205	Calvet, William					x
206	Calvit, Federick		x			
207	Calvit, Joseph					x
208	Calvit, Thomas		x		x	x
209	Calvit, William		x			
210	Campbell, James	x				
211	Campbell, Robert					x
212	Camus, Pedro					x
213	Carpenter, Mary		x			
214	Carpenter, the Widow					x
215	Carradine, Parker		x		x	x
216	Carrel, Jaime			x		
217	Carrell, Benjamin					x
218	Cart, Samuel				x	
219	Carter, Charles				x	x
220	Carter, Jesse		x		x	x
221	Carter, Nehemiah		x			x
222	Carter, Robert		x		x	
223	Carter, Roberto				x	x
224	Cason, Charles					x
225	Cathran, Jayme				x	
226	Catton, Roberto					x
227	Caverly, Isaac	x				
228	Cembrely, Estevan					x
229	Chabenaux, Louis		x			
230	Chacach, Elisabeth			x		
231	Chambers, Benjamin	x				
232	Chambers, Daniel		x			x
233	Chambers, John					x
234	Chambers, William			x		x

	Name	1789a	1789b	1790a	1790b	1792
235	Charlin, John		X			
236	Cheney, Guillermo					X
237	Chevey, William	X				
238	Chisper, Juan			X		
239	Christian, Augustus	X				
240	Ciasgen, John			X		
241	Cilond, Adam					X
242	Clafford, William	X				
243	Clair, George	X				
244	Clark, Daniel		X			X
245	Clark, Gibson		X		X	
246	Clark, Jaime					X
247	Clark, John	X			X	
248	Clark, Lucia					X
249	Clark, William	X			X	X
250	Clarke, Gibson					X
251	Clasoson, Abram	X				
252	Claugh, Abraham				X	
253	Cleary, Jorge					X
254	Cleaver, Stephen	X				
255	Clever, Estevan				X	
256	Cloud, Adam			X		
257	Cobb, Arthur		X			X
258	Cobe, Juan				X	
259	Cobin, Jacob				X	X
260	Cobin, Samuel				X	X
261	Cobun, Jacob				X	
262	Coburn, Jacob		X			
263	Cochran, Roberto					X
264	Cogan, John	X				
265	Cogan, Patricio					X
266	Coil, Marcos					X
267	Colbertson, the Widow					X
268	Cole, Guillermo					X
269	Cole, James	X				
270	Cole, James	X				
271	Cole, James (father)		X			X
272	Cole, James (son)		X		X	X
273	Cole, Mark		X			

	Name	1789a	1789b	1790a	1790b	1792
274	Cole, Salomon					X
275	Cole, Stephen		X		X	
276	Coleco, William			X		
277	Coleman, Ephraim				X	X
278	Coleman, Henry	X				
279	Coleman, Israel				X	X
280	Coleman, Jeremiah		X		X	X
281	Coleman, John		X			
282	Coleman, Peter	X				
283	Coleman, William		X			
284	Collender, Alexandro					X
285	Collerman, Guillermo					X
286	Collins, Carlos	X				X
287	Collins, Denis	X				X
288	Collins, James	X				
289	Collins, Josua				X	X
290	Collins, William		X		X	X
291	Conely, Redman					X
292	Conneghan, Thomas	X				
293	Connel, Daniel	X				
294	Connells, Robert			X		
295	Conner, Juan				X	X
296	Connor, Peter			X		
297	Conoly, Patrick	X				
298	Constonck, William	X				
299	Cook, George				X	
300	Cooper, Henry		X			X
301	Cooper, Jaime					X
302	Cooper, Jesse				X	
303	Cooper, Samuel				X	X
304	Cooper, Samuel		X		X	X
305	Cooper, William		X		X	X
306	Coots, Jacobo	X				
307	Corner, Juan	X				
308	Correl, Juan					X
309	Correl, Juan					X
310	Corry, Jeremiah					X
311	Corry, Job					X
312	Corte, Marcos				X	

	Name	1789a	1789b	1790a	1790b	1792
313	Cory, Job				X	
314	Cory, Ricardo				X	X
315	Cott, Daniel	X				
316	Cott, Estevan					X
317	Cott, Juan					X
318	Courtney, John		X		X	X
319	Cowan, John			X		
320	Cowel, Juan					X
321	Coyl, John			X		
322	Coyleman, Jacobo					X
323	Coyles, Hugh					X
324	Crafford, William	X				
325	Crane, Waterman		X			X
326	Cravin, John					X
327	Crawford, Joseph	X				
328	Crayton, Roberto					X
329	Crumhott, Jacobo					X
330	Crump, William	X				
331	Crutheirs, Juan					X
332	Cruthus, Thomas			X		
333	Cruz, Waterman				X	
334	Cumingham, Thomas	X				
335	Cummins, Thomas		X			X
336	Cumstick, David			X		
337	Cunninghan, Catalina					X
338	Curtis, Benjamin		X			X
339	Curtis, M.					X
340	Curtis, Richard		X		X	X
341	Curtis, William		X			X
342	Danah, Tomas					X
343	Daniels, Thomas			X		X
344	Darlington, Joseph	X				
345	Darron, Thomas				X	
346	Daugherty, Antonio					X
347	Davenport, Jaime					X
348	Davenport, John			X		
349	Davies, Francisco			X		
350	Davis, Elisha		X			
351	Davis, Guillermo			X		X

	Name	1789a	1789b	1790a	1790b	1792
352	Davis, John			x		
353	Davis, Landard Hugh		x			
354	Davis, Samuel		x		x	x
355	Days, James		x			
356	Dayton, Ebenezer		x		x	x
357	De Brady, Juan					x
358	Deaderick, Juan			x		
359	Dervin, Elizabet					x
360	Dicks, Nathan			x		
361	Dickson, Roger	x				
362	Dirhussen, Juan			x		
363	Divet, Ezekiel					x
364	Dix, Juan					x
365	Dix, Nathan			x		
366	Dixon, Roger					x
367	Docthy, Linthy			x		
368	Doddy, Hediak	x				
369	Dodge, Ysrael	x				
370	Domange, Jorge					x
371	Domeng, James			x		
372	Donaldson, Juan					x
373	Doren, Miguel					x
374	Doton, Valentin T.	x				
375	Douglas, Ana					x
376	Douglas, Archival					x
377	Douglas, Daniel				x	x
378	Douglas, David	x			x	x
379	Douglas, Estevan					x
380	Douslen, Carlos				x	
381	Dove, Mistress		x			
382	Dow, Jose					x
383	Duesbery, Juan					x
384	Duitt, Ezekiel		x			
385	Dumbar, Guillermo					x
386	Dun, Richard					x
387	Dunavan, Daniel	x				
388	Dunbar, Robert		x			x
389	Dunbarr, William		x			
390	Duncan, Benjamin			x		

	Name	1789a	1789b	1790a	1790b	1792
391	Duncan, George			X		
392	Duncan, Joseph					X
393	Dunlap, John	X				
394	Dunman, Reuben					X
395	Dunn, John	X				
396	Durang, John	X				
397	Durch, Guillermo					X
398	Durond, Rogero				X	
399	Durr, Sebastian		X			
400	Duwitt, William			X		
401	Dviny, Hugh			X		
402	Dwet, Jese					X
403	Dyson, Clement		X		X	X
404	Dyson, John		X		X	
405	Dyson, Joseph		X			X
406	Dyson, Thomas		X		X	X
407	Earheart, Jacobo					X
408	Eason, Charles		X			
409	Eastman, Abel					X
410	Edmonds, Timothy			X		
411	Edward, Jaime					X
412	Eleaver, James	X				
413	Elliot, Guillermo					X
414	Elliot, James		X		X	
415	Ellis, Abraham		X			X
416	Ellis, Harde		X			
417	Ellis, Jacob				X	
418	Ellis, John		X			
419	Ellis, John (father)					X
420	Ellis, John (son)					X
421	Ellis, Ricardo				X	X
422	Ellis, Richard					X
423	Ellis, Richard		X			
424	Ellsworth, John			X		
425	Elmore, Juan					X
426	Enrusty, John			X		
427	Ervin, James		X		X	X
428	Ervin, Juan					X
429	Erving, Roberto	X				

	Name	1789a	1789b	1790a	1790b	1792
430	Erwin, William		x			x
431	Essex, Thomas	x	x			
432	Estello, William	x				
433	Euing, Carlos			x		
434	Euing, Samuel	x				
435	Evans, Lewis			x	x	
436	Evans, Luis			x		
437	Ever, Thomas				x	
438	Fairbanks, William		x		x	x
439	Falconer, Guillermo					x
440	Farmer, William			x		
441	Farnis, Guillermo			x		
442	Farroco, Alexandro					x
443	Farrow, Alexande		x			
444	Ferguson, Juan				x	x
445	Ferguson, William		x		x	x
446	Fermount, George		x			
447	Fery, James			x		
448	Fields, Daniel			x		
449	Fields, Phillip			x		
450	Fife, Isaac		x		x	
451	Filer, Guillermo				x	
452	Finley, Samuel	x				
453	Finn, Jaime					x
454	Finnan, Daniel	x				
455	Finny, Hugh D.			x		
456	Fisher, John	x				
457	Fitzgerald, George		x			x
458	Fitzgerald, Jaime					x
459	Five, Isaac					x
460	Fletcher, William		x			x
461	Fletcher, Benjamin					x
462	Fleye, Nicolas	x				
463	Flower, Isias				x	
464	Flowers, Doctor		x			
465	Flowers, Elijah					x
466	Flowers, Elijah				x	
467	Flowers, Elisha		x			
468	Flowers, John		x			

	Name	1789a	1789b	1790a	1790b	1792
469	Flowers, Josiah				x	
470	Flowers, Samuel					x
471	Flyng, Jorge			x		
472	Foard, Juan					x
473	Foard, Tomas					x
474	Folbert, Edmund			x		
475	Foley, Patricio					x
476	Fonk, Jacobo			x		
477	Fooy, Benjamin				x	x
478	Ford, John		x			
479	Ford, Joseph		x		x	
480	Ford, Robert		x			
481	Fordler, John	x				
482	Forman, Ezekiel			x		x
483	Forman, Ismy					x
484	Forman, Jorge					x
485	Forman, Samuel S.			x		
486	Forster, James					x
487	Forsyth, James	x				
488	Foster, James		x		x	x
489	Foster, John		x		x	x
490	Foster, Mary					x
491	Foster, Thomas		x		x	x
492	Foster, William		x	x	x	x
493	Fourone, Alexandre				x	
494	Fowler, Alexandre			x		
495	Fowler, John	x			x	
496	Fowler, Jose					x
497	Foye, Benjamin		x			
498	Frahise, George	x				
499	Frail, Eduardo					x
500	Freeman, Thomas				x	x
501	French, Henry			x		
502	Fulds, Daniel			x		
503	Fulds, Felipe			x		
504	Fulds, John	x				
505	Fulley, Yrael			x		
506	Fulton, Alexis	x				
507	Fur, John	x				

	Name	1789a	1789b	1790a	1790b	1792
508	Furman, John	x				
509	Gaeyce, Miguel				x	
510	Gaillard, Ysac					x
511	Gains, Ambrosio	x				
512	Gallagher, William	x				
513	Gallcher, John	x				
514	Gallican, William	x				
515	Gallimore, David					x
516	Garad, Juan				x	
517	Gardener, Henry	x				
518	Gardor, Roberto			x		
519	Garet, Juan					x
520	Garkind, Juan					x
521	Garlan, William	x				
522	Garon, Uriak			x		
523	Gascon, Juan				x	
524	Geaphert, Jacob		x			
525	Geomit, Patrick	x				
526	Geonel, Patrick	x				
527	Gibson, Gabriel		x			
528	Gibson, Gil					x
529	Gibson, John	x				
530	Gibson, Reuben		x		x	x
531	Gibson, Samuel				x	x
532	Gibson, Samuel		x		x	x
533	Gilbert, Cristobal					x
534	Gilbert, Juan				x	
535	Gilbert, William					x
536	Gillaird, Mistress		x			
537	Gillaspie, Guillermo				x	x
538	Gilliard, Isaac		x			
539	Gillmore, Samuel	x				
540	Gilmore, John	x				
541	Gilmore, Samuel	x				
542	Gilsbey, Jayme				x	
543	Glascock, Juan				x	
544	Glascock, M.		x			
545	Glascock, Richard				x	
546	Glascock, William				x	x

	Name	1789a	1789b	1790a	1790b	1792
547	Glascok, Jaime				X	
548	Glascok, Jaime				X	X
549	Glason, Abraam					X
550	Goodwin, Mistress		X			
551	Goodwind, Pheby					X
552	Gookins, Juan				X	
553	Gorden, Robert			X		
554	Gounger, Gilbert	X				
555	Gown, James	X				
556	Grace, Juan				X	
557	Grace, Richard			X		
558	Grafton, Daniel		X			X
559	Grant, Alexandro				X	X
560	Gras, Antonio					X
561	Graudt, Juan				X	
562	Gredy, Juan					X
563	Green, Abner		X			X
564	Green, Abraam					X
565	Green, Henry		X			X
566	Green, John					X
567	Green, Joseph		X		X	
568	Green, Nathan					X
569	Green, Thomas		X			
570	Green, Thomas Masten					X
571	Greenfield, Jesse					X
572	Greenleaf, David			X	X	X
573	Greffin, Juan					X
574	Greham, Thomas	X				
575	Grey, Buflin					X
576	Grey, James			X		
577	Grey, Ruffin		X			
578	Griffin, Daniel	X				
579	Griffin, Gabriel		X		X	X
580	Griffin, John				X	
581	Griffin, John		X			
582	Grifin, Francis	X				
583	Grims, Ricardo					X
584	Griswelle, Stephen			X		
585	Grub, Nicholas			X		

	Name	1789a	1789b	1790a	1790b	1792
586	Grubb, Benjamin				x	
587	Grubb, Nicolas				x	
588	Gruel, Benjamin			x		
589	Guff, Nic			x		
590	Guff, Tomas			x		
591	Guilford, Jeremiah	x				
592	Guise, Miguel					x
593	Gunnels, Federico					x
594	Hagel, Caleb	x				
595	Hains, John	x				x
596	Hains, Stephen	x				x
597	Halbrodk, Daniel	x				
598	Halkenson, Guillermo			x		
599	Hamberlin, William		x			x
600	Hamberling, Juan					x
601	Hamilton, Jesse		x		x	x
602	Hamilton, William	x				
603	Hamphars, Ralph		x			
604	Handerson, James			x		
605	Hansfeld, Guillermo					x
606	Haral, John			x		
607	Hare, Andres	x				
608	Harkins, Guillermo					x
609	Harkins, William	x				
610	Harltock, Christian			x		
611	Harman, Cristian					x
612	Harman, Ezekiel		x			
613	Harman, James		x			x
614	Harrigal, Daniel					x
615	Harrison, John	x	x			
616	Harrison, Joseph					x
617	Harrison, Richard		x			x
618	Hartley, Jacob					x
619	Hartley, Juan				x	
620	Harvard, Carlos					x
621	Harvison, Thomas	x				
622	Hathorn, William	x				
623	Hauser, Gasper			x		
624	Havve, William	x				

	Name	1789a	1789b	1790a	1790b	1792
625	Hawley, Daniel				X	
626	Hayes, James				X	
627	Hays, David	X				
628	Hays, James		X			
629	Heady, Samuel					X
630	Headycorn, Simon			X		
631	Heartley, John		X			
632	Hellbrand, David	X				X
633	Hemell, Carlos					X
634	Hencock, Alexandro	X				
635	Henderson, Alexander		X		X	X
636	Henderson, Henrique				X	
637	Henderson, Juan				X	
638	Henderson, William		X			X
639	Henry, Mitchel	X				
640	Here, Andres					X
641	Hernois, Joseph	X				
642	Herrsan, Guilermo				X	
643	Heword, Jaime	X				
644	Hichison, Stewart	X				
645	Higdon, Jepthah		X		X	X
646	Higdon, Mary		X			
647	Higgins, Barney					X
648	Higginson, Stuart					X
649	Hill, Pedro					X
650	Hill, William			X		
651	Hiller, Margarita					X
652	Hilonds, Jaime					X
653	Hilot, Ricardo				X	
654	History, Ephraim					X
655	Hobbard, Tomas					X
656	Hogan, John			X		
657	Hoirn, Samuel	X				
658	Holladay, Juan					X
659	Holland, Jeremias			X		
660	Holland, Jorge					X
661	Holly, John	X				
662	Holly, Rolan	X				
663	Holmes, Benjamin		X		X	X

	Name	1789a	1789b	1790a	1790b	1792
664	Holmes, Joseph		X			
665	Holmes, Sarah					X
666	Holms, Lubis			X		
667	Holoom, Nataniel				X	
668	Holt, David		X		X	X
669	Holt, Dibdal				X	X
670	Holt, John		X		X	
671	Holy, John	X				
672	Hopkins, Gideon			X	X	
673	Horine, Samuel	X				
674	Horris, Groves				X	
675	Hortin, Abraham		X			X
676	Hoskinson, Ezechiel				X	
677	House, Casper			X		
678	Houvam, Jacques			X		
679	Hover, Jacob			X		
680	Howard, Joshua		X		X	X
681	Howe, William	X	X			X
682	Hubbard, Ephrain			X		
683	Hubbard, Thomas		X		X	
684	Hubbell, John			X		
685	Hudsell, William		X			
686	Hufman, Jacobo					X
687	Huggs, Tomas					X
688	Hughs, Thomas	X			X	
689	Huittler, Daniel					X
690	Hukison, Steward	X				
691	Humphrey, Ana					X
692	Humphrey, Jorge					X
693	Humphreys, Eustice		X		X	X
694	Humphreys, Jorge G.				X	
695	Humphreys, Ralph	X				
696	Hunter, Enrique					X
697	Hunter, John	X				
698	Hunter, Narcisco					X
699	Hush, Little Beay					X
700	Husman, Pedro	X				
701	Hutchins, Anthony		X			X
702	Igdom, Maria					X

	Name	1789a	1789b	1790a	1790b	1792
703	Innis, Alexander			x		
704	Innis, Francis	x				
705	Irwin, William		x			
706	Isenhoot, Bernabe					x
707	Isinhood, Barney		x			
708	Ismund, Ebenezer			x		
709	Ivers, Juan					x
710	Ives, William	x				
711	Jacken, Tomas					x
712	Jackson, George	x				
713	Jacobs, Henry		x		x	
714	Jacobs, Miguel			x		
715	Jaikson, Ahduio	x				
716	James, David		x			
717	Jennings, Roberto	x				
718	John, George	x				x
719	John, James	x				x
720	John, Thomas	x				
721	Johns, Carlos					x
722	Johns, David	x				x
723	Johnson, Edmund			x		x
724	Johnston, Issac		x		x	x
725	Johnston, James	x				
726	Johnston, Juan				x	
727	Jones, Charles		x			
728	Jones, Conrado				x	
729	Jones, David	x				
730	Jones, Francis			x		
731	Jones, Francisco			x		
732	Jones, George	x				
733	Jones, John		x		x	x
734	Jones, Mateo				x	x
735	Jorden, James	x			x	
736	Jorden, Thomas		x		x	x
737	Jus, Juan	x				
738	Jusy, Thomas	x				
739	Kannady, David					x
740	Karr, Samuel					x
741	Keen, Antonio	x				

	Name	1789a	1789b	1790a	1790b	1792
742	Keen, Wilha	x				
743	Kelgar, Tacy			x		
744	Kelly, James					x
745	Kelly, Miguel			x		
746	Kelly, Thomas	x				x
747	Kelsus, Ysaak	x				
748	Kennson, Nataniel					x
749	Kenty, Jaime					x
750	Killian, George		x		x	x
751	Killon, Peter	x				
752	Killor, Peter	x				
753	Killpatrick, Hugh	x				
754	Kindrick, John			x		
755	King, Caleb		x			
756	King, Caleb		x		x	x
757	King, Charles				x	x
758	King, Henrique				x	
759	King, Juan					x
760	King, Justice		x			
761	King, Justo				x	x
762	King, Prosper				x	x
763	King, Ricardo		x		x	x
764	Kinrick, Juan					x
765	Kirk, James		x			x
766	Kirk, Patrick	x				
767	Kirkland, Guillermo					x
768	Kirkland, Samuel					x
769	Koflay, John	x				
770	Kulen, John	x				
771	Lacaman, Nicolas	x				
772	Lafough, Joseph	x				
773	Lambert, David		x		x	x
774	Lamens, James	x				
775	Landon, Davis					x
776	Landphier, Tomas					x
777	Laneer, Benjamin					x
778	Lanhart, Adam					x
779	Larget, Charles		x			
780	Lauman, John	x				

	Name	1789a	1789b	1790a	1790b	1792
781	Leanheart, Adam				x	x
782	Ledyear, George	x				
783	Lee, John			x		
784	Lee, Mark	x				
785	Lee, Peter			x		
786	Lee, William	x	x		x	x
787	Lelly, Thomas	x				
788	Leman, John	x				
789	Lenhart, Adam		x			
790	Leonard, Israel					x
791	Letty, Thomas	x				
792	Levins, Nicolas	x				
793	Lewis, Isaac				x	x
794	Lewis, Jayme				x	
795	Leyeune, David					x
796	Leyeune, Salomon					x
797	Likins, James	x				
798	Linch, Rud	x				
799	Lindsay, James			x		
800	Lintot, Bernard		x			x
801	Livayze, Elisha				x	
802	Lloyd, Thomas				x	
803	Lobdell, James					x
804	Lobellas, Eduardo					x
805	Lobellas, Juan					x
806	Lobellas, Tomas					x
807	Locaman, Nicolas	x				
808	Lord, Richard				x	x
809	Love, Jesse			x		
810	Lovelace, Edward		x			
811	Lovelace, John		x			
812	Lovelace, Thomas		x			
813	Lovell, James				x	
814	Lovill, Louis	x				
815	Luis, Albert	x				
816	Luis, John	x				
817	Lum, Guillermo				x	x
818	Lum, John				x	x
819	Lum, William		x			

	Name	1789a	1789b	1790a	1790b	1792
820	Lusk, James			X		
821	Lusk, John		X			X
822	Lusy, Samuel			X		
823	Luzer, Solomon	X				
824	Lyaton, Jaime					X
825	Lyon, Matheu			X		
826	Lyons, Jermas					X
827	Lyy, John	X				
828	Madden, Emaniel		X		X	X
829	Man, Frederick	X				X
830	Man, Samuel	X				
831	Manachie, Hugo				X	
832	Manadace, Henry		X			
833	Manadne, Enrrique					X
834	Manadne, Enrrique (jr.)					X
835	Mandall, Samuel				X	
836	Manie, Andas		X			
837	Mansco, Federico					X
838	Marbel, Earl					X
839	Marbles, Ezra		X			
840	Marchal, Juan	X				
841	Marcos, Frederick			X		
842	Marcus, Frederick			X		
843	Marshall, John	X				
844	Marter, Hugo Ricardo				X	
845	Martin, Abner	X				
846	Martin, Juan				X	X
847	Martin, Juan Baptista			X		
848	Martin, Samuel			X	X	
849	Martin, Thomas			X		X
850	Martin, Thomas			X	X	X
851	Martin, William	X				
852	Marton, Abner	X				
853	Marvill, Abner					X
854	Masters, Jonathan					X
855	Mather, Guillermo					X
856	Mather, Jaime					X
857	Mathews, Hugh			X		
858	Matus, Hugh			X		

	Name	1789a	1789b	1790a	1790b	1792
859	Max, George	X				
860	May, Humphrey	X				
861	May, Nielis	X				
862	Mays, Abraham					X
863	Mays, Antonio				X	
864	Mays, Stephen				X	X
865	Mazaes, John	X				
866	McBey, Silas			X		
867	McBilland, Thomas	X				
868	McBluce, Thomas			X		
869	McBride, John	X				
870	McCabe, Edward		X			X
871	McCartney, John	X				
872	McClentiek, William	X				
873	McClor, James	X				
874	McCollock, James	X				
875	McComohy, Anthony			X		
876	McCormack, John	X				
877	McCoy, Donald					X
878	McCullock, Mateo					X
879	McDermot, Patricio					X
880	McDermot, Thomas			X		
881	McDougle, Guillermo					X
882	McDouyel, Alexander	X				
883	McDuffey, Arch					X
884	McElroy, James	X				
885	Mceter, John			X		
886	McFagin, John	X				
887	McFarland, David				X	X
888	McFee, Juan					X
889	McGaney, Hugh			X		
890	McGerg, Hugh			X		
891	McGill, Daniel					X
892	McGill, James	X				
893	McGreen, Thomas				X	
894	McHatin, John	X				
895	McHeath, Patricio					X
896	McIntoche, Guillermo					X
897	McIntosh, Eunice					X

	Name	1789a	1789b	1790a	1790b	1792
898	McIntosh, Guillermo			x		
899	McIntosh, James		x			
900	McIntosh, William		x			
901	McIntyre, James				x	x
902	McIntyre, John	x				
903	McKenzey, James	x				
904	McKey, Daniel		x			
905	McKnight, Jorge				x	
906	McLaughlin, Henry	x				
907	Mconohy, Anthony			x		
908	McVoy, Eduard	x				
909	McYnfere, George	x				
910	Melln, William		x			
911	Menjiez, Archibald			x		
912	Merier, Thomas	x				
913	Mettord, Jacob	x				
914	Mguay, Samuel			x		
915	Michel, Alexandro			x		
916	Migal, Daniel				x	
917	Migrot, Roswell				x	
918	Milburn, Enrrique					x
919	Milchez, Lawrence			x		
920	Miler, Arch.		x			
921	Milkoy, David				x	
922	Mille, Mateo			x		
923	Miller, Daniel			x	x	x
924	Miller, Jacobo					x
925	Miller, Jose					x
926	Miller, Richard					x
927	Miller, Robert				x	x
928	Miller, William					x
929	Mills, James	x				
930	Minor, Estevan					x
931	Minor, Guillermo			x		
932	Minor, John		x			
933	Minor, Thiophilus			x		
934	Minor, Thomas	x				
935	Minor, William	x		x		
936	Minorby, Miguel					x

	Name	1789a	1789b	1790a	1790b	1792
937	Mitchel, David				X	X
938	Mitchel, Lauren			X		
939	Mitchell, David		X			
940	Molony, Morris	X				
941	Molson, Augusto	X				
942	Monrroy, La subcere.					X
943	Monsanto, Benjamin					X
944	Monson, Jesse					X
945	Monson, Roberto					X
946	Montgomey, Juan				X	
947	Moore, Alexandro					X
948	Moore, Ruben	X				
949	Moore, Tomas					X
950	Moore, William	X				
951	Morgan, Guillermo					X
952	Morgan, Thomas		X		X	X
953	Morning, Guillermo					X
954	Morrison, James	X				
955	Morrison, William	X				
956	Moses, Abraham				X	
957	Mulhollon, the Widow					X
958	Mulkey, David		X			X
959	Muray, James	X				
960	Muris, Groves					X
961	Murphy, John	X				
962	Murray, Guillermo					X
963	Murray, Jorge					X
964	Murray, Tomas					X
965	Murry, James	X				
966	Myer, Federico					X
967	Mygatt, Margarita					X
968	Nailey, Francisco				X	
969	Nash, Webb	X				
970	Nash, Will	X				
971	Nayler, John	X			X	
972	Naylor, Francisco	X				X
973	Naylor, Juan					X
974	Neeton, John		X			
975	Nelson, Elya	X				

	Name	1789a	1789b	1790a	1790b	1792
976	Nelson, Peter		x		x	x
977	Nevel, Dennes	x				
978	Newman, Ezekiel				x	x
979	Newman, William	x				
980	Newman, Ysac					x
981	Newton, John				x	x
982	Nichols, Tomas					x
983	Nicholson, Enrrique					x
984	Nicholson, James		x			x
985	Night, Jacob	x				
986	Norton, Abraham					x
987	Noskins, Ezekiel					x
988	Novres, Jorge					x
989	Oconnor, Guillermo			x		
990	Oconnor, James			x		
991	Oconor, Juan					x
992	Odam, John		x			
993	Odum, David				x	x
994	Odum, John					x
995	Ogdem, Daniel					x
996	Ogdon, Daniel		x			
997	Oglesbery, William	x				
998	Oglesby, James		x			x
999	Oharah, Charles			x		
1000	Oiler, the Widow					x
1001	Oliver, Russel			x		
1002	Ophil, Eliza					x
1003	Orange					x
1004	Overaton, Jorge				x	
1005	Overrake, George			x		
1006	Owens, William		x			
1007	Owings, William				x	x
1008	Oxbury, John					x
1009	Paiper, Esep	x				
1010	Pallirson, William			x		
1011	Palmer, Archivaldo		x			x
1012	Parkins, Jonathan		x			
1013	Paterson, Guillermo			x		x
1014	Paton, James	x				

	Name	1789a	1789b	1790a	1790b	1792
1015	Patrick, Robert	x				
1016	Patterson, John			x	x	x
1017	Pauling, William	x				
1018	Paulset, Francisco					x
1019	Paulus, Pedro	x				
1020	Peary, Bernabe				x	
1021	Peat, William	x				
1022	Peck, Charles			x		
1023	Penery, Roberto			x		
1024	Penkly, Juan			x		
1025	Perales, Pedro	x				
1026	Peray, Hardy	x				
1027	Percey, Carlos					x
1028	Percey, Jacobo					x
1029	Perkins, John			x		x
1030	Perkins, Jonathan					x
1031	Perkins, Joseph		x			x
1032	Perkins, William			x		
1033	Perleney			x		
1034	Perry, Daniel		x		x	x
1035	Perry, Maydelen					x
1036	Peters, Juan	x				
1037	Peterson, William	x				
1038	Pexdry, Charles		x			
1039	Pext, William	x				
1040	Phelips, Theop	x				
1041	Phelips, Thomas	x				
1042	Philipe, Joseph	x				
1043	Phipps, Elijah				x	
1044	Phipps, Samuel		x		x	x
1045	Phips, Henry				x	x
1046	Pierce, John			x		
1047	Pipes, Windsor		x			x
1048	Pips, Abner					x
1049	Pips, Guillermo Nesey				x	
1050	Pittman, Boner	x				
1051	Pittman, Bukner					x
1052	Platner, Henry		x		x	x
1053	Polter, Ebenezer				x	

	Name	1789a	1789b	1790a	1790b	1792
1054	Polter, Juan				x	
1055	Porter, Andrew	x				
1056	Porter, Samuel					x
1057	Potter, Ebenezer	x				x
1058	Pourchous, Antonio					x
1059	Presler, Pedro				x	
1060	Presley, Pedro					x
1061	Preston, Guillermo					x
1062	Price, Leonardo					x
1063	Price, Lurvilling	x				
1064	Pringle, James			x		
1065	Pritchards, Job					x
1066	Proctor, Reuben					x
1067	Protzman, Enry			x		
1068	Pruett, Beezely		x			
1069	Pruit, Beesley					x
1070	Pughs, David	x				
1071	Puller, Nataniel			x		
1072	Putman, Buckey				x	
1073	Pyatte, Jacobo					x
1074	Quin, Patrick	x				
1075	Raby, Cader					x
1076	Raley, Cader		x			
1077	Ramer, Miguel					x
1078	Randell, Tensa					x
1079	Ranmeson, Martin	x				
1080	Ranner, Samuel					x
1081	Rapalise, Juana					x
1082	Rapalye, Garet					x
1083	Rapalye, Isaac					x
1084	Rapalye, Santiago					x
1085	Rasmus, Daniel	x				
1086	Ratcliffe, John		x		x	x
1087	Ratcliffe, William		x		x	x
1088	Ravas, Samuel		x			
1089	Reaid, Juan				x	
1090	Redick, Samuel				x	
1091	Reed, Thomas				x	x
1092	Reilly, Tomas					x

	Name	1789a	1789b	1790a	1790b	1792
1093	Reynolds, James	x				
1094	Rice, Manuel					x
1095	Rice, Reuben					x
1096	Rich, Jorge					x
1097	Rich, Juan					x
1098	Richards, Eliphtatet	x				
1099	Richards, Estevan				x	x
1100	Richards, Joshua			x		
1101	Richards, Mordica					x
1102	Richards, Morduar	x				
1103	Richardson, George		x		x	
1104	Richardson, Henry		x		x	
1105	Richardson, James		x			x
1106	Ridd, Juan			x		
1107	Ridley, George	x				
1108	Rigthy, John T.	x				
1109	Rigtt, Juan Federico	x				
1110	Riom, Adam				x	
1111	Rit, Guillermo	x				
1112	Ritchards, John			x		
1113	Roach, Enrrique					x
1114	Roach, Henry		x			
1115	Road, Jacob			x		
1116	Rob, Nicolas		x			x
1117	Rob, Nicolas (son)					x
1118	Robens, George			x		
1119	Robert, John			x		
1120	Roberto, Anthony			x		
1121	Roberts, Abraham				x	
1122	Roberts, John			x		
1123	Roberts, John			x		x
1124	Robeson, Tomas					x
1125	Robins, Carlos				x	
1126	Robinson, Archivald					x
1127	Robold, Lenhart			x		
1128	Roddy, Augustus	x				x
1129	Roddy, Ricardo				x	x
1130	Rols, David					x
1131	Rols, Thomas	x				

	Name	1789a	1789b	1790a	1790b	1792
1132	Roper, George	x				
1133	Ros, Hugh	x				
1134	Ros, Thomas	x				
1135	Ross, Guillermo			x		
1136	Ross, Hugh	x				
1137	Ross, Robert			x		
1138	Routh, Elias					x
1139	Routh, Jeremiah				x	x
1140	Routh, Job					x
1141	Routh, Margaret					x
1142	Row, Margarita					x
1143	Row, Mistress		x			
1144	Rox, Roberto			x		
1145	Rubel, Luis	x				
1146	Ruen, Guillermo	x				
1147	Ruker, Jonathan					x
1148	Rule, Thomas					x
1149	Rumsey, Jean		x			
1150	Rundell, Seth				x	x
1151	Rutly, John			x		
1152	Ryan, James			x		
1153	Ryan, William		x		x	x
1154	Ryland, James					x
1155	Ryon, Timothy	x				
1156	Sallier, Juan Baptista			x		
1157	Sanders, James					x
1158	Savage, Ana					x
1159	Savage, Mistress		x			
1160	Savage, Peter	x				
1161	Sayr, Guillermo			x		
1162	Scandling, Andreu	x				x
1163	Scoggins, Juan					x
1164	Scophil, Jose					x
1165	Scott, David			x		
1166	Scott, William		x			
1167	Scriber, Estevan					x
1168	Sekins, James	x				
1169	Selater, Hirve	x				
1170	Serlot, Pedro					x

	Name	1789a	1789b	1790a	1790b	1792
1171	Seur, Jayne Cole				X	
1172	Shanly, Bernardo	X				
1173	Shanower, John	X				
1174	Sharky, Patrick			X		
1175	Shaver, Michael	X				
1176	Shaw, Cornelio					X
1177	Shelivey, Jacob	X				
1178	Shepman, Maria					X
1179	Shey, Joseph			X		
1180	Shilling, Bolser		X			
1181	Shilling, Jacob		X		X	X
1182	Shilling, Palser					X
1183	Shirky, Patrick			X		
1184	Shonaner, Juan					X
1185	Short, William		X			
1186	Show, Hugh	X				
1187	Shunk, John		X			
1188	Shvoly, John	X				
1189	Siliven, Tomas			X		
1190	Silkreg, Guillermo					X
1191	Simmons, Charles		X		X	X
1192	Sinclair, Gaspar		X			
1193	Sinclair, Gaspar M.					X
1194	Singleton, Jayne				X	
1195	Sivesay, David					X
1196	Sivezay, Gabriel					X
1197	Slater, Hugh					X
1198	Slater, Joseph					X
1199	Slats, Antony	X				
1200	Slaughter, John	X				
1201	Sloan, Archibel					X
1202	Sloan, James			X		
1203	Sloan, Patrick			X		
1204	Slone, Arthur			X		
1205	Slone, Joseph			X		
1206	Slory, Sprint	X				
1207	Sluter, Juan					X
1208	Small, Joseph	X				
1209	Smiley, Thomas	X	X		X	X

	Name	1789a	1789b	1790a	1790b	1792
1210	Smily, Juan (son)				X	
1211	Smit, Benjamin	X				
1212	Smith, Calvin					X
1213	Smith, Carlos	X				
1214	Smith, Catalina					X
1215	Smith, Christopher			X		
1216	Smith, David		X			X
1217	Smith, Ebenezer		X		X	X
1218	Smith, Eduardo	X				
1219	Smith, Eleaezer				X	
1220	Smith, Elias					X
1221	Smith, Elisha	X			X	
1222	Smith, Elisha	X			X	
1223	Smith, Godfrey			X		
1224	Smith, Hugh			X		
1225	Smith, James	X			X	X
1226	Smith, John					X
1227	Smith, John	X	X	X	X	X
1228	Smith, Joseph	X				
1229	Smith, Lucins					X
1230	Smith, Luis				X	
1231	Smith, Pedro					X
1232	Smith, Phel.		X			
1233	Smith, Philander		X			X
1234	Smith, Philinu					X
1235	Smith, Philitus					X
1236	Smith, Reuben	X				
1237	Smith, Robert	X				
1238	Smith, Tere					X
1239	Smith, the Widow					X
1240	Smith, Thomas			X		X
1241	Smith, William		X			X
1242	Smith, William		X			X
1243	Smith, Zacarias		X			X
1244	Smith, Zacarias (son)					X
1245	Snody, Andy	X				
1246	Solivester					X
1247	Soloven, Daniel			X		
1248	Spaekman, Juan	X				

	Name	1789a	1789b	1790a	1790b	1792
1249	Spain, Francis		x		x	x
1250	Spain, Jaime				x	x
1251	Spain, Jayme				x	
1252	Spalden, James		x			
1253	Spins, Juan				x	
1254	Spires, Juan					x
1255	Splun, Tomas					x
1256	Springel, Jacob	x				
1257	Sta Maria, Pedro			x		
1258	Stampley, George		x		x	x
1259	Stampley, Jacob				x	x
1260	Stampley, John		x		x	x
1261	Stampley, Margarita					x
1262	Stark, Robert			x		x
1263	Staybraker, John		x			
1264	Stefen, Jacob	x				
1265	Stellinger, Jacob	x				
1266	Stephens, Jacob	x				
1267	Stephenson, Stephen		x		x	x
1268	Sterret, Steven	x				
1269	Stevenson, Samuel	x	x			
1270	Stewart, James			x		x
1271	Stiles, William	x				
1272	Stilinger, Jacob	x				
1273	Still, Benjamin					x
1274	Still, William	x				
1275	Stock, Guillermo					x
1276	Stockstill, Jose					x
1277	Stodt, Benjamin	x				
1278	Stogan, John			x		
1279	Stokman, Federico					x
1280	Stoner, Michel	x				
1281	Stoop, Jacobo					x
1282	Story, Ephrin	x				
1283	Stout, Abel			x		
1284	Stout, Juan					x
1285	Stowars, Juan					x
1286	Stowars, Juan					x
1287	Strawbraker, John					x

	Name	1789a	1789b	1790a	1790b	1792
1288	Strong, Juan Conrad					x
1289	Stucktile, Josua				x	
1290	Stuvart, Charles	x				
1291	Sullivan, Daniel					x
1292	Sullivan, Patricio					x
1293	Sullivan, Patricio					x
1294	Sullivan, Patrick	x			x	
1295	Sullivan, Thomas			x		
1296	Surget, Pedro					x
1297	Swayze, David				x	
1298	Swazey, Gabriel		x		x	
1299	Swazey, Nathan		x		x	x
1300	Swazey, Richard		x		x	x
1301	Swazey, Samuel		x		x	x
1302	Sweyze, Evan				x	
1303	Tabor, Isaac					x
1304	Tabor, William					x
1305	Taitt, Guillermo			x		
1306	Take, Juan					x
1307	Take, Miguel					x
1308	Talet, William		x			
1309	Tambleston, Vath N.		x			
1310	Tarinton, Tomas					x
1311	Tate, John			x		
1312	Tate, John	x				
1313	Taylor, Isac					x
1314	Taylor, Peter	x				
1315	Tennan, Daniel	x				
1316	Tepeltylas, Daniel			x		
1317	Terry, Jaime					x
1318	Terry, John		x		x	x
1319	Thockmorton, Mordica				x	
1320	Thomas, William		x			x
1321	Thorn, Cornelius	x				
1322	Thorn, William	x				
1323	Thorns, John			x		
1324	Thorton, Abraham		x			
1325	Throckmorten, Mordeca	x				
1326	Throckmorton, Robert				x	x

	Name	1789a	1789b	1790a	1790b	1792
1327	Thuns, Beray			X		
1328	Tibbs, John	X				
1329	Tinsley, Prestney			X		
1330	Todd, Charles			X		
1331	Todd, Roberto					X
1332	Todo, Charles			X		
1333	Tomas, Juan			X		X
1334	Tomlinson, Nathaniel				X	X
1335	Tomlston, Nataniel					X
1336	Tomlston, Nataniel					X
1337	Tompson, Theophelus			X		
1338	Tomson, William	X				
1339	Toogins, Jonas				X	
1340	Tool, Patrick		X			
1341	Tooy, Isaac					X
1342	Torman, Ezikiel			X		
1343	Torret, Jacob	X				
1344	Trasher, Juan					X
1345	Travellion, Richard		X			
1346	Trevilion, Temple S.				X	
1347	Trimble, Jacob			X		
1348	Trockmorton, Mordica					X
1349	Troop, Jorge					X
1350	Truely, Benet					X
1351	Truely, Benet				X	
1352	Truely, James				X	X
1353	Truley, James		X			
1354	Truvins, John	X				
1355	Tunlof, Presting				X	
1356	Turner, Roberto				X	
1357	Turney, Mathew		X			
1358	Turpin, Philip P.				X	
1359	Tuvis, Juan	X				
1360	Tux, John	X				
1361	Twely, Nataniel					X
1362	Twins, Tomas					X
1363	Uph, Jacob	X				
1364	Vallepet, Luis				X	
1365	Vancheret, Jose					X

	Name	1789a	1789b	1790a	1790b	1792
1366	Vancheret, Juan					x
1367	Vandevoas, John	x				
1368	Vannalson, Elijak	x				
1369	Vardeman, William	x				
1370	Vass, Thomas		x			
1371	Vaude, Thomas				x	
1372	Vebn, Juan				x	
1373	Veleroit, John	x				
1374	Vilaret, Luis					x
1375	Villeret, Juan B.			x		
1376	Voice, Tomas					x
1377	Vousdan, Guillermo					x
1378	Wade, James		x			x
1379	Wadkins, Andres					x
1380	Wales, Samuel	x				
1381	Walker, George			x		
1382	Walker, Joseph			x		
1383	Walker, Joseph			x		
1384	Wall, Juan					x
1385	Walles, James	x				
1386	Walles, Whitington	x				
1387	Walther, George			x		
1388	Walton, William	x				
1389	Warck, Juan				x	
1390	Ward, Levis	x				
1391	Waths, Roberto					x
1392	Watson, James			x		
1393	Watts, Gideon	x				
1394	Watts, James	x				
1395	Watts, Robert	x				
1396	Waunos, Luis			x		
1397	Weasner, Jorge					x
1398	Weed, Joel					x
1399	Weed, Joel				x	
1400	Weedon, Guillermo	x				
1401	Weeks, William		x			x
1402	Weeve, Guillermo				x	
1403	Welch, Thomas	x				
1404	Welck, Jacob	x				

	Name	1789a	1789b	1790a	1790b	1792
1405	Weley, Jaimes	x				
1406	Welton, Juan					x
1407	Wenchefrer, George	x				
1408	Wenshey, Christian	x				
1409	Wenters, Stephan	x				
1410	Wery, Adan	x				
1411	West, Abner	x				
1412	West, Cato		x		x	x
1413	West, Little Berry					x
1414	West, William				x	x
1415	Wethers, Jese					x
1416	Whitaker, Daniel		x		x	
1417	White, Lily					x
1418	White, Mateo					x
1419	White, Mathew		x			
1420	White, Thomas	x				
1421	Whithers, Roberto				x	
1422	Whitley, Solomon	x			x	
1423	Wibles, John	x				
1424	Wilcox, Jereus	x				
1425	Wiley, John	x			x	x
1426	Wilkenson, William	x				
1427	Wilkerson, Juan					x
1428	Wilkey, Noble	x				
1429	Wilkins, Carlos	x				
1430	Wilkinson, George	x			x	
1431	Wilky, Noble	x				
1432	Willey, James	x	x		x	x
1433	William, John	x				
1434	Williams, David		x			x
1435	Williams, Edward	x				
1436	Williams, Hezekiah				x	
1437	Williams, John	x		x		x
1438	Williams, Juan			x		
1439	Williams, Matheo			x		
1440	Williams, Miguel			x		x
1441	Williams, Thomas	x				
1442	Willis, Henry	x				
1443	Willson, Michael			x		

	Name	1789a	1789b	1790a	1790b	1792
1444	Willson, William					x
1445	Wilson, James	x				
1446	Wilson, Juan				x	x
1447	Wilson, Roberto	x				
1448	Winchinsior, George			x		
1449	Winchinster, David			x		
1450	Winllis, George	x				
1451	Winskey, Christian	x				
1452	Winter, George	x				
1453	Wintirs, Stevan	x				
1454	Wintors, Elisha			x		
1455	Wise, David	x				
1456	Withers, Robert					x
1457	Withon, Jesse				x	
1458	Witley, Salomon					x
1459	Witsel, Luis			x		
1460	Wnama, Matias A.	x				
1461	Wolph, George			x		
1462	Woods, James			x		
1463	Woolley, Melling					x
1464	Worner, Luis			x		
1465	Wright, Alexander			x		
1466	Yorther, John			x		
1467	Young, Elizabet					x
1468	Young, Guillermo				x	x
1469	Young, Juan				x	x
1470	Young, Juan				x	
1471	Yoy, Nataniel				x	
1472	Zeines, Juan					x
1473	Zuglas, John	x				

Table 19. 1795/1799

	Name	1795	1796	1799
1	Alston, John			x
2	Alston, Solomon			x
3	Alston, William			x
4	Baird, Isham	x		
5	Baker, John			x
6	Barnes, John	x		
7	Biggs, Caleb			x
8	Bord, William	x		
9	Broderick, Guillermo			x
10	Bryan, William	x		
11	Buasfield, Rowlen	x		
12	Calliham, David	x		
13	Calliham, John	x		
14	Carnly, Thomas	x		
15	Clark, Daniel		x	
16	Clarksond, William	x		
17	Clasher, John	x		
18	Coleman, John R.			x
19	Collins, Jno.		x	
20	Collins, William			x
21	Craw, James	x		
22	Diane, Cornelius	x		
23	Dions, Cornelius	x		
24	Gardnhart, Michal			x
25	Girault, Juan	x		
26	Griffin, Absalom	x		
27	Griffin, James	x		
28	Grunwell, Jeremiah	x		
29	Harbour, Thomas	x		x
30	Hart, George	x		
31	Hutchinson, Samuel			x
32	Huubour, Adonyah	x		
33	Jones, David		x	
34	Jones, James		x	
35	Jones, James (son)		x	
36	Knight, John	x		
37	Leen, Daniel	x		
38	Linde, John	x		
39	Lloyd, Robert	x		

	Name	1795	1796	1799
40	Lovelace, Edward		x	
41	Lovelace, George		x	
42	Lovelace, John (father)		x	
43	Lovelace, John (son)		x	
44	Lovelace, Richard		x	
45	Lovelace, Thomas		x	
46	Lovelace, William		x	
47	Lutz, Johan Abraham	x		
48	Manadue, Henry			x
49	Mayes, Stephen			x
50	McLane, Malcolm	x		
51	Mims, Samuel	x		
52	Mojo, William	x		
53	Montgomery, Jasper	x		
54	Montgomery, Thomas	x		
55	Moore, Ruben			x
56	Nelson, Christian			x
57	Ogden, Daniel		x	
58	Ogden, Isac		x	
59	Ogden, Richard		x	
60	Ogden, William		x	
61	Pendergrap, Robert	x		
62	Percy, Charles Luke		x	
63	Percy, Thomas G.		x	
64	Phaves, William	x		
65	Pipes, Gill			x
66	Pollock, Thomas	x		
67	Roach, Henry		x	
68	Roach, John		x	
69	Roach, William		x	
70	Sewkles, Adam			x
71	Sims, Mathew	x		
72	Smith, Adolphfus F.		x	
73	Smith, Israel	x		
74	Smith, John Moses		x	
75	Smith, William		x	
76	Smith, Zachariah (father)		x	
77	Smith, Zachariah (son)		x	
78	Stephens, John	x		

	Name	1795	1796	1799
79	Stephens, John	x		x
80	Stephens, John	x		x
81	Stite, Richard	x		
82	Storup, George P.			x
83	Swayze, Stephen			x
84	Thorp, Robert			x
85	Wall, John		x	
86	Weed, Joel			x
87	Welton, Patience			x
88	Wimlish, James	x		
89	Wirs, Guillermo			x
90	Young, Mosco	x		
91	Younge, Samuel	x		

Table 20. Natchez Origins

	Names	Dates	Origins	Destination
1	Abercromedi, Jayme	1794	Ireland	
2	Abercromedi, Juan	1794	Ireland	
3	Adam, Armotead	1795	Americano	USA
4	Adrair, Guillermo	1795	Americano	USA
5	Aldeston, Jayme	1793	Ireland	USA
6	Aldin, Benjamin	1795	Americano	Louisiana
7	Amer, Jamery	1794	France	
8	Amistron, Guillermo	1795	Ireland	Louisiana
9	Anderson, Andres	1795	Americano	Louisiana
10	Anderson, Guillermo	1795	Americano	USA
11	Andn, Joaquin	1795	Americano	USA
12	Andres, Santiago	1794	Canada	New Orleans
13	Aoche, Silbestre	1794	Germany	Louisiana
14	Arkley, Roberto	1794	Americano	Natchez
15	Arman, Juan	1794	Americano	
16	Armstead, Benjamin	1795	Americano	USA
17	Armstrong, Salomon	1795	Americano	USA
18	Ashluay, Tomas	1794	Americano	Natchez
19	Astin, Jose	1795	Ireland	Louisiana
20	Aynw, Bernardo	1794	Ireland	USA
21	Bacon, David	1795	Americano	USA
22	Bail, Conel	1794	Ireland	New Madrid
23	Ballanuz, Guillermo	1795	Americano	USA
24	Ballis, Guillermo	1795	Americano	USA
25	Bancagrime, James	1795	Americano	Louisiana
26	Bartelet, Piam	1794	Americano	USA
27	Bartlet, James	1795	Americano	USA
28	Barton, Carlos	1795	Americano	USA
29	Bauchanp, Juan	1793		USA
30	Baucher, Tomas	1794	Ireland	Louisiana
31	Becas, Antonio	1795	France	USA
32	Bedger, Davis	1795	Americano	USA
33	Bell, Jose	1794	Americano	USA
34	Bell, Jose	1795	Americano	USA
35	Bell, Simeon	1795	Americano	USA
36	Benechan, Patricio	1794	Ireland	USA
37	Benglyuu, Housal	1794	Americano	USA
38	Berhinshire, Jose	1795	Americano	USA
39	Bigg, Guillermo	1794	Americano	USA

	Names	Dates	Origins	Destination
40	Bingham, Silas	1794	Americano	USA
41	Bingham, Taubes	1794	Americano	USA
42	Blain, James	1794	Ireland	USA
43	Blanetut, Silbestre	1795	France	USA
44	Blein, Jayme	1794	Americano	USA
45	Blek, Daniel	1795	Americano	USA
46	Blue, Ysac	1795	Americano	USA
47	Boaed, Handrason	1795	Americano	USA
48	Bocah, Juan	1795	Americano	USA
49	Boiw, Roberto	1794	Americano	Natchez
50	Bols, James	1794	Americano	Natchez
51	Boman, Daniel	1793	Americano	USA
52	Borget, Jose	1794	Americano	Natchez
53	Bouland, Roberto	1794	Americano	USA
54	Bowsoearingen, Tomas	1793		USA
55	Boyle, Connel	1793	Ireland	USA
56	Bradly, John	1793	Ireland	USA
57	Branan, Jose	1794	Americano	USA
58	Brand, Jorge	1794	Americano	USA
59	Branle, Federico	1794	Americano	USA
60	Bratson, Guillermo	1795	Americano	USA
61	Brayen, Juan	1795	Americano	USA
62	Brest, Juan	1793	Ireland	USA
63	Brian, John	1794	Fort Pitt	USA
64	Briton, Jose	1795	Americano	USA
65	Brokes, David	1794	Americano	USA
66	Brovim, Jus	1794	Ireland	USA
67	Brown, James	1795	Americano	USA
68	Brown, Samuel	1795	Americano	USA
69	Bullol, Etien	1793	Italian	
70	Burk, Stephen	1793	Ireland	USA
71	Burke, Tomas	1795	Americano	USA
72	Burnet, Juan	1795	Americano	USA
73	Bursly, James	1795	Americano	USA
74	Butin, Samuel	1795	Americano	USA
75	Calduel, Juan	1795	Americano	
76	Calen, Thomas	1795	England	Louisiana
77	Cambell, Santiago	1795	Americano	USA
78	Cannes, Jon	1795	Americano	USA

	Names	Dates	Origins	Destination
79	Canney, Juan	1794	Americano	USA
80	Canscild, Bewen	1795	Americano	USA
81	Cantel, Gui	1793	Scotland	USA
82	Canue, Guillermo	1794	Ireland	USA
83	Carril, Hercules	1795	Americano	USA
84	Carril, Jorge	1795	Americano	USA
85	Carter, Jose	1794	Americano	USA
86	Chaffins, David	1795	France	USA
87	Chambers, Guillermo	1793	Americano	USA
88	Chambers, Juan	1794	Americano	USA
89	Chanon, Juan	1794	Americano	USA
90	Charp, Jose	1794	Americano	USA
91	Chayber, Guillermo	1794	Americano	Natchez
92	Chefue, Juan	1794	Germany	
93	Cheval, Wilcan	1795	Americano	USA
94	Chiera, Juan Bautista	1794	France	
95	Chines, Juan	1793	Ireland	Louisiana
96	Chumeca, Guillermo	1795	Americano	Louisiana
97	Clark, Elms	1795	Americano	USA
98	Clark, John	1795	Americano	USA
99	Claud, Adan	1793	Americano	Natchez
100	Cleavns, Estevan	1795	Americano	USA
101	Clemente, Juan	1795	Americano	USA
102	Clindsall, Roberto	1794	Ireland	USA
103	Cliver, Estevan	1794	Americano	USA
104	Coba, Coba	1794	Americano	USA
105	Cokler, Juan	1794	England	USA
106	Colbert, John	1795	Americano	USA
107	Colbert, Juan	1795	Americano	USA
108	Colbert, Simon	1795	Americano	USA
109	Colbert, Simon	1795	Americano	USA
110	Colem, Guillermo	1794	Ireland	USA
111	Coleman, Esmaelen	1794	Americano	USA
112	Colems, Tomas	1794	Ireland	
113	Colens, Juan	1794	Ireland	
114	Coliben, Samuel	1794	Ireland	USA
115	Collin, Tomas V.	1795	Americano	USA
116	Collins, Jose	1794	Americano	USA
117	Colwel, Diego	1793	Ireland	USA

	Names	Dates	Origins	Destination
118	Comens, Juan	1794	Ireland	USA
119	Comes, Ygnacio	1795	Americano	USA
120	Comor, Miguel	1795	Americano	USA
121	Coner, Guillermo	1794	Americano	USA
122	Connal, Carlos	1795	Americano	USA
123	Conoby, Jacobo	1795	Americano	USA
124	Cooper, Jacobo	1794	Americano	USA
125	Coris, Juan	1794	Americano	USA
126	Crave, Josiah	1795	Americano	USA
127	Crawford, Andres	1794	Americano	USA
128	Crawford, Tomas	1794	Americano	USA
129	Cruz, Jacobo	1794	Americano	USA
130	Currau, Guillermo	1795	Americano	USA
131	Cuus, Tomas	1795	Americano	USA
132	Cuwy, William	1795	Americano	USA
133	Daughtel, Jose	1794	Americano	USA
134	Davien, Juan	1793	Germany	New Orleans
135	Deaivonge, Jose	1794	France	Louisiana
136	Deken, Jorpe	1795	Americano	
137	Delin, Juan	1794	Americano	USA
138	Delon, Federico	1794	Germany	USA
139	Denuelle, Francisco	1793	St. Louis	St. Louis
140	Deruin, Estevan	1793	Canada	
141	Devis, Leiua	1794	Americano	USA
142	Devis, Pedro	1793	Kentucky	USA
143	Devoir, Samuel	1795	Americano	USA
144	Diekles, Carlos	1795	Americano	USA
145	Dobert, Pedro	1794	Americano	
146	Doget, Miguel	1795	Ireland	USA
147	Dorvin, Hosien	1795	Americano	USA
148	Dorvins, Tomas	1795	Americano	USA
149	Dosten, Guillermo	1794	England	USA
150	Dougan, Enrique	1795	Americano	USA
151	Dreit, Francisco	1794	Americano	USA
152	Dunahow, James	1795	Americano	USA
153	Duting, Juan	1794	England	USA
154	Eddy, Samuel	1795	Americano	USA
155	Empel, Juan	1793	New Madrid	New Madrid
156	Esgr, Jonatan	1794	Americano	USA

	Names	Dates	Origins	Destination
157	Eslignan, Madama	1794	Americano	New Orleans
158	Esmael, Guillermo	1794	Americano	USA
159	Estan, Juan	1794	Americano	New Madrid
160	Estan, Ranzon	1794	Americano	New Madrid
161	Estidier, Jose	1795	Americano	USA
162	Estimal, Madama	1794	Americano	Natchez
163	Estod, Samiel	1794	Americano	Natchez
164	Estuard, Guillermo	1795	Americano	USA
165	Fabuel, Samuel	1794	Americano	USA
166	Fageson, Samuel	1794	Americano	USA
167	Faghy, John	1793	Ireland	USA
168	Falknen, John	1795	Americano	USA
169	Far, Estevan	1794	Americano	USA
170	Farsel, Jose	1794	Americano	Natchez
171	Felipe, Samuel	1794	Americano	
172	Feple, Pedro	1794	Americano	Louisiana
173	Ferril, Tomas	1795	Americano	USA
174	Ferrol, James	1794	Americano	Louisiana
175	Fiamen, Elias	1795	Americano	USA
176	Filipis, Aysik	1794	Americano	Louisiana
177	Flin, Eduardo	1795	Americano	USA
178	Flin, Hugh	1795	Americano	USA
179	Flincher, Benjamin	1795	England	Louisiana
180	Floier, Tomas	1793	Americano	USA
181	Fon, John	1795	Americano	USA
182	Forster, Juan	1794	Americano	Natchez
183	Forthize, Roberto	1794	Americano	USA
184	Foy, Pedro	1794	Ireland	USA
185	Frances, Jose Gordon	1794	Americano	New Madrid
186	Frannin, Jayme	1794	Americano	USA
187	Fraye, Jose	1795	Americano	USA
188	Frons, Juan	1795	Americano	USA
189	Fulton, Alexandro	1795	Americano	USA
190	Galguera, Juan	1794	Ireland	USA
191	Gallaghen, Carlos	1794	Ireland	USA
192	Garnet, Juan	1794	Fort Pitt	USA
193	Gati, Juan	1793	Kentucky	USA
194	Gawen, Jesse	1795	Americano	USA
195	Gilekust, Guillermo	1795	Americano	

	Name	Origin	Date
196	Holsten, George	Fort Pitt	a
197	Horine, Samuel	Kentucky	b
198	House, Casper	Pennsylvania	b
199	Hover, Jacob	Kentucky	b
200	Hubbard, Ephrain	Virginia	b
201	Hughs, Thomas	Kentucky	b
202	Hukison, Steward	Kentucky	b
203	Humphreys, Ralph	Kentucky	b
204	Hunter, John	Kentucky	b
205	Innis, Francis	Kentucky	b
206	Isenhood, Barnet	North Carolina	a
207	Ismund, Ebenezer	Pennsylvania	b
208	Ives, William	Kentucky	b
209	Jackson, George	Kentucky	b
210	Jacobs, Miguel	Pennsylvania	b
211	Jennings, Roberto	Kentucky	b
212	John, George	Kaskakia [Illinois]	b
213	John, James	Kaskakia [Illinois]	b
214	John, Thomas	Kaskakia [Illinois]	b
215	Johns, David	Kaskakia [Illinois]	b
216	Johnson, Edmund	Virginia	b
217	Johnston, James	Kentucky	b
218	Jones, Charles	North Carolina	a
219	Jones, Charles	Kentucky	b
220	Jones, David	Kentucky	b
221	Jones, Henry	North Carolina	a
222	Jones, Robert	North Carolina	a
223	Jorden, James	Kentucky	b
224	Jus, Juan	Pennsylvania	b
225	Karnis, Richard	North Carolina	a
226	Keen, Wilha	Pennsylvania	b
227	Kelly, Miguel	Cumberland	b
228	Kelly, Thomas	Kentucky	b
229	Killian, George	North Carolina	b
230	Killian, George	North Carolina	a
231	Killor, Peter	Kentucky	b
232	Killpatrick, Hugh	Kentucky	b
233	Kirk, Patrick	Kentucky	b
234	Koflay, John	Pennsylvania	b

	Name	Origin	Date
235	Kulen, John	Kentucky	b
236	Lacaman, Nicolas	Kentucky	b
237	Lafough, Joseph	Kentucky	b
238	Land, John	Fort Pitt	a
239	Lauman, John	Kentucky	b
240	Ledyear, George	Kentucky	b
241	Lee, Mark	Kentucky	b
242	Lee, William	Kentucky	b
243	Leman, John	Kentucky	b
244	Letty, Thomas	Kentucky	b
245	Levins, Nicolas	Kentucky	b
246	Linch, Rud	Pennsylvania	b
247	Liveing, Lovis	Fort Pitt	a
248	Lord, Tomas	Kentucky	a
249	Lovill, Louis	Kentucky	b
250	Luzer, Solomon	Kentucky	b
251	Lyon, Matheu	Fort Pitt	b
252	Man, Frederick	Kentucky	b
253	Manadiac, Henry	North Carolina	a
254	Manie, Andas	Puesto Vencen	b
255	Marbal, Ezra	Kentucky	a
256	Marbel, Abner	Kentucky	a
257	Marchal, Juan	Illinois	b
258	Marcus, Frederick	Pennsylvania	b
259	Marn, Martin	North Carolina	a
260	Marney, John	Cumberland	a
261	Martin, Juan Baptista	Puesto Vencen	b
262	Martin, William	Kentucky	b
263	Marton, Abner	Kentucky	b
264	Matus, Hugh	Kentucky	b
265	Max, George	Kentucky	b
266	May, Humphrey	Kentucky	b
267	McBilland, Thomas	Kentucky	b
268	McBluce, Thomas	Virginia	b
269	McBride, John	Kentucky	b
270	McCartney, John	Kentucky	b
271	McClentiek, William	Kentucky	b
272	McCollock, James	Kentucky	b
273	McDermot, Thomas	Pennsylvania	b

	Name	Origin	Date
274	McDouyel, Alexander	Pennsylvania	b
275	McDugall, William	Cumberland	a
276	McElroy, James	Cumberland	b
277	McFagin, John	Kentucky	b
278	McGaney, Hugh	Kentucky	b
279	McGill, James	Kentucky	b
280	McGill, Thomas	North Carolina	a
281	McGovebick, Rubin	Cumberland	a
282	McGuore, Hugh	Cumberland	a
283	McHatin, John	Kentucky	b
284	McIntosh, Guillermo	Puesto Vencen	b
285	McIntyre, John	Kentucky	b
286	McKenzey, James	Kentucky	b
287	McLaughlin, Henry	Kaskakia [Illinois]	b
288	Mconohy, Anthony	Pennsylvania	b
289	McVoy, Eduard	Kentucky	b
290	McYnfere, George	Kentucky	b
291	Menjiez, Archibald	Kentucky	b
292	Merier, Thomas	Kentucky	b
293	Mettord, Jacob	Pennsylvania	b
294	Milchez, Lawrence	Pennsylvania	b
295	Miller, Daniel	North Carolina	a
296	Miller, William	Choctaw Nation	a
297	Mills, James	Kentucky	b
298	Minor, Estevan	North Carolina	a
299	Minor, Estevan	North Carolina	b
300	Minor, Guillermo	Pennsylvania	b
301	Minor, Thiophilus	Pennsylvania	b
302	Minor, William	Pennsylvania	b
303	Moore, William	Kentucky	b
304	Moran, William	North Carolina	a
305	Mordock, John	Kentucky	a
306	Morgan, David	Kentucky	a
307	Morrison, William	Kentucky	b
308	Muray, James	Kentucky	b
309	Murphy, John	Kentucky	b
310	Murry, Edward	North Carolina	a
311	Nash, Webb	Kentucky	b
312	Nevel, Dennes	Kentucky	b

	Name	Origin	Date
313	Oconnor, Guillermo	Pennsylvania	b
314	Oconnor, James	Kentucky	b
315	Oglesbery, William	Kaskakia [Illinois]	b
316	Olifunt, John	North Carolina	a
317	Paterson, Guillermo	Kentucky	b
318	Paton, James	Kentucky	b
319	Patrick, Robert	Kentucky	b
320	Pauling, William	Kentucky	b
321	Paulus, Pedro	Pennsylvania	b
322	Peck, Charles	Kentucky	b
323	Penkly, Juan	Cumberland	b
324	Perales, Pedro	Kaskakia [Illinois]	b
325	Perleney	Cumberland	b
326	Peters, Juan	Illinois	b
327	Peterson, William	Kentucky	b
328	Pext, William	Kentucky	b
329	Phelips, Theop	Pennsylvania	b
330	Philipe, Joseph	Kaskakia [Illinois]	b
331	Pichins, David	North Carolina	a
332	Pichins, John	North Carolina	a
333	Piernas, Pedro	North Carolina	a
334	Pittman, Boner	Pennsylvania	b
335	Pittman, Noah	North Carolina	a
336	Porter, Andrew	Kentucky	b
337	Price, Lurvilling or Luvillin	Kentucky	b
338	Pughs, David	Pennsylvania	b
339	Puller, Nataniel	Cumberland	b
340	Quin, Patrick	Kentucky	b
341	Rahos, William	North Carolina	a
342	Ranmeson, Martin	Pennsylvania	b
343	Rasmus, Daniel	Kentucky	b
344	Ray, Archibel	North Carolina	a
345	Reynolds, James	Kentucky	b
346	Richards, Eliphtatet	Pennsylvania	b
347	Richards, Joshua	Kentucky	b
348	Richards, Stephen	Kentucky	a
349	Richardson, George	North Carolina	a
350	Richardson, George	North Carolina	b
351	Richardson, James	North Carolina	a

	Name	Origin	Date
352	Ridd, Juan	Kentucky	b
353	Ridley, George	Cumberland	b
354	Rigthy, John Treaercets	Kentucky	b
355	Rit, Guillermo	Kaskakia [Illinois]	b
356	Road, Jacob	Kentucky	b
357	Robens, George	Pennsylvania	b
358	Roberto, Anthony	Kentucky	b
359	Roberts, John	Virginia	b
360	Rockler, Rubin	Kentucky	a
361	Roddy, Augustus	Kentucky	b
362	Rols, Thomas	Kentucky	b
363	Roper, George	Kentucky	b
364	Ros, Hugh	Pennsylvania	b
365	Ross, Guillermo	Kentucky	b
366	Rox, Roberto	Kentucky	b
367	Rud, Thomas	Kentucky	a
368	Rundell, Josiah	Cumberland	a
369	Rundell, Seth	Cumberland	a
370	Ryon, Timothy	Pennsylvania	b
371	Sallier, Juan Baptista	Puesto Vencen	b
372	Sayr, Guillermo	Kentucky	b
373	Scandling, Andreu	Kentucky	b
374	Sekins, James	Kentucky	b
375	Selater, Hirve	Kaskakia [Illinois]	b
376	Selden, George	Connecticut	a
377	Shanower, John	Kentucky	b
378	Sharky, Patrick	Virginia	b
379	Shaver, Michael	Kentucky	b
380	Shelivey, Jacob	Kaskakia [Illinois]	b
381	Shever, Leval	North Carolina	a
382	Shey, Joseph	Pennsylvania	b
383	Shoals, Christopher	North Carolina	a
384	Short, William	Kentucky	a
385	Shvoly, John	Pennsylvania	b
386	Slats, Antony	Kentucky	b
387	Slaughter, John	Kentucky	b
388	Sloan, Archibel	North Carolina	a
389	Sloan, Archibel	North Carolina	b
390	Slone, Arthur	Kentucky	b

	Name	Origin	Date
391	Slone, Joseph	Kentucky	b
392	Slory, Sprint	Kaskakia [Illinois]	b
393	Smith, Christopher	Fort Pitt	b
394	Smith, Eduardo	Kentucky	b
395	Smith, Elisha	Kaskakia [Illinois]	b
396	Smith, Godfrey	Kentucky	b
397	Smith, James	Kentucky	b
398	Smith, John	Pennsylvania	b
399	Smith, Joseph	Kentucky	b
400	Smith, Reuben	Kentucky	b
401	Smith, Richard	North Carolina	a
402	Smith, Robert	Kentucky	b
403	Smith, Thomas	Virginia	b
404	Snody, Andy	Cumberland	b
405	Spaekman, Juan	Kaskakia [Illinois]	b
406	Spalding, James	Cumberland	a
407	Sta Maria, Pedro	Puesto Vencen	b
408	Stellinger, Jacob	Kentucky	b
409	Stephens, Jacob	Kentucky	b
410	Sterret, Steven	Kentucky	b
411	Stevenson, Samuel	Kaskakia [Illinois]	b
412	Stewart, James	Kentucky	b
413	Stiles, William	Kentucky	b
414	Stodt, Benjamin	Kentucky	b
415	Stogan, John	Virginia	b
416	Stoner, Michel	Kentucky	b
417	Stricklin, Daniel	Cumberland	a
418	Sullivan, Patrick	Kentucky	b
419	Sullivan, Thomas	Virginia	b
420	Taitt, Guillermo	Cumberland	b
421	Tate, John	Pennsylvania	b
422	Tate, John	Kentucky	b
423	Taylor, Isaac	Kentucky	a
424	Taylor, Peter	Kentucky	b
425	Tell, Stephen	North Carolina	a
426	Tennan, Daniel	Kentucky	b
427	Tepeltylas, Daniel	Pennsylvania	b
428	Thompson, Cristobal	Kentucky	a
429	Thuns, Beray	Virginia	b

	Name	Origin	Date
430	Tibbs, John	Kentucky	b
431	Todd, Charles	Kentucky	b
432	Tomas, Juan	Fort Pitt	b
433	Tomson, William	Kentucky	b
434	Torman, Ezikiel	Pennsylvania	b
435	Trenthan, Martin	Cumberland	a
436	Truvins, John	Kentucky	b
437	Uph, Jacob	Kentucky	b
438	Vandevoas, John	Kentucky	b
439	Vannalson, Elijak	Kaskakia [Illinois]	b
440	Vardeman, William	Kentucky	b
441	Veleroit, John	Kentucky	b
442	Villeret, Juan Baptista	Puesto Vencen	b
443	Wales, Samuel	Cumberland	b
444	Walker, Andreu	Pennsylvania	a
445	Walker, George	Kentucky	b
446	Walker, Joseph	Kentucky	b
447	Walton, William	Kentucky	b
448	Ward, Levis	Kentucky	b
449	Watts, Gideon	Kentucky	b
450	Watts, James	Kentucky	b
451	Watts, Robert	Illinois	b
452	Waunos, Luis	Pennsylvania	b
453	Weathers, Zebulon	North Carolina	a
454	Welch, Thomas	Kentucky	b
455	Welck, Jacob	Kentucky	b
456	Weley, Jaimes	Kentucky	b
457	Wenchefrer, George	Kentucky	b
458	Wenshey, Christian	Kentucky	b
459	Wenters, Stephan	Kentucky	b
460	Wery, Adan	Kentucky	b
461	West, Abner	Georgia	b
462	West, John	Cumberland	a
463	White, Thomas	Kentucky	b
464	Wibles, John	Kentucky	b
465	Wilcox, Jereus	Pennsylvania	b
466	Wiley, John	Kentucky	b
467	Wilkenson, William	Kentucky	b
468	Wilkinson, George	Kentucky	b

	Name	Origin	Date
469	Wilky, Noble	Kentucky	b
470	Williams, Edward	Kentucky	b
471	Williams, John	Kentucky	b
472	Williams, Juan	South Carolina	b
473	Williams, Matheo	Kentucky	b
474	Williams, Thomas	Pennsylvania	b
475	Willis, Henry	Georgia	b
476	Willson, William	North Carolina	b
477	Wilson, James	Kentucky	b
478	Wilson, William	North Carolina	a
479	Winchinsior, George	Cumberland	b
480	Winchinster, David	Cumberland	b
481	Winllis, George	Cumberland	b
482	Wise, David	Kentucky	b
483	Witsel, Luis	Kentucky	b
484	Wnama, Matias A.	Pennsylvania	b
485	Wolph, George	Pennsylvania	b
486	Woods, John	North Carolina	a

Table 21. Nogales Names

	Names	Dates	Origins	Destination
1	Abercromedi, Jayme	1794	Ireland	
2	Abercromedi, Juan	1794	Ireland	
3	Adam, Armotead	1795	Americano	USA
4	Adrair, Guillermo	1795	Americano	USA
5	Aldeston, Jayme	1793	Ireland	USA
6	Aldin, Benjamin	1795	Americano	Louisiana
7	Amer, Jamery	1794	France	
8	Amistron, Guillermo	1795	Ireland	Louisiana
9	Anderson, Andres	1795	Americano	Louisiana
10	Anderson, Guillermo	1795	Americano	USA
11	Andn, Joaquin	1795	Americano	USA
12	Andres, Santiago	1794	Canada	New Orleans
13	Aoche, Silbestre	1794	Germany	Louisiana
14	Arkley, Roberto	1794	Americano	Natchez
15	Arman, Juan	1794	Americano	
16	Armstead, Benjamin	1795	Americano	USA
17	Armstrong, Salomon	1795	Americano	USA
18	Ashluay, Tomas	1794	Americano	Natchez
19	Astin, Jose	1795	Ireland	Louisiana
20	Aynw, Bernardo	1794	Ireland	USA
21	Bacon, David	1795	Americano	USA
22	Bail, Conel	1794	Ireland	New Madrid
23	Ballanuz, Guillermo	1795	Americano	USA
24	Ballis, Guillermo	1795	Americano	USA
25	Bancagrime, James	1795	Americano	Louisiana
26	Bartelet, Piam	1794	Americano	USA
27	Bartlet, James	1795	Americano	USA
28	Barton, Carlos	1795	Americano	USA
29	Bauchanp, Juan	1793		USA
30	Baucher, Tomas	1794	Ireland	Louisiana
31	Becas, Antonio	1795	France	USA
32	Bedger, Davis	1795	Americano	USA
33	Bell, Jose	1794	Americano	USA
34	Bell, Jose	1795	Americano	USA
35	Bell, Simeon	1795	Americano	USA
36	Benechan, Patricio	1794	Ireland	USA
37	Benglyuu, Housal	1794	Americano	USA
38	Berhinshire, Jose	1795	Americano	USA
39	Bigg, Guillermo	1794	Americano	USA

	Names	Dates	Origins	Destination
40	Bingham, Silas	1794	Americano	USA
41	Bingham, Taubes	1794	Americano	USA
42	Blain, James	1794	Ireland	USA
43	Blanetut, Silbestre	1795	France	USA
44	Blein, Jayme	1794	Americano	USA
45	Blek, Daniel	1795	Americano	USA
46	Blue, Ysac	1795	Americano	USA
47	Boaed, Handrason	1795	Americano	USA
48	Bocah, Juan	1795	Americano	USA
49	Boiw, Roberto	1794	Americano	Natchez
50	Bols, James	1794	Americano	Natchez
51	Boman, Daniel	1793	Americano	USA
52	Borget, Jose	1794	Americano	Natchez
53	Bouland, Roberto	1794	Americano	USA
54	Bowsoearingen, Tomas	1793		USA
55	Boyle, Connel	1793	Ireland	USA
56	Bradly, John	1793	Ireland	USA
57	Branan, Jose	1794	Americano	USA
58	Brand, Jorge	1794	Americano	USA
59	Branle, Federico	1794	Americano	USA
60	Bratson, Guillermo	1795	Americano	USA
61	Brayen, Juan	1795	Americano	USA
62	Brest, Juan	1793	Ireland	USA
63	Brian, John	1794	Fort Pitt	USA
64	Briton, Jose	1795	Americano	USA
65	Brokes, David	1794	Americano	USA
66	Brovim, Jus	1794	Ireland	USA
67	Brown, James	1795	Americano	USA
68	Brown, Samuel	1795	Americano	USA
69	Bullol, Etien	1793	Italian	
70	Burk, Stephen	1793	Ireland	USA
71	Burke, Tomas	1795	Americano	USA
72	Burnet, Juan	1795	Americano	USA
73	Bursly, James	1795	Americano	USA
74	Butin, Samuel	1795	Americano	USA
75	Calduel, Juan	1795	Americano	
76	Calen, Thomas	1795	England	Louisiana
77	Cambell, Santiago	1795	Americano	USA
78	Cannes, Jon	1795	Americano	USA

	Names	Dates	Origins	Destination
79	Canney, Juan	1794	Americano	USA
80	Canscild, Bewen	1795	Americano	USA
81	Cantel, Gui	1793	Scotland	USA
82	Canue, Guillermo	1794	Ireland	USA
83	Carril, Hercules	1795	Americano	USA
84	Carril, Jorge	1795	Americano	USA
85	Carter, Jose	1794	Americano	USA
86	Chaffins, David	1795	France	USA
87	Chambers, Guillermo	1793	Americano	USA
88	Chambers, Juan	1794	Americano	USA
89	Chanon, Juan	1794	Americano	USA
90	Charp, Jose	1794	Americano	USA
91	Chayber, Guillermo	1794	Americano	Natchez
92	Chefue, Juan	1794	Germany	
93	Cheval, Wilcan	1795	Americano	USA
94	Chiera, Juan Bautista	1794	France	
95	Chines, Juan	1793	Ireland	Louisiana
96	Chumeca, Guillermo	1795	Americano	Louisiana
97	Clark, Elms	1795	Americano	USA
98	Clark, John	1795	Americano	USA
99	Claud, Adan	1793	Americano	Natchez
100	Cleavns, Estevan	1795	Americano	USA
101	Clemente, Juan	1795	Americano	USA
102	Clindsall, Roberto	1794	Ireland	USA
103	Cliver, Estevan	1794	Americano	USA
104	Coba, Coba	1794	Americano	USA
105	Cokler, Juan	1794	England	USA
106	Colbert, John	1795	Americano	USA
107	Colbert, Juan	1795	Americano	USA
108	Colbert, Simon	1795	Americano	USA
109	Colbert, Simon	1795	Americano	USA
110	Colem, Guillermo	1794	Ireland	USA
111	Coleman, Esmaelen	1794	Americano	USA
112	Colems, Tomas	1794	Ireland	
113	Colens, Juan	1794	Ireland	
114	Coliben, Samuel	1794	Ireland	USA
115	Collin, Tomas V.	1795	Americano	USA
116	Collins, Jose	1794	Americano	USA
117	Colwel, Diego	1793	Ireland	USA

	Names	Dates	Origins	Destination
118	Comens, Juan	1794	Ireland	USA
119	Comes, Ygnacio	1795	Americano	USA
120	Comor, Miguel	1795	Americano	USA
121	Coner, Guillermo	1794	Americano	USA
122	Connal, Carlos	1795	Americano	USA
123	Conoby, Jacobo	1795	Americano	USA
124	Cooper, Jacobo	1794	Americano	USA
125	Coris, Juan	1794	Americano	USA
126	Crave, Josiah	1795	Americano	USA
127	Crawford, Andres	1794	Americano	USA
128	Crawford, Tomas	1794	Americano	USA
129	Cruz, Jacobo	1794	Americano	USA
130	Currau, Guillermo	1795	Americano	USA
131	Cuus, Tomas	1795	Americano	USA
132	Cuwy, William	1795	Americano	USA
133	Daughtel, Jose	1794	Americano	USA
134	Davien, Juan	1793	Germany	New Orleans
135	Deaivonge, Jose	1794	France	Louisiana
136	Deken, Jorpe	1795	Americano	
137	Delin, Juan	1794	Americano	USA
138	Delon, Federico	1794	Germany	USA
139	Denuelle, Francisco	1793	St. Louis	St. Louis
140	Deruin, Estevan	1793	Canada	
141	Devis, Leiua	1794	Americano	USA
142	Devis, Pedro	1793	Kentucky	USA
143	Devoir, Samuel	1795	Americano	USA
144	Diekles, Carlos	1795	Americano	USA
145	Dobert, Pedro	1794	Americano	
146	Doget, Miguel	1795	Ireland	USA
147	Dorvin, Hosien	1795	Americano	USA
148	Dorvins, Tomas	1795	Americano	USA
149	Dosten, Guillermo	1794	England	USA
150	Dougan, Enrique	1795	Americano	USA
151	Dreit, Francisco	1794	Americano	USA
152	Dunahow, James	1795	Americano	USA
153	Duting, Juan	1794	England	USA
154	Eddy, Samuel	1795	Americano	USA
155	Empel, Juan	1793	New Madrid	New Madrid
156	Esgr, Jonatan	1794	Americano	USA

	Names	Dates	Origins	Destination
157	Eslignan, Madama	1794	Americano	New Orleans
158	Esmael, Guillermo	1794	Americano	USA
159	Estan, Juan	1794	Americano	New Madrid
160	Estan, Ranzon	1794	Americano	New Madrid
161	Estidier, Jose	1795	Americano	USA
162	Estimal, Madama	1794	Americano	Natchez
163	Estod, Samiel	1794	Americano	Natchez
164	Estuard, Guillermo	1795	Americano	USA
165	Fabuel, Samuel	1794	Americano	USA
166	Fageson, Samuel	1794	Americano	USA
167	Faghy, John	1793	Ireland	USA
168	Falknen, John	1795	Americano	USA
169	Far, Estevan	1794	Americano	USA
170	Farsel, Jose	1794	Americano	Natchez
171	Felipe, Samuel	1794	Americano	
172	Feple, Pedro	1794	Americano	Louisiana
173	Ferril, Tomas	1795	Americano	USA
174	Ferrol, James	1794	Americano	Louisiana
175	Fiamen, Elias	1795	Americano	USA
176	Filipis, Aysik	1794	Americano	Louisiana
177	Flin, Eduardo	1795	Americano	USA
178	Flin, Hugh	1795	Americano	USA
179	Flincher, Benjamin	1795	England	Louisiana
180	Floier, Tomas	1793	Americano	USA
181	Fon, John	1795	Americano	USA
182	Forster, Juan	1794	Americano	Natchez
183	Forthize, Roberto	1794	Americano	USA
184	Foy, Pedro	1794	Ireland	USA
185	Frances, Jose Gordon	1794	Americano	New Madrid
186	Frannin, Jayme	1794	Americano	USA
187	Fraye, Jose	1795	Americano	USA
188	Frons, Juan	1795	Americano	USA
189	Fulton, Alexandro	1795	Americano	USA
190	Galguera, Juan	1794	Ireland	USA
191	Gallaghen, Carlos	1794	Ireland	USA
192	Garnet, Juan	1794	Fort Pitt	USA
193	Gati, Juan	1793	Kentucky	USA
194	Gawen, Jesse	1795	Americano	USA
195	Gilekust, Guillermo	1795	Americano	

	Names	Dates	Origins	Destination
196	Glas, Juan	1795	Ireland	Louisiana
197	Gol, Milen	1793	Kentucky	USA
198	Gold, James	1794	Americano	New Madrid
199	Gomes, Juan	1795	Spain	USA
200	Graven, Patricio	1795	Americano	USA
201	Gregor, Benjamin	1794	Americano	USA
202	Grmitenan, Guillermo	1794	Americano	USA
203	Guidony, Pedro	1793	Italy	USA
204	Guimlien, Simon	1794	Americano	Natchez
205	Guisou, Andres	1794	Canada	New Madrid
206	Gustey, Jonathan	1793	Americano	USA
207	Halen, Thun	1795	Americano	USA
208	Hall, Juan	1795	Americano	USA
209	Hallaway, Isac	1795	Americano	USA
210	Hamilton, Enrique	1795	Americano	USA
211	Hamilton, Juan	1794	Ireland	USA
212	Harrie, Jose	1795	Americano	USA
213	Hatton, Demy	1795	Americano	USA
214	Hay, John	1795	Americano	USA
215	Henning, Guillermo	1795	Americano	USA
216	Hibbs, John	1795	Americano	USA
217	Higgins, Jose	1795	Americano	USA
218	Hinds, Guillermo	1795	Americano	USA
219	Hiton, John	1795	Americano	USA
220	Hoben, John	1795	Americano	USA
221	Hollingsworth, Juan	1795	Americano	USA
222	Holsce, Juan	1794	Kentucky	
223	Hough, Benjamin	1795	Americano	USA
224	Hovent, Bolen	1795	Americano	USA
225	Hublard, Tonatas	1795	Americano	USA
226	Huet, Roxel	1793	Rechton	USA
227	Huling, Jonatas	1795	Americano	USA
228	Hunter, Juan	1795	Americano	USA
229	Huts, Juan	1794	Americano	Louisiana
230	Jacoc, Roberto	1795	Americano	Louisiana
231	Johston, Roberto	1795	Americano	Louisiana
232	Jones, Jose	1795	Americano	USA
233	Jones, Tomas	1795	Americano	USA
234	Juanarts, Carlos	1794	Germany	

	Names	Dates	Origins	Destination
235	Keses, Tomete	1794	Ireland	USA
236	Kethey, Jorge	1795	Americano	USA
237	Kinberlin, Juan	1795	Americano	USA
238	King, Carlos	1794	Americano	USA
239	King, Carlos	1795	Americano	USA
240	King, John	1795	Americano	USA
241	King, Juan	1794	Americano	USA
242	La Forina, Hipolita	1794	Canada	Natchez
243	Lachance, Bautis	1793	St. Louis	St. Louis
244	Lachanse, Antonio	1793	St. Louis	St. Louis
245	Lachenes, Santiago	1793	Canada	
246	Lacoyen, Jede	1795	Americano	USA
247	Lanchast, Adam	1795	Americano	USA
248	Landois, Pedro	1794	Canada	Punta Cortada
249	Langlois, Juan Adrian	1793	French	New Madrid
250	Larnich, Igroe	1795	Americano	USA
251	Lau, Aboun	1795	Americano	USA
252	Lavery, Pedro	1794	Americano	USA
253	Lavery, Samuel	1794	Americano	USA
254	Leming, Jose	1794	Americano	USA
255	Leny, Jose	1793	Ireland	USA
256	Lervantes, Pedro	1793	Canada	
257	Lery, Cornelio	1794	Ireland	
258	Lic, Juan	1794	Americano	Louisiana
259	Lic, Pedro	1794	Americano	Louisiana
260	Lic, Ricardo	1794	Americano	Louisiana
261	Limins, Jose	1793	Kentucky	USA
262	Linchi, Patricio	1794	Americano	USA
263	Lit, Nicolas	1795	Americano	USA
264	Litle, Juan	1794	Americano	USA
265	Long, Jorge	1795	Americano	USA
266	Lono, Adan	1795	Americano	USA
267	Loorte, Manuel	1793	Ireland	
268	Lotterman, Enrique M.	1795	Americano	USA
269	Lucas, Marco	1795	Americano	USA
270	Lucas, William	1795	Americano	USA
271	Madres, Jose	1793	Ireland	USA
272	Maileng, Alexandro	1794	Ireland	
273	Manchan, Francisco	1793	Canada	

	Names	Dates	Origins	Destination
274	Mandeler, Guillermo	1794	Americano	USA
275	Manily, Jayme	1794	Americano	USA
276	Mans, Larans	1794	England	USA
277	Marchal, Guillermo	1794	England	
278	Marten, Genere	1794	Americano	USA
279	Marten, Guillermo	1794	Americano	USA
280	Martimon, Daniel	1795	Americano	USA
281	Martin, Alexandro	1794	Americano	USA
282	Marty, Femous	1794	Kentucky	USA
283	McClachlan, Patricio	1795	Americano	USA
284	McClur, Jose	1794	Americano	USA
285	McComas, Tomas	1795	Americano	USA
286	McCome, Juan	1794	Ireland	USA
287	McDewal, Azon	1795	Americano	Louisiana
288	McDonal, James	1795	Americano	USA
289	McFarlan, Samuel	1794	Americano	USA
290	McLeary, Hugo	1795	Americano	Louisiana
291	McLen, Juan	1794	Americano	USA
292	McMulen, Jayme	1794	Kentucky	
293	McPin, Miguel	1795	Americano	USA
294	McPin, Roveut	1795	Americano	USA
295	McPurg, Alexandro	1793	Ireland	USA
296	McRuite, Juan	1794	Ireland	USA
297	Mecanty, Juan	1793	Ireland	Louisiana
298	Mecleman, Jayme	1793	Ireland	USA
299	Meek Falam, Juan	1794		Natchez
300	Meloni, Patricio	1795	Ireland	Louisiana
301	Merel, Johon	1793	Americano	USA
302	Merient, Juan Francisco	1794	France	New Orleans
303	Mescen, William	1793		Natchez
304	Mice, Juan	1795	Americano	USA
305	Miguel, Andres	1793	Ireland	USA
306	Miguel, Francisco	1793	Italian	
307	Milord, Carlos	1794	Americano	
308	Mimbres, Guillermo	1794	Americano	USA
309	Mimphey, Owen	1795	Americano	USA
310	Mogew, Jayme	1793	Ireland	USA
311	Moor, Juan	1793	Americano	USA
312	Moor, Samuel	1794	Americano	USA

	Names	Dates	Origins	Destination
313	Moore, Anir	1794	Ireland	New Orleans
314	Moore, Daniel	1795	Americano	USA
315	Moore, Enrique	1795	Americano	USA
316	Mooy, James	1794	Ireland	USA
317	Moresen, Juan	1794	Americano	USA
318	Morfil, David	1793	Americano	USA
319	Morgren, Moses	1794	Americano	USA
320	Mortemon, Francisco	1795	Americano	USA
321	Mouyan, Rubin	1795	Americano	USA
322	Movr, Juan	1794	Ireland	Natchez
323	Muekleroy, John	1793	Ireland	USA
324	Nagle, Christian	1795	Americano	USA
325	Nalkone, Jose	1795	Americano	USA
326	Ndet, Juan	1793	Kentucky	USA
327	Neaman, Ezequial	1794	Americano	Natchez
328	Nelck, Bolust	1795	Americano	USA
329	Newhum, Mateo	1795	Americano	
330	Newhure, Eduardo	1795	Americano	
331	Niay, John	1795	Americano	USA
332	Nicol, Bautista	1793	France	USA
333	Nigelson, Tomas	1793	England	USA
334	Noan, Arturo	1795	Americano	USA
335	Noble, Guillermo	1794	Americano	Natchez
336	Nomenson, Roberto	1793	Kentucky	USA
337	Norman, Carlos	1794	Canada	St. Louis
338	Nul, Tomas	1794	Americano	USA
339	Numan, Guillermo	1794	Ireland	
340	Onden, Jeremiah	1794	Americano	USA
341	Oneal, Jorge	1795	Americano	USA
342	Orn, Guillermo	1795	Americano	USA
343	Ott, Juan	1793	Germany	
344	Owen, Enrrique	1794	Ireland	USA
345	Peansy, Roberto	1794	Ireland	New Orleans
346	Pero, Peden	1794	France	
347	Perry, Guillermo	1795	Americano	USA
348	Peter, John	1795	Americano	USA
349	Petty, Juan	1795	Americano	USA
350	Picard, Francisco	1794	France	New Madrid
351	Piketen, Guillermo	1794	Americano	USA

	Names	Dates	Origins	Destination
352	Pipi, Guillermo	1795	England	USA
353	Plesent, Nara	1795	Americano	Louisiana
354	Pok, Alexandro	1795	Americano	USA
355	Pomry, Tomas	1795	Americano	USA
356	Porcer, Hugo	1794	Ireland	USA
357	Power, Enrique	1795	Americano	USA
358	Prather, Ricardo	1794	Americano	USA
359	Principe, Francisco	1794		USA
360	Principe, Ynico	1794	Americano	
361	Profit, Carlos	1794	Americano	
362	Progene, Jose	1795	Americano	USA
363	Purdon, Guillermo	1795	Americano	USA
364	Pusly, Abil	1795	Americano	USA
365	Quin, Juan	1793	Ireland	
366	Quin, William	1795	Americano	USA
367	Quinlin, Jayme	1794	Ireland	Louisiana
368	Ragan, Thomas	1795	Americano	USA
369	Rain, Jose	1795	England	Louisiana
370	Rain, Roberto	1794	Ireland	
371	Ratler, Juan	1794	Germany	Louisiana
372	Rayan, Daniel	1794	England	USA
373	Read, Jose	1795	Americano	Louisiana
374	Reflen, Carlos	1794	Germany	Arkansas
375	Renato, Jesse	1794	England	St. Louis
376	Renekin, Enrrique	1794	Ireland	USA
377	Reyen, Miguel	1794	Ireland	Natchez
378	Richele, Jorge	1794	Americano	USA
379	Richer, Guillermo	1793	England	USA
380	Ridmeand, James	1794	Americano	USA
381	Ries, Samuel	1793	Ireland	USA
382	Rigle, Roberto	1794	Americano	USA
383	Robeson, Guillermo	1794	England	USA
384	Ros, Francisco	1795	Americano	USA
385	Rosb, David	1794	Fort Pitt	USA
386	Royen, Juan	1795	Ireland	Louisiana
387	Ruian, Guillermo	1795	Americano	USA
388	Ruw, Ruth	1794	Americano	USA
389	Sale, Luis	1793	Kentucky	USA
390	Santa Maria, Juan Bapt.	1793	Criollo	New Madrid

	Names	Dates	Origins	Destination
391	Sanz, Jime	1793	Americano	USA
392	Sarlet, Nicolas	1794	Germany	Bayou Pierre
393	Seget, Denis	1793	Kentucky	USA
394	Serre, Juan	1793	Ireland	Louisiana
395	Sersel, Jorge	1794	Americano	Natchez
396	Shackler, Ricardo	1794	Americano	
397	Shrank, Thomas	1795	Americano	USA
398	Simms, Eduardo	1795	Americano	USA
399	Sinson, Tomas	1795	Americano	USA
400	Six, Adams	1795	Americano	USA
401	Slockhowe, Anos	1795	Americano	USA
402	Small, Juan	1794	Kentucky	USA
403	Smides, Juan	1794	Americano	USA
404	Smit, Jorge	1795	Americano	USA
405	Smit, Juan	1793	England	USA
406	Smit, Tomas	1795	England	Louisiana
407	Smith, Guillermo	1794	Americano	USA
408	Snoddy, Andres	1793	Cumberland	Opelusas
409	Soudre, Carlos	1793	Canada	New Madrid
410	Stephen, Amos	1795	Americano	USA
411	Stones, John	1795	Americano	USA
412	Stuly, Enrique	1795	Americano	USA
413	Tacheu, Jonas	1794	Americano	USA
414	Talkiner, Enrique	1795	Americano	Louisiana
415	Tardiveau, Bartolome	1794	France	New Madrid
416	Tasaid, Samuel	1795	Ireland	USA
417	Taylor, Juan	1794	Ireland	Louisiana
418	Telar, Nicolas	1794	Americano	USA
419	Temple, Guillermo	1794	Americano	USA
420	Teneron, Patricio	1794	Ireland	Louisiana
421	Tepedor, Andres	1794	Americano	USA
422	Tete, Jayme	1793	Ireland	USA
423	Thomioz, Guillermo	1795	Americano	USA
424	Thomson, Juan	1795	France	USA
425	Tickling, Gulillermin	1795	Americano	USA
426	Toleston, Matias	1794	Americano	USA
427	Tomas, Guillermo	1793		
428	Tomas, Jorge	1795	Americano	USA
429	Tomas, Samuel	1794	Americano	

	Names	Dates	Origins	Destination
430	Tompson, Samuel	1795	Americano	USA
431	Touten, Antonio	1794	Fort Pitt	USA
432	Toy, Juan	1795	Americano	USA
433	Tule, Juan	1794	Americano	USA
434	Tuluje, Noel	1794		St. Genovieve
435	Ublesilde, Enrique	1795	Americano	USA
436	Urchy, Juan	1794	Ireland	Punta Cortada
437	Vatrie, Carlos	1795	Americano	USA
438	Veau, Pedro	1794	Canada	
439	Vellimse, Francisco	1794	Canada	New Orleans
440	Verenu, Jose	1793	Kentucky	USA
441	Vinteru, Jose	1795	Americano	USA
442	Vounly, Jaime	1795	Americano	USA
443	Walker, Jose	1795	Americano	USA
444	Ward, Juin	1795	Americano	USA
445	Water, Richard	1794	Kentucky	USA
446	Waters, Ricardo Y.	1793	New Madrid	
447	Welche, Roberto	1794	Americano	USA
448	Welckern, Robert	1795	Americano	USA
449	Whigly, Andres	1795	Americano	USA
450	Whitathon, Tomas	1795	Americano	USA
451	Wilcok, Jayme	1794	Americano	USA
452	Wilcoks, Aysik	1794	Americano	USA
453	Wilems, Juan	1794	Americano	USA
454	Wilson, Amos	1795	Americano	USA
455	Wilson, Amos	1793	Americano	USA
456	Wilson, Guillermo	1795	Ireland	Louisiana
457	Windres, Joe	1794	Americano	USA
458	Winteru, Jose	1795	Americano	USA
459	Winteru, Samuel	1795	Americano	USA
460	Wol, Antonio	1793	Canada	New Oreleans
461	Wright, Tomas	1794	Americano	USA
462	Yblenotelesen, Achils	1793	Kentucky	USA
463	Yndreson, Jayme	1794	Ireland	USA
464	Ynglatera, Juan	1794	Americano	USA
465	Ynglatera, Ysrael	1794	Americano	USA
466	Yonsson, Jayme	1794	Ireland	USA

In 1779 the militia of St. Louis were either French or of French ancestry and so have been omitted from the present work.[18] In Table 23 (New Madrid Militia) the ranks are corporal (cabo1 and cabo 2), sergeant (sargento), second lieutenant (subteniente), lieutenant (teniente) and captain (capitan). The term "militia" is here used to indicate all other individuals without a rank in the manuscript. The following abbreviations and symbols are used in Missouri tables: p (Protestant), c (Catholic), M.C. (male children), F.C. (female children), m (married), w (widowed), n (no spouse). The town of Sta. Genoveva is the modern Saint Genevieve. New Madrid, which was founded in 1789, still exists under that name in southeast Missouri.

---

[18]A list of these soldiers with their birthplaces (from AGI Cuba 213), and another of the same militia in 1780 (from AGI Cuba 2) has been published by McDermott (1974:373-386).

Table 22. New Madrid Names

	Names	M.C.	F.C.	Date	Spouse	Religion
1	Abelino, Lorenzo			1793-09-19		
2	Abelino, Lorenzo			1795-11-20		c
3	Adams, Jacobo	2	1	1793-11-20	m	p
4	Adams, Jacobo			1796-07-01		
5	Adams, Jacobo	1	3	1796-12-21	m	p
6	Adams, Jacobo	0	3	1797-12-01	m	
7	Adams, Jorge			1789-04-22		
8	Adams, Juan	0	3	1795-11-20	m	p
9	Adams, Santiago	0	3	1794-12-02	m	p
10	Adelhison, David			1793-03-31		p
11	Aimenic, Juan Bautista			1793-11-20		c
12	Alellet, Juan Bautista	3	3	1797-12-01	m	
13	Alley, Juan	2	4	1795-11-20	m	p
14	Amelin, Francisco			1790-12-31	m	
15	Amelin, Francisco	0	0	1793-03-31	m	c
16	Amelin, Francisco	0	0	1793-11-20	m	c
17	Amelin, Madama			1794-12-02		c
18	Amelon, Lorenzo			1794-12-02		c
19	Andreson, Davies			1790-04-15		
20	Anelinet, Lorenzo	2	0	1793-11-20	m	c
21	Ange, Nicolas			1795-11-20		c
22	Apten, Roberto			1796-07-01		
23	Archambeau, Francisco			1796-07-01		
24	Archambeau, Francisco			1796-12-21		c
25	Archambeau, Francisco			1797-12-01		
26	Archanbeaut, Pedro			1793-03-31		c
27	Ashley, William			1792-09-16		
28	Aubin, Joseph			1791-04-31		
29	Aubin, Juan Bauptista			1791-04-30	m	
30	Aubouchon, Luis Antonio			1793-11-20		c
31	Auger, Nicolas			1794-12-02		c
32	Auger, Nicolas			1796-07-01		
33	Augfollue, Alex			1796-07-01		
34	Aveline, Lorenzo	0	1	1793-11-20	m	c
35	Aveline, Lorenzo			1794-12-02		c
36	Aveline, Lorenzo			1796-07-01		
37	Aveline, Lorenzo			1796-12-21		c
38	Aveline, Lorenzo			1797-12-01		
39	Babigni, Veronica	1	0	1793-03-31	n	c

231

	Names	M.C.	F.C.	Date	Spouse	Religion
40	Baby, Louis			1792-06-24		
41	Bachant, Antonio	1	0	1795-11-20	m	c
42	Bachet, Francisco	3	2	1793-11-20	m	c
43	Badiwell, Inigo			1794-12-02		p
44	Bagley, Henry			1792-05-07		
45	Balgouchis, Cirilo	0	0	1793-03-31	m	c
46	Baker, Joel			1790-10-25		
47	Baker, Joel			1790-12-31	m	
48	Baly, Luis			1796-07-01		
49	Baly, Luis	2	0	1797-12-01	m	
50	Banbien, Jose	0	1	1793-11-20	m	c
51	Bankson, James			1795-05-07		
52	Barbien, Jose			1793-06-26		
53	Barceloux, (widow of)			1790-12-31		
54	Barceloux, Juan Bautista			1790-12-31		
55	Barceloux, Juan Bautista			1793-03-31		c
56	Barceloux, Juan Bautista			1793-11-20		c
57	Barceloux, Luis			1795-02-16		
58	Barker, Joel			1790-01-27		
59	Barry, Juan			1796-07-01		
60	Barry, Juan			1797-12-01		
61	Barsaloux, Juan Bautista	0	0	1794-12-02	m	c
62	Barsaloux, Juan Bautista			1795-11-20		c
63	Barsaloux, Juan Bautista			1796-07-01		
64	Barsaloux, Juan Bautista			1796-12-21		c
65	Barsaloux, Juan Bautista			1797-12-01		
66	Bartholomew, William			1796-07-28		
67	Batlail, Daniel			1793-11-20		p
68	Baudeauvincs, Jose			1793-11-20		c
69	Baudouin, Jose			1794-12-02		c
70	Baudouin, Jose			1795-11-20		c
71	Baugase, Jacobo	4	4	1796-12-21	m	p
72	Baviny, Mad.a			1791-04-30		
73	Baxet, Antonio	4	2	1795-11-20	m	c
74	Bayan, Christopher			1797-05-07		
75	Bayle, James			1790-10-25		
76	Baylon, Avon			1794-05-15		
77	Baylon, Robert			1797-06-28		
78	Beard, Guillermo			1790-01-27		

	Names	M.C.	F.C.	Date	Spouse	Religion
79	Beaugard, Jacobo			1796-07-01		
80	Beaugard, Jacobo	4	3	1797-12-01	m	
81	Becker, Benjamin	1	0	1793-11-20	n	p
82	Beker, Jorge			1791-08-10		
83	Belli, Waters			1793-11-20		p
84	Benguiome, Francisco			1792-06-24		
85	Benguiome, Francisco			1795-11-20		c
86	Benguiome, Jacinto			1794-07-09		
87	Benguiome, Jacinto	0	1	1794-12-02	m	c
88	Benguiome, Jacinto	0	1	1795-11-20	m	c
89	Benguiome, Natal	1	1	1793-11-20	n	c
90	Benguiome, Natal			1795-11-20		c
91	Bennet, Benjamin			1789-04-22		
92	Benton, Juan Bautista			1793-03-31		c
93	Berdon, Thomas			1790-04-15		
94	Bergand, Carlos			1791-04-30	m	
95	Bermet, Antonio			1790-12-31		
96	Bernardo, Pedro M.	0	0	1794-12-02	m	c
97	Berni, Guillermo	0	3	1793-03-31	m	p
98	Berry, William			1792-03-05		
99	Berthlaume, Francisco	2	0	1794-12-02	m	c
100	Berthlaume, Francisco			1796-07-01		
101	Berthlaume, Francisco	2	1	1796-12-21	m	c
102	Berthlaume, Francisco			1797-12-01		
103	Berthlaume, Hiacinthe			1796-07-01		
104	Berthlaume, Jose			1796-07-01		
105	Berthlaume, Jose			1797-12-01		
106	Besenet, Juan			1795-11-20		c
107	Besmet, Joel	3	2	1796-12-21	m	p
108	Bettés, Nancy			1796-12-21		p
109	Biggle, Caleb			1793-11-20		p
110	Biggs, Caleb			1792-03-05		
111	Biggs, Juan	1	0	1793-11-20	m	p
112	Biggs, Juan	0	0	1794-12-02	m	p
113	Biggs, Pa.			1796-07-01		
114	Biggs, Teresa	1	0	1795-11-20		p
115	Biggs, Teresa (widow)	1	0	1796-12-21	w	p
116	Binelle, Juan Bauptista			1791-04-30	m	
117	Binelli, Jeun			1791-04-31		

	Names	M.C.	F.C.	Date	Spouse	Religion
118	Biyguer, Juan	1	0	1795-11-20		c
119	Black, Samuel	1	0	1793-11-20	n	p
120	Black, Samuel	0	0	1794-12-02	m	p
121	Black, Samuel			1795-11-20		p
122	Black, Samuel			1796-12-21		p
123	Blackburn, Joseph			1790-12-31		
124	Block, Andre	1	2	1797-12-01	m	
125	Bodoy, Louis			1791-04-31		
126	Bodwell, Enoch			1793-04-07		
127	Bogan, Jacob			1794-01-03		
128	Bogand, Basilio	3	0	1795-11-20	m	p
129	Bogard, Jacobo	3	3	1794-12-02	m	p
130	Bogard, Joseph			1794-01-03		
131	Bolon, Amable			1790-12-31	m	
132	Bolquet, Francisco			1795-12-13		
133	Bolton, Guillermo			1796-07-01		
134	Bolton, Guillermo			1797-12-01		
135	Bolton, William			1797-05-07		
136	Bomo, Luis de la	0	1	1795-11-20	m	c
137	Bonneau, Carlos			1791-04-30		
138	Bonneau, Carlos			1791-04-31		
139	Bonneau, Carlos			1792-06-24		
140	Bonneau, Carlos	3	3	1793-03-31	m	c
141	Bonneau, Carlos	3	4	1793-11-20	m	c
142	Bonneau, Carlos	3	2	1794-12-02	m	c
143	Bonneau, Carlos	3	2	1795-11-20	m	c
144	Bonneau, Carlos			1796-07-01		
145	Bonneau, Carlos	3	2	1796-12-21	m	c
146	Bonneau, Carlos	3	2	1797-12-01	m	
147	Bonneau, Nicolas			1791-04-30		
148	Bonneau, Nicols			1791-04-31		
149	Boquel, Francisco			1795-11-20		c
150	Borbon, Santa Maria			1790-12-31	m	
151	Bordeau, Joseph			1791-04-31		
152	Bordeleau, Miguel			1791-04-30		
153	Bordeleru, Michel			1791-04-31		
154	Boudauville, Geronimo	2	4	1793-11-20	m	c
155	Bouillette, Guillermo			1797-12-01		
156	Bouiltelle, Guillermo			1796-07-01		

	Names	M.C.	F.C.	Date	Spouse	Religion
157	Bovias, Joseph			1791-04-31		
158	Bowen, Jacobo			1797-12-01		
159	Bowin, Bernardo	1	3	1795-11-20	m	p
160	Boyer, Andres			1791-04-30		
161	Boyer, Francisco			1791-04-30		
162	Boyer, Francois			1791-04-31		
163	Boyer, Santos			1791-04-30		
164	Boyers, Coupaints			1791-04-31		
165	Boyle, Connel			1794-12-02		c
166	Boyle, Guillermo			1793-11-20		c
167	Boyle, Philip			1793-06-07		
168	Boylon, Aron			1794-12-02		p
169	Branard, Jacobo	3	3	1795-11-20	m	p
170	Brouillet, Louis			1792-06-24		
171	Brouillet, Luis			1791-04-30	m	
172	Brouillet, Luis	2	0	1793-03-31	m	c
173	Brouillet, Luis	3	0	1793-11-20	m	c
174	Brouillet, Luis	1	0	1795-11-20	m	c
175	Brouillet, Luis (hijo)			1793-03-31		c
176	Brouillet, Luis (hijo)			1794-12-02		c
177	Brouillet, Luis (hijo)			1795-11-20		c
178	Brouillet, Luis (padre)	1	0	1794-12-02	m	c
179	Brouillette, Luis			1796-07-01		
180	Brouillette, Luis	2	1	1796-12-21	m	c
181	Brouillette, Luis	x	0	1797-12-01	m	
182	Brouin, Francisco			1796-07-01		
183	Brouin, Francisco			1797-12-01		
184	Brown, Juan	0	2	1795-11-20		p
185	Brown, Julian	2	1	1793-11-20	m	p
186	Brown, William			1796-07-28		
187	Bruiet, Francisco			1795-04-24		
188	Bruiet, Miguel	2	3	1795-11-20	m	c
189	Brulli, Louis			1791-04-31		
190	Bryan, Dave			1797-05-07		
191	Buraw, George			1797-12-01		
192	Burke, Stephen			1793-06-18		
193	Burns, Miguel	5	4	1795-11-20	m	p
194	Burry, Nicholas			1791-04-31		
195	Butayllen, Francisco	2	0	1795-11-20		c

	Names	M.C.	F.C.	Date	Spouse	Religion
196	Byrne, Michael			1790-10-25		
197	Caldwel, Jayme			1790-01-27		
198	Calue, Juan Francisco			1793-11-20		c
199	Camell, Carlos			1795-11-20	m	p
200	Cammack, Christopher			1792-12-30		
201	Campbell, Catalina			1796-07-01		
202	Campbell, Catalina			1796-12-21		p
203	Campbell, Peter			1792-09-16		
204	Campeat, Joseph			1791-04-30		
205	Campeau, Joseph			1791-04-31		
206	Campo, Ypolito			1790-12-31		
207	Campo, Ypolito			1793-03-31		c
208	Canen, Guillermo			1793-11-20		p
209	Carjon, Thomas			1792-06-24		
210	Caron, Juan Bautista			1796-07-01		
211	Caron, Juan Bautista			1797-12-01		
212	Carpenter, Conrad			1796-07-01		
213	Carpenter, Conrad	2	2	1797-12-01	n	
214	Carron, Juan Bauptista			1791-04-30		
215	Carsen, Guillermo			1794-12-02		p
216	Cartard, Mauricio			1790-01-27		
217	Casidy, Patrick			1796-07-01		
218	Casidy, Patrick			1797-12-01		
219	Catey, John			1797-05-07		
220	Caulk, Tomas W.			1796-07-01		
221	Caulk, Tomas W.			1797-05-07		
222	Caulk, Tomas W.	3	3	1797-12-01	m	
223	Causin, Noel			1791-04-31		
224	Cavanaugh, Santiago			1796-07-01		
225	Cavenaugh, Santiago	2	1	1797-12-01	m	
226	Cayol, Francisco			1793-11-20		c
227	Cayote, Francisco			1793-04-07		
228	Cemins, Juan			1790-01-27		
229	Champagne, Francisco	0	0	1793-03-31	m	c
230	Champagne, Francisco			1793-11-20		c
231	Chararone			1796-07-01		
232	Charaud...	0	1	1797-12-01	m	
233	Charlier, Juan Bautista			1794-12-02		c
234	Charlier, Juan Bautista			1796-07-01		

236

	Names	M.C.	F.C.	Date	Spouse	Religion
235	Charnetier, Juan			1795-11-20		c
236	Charnetier, Paula	0	1	1795-11-20		c
237	Charrelier, Catalina	1	1	1793-11-20	n	c
238	Charretiers, Juana (widow)	1	1	1793-03-31	w	c
239	Chartier, (widow of)	0	1	1794-12-02	w	c
240	Chartier, (widow of)			1796-07-01	w	
241	Chartier, Ve.	2	1	1796-12-21		c
242	Chatigni, Ygnacio	1	0	1793-03-31	m	c
243	Chaudillon, Juan Bautista			1796-07-01		
244	Chaudillon, Juan Bautista			1796-12-21		c
245	Chaudillon, Juan Bautista			1797-12-01		
246	Chavam			1795-11-20		Indian
247	Chemin, Juan Bautista			1793-11-20		p
248	Cheraky, (widow of)	1	0	1794-12-02	w	Indian
249	Cheraky, Maria	1	2	1795-11-20	n	Indian
250	Chéraquise			1796-07-01		
251	Cheraquite, Maria	1	1	1796-12-21		Indian
252	Chiesom, Joseph			1790-12-31	m	
253	Chiflen, Felipe			1793-03-31		c
254	Chiland, Francisco Michel	2	0	1793-11-20	m	c
255	Chiland, Francisco Michel			1795-11-20		c
256	Chilard, Francisco Michel			1794-12-02		c
257	Chiriot, Juan			1796-07-01		
258	Chisem, Miguel	0	2	1793-03-31	m	p
259	Chissem, Miguel Uyo	0	4	1795-11-20	m	p
260	Chodillon, Juan			1795-11-20		c
261	Chodillon, Juan Bautista			1793-03-31		c
262	Chodillon, Juan Bautista	0	3	1793-11-20	m	c
263	Christy, Thomas			1789-11-30		
264	Clark			1790-01-27		
265	Cleghornes, Jayme			1789-04-22		
266	Clerissout, muger	2	0	1797-12-01	m	
267	Clermont, Benjamin	1	0	1793-11-20	m	c
268	Clermont, Benjamin			1795-11-20		c
269	Clermont, Juan Bautista	1	0	1794-12-02	m	c
270	Clermont, Michel	2	0	1796-12-21	m	c
271	Clibelin, Johen			1790-12-31		
272	Coder Petis, Andre			1796-12-21		c
273	Coder, Andre			1791-04-31		

	Names	M.C.	F.C.	Date	Spouse	Religion
274	Coder, Andres			1794-12-02		c
275	Coder, Enrique			1791-04-30		
276	Coder, Henrique			1794-12-02		c
277	Coder, Joseph			1792-06-24		
278	Coder, Juan Bautista			1791-04-30		
279	Coder, Juan Bautista	0	0	1793-03-31	m	c
280	Coder, Pedro			1791-04-30		
281	Coder, Pierre			1791-04-31		
282	Coder, Renato			1791-04-30	m	
283	Coder, Renato	4	3	1793-03-31	m	c
284	Coder, Santos			1791-04-30	m	
285	Coder, Toupauits			1791-04-31		
286	Coder, Tusen	2	5	1793-03-31	m	c
287	Collot, Juan Luis			1791-04-31		
288	Collu, Jacobo			1796-07-01		
289	Colo, James			1792-06-24		
290	Compagnot, Francisco			1791-04-30	m	
291	Compagnot, Francisco	3	0	1793-03-31	m	c
292	Compagnot, Pedro			1793-11-20		c
293	Compagnot, Pierre			1792-06-24		
294	Companoy, Ma. (widow)			1791-04-30		
295	Compin, Claudio Gabriel			1793-11-20		c
296	Compugnol, Francois			1791-04-31		
297	Connor, Ephraim	0	0	1793-11-20	m	p
298	Connor, Ephraim			1794-12-02		p
299	Connor, Ephraim			1795-11-20		p
300	Connor, Juan			1793-03-31		p
301	Connors, Juan			1794-12-02		p
302	Conrad, John			1792-09-16		
303	Cook, Jacobo			1795-11-20	m	p
304	Cool, Jacobo			1796-12-21		p
305	Cooper, James			1790-04-15		
306	Corey, James			1792-05-07		
307	Cormatek, Thomas			1790-10-25		
308	Cortner, Juan			1796-07-01		
309	Costero, George			1796-07-01		
310	Cotta, Jacobo	0	1	1796-12-21	m	c
311	Couguenil, Francisco			1793-03-31		c
312	Couke, Andres			1796-12-21	m	p

	Names	M.C.	F.C.	Date	Spouse	Religion
313	Coulo, Santiago			1794-12-02		p
314	Counnien, Pasgual			1795-02-16		
315	Courent, Guillermo			1793-03-31		p
316	Cournai, Juan			1793-11-20		c
317	Cousley, Francisco			1796-12-21		c
318	Couteley, Francisco			1796-07-01		
319	Couteley, Francisco	1	0	1797-12-01	m	
320	Couteux, Diego	0	0	1794-12-02	m	c
321	Coutrie, Jacquet			1792-06-24		
322	Cowan, William			1792-02-06		
323	Cox, Andres	1	3	1795-11-20	m	p
324	Crabin, Carlos			1796-07-01		
325	Crabin, Carlos			1797-12-01		
326	Crispin, Tomas			1796-07-01		
327	Crispin, Tomas			1797-05-07		
328	Crispin, Tomas			1797-12-01		
329	Cristianem, Juan			1793-01-11		
330	Crock, Edouard			1792-06-24		
331	Crow, Jacobo			1796-07-01		
332	Crow, Jacobo	1	1	1796-12-21		p
333	Crow, Jacobo	1	0	1797-12-01	m	
334	Cruik, Faquin	2	2	1797-12-01	m	
335	Cueteau, Jacobo			1795-11-20	m	c
336	Cuetue, Jacobo	0	0	1793-11-20	m	c
337	Cuetue, Santiago	0	0	1793-03-31	m	c
338	Culbert, John			1790-10-25		
339	Culbert, William			1791-04-31		
340	Cunninghams, Juan			1789-04-22		
341	Cuntow, Roque	2	4	1795-11-20	m	c
342	Cury, Andres			1790-01-27		
343	Dairmont, Juan			1796-12-21		p
344	Danise, Juan			1793-03-31		c
345	Daperou, Jose	1	0	1793-11-20	n	c
346	Daure, Jean			1791-04-31		
347	Davidson, Thomas			1789-11-30		
348	Davidson, Thomas			1790-12-31		
349	Davies, Samuel			1790-04-15		
350	Davis (widow of)			1796-07-01		
351	Davis, (widow of)	1	0	1796-12-21		p

	Names	M.C.	F.C.	Date	Spouse	Religion
352	Davis, (widow of)	1	1	1797-12-01	w	
353	Davis, Benjamin			1789-04-22		
354	Davis, Benjamin			1793-03-31		p
355	Davis, Berij			1789-11-30		
356	Davis, Guillermo			1793-11-20		p
357	Davis, Guillermo			1794-12-02		p
358	Davis, Guillermo			1795-11-20		c
359	Davis, Guillermo			1796-12-21		p
360	Davis, John			1794-03-31		
361	Davis, Juan, (widow of)	1	0	1794-12-02	w	p
362	Davis, Samuel			1790-12-31		
363	Davis, Samuel			1793-03-31		p
364	Davis, Tomas			1789-04-22		
365	Davison, William			1797-05-07		
366	Day, Aaron			1790-04-15		
367	Day, Aaron			1790-12-31		
368	Daybread, Andres	0	0	1797-12-01	m	
369	Daybread, Juan	0	1	1797-12-01	n	
370	de Frontenac			1790-12-31		
371	Dearmits, Alexandro			1789-04-22		
372	Decker, Lucas			1789-04-22		
373	Degan, Jose	2	2	1793-03-31	m	c
374	Degano, Joseph			1791-04-31		
375	Delisle, Carlos			1791-04-30		
376	Delislo, Charles			1791-04-31		
377	Denisse, Juan			1793-11-20		c
378	Denoyom, Silvestre			1793-03-31		c
379	Denoyon, Luis			1791-04-30		
380	Denoyon, Luis			1791-04-31		
381	Denoyon, Luis			1793-03-31		c
382	Denoyon, Luis	0	0	1793-11-20	m	c
383	Denoyon, Luis			1794-12-02		c
384	Denoyon, Luis	1	0	1795-11-20	m	c
385	Denoyon, Luis			1796-12-21		c
386	Deny, Juan			1790-12-31		
387	Derlac, Girardo			1796-12-21	m	c
388	Derlac, Juan			1793-11-20		c
389	Derlac, Juan			1794-12-02		c
390	Derlac, Juan			1795-11-20		c

	Names	M.C.	F.C.	Date	Spouse	Religion
391	Derlac, Juan			1796-07-01		
392	Derlac, Juan	0	1	1797-12-01	m	
393	Derlacqus, Jean			1792-06-24		
394	Deroche, Pedro			1790-04-15		
395	Deroche, Pedro	1	0	1793-03-31	m	c
396	Deroche, Pedro	0	0	1793-11-20	m	c
397	Deroche, Pedro			1794-12-02		c
398	Deroche, Pedro	1	1	1795-11-20	m	c
399	Deroche, Pedro			1796-07-01		
400	Deroche, Pedro	0	1	1796-12-21	m	c
401	Deroche, Pedro	0	1	1797-12-01	m	
402	Derrous, Francis	1	1	1795-11-20		c
403	Derrouse, Francisco	1	3	1793-11-20	n	c
404	Derusver, Francisco	1	3	1793-03-31	m	c
405	Desbigny, Pedro	2	0	1795-11-20	m	c
406	Desbigny, Pedro			1796-07-01		
407	Desbigny, Pedro	2	0	1796-12-21	m	c
408	Despeintreux, Lucas			1793-06-26		
409	Desroussee, Francisco	0	1	1797-12-01	n	
410	Desrousserd, Francisco			1796-07-01		
411	Desrousserd, Francisco			1796-07-01		
412	Detaillis, Fr.	2	0	1794-12-02	m	c
413	Detallie, Joseph			1791-04-30	m	
414	Deuimtes, Benjamin	1	1	1797-12-01	m	
415	Devores, Nicolas			1797-12-01		
416	Dobbns, David			1794-12-02		p
417	Dodd, Mathew			1792-09-16		
418	Dominguez, Diego			1792-09-16		
419	Donson, Guillermo			1797-12-01		
420	Doran, Michael			1792-06-24		
421	Dorete, Ama			1796-12-21		p
422	Dorman, ...	1	1	1797-12-01	m	
423	Dorman, Jorge			1797-05-07		
424	Dorsey, Samuel			1792-03-10		
425	Dorsey, Samuel			1794-12-02		p
426	Dorsey, Samuel			1795-11-20	m	c
427	Dorsey, Samuel			1796-07-01		
428	Dorsey, Samuel			1796-12-21	m	c
429	Dorsey, Samuel	1	0	1793-03-31	m	c

	Names	M.C.	F.C.	Date	Spouse	Religion
430	Douairon, Jose			1796-12-21		p
431	Dougannes, Juan			1796-12-21		c
432	Dougherty, Jayme			1789-04-22		
433	Doukoubrot, Joseph			1792-06-27		
434	Dounien, Pedro	1	0	1793-11-20	m	c
435	Douns, Miguel			1793-03-31		p
436	Drayon, Pedro			1795-04-24		
437	Droubin, Estevan	2	0	1793-11-20	m	c
438	Drouilly, Juan Bautista			1794-12-02		c
439	Droullard, Pedro			1793-05-27		
440	Druiant, Juan Bautista	1	0	1793-11-20	m	c
441	Drybread, Juan			1794-12-02		p
442	Drybread, Juan			1795-11-20		c
443	Drybread, Juan			1796-07-01		
444	Dublin, David			1793-11-20		p
445	Duboi, Luis	2	2	1797-12-01	m	
446	Dubois, Luis			1796-07-01		
447	Ducomb (widow of)			1796-12-21		c
448	Ducomb, (widow of)			1796-07-01		
449	Ducomb, Felipe	1	0	1793-11-20	m	c
450	Ducomb, muger	0	1	1797-12-01	m	
451	Ducomb, Philip			1793-06-26		
452	Ducomb, woman			1796-07-01		
453	Ducombe, Magdalena			1795-11-20		c
454	Duffy, Corneilion			1789-11-30		
455	Duggard, Guillermo			1795-03-21		
456	Duinre, Ambrosio			1790-12-31		
457	Dumais, Pedro			1793-03-31		c
458	Dumais, Pedro	1	0	1794-12-02	m	c
459	Dumais, Pedro			1794-12-02		c
460	Dumais, Pierre			1792-06-24		
461	Dumais, Pierre			1793-04-07		
462	Dumay			1797-05-07		
463	Dumay, Ambrosio	1	0	1793-11-20	n	c
464	Dumayo, Ambrosio			1793-03-31		c
465	Dunn, Jayme			1789-04-22		
466	Dunn, Michael			1792-06-24		
467	Dupin, Francisco Riche	1	0	1794-12-02	m	c
468	Dupin, Francisco Riche	1	0	1795-11-20	m	c

	Names	M.C.	F.C.	Date	Spouse	Religion
469	Dupin, Francisco Riche			1796-07-01		
470	Dupin, Francisco Riche	1	0	1797-12-01	m	
471	Dupuig, Juan			1795-11-20		c
472	Dupuis, Isidore			1796-07-01		
473	Dupuis, Isidoro			1794-12-02		c
474	Dupuis, Isidoro			1795-11-20		c
475	Dupuis, Juan Bautista			1793-11-20		c
476	Dupuis, Juan Bautista			1796-07-01		
477	Dupuis, Juan Bautista			1796-12-21		c
478	Dupuis, Juan Bautista			1797-12-01		
479	Dupuiy, Isidro			1795-02-16		
480	Dutaville, Francisco			1796-07-01		
481	Dutreueble, Juan Bautista			1797-12-01		
482	Dutrubler, Juan			1795-11-20		c
483	Dutrumbles, Juan Bautista			1796-07-01		
484	Duvé, Mariana (widow)			1790-12-31		
485	Duver, Josefa (widow)	1	1	1793-03-31	w	c
486	Egaim, Petu			1792-06-24		
487	Eguins, Pedro			1793-11-20		c
488	Eichard, Vern			1791-04-31		
489	Elioten, Juan			1795-11-20		p
490	Elliot, Guillermo			1793-03-31		p
491	Elliot, William			1792-04-02		
492	Empfil			1790-12-31		
493	Emphill, Jones			1793-03-31		p
494	Engele, Philip			1795-04-19		
495	Ensor, George			1792-11-30		
496	Estan, Juan			1793-11-20		p
497	Eudems, Nicolas			1793-11-20		c
498	Evens, William			1797-05-30		
499	Faith, Jose			1796-07-01		
500	Faith, Jose			1796-12-21		c
501	Falconer, Francisco	0	1	1794-12-02	m	p
502	Falconer, Francisco	0	1	1795-11-20	m	p
503	Falconer, Francisco	0	1	1796-12-21	m	c
504	Fallan, James			1792-09-16		
505	Farney, Antonio			1789-04-22		
506	Faullo, Joseph	0	0	1797-12-01	m	
507	Feille, Juan			1795-11-20		c

	Names	M.C.	F.C.	Date	Spouse	Religion
508	Fernandez, Jose			1793-03-31		c
509	Filverid, Pedro			1790-12-31	m	
510	Finky, Robert			1792-05-07		
511	Firand, Luis			1795-02-16		
512	Fitch, Walling			1797-05-07		
513	Folan, James M.			1797-05-07		
514	Fondan, Juan			1795-11-20		c
515	Fool, Nancy	0	0	1797-12-01	m	
516	Formosa, William			1790-04-15		
517	Fouchet, Ventura			1793-03-31		c
518	Fouchet, Ventura			1793-11-20		c
519	Fouedsey, B.			1792-06-24		
520	Fouliniount, Richard	1	0	1793-03-31	m	c
521	Fourdain, Jevis			1792-06-24		
522	Fremont, Agustin Ch.			1794-12-02		c
523	Frison, Juan			1795-11-20		c
524	Fulham, John			1792-05-07		
525	Fulham, Juan			1793-11-20		c
526	Funlison, Richard			1792-03-05		
527	Furney, Matias			1789-04-22		
528	Furney, Matias			1789-04-22		
529	Gabeant, Pedro	0	1	1795-11-20		c
530	Galbeau, Carlos			1795-11-20		c
531	Gamelin, (widow of)	2	3	1794-12-02	w	c
532	Gamelin, (widow of)			1796-07-01		
533	Gamelin, (widow of)	2	3	1796-12-21	w	c
534	Gamelin, Antoine			1791-04-31		
535	Gamelin, Antonio			1791-08-19		
536	Gamelin, Antonio	1	3	1793-03-31	m	c
537	Gamelin, Antonio	1	0	1793-11-20	m	c
538	Gamelin, Margarita	2	3	1795-11-20	n	c
539	Garan, Pedro			1796-07-01		
540	Garau, Pierre	1	0	1797-12-01	m	
541	Garill, Nicolas	1	0	1795-11-20	m	p
542	Garlia, Maria	1	1	1793-11-20	n	Indian
543	Garques, Juan	1	5	1796-12-21	m	p
544	Gaulin, Louis			1791-04-31		
545	Gaultien, Louis			1791-04-31		
546	Gavenir, Pedro			1795-11-20		c

	Names	M.C.	F.C.	Date	Spouse	Religion
547	Gayo, Antonio			1794-12-02		p
548	Gazoiche, Juim...			1790-10-25		
549	Geneocux, Jose			1796-07-01		
550	Geoffroy, Pedro			1792-05-30		
551	Geoffroy, Pedro			1794-12-02		c
552	German, Juan	0	3	1796-12-21	m	p
553	Geroult, Andres			1793-11-20		c
554	Geroult, Andres			1795-11-20		c
555	Geroult, Andres			1796-07-01		
556	Geroult, Andres			1796-12-21		c
557	Geroult, Andres			1797-12-01		
558	Gervair, Juan Bautista			1796-12-21		c
559	Gervais, Juan Bautista			1796-07-01		
560	Gervais, Juan Bautista			1797-12-01		
561	Gervaix, Juan Bautista			1796-07-01		
562	Geuouix, Jose	0	0	1797-12-01	m	
563	Gibault, Pedro			1796-07-01		
564	Gibault, Pedro (priest)			1794-12-02		c
565	Gienin, Juan Simon	1	1	1793-11-20	m	c
566	Gille, Jayme	0	1	1793-11-20	m	c
567	Gines, Enrique			1795-11-20		c
568	Giroult, Nicolas			1794-12-02		c
569	Godaufruad, Pedro			1793-11-20		c
570	Goden, Andres			1795-11-20	m	c
571	Goden, Andres			1796-07-01		
572	Goden, Andres			1796-12-21	m	c
573	Goden, Averey	0	0	1797-12-01	m	
574	Goden, Enrique			1795-11-20		c
575	Goden, Tiberio			1795-11-20		c
576	Godes, Toussaint			1796-07-01		
577	Godes, Toussaint			1797-12-01		
578	Gomez, Juan			1796-12-21		p
579	Gonet, Claudio Jose			1793-11-20		c
580	Gonette, Carlos			1794-12-02		c
581	Gonette, Francisco			1796-12-21		c
582	Gonette, François			1797-12-01		
583	Gonettes, Claudio			1796-07-01		
584	Gore, David			1790-10-25		
585	Gore, Issac			1791-04-31		

		Names	M.C.	F.C.	Date	Spouse	Religion
586		Gotiers, Luis			1793-03-31		c
587		Gounet, Juan			1795-11-20		c
588		Gounete, Carlos Joseph	0	2	1793-03-31	n	c
589		Gow, Jocabo			1795-11-20	m	p
590		Goyeau, Antonio			1793-11-20		c
591		Graham, Aaron			1796-07-01		
592		Grahams, Aaron	2	3	1797-12-01	m	
593		Gran, Henry			1796-12-21		p
594		Grand, Jose			1794-12-02		c
595		Grand-Prie, Alexo			1795-02-16		
596		Grandjean, Juan Francisco			1794-12-02		c
597		Grandjean, Juan Francisco			1795-11-20		c
598		Graset, Juan	0	0	1793-11-20	m	c
599		Gray, David			1791-08-19		
600		Gray, David			1793-03-31		p
601		Gray, David			1793-11-20		p
602		Gray, David			1794-12-02		p
603		Gray, David			1795-11-20		p
604		Gray, David			1796-07-01		
605		Gray, David			1796-12-21		p
606		Green, Benjamin			1795-02-16		
607		Green, Guillermo			1789-04-22		
608		Green, Henry			1796-07-01		
609		Green, Henry			1797-12-01		
610		Green, Juan			1794-12-02		p
611		Griman, Juan			1795-11-20		c
612		Grimard, Juan Bautista			1793-11-20		c
613		Grimard, Juan Bautista			1794-12-02		c
614		Grimard, Juan Bautista			1796-07-01		
615		Grimard, Juan Bautista			1796-12-21		c
616		Grimare, Pierre			1791-04-31		
617		Grimaret, Pedro			1791-04-30		
618		Gromt, Andres			1796-07-01		
619		Gruiden, Benjamin			1795-11-20		p
620		Gualbaud, Francisco	0	2	1794-12-02	m	c
621		Guarlia, Maria			1790-12-31		
622		Guellet, Francisco			1794-12-02		p
623		Guere, Pedro			1790-12-31		
624		Guerin, Juan Simon	1	1	1794-12-02	m	c

	Names	M.C.	F.C.	Date	Spouse	Religion
625	Guerin, Juan Simon	1	1	1795-11-20	m	c
626	Guerin, Juan Simon			1796-07-01		
627	Guerin, Juan Simon	2	1	1796-12-21	m	c
628	Guerin, Juan Simon	2	1	1797-12-01	m	
629	Guierin, Pedro	0	0	1794-12-02	m	c
630	Guierrier, Pedro			1791-04-30	m	
631	Guilbaud, Carlos			1790-12-31	m	
632	Guilbaud, Carlos	0	2	1793-03-31	m	c
633	Guilbaud, Carlos	0	2	1793-11-20	m	c
634	Guilbaud, Carlos			1796-07-01		
635	Guilbaud, Carlos	0	1	1796-12-21	m	c
636	Guilbaud, Carlos	0	2	1797-12-01	m	
637	Guill, Jacobo			1796-07-01		
638	Guill, Jacobo			1796-12-21	m	p
639	Guill, Jacobo	0	0	1797-12-01	m	
640	Guill, Nicolas	0	1	1794-12-02	m	p
641	Guill, Suzana			1796-12-21		p
642	Guillermo			1790-01-27		
643	Guilmore, John			1792-12-30		
644	Guilmore, Juan			1793-11-20		p
645	Guilmore, Juan			1794-12-02		p
646	Guilmore, Juan			1795-11-20		p
647	Guilmore, Juan			1796-07-01		
648	Guilmore, Juan			1796-12-21		p
649	Guilmore, Juan			1797-12-01		
650	Guitant, Pedro			1793-11-20		c
651	Gunderman, F.D.			1796-12-07		
652	Gutier, Luis			1791-04-30		
653	Guture, Jayme			1790-12-31		
654	Hain, Enrique			1793-11-20		p
655	Haley, Nicolas	0	1	1795-11-20	m	c
656	Hall, Jorge			1789-04-22		
657	Hamphille, Juan			1793-11-20		p
658	Hands, Ketey			1796-12-21		Indian
659	Hands, Samy			1796-12-21		Indian
660	Hant, Juan			1793-11-20		p
661	Hanvey, Juan			1793-03-31		c
662	Harper, Guillermo			1797-04-12		
663	Harpin, Francisco			1791-04-30		

	Names	M.C.	F.C.	Date	Spouse	Religion
664	Harpin, Francois			1791-04-31		
665	Harpin, Joseph			1791-04-31		
666	Harris, Nathan			1793-02-16		
667	Harrison, Benjamin			1790-01-27		
668	Harrison, Nicolas			1790-01-27		
669	Hart, Juan			1794-12-02		p
670	Hart, Juan			1796-07-01		
671	Hart, Juan			1796-12-21		p
672	Harvey, J.			1791-12-19		
673	Haubert, Nicolas			1793-11-20		c
674	Haunot, Gabriel	0	0	1793-03-31	m	c
675	Haut, Juan			1797-12-01		
676	Heasly, Juan			1790-01-27		
677	Hempill, Jones			1793-03-31		p
678	Heur, George			1796-12-21		p
679	Hewitt, Kufsell			1792-05-30		
680	Hibernois, Antonio	0	0	1793-11-20	m	c
681	Hibernois, Antonio			1796-07-01		
682	Hibernois, Antonio			1796-12-21	m	c
683	Hibernois, Antonio	0	0	1797-12-01	m	
684	Higgins, Pedro			1794-12-02		p
685	Hikey, Michal			1792-09-30		
686	Hill, Samuel			1794-08-25		
687	Hill, Samuel			1794-12-02		p
688	Hill, Samuel			1796-07-01		
689	Hill, Samuel			1796-12-21		p
690	Hill, Samuel			1797-12-01		
691	Hilliams, Jayme			1789-04-22		
692	Hilo, Jaquin	2	3	1796-12-21	m	p
693	Hilton, William			1796-07-02		
694	Hinkson, Juan			1790-01-27		
695	Hinkson, Roberto			1790-01-27		
696	Hitton, William			1796-12-21		p
697	Hodson, Fes.	2	1	1797-12-01	m	
698	Hood, woman			1796-07-01		
699	Hoplitto, Boston			1789-04-22		
700	Hord, woman			1796-07-01		
701	Horlen, Antonio			1796-12-21		p
702	Horner, Juan			1796-07-01		

	Names	M.C.	F.C.	Date	Spouse	Religion
703	Horner, Juan			1796-12-21	m	c
704	Horner, Juan	0	0	1797-12-01	m	
705	Horsley, Thomas Young			1792-06-24		
706	Horsley, Tomas			1793-11-20		p
707	Horsley, Tomas			1794-12-02		p
708	Horsley, Tomas			1795-11-20		p
709	Horsley, Tomas			1796-07-01		
710	Horsley, Tomas			1796-12-21		p
711	Horsley, Tomas			1797-12-01		
712	Horton, Antonio			1795-12-13		
713	Hudson, Francis			1796-07-28		
714	Hudson, Francisco	1	0	1796-12-21	m	p
715	Hulings, Juan			1789-04-22		
716	Hunot, Jose			1791-04-30	m	
717	Hunot, Jose			1793-03-31		c
718	Hunot, Jose	3	4	1793-03-31	m	c
719	Hunot, Jose	2	3	1793-11-20	m	c
720	Hunot, Jose			1796-07-01		
721	Hunot, Jose	2	3	1797-12-01	m	
722	Hunot, Jose (hijo)			1794-12-02		c
723	Hunot, Jose (padre)	1	3	1795-11-20	m	c
724	Hunot, Jose (padre)	1	3	1796-12-21	m	c
725	Hunt, Jose (hijo)			1796-12-21		p
726	Hunt, Jose Pierre	1	4	1794-12-02	m	c
727	Hurot, D.			1791-04-31		
728	Hutcheson, Henry			1796-07-01		
729	Hutchinson, Henry			1797-06-28		
730	Hutchinson, John			1792-09-16		
731	Huvel, Rufsel	0	0	1794-12-02	m	p
732	Ingrand, Jaime			1790-01-27		
733	Jackson, Elijah			1793-03-31		p
734	Jackson, Elijah			1793-03-31		p
735	Jackson, Elijah			1793-11-20		p
736	Jackson, Elijah	0	0	1794-12-02	m	p
737	Jackson, Elijah			1795-11-20		p
738	Jackson, Elijah			1796-07-01		
739	Jackson, Elijah			1796-12-21		p
740	Jackson, Elijah			1797-12-01		
741	Jackson, Epher			1791-12-19		

	Names	M.C.	F.C.	Date	Spouse	Religion
742	Jackson, Jesse			1793-11-11		
743	Jacob, Tomas	2	0	1793-11-20	m	c
744	Jacob, Tomas			1794-12-02		c
745	Jacob, Tomas			1795-11-20	m	c
746	Jacob, Tomas			1796-07-01		
747	Jacob, Tomas			1796-12-21	m	c
748	Jacob, Tomas	0	0	1797-12-01	m	
749	James, John			1792-05-30		
750	Jequin, Jacque			1791-04-31		
751	Johnson, Peter			1795-03-21		
752	Johnson, Timothy			1789-11-30		
753	Jordans, Edhar			1789-11-30		
754	Josley, William			1792-09-16		
755	Jubtil, Nicolas			1797-12-01		
756	Kaleand, Juan	1	0	1793-11-20	m	p
757	Kang, Juan			1796-07-01		
758	Kang, Juan			1796-12-21		p
759	Kang, William			1797-12-01		
760	Kaunot, José (hijo)			1795-11-20		c
761	Kelle, Juan			1795-11-20		c
762	Kelsy, Isaac			1792-06-24		
763	Kendall, Jerimah			1790-04-15		
764	Kendall, William			1790-04-15		
765	Kendle, Jeremin			1790-12-31	m	
766	Keoette, Jacobo	0	1	1797-12-01	n	
767	Kilwell, Vicenta	5	3	1795-11-20		p
768	King, John			1795-12-13		
769	Klein, Johann			1793-06-26		
770	Klicky, Antonio			1790-04-15		
771	Koud, Juan	3	0	1793-11-20	m	c
772	Kwet, Rowill			1793-11-20		p
773	Labolle, Joseph			1790-12-31		
774	Labousieve, Veronica	1	0	1795-11-20		c
775	Labullive, muger	1	1	1797-12-01	m	
776	Labusiaire, Ma.			1791-04-30		
777	Labussiere, (widow of)	0	1	1796-12-21	w	c
778	Labussiere, woman			1796-07-01		
779	Lac, Jorge	2	1	1793-11-20	m	p
780	Lacosta, Francisco	3	2	1793-03-31	m	c

	Names	M.C.	F.C.	Date	Spouse	Religion
781	Lacoste, Francisco			1791-04-30	m	
782	Lacoste, Francois			1791-04-31		
783	Lacruz, Jayme (widow of)			1791-04-30	w	
784	Laderoute, Jacobo			1795-11-20		c
785	Laderoute, Jacobo			1796-07-01		
786	Laderoute, Jacobo			1796-12-21		c
787	Laderoute, Jacobo			1797-12-01		
788	Laderoute, Pable	1	0	1797-12-01	m	
789	Laderoute, Pablo	0	1	1794-12-02	m	c
790	Laderoute, Pablo	1	1	1795-11-20	m	c
791	Laderoute, Pablo			1796-07-01		
792	Laderoute, Pablo	1	1	1796-12-21	m	c
793	Ladonceur, Juan			1795-11-20		c
794	Laeroix, Luisa			1796-12-21		c
795	Lafleur, Francisco			1791-04-30		
796	Lafleur, Jose			1793-03-31		c
797	Lafleur, Jose			1793-11-20		c
798	Lafleur, Jose			1794-12-02		c
799	Lafleur, Jose			1795-11-20		c
800	Laforge, Pedro Antonio	2	3	1794-12-02	m	c
801	Laforge, Pedro Antonio	2	2	1795-11-20	m	c
802	Laforge, Pedro Antonio			1796-07-01		
803	Laforge, Pedro Antonio	2	2	1796-12-21	m	c
804	Laforge, Pedro Antonio			1797-05-29		
805	Laforge, Pedro Antonio	2	2	1797-12-01	m	
806	Lafrete, Benjamin			1790-04-15		
807	Lafuener, Jose			1795-11-20		c
808	Lagarde, Juan Bauptista			1791-04-30		
809	Lagardo, Jean			1791-04-31		
810	Lagaus, Pedro			1797-12-01		
811	Laguille, Francisco			1793-03-31		c
812	Lainesés, David			1796-07-01		
813	Lainesés, David			1796-12-21		p
814	Lalou, Juan Francisco			1794-12-02		c
815	Lamb, Juan			1796-07-01		
816	Lamb, Juan			1797-12-01		
817	Lambert, Thomas			1792-11-30		
818	Lambert, Thomas	1	2	1793-11-20	m	c
819	Lamoureux, Jose	2	0	1793-11-20	m	c

251

	Names	M.C.	F.C.	Date	Spouse	Religion
820	Lamoureux, José	2	0	1794-12-02	m	c
821	Lamoureux, José	2	0	1795-11-20	m	c
822	Lamoureux, Jose			1796-07-01		
823	Lamoureux, Jose	2	0	1796-12-21	m	c
824	Landoise, Amable			1793-11-20		c
825	Landoise, Amable			1794-12-02		c
826	Landoise, Amable			1795-11-20		c
827	Langbis, Roberto			1793-11-20		c
828	Langlois, Francisco			1791-04-30		
829	Langlois, Francisco	0	0	1793-11-20	m	c
830	Langlois, Francisco			1794-07-09		
831	Langlois, Francisco			1795-11-20		c
832	Langlois, Francisco			1796-07-01		
833	Langlois, Francisco			1796-12-21		c
834	Langlois, Francisco			1797-12-01		
835	Langlois, Françoin			1792-05-26		
836	Langlois, Francois			1791-04-31		
837	Langlois, Juan Bautista			1794-12-02		c
838	Langlois, Juan Bautista			1796-07-01		
839	Langlois, Juan Bautista			1797-05-07		
840	Langlois, Juan Bautista			1797-12-01		
841	Langlois, Tetrudis	1	1	1793-03-31	n	c
842	Langlow, Kento			1795-11-20		p
843	Languille, F.			1792-04-02		
844	Lano, Jacob			1790-12-31		
845	Lansford, Moises			1790-12-31	m	
846	Lansford, Moises	0	0	1793-03-31	m	p
847	Lansford, Moises	2	2	1793-11-20	m	p
848	Lansford, Moises	1	3	1794-12-02	m	p
849	Lansford, Moises	1	3	1795-11-20	m	p
850	Lansford, Moises			1796-07-01		
851	Lansford, Moises	1	3	1796-12-21	m	p
852	Lansford, Moises	1	3	1797-12-01	m	
853	Laplanta, Jose	0	1	1793-11-20	m	c
854	Laplante, Jose	1	0	1793-03-31	m	c
855	Laplante, Jose			1793-11-20		c
856	Laplante, José	3	0	1794-12-02	m	c
857	Laplante, Jose	1	1	1795-11-20	m	c
858	Laplante, Jose			1796-07-01		

	Names	M.C.	F.C.	Date	Spouse	Religion
859	Laplante, Jose	1	1	1796-12-21	m	c
860	Laplante, Jose	0	2	1797-12-01	m	
861	Lardibeau, Bartolome			1797-12-01		
862	Lardibeau, Bartolome			1795-11-20		c
863	Largillon, (widow of)	1	0	1796-12-21	w	c
864	Largillon, muger			1797-12-01		
865	Largillon, woman			1796-07-01		
866	Lariviere, Francisco			1794-12-02		c
867	Lasaurse, Miguel			1791-08-19		
868	Lasfetier, Luis			1793-03-31		c
869	Lataesnay, Jose			1794-12-02		c
870	Lataille, Pedro			1795-04-24		
871	Latauhe, Juan Bautista			1795-04-24		
872	Laternay, Jose			1796-12-21	m	c
873	Lathur, Juan Bautista			1796-12-21		c
874	Latou, Pierre			1791·04-31		
875	Latouche, Juan			1795-11-20		c
876	Lature, Pedro			1791-04-30	m	
877	Lavalle, Juan	1	1	1795-11-20	m	c
878	Lavallé, Juan			1796-07-01		
879	Lavalle, Juan	1	0	1797-12-01	m	
880	Lavalle, Juan Bautista	1	2	1796-12-21	m	c
881	Lavallée, Francisco	1	0	1794-12-02	m	c
882	Lavoix, Francisco			1793-03-31		c
883	LeBan, (widow of)	2	0	1794-12-02	w	c
884	Lebrond, Luis			1791-04-30		
885	Lec Evots, Jacques			1791-04-31		
886	Ledoux, Pedro			1794-12-02		c
887	Ledoux, Pedro			1795-11-20		c
888	Leduc, Cirillo	2	0	1793-11-20	m	c
889	Leduc, Cirillo	0	0	1794-12-02	m	c
890	Leduc, Cirillo			1795-11-20	m	c
891	Leduc, Cirillo (widow of)			1796-07-01	w	
892	Leduc, Cirillo (widow of)	1	0	1796-12-21	w	c
893	Leduc, Cirillo (widow of)	0	0	1797-12-01	w	
894	Leduc, Felipe			1794-12-02		c
895	Leduc, Felipe	2	0	1795-11-20	m	c
896	Leduc, Felipe			1796-07-01		
897	Leduc, Felipe			1797-12-01		

	Names	M.C.	F.C.	Date	Spouse	Religion
898	Leduc, Jose			1795-11-20		c
899	Leduc, Jose			1796-07-01		
900	Leduc, Jose			1797-12-01		
901	Lefebre, Miguel			1793-11-20		c
902	Lefonait, Joseph	1	0	1797-12-01	m	
903	Lefunay, Jose			1796-07-01		
904	Legrand, Jose			1791-04-31		
905	Legrand, Jose			1793-03-31		c
906	Legrand, Jose			1795-11-20		c
907	Legrand, Jose			1796-07-01		
908	Legrand, Jose			1796-12-21		c
909	Legrand, Jose			1797-12-01		
910	Legrand, Juan Bautista			1794-12-02		c
911	Legrand, Juan Maria			1793-03-31		c
912	Legrand, Veronica	3	0	1793-11-20	n	c
913	Legrand, Veronica (widow)	6	2	1793-03-31	w	c
914	Legré, Johen			1790-12-31		
915	Lemoltre, Jacque			1791-04-31		
916	Lemotle, Jayme			1791-04-30		
917	Lenze, Tomas			1796-07-01		
918	Lenze, Tomas			1797-12-01		
919	Leonard, Francisco			1794-12-02		c
920	Leonard, Pedro			1793-11-20		p
921	Leopat, Tibursio			1795-11-20		c
922	Leper, Nicolas			1796-12-21		p
923	Lepten, Robert			1797-12-01		
924	Lesieur (widow of)			1796-07-01	w	
925	Lesieur, Francisco			1790-12-31		
926	Lesieur, Francisco	0	0	1793-03-31	m	c
927	Lesieur, Francisco	1	0	1793-11-20	m	c
928	Lesieur, Francisco	0	1	1794-12-02	m	c
929	Lesieur, Francisco	2	1	1795-11-20	m	c
930	Lesieur, Francisco			1796-07-01		
931	Lesieur, Francisco	0	2	1796-12-21	m	c
932	Lesieur, Francisco	0	2	1797-12-01	m	
933	Lesieur, Jose			1790-12-31		
934	Lesieur, Jose	0	0	1793-03-31	m	c
935	Lesieur, Jose	1	0	1793-11-20	m	c
936	Lesieur, Jose	1	0	1794-12-02	m	c

	Names	M.C.	F.C.	Date	Spouse	Religion
937	Lesieur, Jose			1795-11-20		c
938	Letulipe, Pedro			1790-12-31	m	
939	Levron, Louis			1791-04-31		
940	Levvis, Joseph	0	0	1797-12-01	m	
941	Levy, Cornelius			1794-01-03		
942	Lewars, Jose			1796-07-01		
943	Lgains, Pedro			1796-07-01		
944	Lice, John			1797-05-07		
945	Lices, Juan	0	1	1797-12-01	m	
946	Liebert, Felipe	2	1	1795-11-20	m	c
947	Liebert, Felipe	2	2	1796-12-21	m	c
948	Lindsey, David			1795-04-24		
949	Lion, Humphry			1790-01-27		
950	Lionav, Francois			1792-06-24		
951	Lipas, Christopher			1797-12-01		
952	Locke, Joseph			1790-04-15		
953	Logan, Thomas			1790-04-15		
954	Loierrien, Pierre			1791-04-31		
955	Loigrand, Carlos			1796-07-01		
956	Lojainan, Pedro			1796-12-21		p
957	Loncambroud, Andre			1796-07-01		
958	Loncambroud, Andres	1	2	1796-12-21		c
959	Londernis, Bryant			1789-11-30		
960	Long, Feliz			1794-12-02		p
961	Long, Feliz			1795-11-20		p
962	Longue, Felipe			1796-07-01		
963	Longue, Felipe			1797-12-01		
964	Longwell, James			1794-01-03		
965	Longwell, Santiago			1794-12-02		p
966	Losguon, Carlos	1	0	1797-12-01	m	
967	Lousseant, Francisco			1792-05-26		
968	Louvieren, Philipe			1796-12-21		c
969	Louvisoer, Phelipe			1797-12-01		
970	Lowaros, Minegre	0	0	1797-12-01	m	
971	Lucker, Juan			1797-12-01		
972	Luech, Levi			1790-10-25		
973	Luemnes, Guillermo			1796-07-01		
974	Luenue, William			1797-12-01		
975	Luigron, Carlos			1797-05-07		

	Names	M.C.	F.C.	Date	Spouse	Religion
976	Luintiman, Tomas			1796-07-01		
977	Luneford, Moise			1790-01-27		
978	Lyix, Jaquin			1796-07-01		
979	Mack, Guillermo			1790-01-27		
980	Mackey, Michael			1796-09-08		
981	Macormek, Jones			1793-03-31		p
982	Madonel, Gines			1790-12-31	m	
983	Maguibinne			1790-12-31		
984	Mahon, Robert M.			1792-12-04		
985	Mais, Jose			1790-12-31		
986	Maisonville			1790-12-31	m	
987	Maisonville, Francisco			1795-11-20		c
988	Maisonville, Francisco			1796-07-01		
989	Maisonville, Francisco			1797-12-01		
990	Maisonville, Jose	2	2	1793-03-31	n	c
991	Maisonville, Jose	2	0	1793-11-20	n	c
992	Maisonville, Jose			1794-12-02		c
993	Maisonville, Jose (hijo)			1793-03-31		c
994	Maisonville, Joseph			1792-06-24		
995	Maisonville, Juan			1795-11-20		c
996	Maisonville, Juan Bautista			1794-12-02		c
997	Maisonville, Juan Bautista			1796-07-01		
998	Maisonville, Juan Bautista			1796-12-21		c
999	Maisonville, Juan Bautista			1797-12-01		
1000	Malbete, Juan Moises	1	2	1793-03-31	m	c
1001	Malbete, Moises	1	0	1793-11-20	m	c
1002	Malbete, Moises	0	2	1794-12-02	m	c
1003	Malbete, Moises	0	2	1795-11-20	m	c
1004	Malbete, Moises			1796-07-01		
1005	Malbete, Moises	0	2	1796-12-21	m	c
1006	Malbete, Moises	0	2	1797-12-01	m	
1007	Mallet, Antonio			1791-04-30	m	
1008	Mallet, Antonio	2	1	1793-03-31	m	c
1009	Mallet, Antonio	2	2	1793-11-20	m	c
1010	Mallet, Jose			1793-03-31		c
1011	Mallon, Arturo	0	0	1793-11-20	m	p
1012	Mallvents, Luis			1790-12-31	m	
1013	Mancien, Pedro	0	0	1793-11-20	m	c
1014	Marchard, Didier			1792-05-26		

	Names	M.C.	F.C.	Date	Spouse	Religion
1015	Marchard, Didier			1794-12-02		c
1016	Marguet, (widow of)	0	1	1794-12-02	w	c
1017	Marguet, Madame de	0	1	1795-11-20		c
1018	Marquet, Bernardin			1794-04-09		
1019	Marquet, Louis			1794-04-09		
1020	Martin, Pierre			1792-06-24		
1021	Mason, Joseph			1792-09-30		
1022	Mathews, Daniel			1797-12-01		
1023	Mathews, Guillermo			1796-07-01		
1024	Mathews, Vm.	3	4	1797-12-01	m	
1025	Mathis, Daniel			1797-05-07		
1026	Matunin Bernard, Pedro	0	0	1793-11-20	m	c
1027	Maurice, Juan Bautista			1793-11-20		c
1028	Mayers, Jacobo	1	4	1793-03-31	m	p
1029	Mayers, Jacobo	2	3	1793-11-20	m	p
1030	Mayers, Jacobo	1	4	1794-12-02	m	p
1031	Mayers, Jacobo	2	4	1795-11-20	m	p
1032	Mayers, Jacobo			1796-07-01		
1033	Mayers, Jacobo	2	4	1796-12-21	m	p
1034	Mayers, Jacobo	2	4	1797-12-01	m	
1035	Mc Kay, Pedro			1790-12-31	m	
1036	Mc. Moleo, Pacolo			1796-12-21		p
1037	McCanza, William			1792-06-24		
1038	McCay, Robert			1791-07-25		
1039	McCay, Robert			1792-11-30		
1040	McCay, Roberto			1793-03-31		c
1041	McCay, Roberto	0	2	1793-11-20	m	c
1042	McCay, Roberto	0	1	1794-12-02	m	c
1043	McCay, Roberto	0	1	1795-11-20	m	c
1044	McCay, Roberto			1796-07-01		
1045	McCay, Roberto	1	1	1796-12-21	m	c
1046	McCay, Roberto	1	1	1797-12-01	m	
1047	McChisholm, Hugh			1790-12-31		
1048	McChisholm, Hugh			1796-07-01		
1049	McChisholm, Hugh	1	3	1794-12-02	m	p
1050	McChisholm, Hugh	1	3	1796-12-21	m	p
1051	McChisholm, Hugh	1	3	1797-12-01	m	
1052	McChisholm, Hugh	1	3	1793-11-20	m	p
1053	McCleland, Jacobo			1796-07-01		

	Names	M.C.	F.C.	Date	Spouse	Religion
1054	McCleland, Juan			1797-12-01		
1055	McClelland, John			1797-05-07		
1056	McCoklmeck, Johen			1790-12-31		
1057	McCormick, Mathias			1795-02-16		
1058	McCormick, Mathias	3	0	1795-11-20	m	p
1059	McCormick, Mathias			1796-07-01		
1060	McCormick, Mathias	1	2	1796-12-21	m	p
1061	McCormick, Mathias	1	2	1797-12-01	m	
1062	McCourtney, Jose			1795-01-09		
1063	McCourtney, Jose			1795-11-20	m	p
1064	McCourtney, Jose			1796-07-01		
1065	McCourtney, Jose			1796-12-21	m	p
1066	McCourtney, Jose			1794-12-02		p
1067	McCullock, Jacobo			1793-11-20		p
1068	McCullock, James			1792-05-07		
1069	McCully, Jorge			1789-04-22		
1070	McDonald			1789-11-30		
1071	McDonel, Jayme			1790-01-27		
1072	McDonell, ALexandro			1789-04-22		
1073	McFarlan, Jacobo			1796-07-01		
1074	McFarley, Jacob			1797-12-01		
1075	McKentoche, Abner			1797-12-01		
1076	McKinney, James			1790-10-25		
1077	McKoy, Guillermo	3	5	1795-11-20	m	p
1078	McLaughlin, Batt			1793-06-18		
1079	Mclean, James			1792-06-24		
1080	McMillan, James			1794-01-03		
1081	McMollen, Jacobo	0	0	1797-12-01	m	
1082	Meace, James			1795-03-21		
1083	Meaces, Jacobo			1796-07-01		
1084	Meares, Jacobo			1796-07-01		
1085	Melayes, Luis			1796-07-01		
1086	Meley, Tomas	1	0	1797-12-01	m	
1087	Melivies, Miguel			1796-07-01		
1088	Mellon, Arthur			1790-04-15		
1089	Mellon, Arthur			1790-12-31		
1090	Mellon, Arthur			1794-12-02		p
1091	Mellon, Arthur			1795-11-20		p
1092	Mellon, Arthur			1796-07-01		

	Names	M.C.	F.C.	Date	Spouse	Religion
1093	Mellon, Arthur			1796-12-21		p
1094	Mellon, Arthur			1797-12-01		
1095	Meloche, Antonio			1791-04-30	m	
1096	Meloche, Antonio			1791-04-31		
1097	Meloche, Antonio	0	0	1794-12-02	m	c
1098	Mertuin, Jacobo			1795-11-20		c
1099	Metivi, Luis			1797-12-01		
1100	Mettez, Joseph			1791-04-30	m	
1101	Meuice, George			1795-05-18		
1102	Michel, Francisco	0	0	1793-11-20	m	c
1103	Michel, Francisco			1796-07-01		
1104	Michel, Francisco	1	1	1797-12-01	m	
1105	Michel, Jose			1793-03-31		c
1106	Michel, Jose			1793-11-20		c
1107	Michel, Jose			1794-12-02		c
1108	Michel, Jose			1795-11-20		c
1109	Michel, Jose			1796-07-01		
1110	Michel, Jose			1796-12-21		c
1111	Millan, Florencio			1797-06-28		
1112	Millegrano, Juan Bautista	1	2	1793-11-20	m	c
1113	Miller, Benjamin			1793-04-07		
1114	Millet, Benjamin	0	1	1793-11-20	m	c
1115	Millet, Juan Bautista			1791-04-30	m	
1116	Millet, Juan Bautista	1	0	1793-11-20	m	c
1117	Millom, David	3	0	1793-03-31	m	p
1118	Mock, Vili			1790-12-31		
1119	Mock, Guillermo			1793-11-20		p
1120	Mock, Guillermo			1794-12-02		p
1121	Mock, Guillermo			1795-11-20	m	p
1122	Mock, Guillermo			1796-07-01		
1123	Mock, Guillermo			1796-12-21	m	p
1124	Mock, Guillermo	0	0	1797-12-01	m	
1125	Mock, William			1790-04-15		
1126	MoConnade, Guillermo			1793-11-20		p
1127	Moises, Carlos			1791-04-30		
1128	Moles, Maria			1797-12-01		
1129	Molles, woman			1796-07-01		
1130	Mondor, Juan			1795-11-20		c
1131	Mondor, Nicolas			1794-12-02		c

	Names	M.C.	F.C.	Date	Spouse	Religion
1132	Monemara, James			1797-06-28		
1133	Mongomery, Guillermo			1789-04-22		
1134	Mongomery, Jorge			1789-04-22		
1135	Mongomery, Jugo			1789-04-22		
1136	Montmirel, Joseph			1791-04-30	m	
1137	Montmirel, Joseph			1791-04-31		
1138	Morand, Luis			1791-04-30		
1139	Morclanc, Hugh Luis			1790-10-25		
1140	Morgan, Maria			1790-12-31		
1141	Morgan, Maria			1793-03-31		p
1142	Morin, Francis			1797-05-07		
1143	Morin, Francisco			1797-12-01		
1144	Moris, Tomas			1790-01-27		
1145	Morme, Francisco			1796-07-01		
1146	Morrel, Juan Bautista			1793-03-31		c
1147	Morris, Samuel			1789-11-30		
1148	Moyses, Juan Bautista	2	0	1793-11-20	m	c
1149	Muarmolles			1796-07-01		
1150	Mulatrulle, Sarah	0	1	1796-12-21		p
1151	Murphy, Michel	0	0	1797-12-01	m	
1152	Murphy, William			1796-07-01		
1153	Murphy, William	2	2	1797-12-01	m	
1154	Naheilman, Ketez			1793-11-20		"India"
1155	Neeley, Tomas			1796-07-01		
1156	Nesbill, David			1796-12-07		
1157	Nicholas, Juan			1795-12-13		
1158	Nicolas, Juan			1795-11-20		p
1159	Nicolas, Juan			1796-12-21		p
1160	Nipie, Bernardo			1791-04-30		
1161	Noel, Ambroi			1791-04-31		
1162	Nooden, Guillermo			1790-01-27		
1163	Nugin, John			1792-09-16		
1164	OBryan, Juan			1794-12-02		p
1165	OBune, James			1794-08-25		
1166	Ofman, Frederic			1793-11-20		c
1167	Oneille, Jose			1793-11-20		c
1168	Oneille, Jose			1794-12-02		c
1169	Onraw, George			1796-07-01		
1170	Onraw, George			1796-12-21		c

	Names	M.C.	F.C.	Date	Spouse	Religion
1171	Oubtet, Nicolas			1796-07-01		
1172	Ouelette, Francisco			1791-04-30		
1173	Ouelette, Francois			1791-04-31		
1174	Overby, Boruel			1796-07-01		
1175	Overby, Boruel	1	0	1796-12-21	m	p
1176	Overby, Boruel	0	1	1797-12-01	n	
1177	Owens, David			1789-04-22		
1178	Owens, Jayme			1789-04-22		
1179	Owens, Juan			1789-04-22		
1180	Ozauges, Pierre			1791-04-31		
1181	Packard, Isiah			1795-05-18		
1182	Paguef, Francisco	0	0	1794-12-02	m	c
1183	Paguet, Francisco			1793-11-20		c
1184	Pamard, Romano			1793-11-20		c
1185	Pamard, Romano			1794-12-02		c
1186	Pamard, Romano			1795-11-20		c
1187	Pamard, Romano			1796-07-01		
1188	Paquelle, Francisco			1796-07-01		
1189	Paquette, Francisco	0	0	1797-12-01	m	
1190	Paquin, Francisco			1790-12-31	m	
1191	Paquin, Francisco	5	0	1793-03-31	m	c
1192	Paquin, Francisco	6	0	1793-11-20	m	c
1193	Paquin, Francisco	7	0	1794-12-02	m	c
1194	Paquin, Francisco	6		1795-11-20	m	c
1195	Paquin, Francisco			1795-11-20		c
1196	Paquin, Francisco			1796-07-01		
1197	Paquin, Francisco	7		1796-12-21	m	c
1198	Paquin, Francisco	7	0	1797-12-01	m	
1199	Paquin, Luis			1790-12-31		
1200	Pardon, Tomas	0	0	1794-12-02	m	p
1201	Parker, Azon			1795-11-20		p
1202	Parker, Juan			1796-07-01		
1203	Parker, Samuel	6	4	1795-11-20	m	p
1204	Parkes, Jacobo			1797-12-01		
1205	Parkes, Juan			1797-12-01		
1206	Parkin, John			1797-05-07		
1207	Patterson			1797-05-07		
1208	Patterson, Benjamin	2	2	1797-12-01	m	
1209	Patterson, John			1797-05-30		

	Names	M.C.	F.C.	Date	Spouse	Religion
1210	Payan, Pedro			1795-11-20		c
1211	Payant, Pedro			1794-12-02		c
1212	Pearl, Richard			1790-04-15		
1213	Pedro, Nicolas Juan			1795-11-20		c
1214	Peigay, Nicolas			1796-07-01		
1215	Peigne, Nicolas			1796-07-01		
1216	Peignes, Nicolas	1	1	1797-12-01	m	
1217	Peletieu, Eustaguio	4	2	1793-03-31	m	c
1218	Peltier, Eustaquio			1791-04-30	m	
1219	Peoces, Jacobo			1796-07-01		
1220	Peole, James	1	0	1797-12-01	m	
1221	Perkins, Francisco			1789-04-22		
1222	Perkins, Francisco			1790-01-27		
1223	Perodeau, (widow of)	1	0	1794-12-02	w	c
1224	Perodeau, Jose	2	1	1793-11-20	m	c
1225	Perodeau, Joseph (hijo)			1791-04-30	m	
1226	Perodeau, Joseph (padre)			1791-04-30	m	
1227	Perron, Amable			1791-04-30		
1228	Perron, Amable			1791-04-31		
1229	Perron, Amable			1793-03-31		c
1230	Perron, Amable			1793-11-20		c
1231	Perron, Amable			1794-12-02		c
1232	Perron, Amable			1795-11-20		c
1233	Perrou, Pierre			1792-06-24		
1234	Petit, Antonio			1792-12-30		
1235	Petit, Antonio	1	0	1793-11-20	m	c
1236	Phelviri, Pedro	1	1	1793-03-31	m	c
1237	Philips, Joseph			1789-04-22		
1238	Philips, Juan			1789-04-22		
1239	Phillips, Sylvanius			1797-06-28		
1240	Picard, Alexis			1796-07-01		
1241	Picard, Alexis			1796-07-01		
1242	Picard, Alexis	3	0	1796-12-21	m	c
1243	Picard, Alexo	3	0	1795-11-20	m	c
1244	Picard, Alexo	3	0	1797-12-01	m	
1245	Picard, Francisco	1	0	1793-11-20	m	c
1246	Pierre, Nicolas Jean	2	0	1793-11-20	m	c
1247	Pierre, Nicolas Jean	1	1	1794-12-02	m	c
1248	Pierse, Maria Sn.			1796-12-21		c

	Names	M.C.	F.C.	Date	Spouse	Religion
1249	Pinueta, Leandro	4	1	1795-11-20	m	c
1250	Poirier, Pedro	1	0	1793-03-31	m	c
1251	Poirier, Pedro	1	1	1793-11-20	m	c
1252	Poirier, Pedro			1793-11-20		c
1253	Poirier, Pedro	1	0	1794-12-02	m	c
1254	Poirier, Pedro	1	0	1795-11-20	m	c
1255	Poirier, Pedro			1796-07-01		
1256	Poirier, Pedro	1	0	1796-12-21	m	c
1257	Poldevin, Roberto			1797-12-01		
1258	Pontbent, Francisco	1	2	1793-11-20	m	c
1259	Pontell, Tomas			1791-07-25		
1260	Pouneuf, Pablo	0	1	1793-11-20	m	c
1261	Power, Samuel			1791-07-25		
1262	Power, Tomas			1794-05-15		
1263	Power, Tomas			1795-11-20		c
1264	Power, Tomas			1796-07-01		
1265	Power, Tomas			1796-12-21	m	c
1266	Pressete, Juan			1793-03-31		c
1267	Pretchet, Juan	3	1	1795-11-20		p
1268	Pretchet, Juan			1796-07-01		
1269	Pretchet, Juan	2	1	1796-12-21		p
1270	Pretchet, Juan	3	1	1797-12-01	n	
1271	Prethon, Juan	3	3	1793-11-20	m	c
1272	Pride, Jaime			1790-01-27		
1273	Pride, Jayme			1789-04-22		
1274	Pritchard, Juan	4	2	1794-12-02	n	p
1275	Provem, Samuel	1	1	1793-03-31	m	p
1276	Prudome, Tomas			1793-11-20		p
1277	Pupu, Francisco Maria	0	6	1793-11-20	m	c
1278	Queburne, Jones			1793-03-31		p
1279	Quenez, Antonio	2	3	1793-03-31	m	c
1280	Quenez, Pedro	2	2	1793-03-31	m	c
1281	Quibau, Carls			1790-12-31		
1282	Quirot, Juan			1795-11-20		c
1283	Racine, Francisco			1791-04-30	m	
1284	Racine, Francisco	1	3	1793-03-31	m	c
1285	Racine, Francisco	1	3	1793-11-20	m	c
1286	Racine, Francisco	3	1	1794-12-02	m	c
1287	Racine, Francisco	2	3	1795-11-20	m	c

	Names	M.C.	F.C.	Date	Spouse	Religion
1288	Racine, Francisco			1796-07-01		
1289	Racine, Francisco	2	3	1796-12-21	m	c
1290	Racine, Francisco	2	3	1797-12-01	m	
1291	Racine, Juan Baptista			1791-04-30	m	
1292	Racine, Juan Baptista	1	1	1794-12-02	m	c
1293	Racine, Juan Baptista	1	2	1796-12-21	m	c
1294	Racine, Juan Bautista	1	1	1793-11-20	m	c
1295	Racine, Juan Bautista			1796-07-01		
1296	Racine, Juan Bautista	1	2	1797-12-01	m	
1297	Railli, Miguel			1795-11-20		p
1298	Rajer, Alexandro			1790-01-27		
1299	Ramsey, Geoffroy			1794-04-09		
1300	Randal, Samuel			1797-05-30		
1301	Rangez, Pedro			1791-04-30	m	
1302	Rayen, Jacobo	1	0	1793-11-20	m	p
1303	Rayen, Jacobo	1	2	1794-12-02	m	p
1304	Rayen, Jacoby			1796-12-21		c
1305	Rayen, James			1796-07-01		
1306	Rayen, James			1797-12-01		
1307	Reagan, George			1796-07-01		
1308	Reagan, George N.	2	2	1796-12-21	m	p
1309	Reagan, George N.	1	0	1797-12-01	m	
1310	Reburn, John			1791-07-25		
1311	Reed, Juan			1795-02-16		
1312	Rees, (widow of)			1797-12-01	m	
1313	Rees, Arturo			1790-01-27		
1314	Rees, Azon			1790-04-15		
1315	Rees, Azon			1790-12-31	m	
1316	Rees, Azon	0	1	1793-03-31	m	p
1317	Rees, Azon	0	1	1793-11-20	m	p
1318	Rees, Azon	0	1	1794-12-02	m	p
1319	Rees, Azon	0	1	1795-11-20	m	p
1320	Rees, Azon			1796-07-01		
1321	Rees, Azon	0	1	1796-12-21	m	p
1322	Regh, Morris			1790-10-25		
1323	Reilley, Mathias			1796-12-21		p
1324	Rendeau, Joachin	4	1	1794-12-02	m	c
1325	Rendeau, Jose	4	1	1793-03-31	m	c
1326	Rendeau, Jose	4	1	1793-11-20	m	c

	Names	M.C.	F.C.	Date	Spouse	Religion
1327	Rendeau, Jose	4	1	1795-11-20	m	c
1328	Rendeau, Jose			1796-07-01		
1329	Rendeau, Jose	4	1	1797-12-01	m	
1330	Reyan, George			1797-05-29		
1331	Rice, Daniel			1796-07-01		
1332	Rice, Daniel			1797-05-31		
1333	Rice, Daniel			1797-12-01		
1334	Richard, Juan Baptista			1791-04-30	m	
1335	Richard, Juan Bautista	1	0	1793-03-31	m	c
1336	Richard, Juan Bautista	1	0	1793-11-20	m	c
1337	Richeduvois, Glot Sr. co			1796-12-21	m	c
1338	Riley, Matéo			1794-12-02		c
1339	Robinson, Guillermo			1789-04-22		
1340	Robot, Georges			1793-02-16		
1341	Robot, Georges			1796-07-01		
1342	Robot, Georges			1796-12-21	m	p
1343	Robuch, Jorge	0	0	1794-12-02	m	p
1344	Roburck, Jorge	0	0	1793-11-20	m	p
1345	Roche, Cristoval			1793-11-20		c
1346	Rodeller, Guillermo			1793-03-31		c
1347	Rodgers, Michael			1796-07-24		
1348	Rodriguez, Francisco			1791-08-10		
1349	Rogers, Robert			1797-05-29		
1350	Rogers, Robert	0	0	1797-12-01	m	
1351	Rogers, Roberto			1796-07-01		
1352	Rouin, Juan Bautista	1	1	1795-11-20	m	c
1353	Rousse, Francisco			1791-04-30	m	
1354	Rowen, Roses			1796-07-01		
1355	Rowen, Roses			1797-12-01		
1356	Roze, Guillermo			1797-12-01		
1357	Rozoce, Pedro			1790-12-31	m	
1358	Rubu, Antonio Jose	0	1	1793-11-20	m	c
1359	Ruddell, George			1796-07-01		
1360	Ruddell, George	2	5	1796-12-21	m	p
1361	Ruddell, George	4	2	1797-12-01	m	
1362	Russel, Jacobo			1796-07-01		
1363	Ryan, Michael			1794-08-25		
1364	Sabourin, Pedro	0	0	1793-03-31	m	c
1365	Sabourin, Pedro	1	0	1793-11-20	m	c

	Names	M.C.	F.C.	Date	Spouse	Religion
1366	Sabourin, Pedro			1794-12-02		c
1367	Sabourin, Pedro	1	1	1795-11-20	m	c
1368	Sabourin, Pedro			1796-07-01		
1369	Sabourin, Pedro	1	1	1797-12-01	m	
1370	Safray, Pedro			1793-03-31		c
1371	Safray, Pedro			1793-11-20		c
1372	Safray, Pedro	0	2	1794-12-02	m	c
1373	Safray, Pedro			1795-11-20		c
1374	Safray, Pedro			1796-07-01		
1375	Safray, Pedro			1796-12-21		c
1376	Sagres, Tibo St.			1790-12-31	m	
1377	Saint Aubin, Luis			1791-04-30	m	
1378	Saint Aubin, Luis	1	2	1793-03-31	m	c
1379	Saint Aubin, Luis	1	3	1793-11-20	m	c
1380	Saint Aubin, Luis	1	3	1794-12-02	m	c
1381	Saint Aubin, Luis	2	3	1795-11-20	m	c
1382	Saint Aubin, Luis			1796-07-01		
1383	Saint Aubin, Luis	1	1	1797-12-01	m	
1384	Saint Aubin, Luis	2	3	1796-12-21	m	c
1385	Salé (free black)	2	0	1795-11-20	m	p
1386	Saler, woman			1796-07-01		
1387	Sales Jones, Benjamine			1796-07-01		
1388	Salier, Juan			1795-11-20		c
1389	Salier, Juan Bautista	2	0	1793-11-20	m	c
1390	Salier, Juan Bautista			1794-12-02		c
1391	Sallui, Joseph			1791-04-31		
1392	Samson, Alexandro			1790-12-31	m	
1393	Samson, Alexandro	1	0	1793-03-31	m	c
1394	Samson, Alexandro	1	1	1793-11-20	m	c
1395	Samson, Alexandro	1	1	1794-12-02	m	c
1396	Samson, Alexandro	2	1	1795-11-20	m	c
1397	Samson, Alexandro			1796-07-01		
1398	Samson, Alexandro	1	1	1796-12-21	m	c
1399	Samson, Alexandro	1	0	1797-12-01	m	
1400	San Antonio			1790-12-31	m	
1401	Sanidin, Francisco			1793-03-31		c
1402	Sanpaña, Francisco			1790-12-31		
1403	Sanson Aroche, (widow of)	2	3	1797-12-01	w	
1404	Santa Maria, Estevan	1	2	1793-03-31	m	c

	Names	M.C.	F.C.	Date	Spouse	Religion
1405	Santa Maria, Estevan	3	3	1793-11-20	m	c
1406	Santa Maria, Estevan	4	3	1794-12-02	m	c
1407	Santa Maria, Estevan	5	3	1795-11-20	m	c
1408	Santa Maria, Estevan			1796-07-01		
1409	Santa Maria, Estevan	3	2	1797-12-01	n	
1410	Santa Maria, Etienic	5	2	1796-12-21	m	c
1411	Santa Maria, Francisco	1	2	1793-03-31	m	c
1412	Santa Maria, Francisco	2	2	1793-11-20	m	c
1413	Santa Maria, Francisco	2	2	1794-12-02	m	c
1414	Santa Maria, Francisco	2	3	1795-11-20	m	c
1415	Santa Maria, Francisco			1796-07-01		
1416	Santa Maria, Francisco	2	3	1796-12-21	m	c
1417	Santa Maria, Francisco	2	3	1797-12-01	m	
1418	Santa Maria, Jose			1791-04-30	m	
1419	Santa Maria, Jose	1	1	1793-03-31	m	c
1420	Santa Maria, Jose	1	1	1793-11-20	m	c
1421	Santa Maria, José	2	1	1794-12-02	m	c
1422	Santa Maria, Jose	2	1	1795-11-20	m	c
1423	Santa Maria, Jose			1796-07-01		
1424	Santa Maria, Jose	3	1	1796-12-21	m	c
1425	Santa Maria, Jose	2	1	1797-12-01	m	
1426	Sarsamen, Luis			1790-12-31		
1427	Savul, Luis			1790-12-31	m	
1428	Saxton, Joseph	2	1	1797-12-01	m	
1429	Scaler, Jacobo			1795-11-20		p
1430	Scaler, woman			1796-07-01		
1431	Selby, David	5	3	1795-11-20	m	p
1432	Serafim, Ambrosio			1796-07-01		
1433	Serafin, Ambrosio			1795-11-20		c
1434	Serafin, Ambrosio			1797-12-01		
1435	Serafin, Angel			1795-11-20		c
1436	Seraphim, Agnes			1796-07-01		
1437	Seraphim, Agnes	0	0	1797-12-01	m	
1438	Seré, Antonio			1790-12-31		
1439	Serres, James			1797-12-01		
1440	Servant, Pedro			1794-12-02		c
1441	Shelby, David			1796-07-01		
1442	Shelby, David	6	4	1796-12-21	m	p
1443	Shelby, David	6	2	1797-12-01	m	

	Names	M.C.	F.C.	Date	Spouse	Religion
1444	Shelly			1789-11-30		
1445	Shepard, John			1797-05-31		
1446	Shepard, Samuel			1797-05-07		
1447	Sheves, Pedro			1797-12-01		
1448	Shreeve, Ysrael			1789-04-22		
1449	Siebert, Phelipe	2	1	1794-12-02	m	c
1450	Siebert, Philip			1794-07-11		
1451	Sieur, Noel Antoine			1793-06-26		
1452	Silch, Waling	0	0	1797-12-01	m	
1453	Simple, David			1797-06-28		
1454	Simple, David			1797-12-01		
1455	Sincops, Josepha			1797-12-01		
1456	Skerelles, Jacobo			1796-07-01		
1457	Skerettes, Jacobo			1796-07-01		
1458	Skerrett, Isidore			1795-05-07		
1459	Slites, Juan			1797-12-01		
1460	Smith, Mathew			1796-07-24		
1461	Smith, Tomas			1797-06-28		
1462	Smith, William			1793-03-05		
1463	Smiz, Jacobo	1	0	1797-12-01	m	
1464	Soasen, Joseph			1790-12-31	m	
1465	Soldener, Francisco			1796-07-01		
1466	Soles, Moses			1790-10-25		
1467	Sollin, Alexo Auguste			1797-12-01		
1468	Sommers, Juan			1796-07-01		
1469	Sommers, Juan			1797-12-01		
1470	Soues, Juan			1795-11-20		p
1471	St. Jean, Luis			1797-12-01		
1472	St. Martin, Madama			1794-12-02		c
1473	Starkey, Jayme			1789-04-22		
1474	Ste Mair, Joseph			1791-04-31		
1475	Stevart, Juan			1789-04-22		
1476	Steward, Juan			1790-01-27		
1477	Stewart, John			1790-04-15		
1478	Stierette, Isidor			1796-12-21		c
1479	Stillman, John			1790-12-31	m	
1480	Stilman, Jones	3	4	1793-03-31	m	p
1481	Stockeley, Francisco			1791-04-30		
1482	Stockky, Franky			1791-04-31		

	Names	M.C.	F.C.	Date	Spouse	Religion
1483	Stofle, Henrico	1	0	1797-12-01	m	
1484	Stofler, Henrico			1796-07-01		
1485	Stopman, Federico			1790-12-31	m	
1486	Story, Jose			1789-11-30		
1487	Story, Jose			1790-12-31		
1488	Story, Jose			1793-03-31		p
1489	Story, Jose			1793-11-20		p
1490	Story, Jose	0	0	1794-12-02	m	p
1491	Story, Jose			1795-11-20	m	p
1492	Story, Jose			1796-07-01		
1493	Story, Jose			1796-12-21	m	c
1494	Story, Jose	0	0	1797-12-01	m	
1495	Story, Joseph			1789-04-22		
1496	Strickland Power, Tomas			1794-12-02		c
1497	Strickley, Juan	2	0	1797-12-01	m	
1498	Sualer, Lamberto	1	3	1795-11-20	m	c
1499	Subourin, Pierre			1792-06-24		
1500	Sudiñon, Juan Baptista			1790-12-31		
1501	Sulivan, M.			1792-06-24		
1502	Sullivan, Federico			1792-03-10		
1503	Sullivan, Federico			1793-03-31		c
1504	Talbert, Juan			1793-11-20		c
1505	Taner, Jose	0	1	1793-03-31	m	p
1506	Tardiveau, Bartholome			1793-12-15		
1507	Tardiveau, Bartholome			1794-12-02		c
1508	Tardiveau, Bartholome			1796-07-01		
1509	Tardiveau, Bartholome			1796-12-21		c
1510	Tarteron de Labeaume, Luis	0	1	1793-11-20	m	c
1511	Tarteron de labeaume, Luis	1	1	1794-12-02	m	c
1512	Tastelly, Antonio			1792-06-24		
1513	Taylor, Guillermo			1797-12-01		
1514	Taylor, Roberto			1796-07-01		
1515	Tebbs, James			1792-06-24		
1516	Tengleton, Joseph			1790-10-25		
1517	Tesien, Nicolas			1793-11-20		c
1518	Tetro, Juan Bautista	0	0	1793-03-31	m	c
1519	Tetroic, Juan Bautista	1	1	1793-11-20	m	c
1520	Thechelet, Levi	1	0	1793-03-31	m	p
1521	Thiriet, Claudio			1796-07-01		

	Names	M.C.	F.C.	Date	Spouse	Religion
1522	Thiriet, Claudio			1796-12-21		c
1523	Thiriet, Claudio			1797-12-01		
1524	Thiriot, Juan			1794-12-02		c
1525	Thiriot, Juan			1797-12-01		
1526	Thompson			1789-11-30		
1527	Thompson			1790-12-31	m	
1528	Thompson, Frank			1796-12-21	m	p
1529	Thompson, Isaac			1790-01-27		
1530	Thompson, Isaac	0	0	1793-03-31	m	p
1531	Thompson, Isaac	0	0	1793-11-20	m	p
1532	Thompson, Isaac	0	2	1794-12-02	m	p
1533	Thompson, Isaac			1795-11-20	m	p
1534	Thompson, Isaac			1796-07-01		
1535	Thompson, Isaac	0	0	1797-12-01	m	
1536	Thompson, Juan			1790-01-27		
1537	Tibeau, Nicolas	1	1	1793-11-20	m	c
1538	Tibre, Juan			1793-11-20		c
1539	Ticos, Juan			1796-07-01		
1540	Tifo, Francisco			1790-12-31		
1541	Timen, Tomas Luis	3	2	1797-12-01	m	
1542	Tippy, Abram			1790-10-25		
1543	Tison, Alberto			1796-07-01		
1544	Tison, Alberto			1796-07-01		
1545	Tison, Alberto			1796-12-21		c
1546	Tison, Alberto			1797-12-01		
1547	Todd, Tomas			1789-04-22		
1548	Tolon, Juan			1791-04-30	m	
1549	Tonuwates, Richard			1796-12-21		p
1550	Toope, Frederico			1790-04-15		
1551	Torn, Simon	1	0	1793-11-20	n	p
1552	Tostell, Antonio			1793-11-20		c
1553	Touinay, Francisco			1794-12-02		c
1554	Toulleni, Guillermo			1793-11-20		p
1555	Toulon, Juan	0	0	1793-03-31	m	c
1556	Tourdain, Juan			1794-12-02		c
1557	Tournay, Françon Xavie			1794-03-31		
1558	Tremble, Juan Bautista Du			1794-12-02		c
1559	Tribeaut, Nicolas	1	1	1793-03-31	m	c
1560	Trocaubrout, Andres	1	3	1793-03-31	m	c

	Names	M.C.	F.C.	Date	Spouse	Religion
1561	Trocaubrout, Andres	1	2	1793-11-20	n	c
1562	Trocaubrout, Andres	0	2	1794-12-02	n	p
1563	Trocaubrout, Andres	0	2	1795-11-20		p
1564	Troclebroad, Juan			1789-04-22		
1565	Tucanbrote, Julian (hijo)	0	0	1793-03-31	m	c
1566	Tuertiment, Tomas			1795-02-16		
1567	Tuncote, Jose	1	0	1793-03-31	m	c
1568	Tunnay, Francisco			1795-11-20		c
1569	Turboys, Juan			1790-01-27		
1570	Turent, Jose	0	0	1793-11-20	m	c
1571	Tustiman, Tomas	3	3	1796-12-21	m	p
1572	Tuuceret, Antorire			1791-04-31		
1573	Upham, Roberto			1796-12-21		p
1574	Vachard, Antonio			1796-07-01		
1575	Vachard, Antonio	1	0	1796-12-21	m	c
1576	Vachard, Antonio	1	1	1797-12-01	m	
1577	Vachet, Francisco	3	2	1793-03-31	m	c
1578	Vachette, Antonio	4	2	1794-12-02	m	c
1579	Vachette, Antonio	3	2	1796-12-21	m	c
1580	Vadeboncoeur			1796-12-21	m	c
1581	Vadeboncoeur, Pedro			1794-12-02		c
1582	Vadeboncon, Pedro			1795-11-20	m	c
1583	Valbenda, Antonio			1793-03-31		c
1584	Valete, Francisco	0	0	1793-03-31	m	c
1585	Valete, Francisco	0	0	1793-11-20	m	c
1586	Vallancurt, Francisco			1793-11-20		c
1587	Valois, Luis			1793-03-31		c
1588	Valrelimant, Ketez			1793-03-31		c
1589	Van Hooke, Samuel			1789-11-30		
1590	Vandenbemden			1792-04-02		
1591	Vandenbemden, Jose			1795-11-20		c
1592	Vandenbemden, Jose			1796-12-21		c
1593	Vandenbemden, Jose			1797-12-01		
1594	Vandenbemden, Julian			1793-03-31		c
1595	Vandenbemden, Luis	1	0	1794-12-02	m	c
1596	Vandenbemden, Luis	1	0	1795-11-20	m	c
1597	Vandenbemden, Luis			1796-07-01		
1598	Vandenbemden, Luis			1796-12-21	m	c
1599	Vandenbemden, Luis	0	0	1797-12-01	m	

	Names	M.C.	F.C.	Date	Spouse	Religion
1600	Vandenlenden, Jose			1796-07-01		
1601	Vandernaiy, Pedro			1796-12-21		p
1602	Vanderstines, Pedro			1796-07-01		
1603	Vanidesline, Pedro			1797-12-01		
1604	Vaugham, Daniel			1797-12-01		
1605	Verours, Francois			1791-04-31		
1606	Villeneuve, Charles			1791-04-31		
1607	Viot, Juan			1796-07-01		
1608	Viot, Juan			1796-07-01		
1609	VirtdeGascon, Jean	2	3	1797-12-01	m	
1610	Vives, Pedro	1	2	1797-12-01	m	
1611	Walace, Jaime			1790-01-27		
1612	Walde, John			1794-01-03		
1613	Walen, Juan			1796-07-01		
1614	Walis, Sales			1797-12-01		
1615	Walker, Roberto			1789-04-22		
1616	Wallix, Sales			1796-07-01		
1617	Wallix, Soles			1796-07-01		
1618	Walls, Juan			1796-07-01		
1619	Walls, Juan			1797-12-01		
1620	Wals, Juan			1794-12-02		p
1621	Wals, Juan			1796-12-21		p
1622	Wals, Salé	0	1	1795-11-20		p
1623	Wanfox, Cristopher	2	0	1797-12-01	m	
1624	Wanhooks, Samuel			1790-01-27		
1625	Waters, Ricardo Juan			1790-10-25		
1626	Waters, Ricardo Juan			1790-12-31		
1627	Waters, Ricardo Juan			1793-11-20		p
1628	Waters, Ricardo Juan			1794-12-02		p
1629	Waters, Ricardo Juan			1795-11-20		p
1630	Waters, Ricardo Juan			1796-07-01		
1631	Waters, Ricardo Juan			1797-12-01		
1632	Waters, Ricardo Juan			1793-03-31		p
1633	Watson, Juan			1795-11-20		p
1634	Watson, Juan			1796-07-01		
1635	Watson, Juan			1796-12-21		p
1636	Watson, Juan			1797-12-01		
1637	Wegins, John			1790-12-31		
1638	Wenwe, Samuel			1790-12-31		

	Names	M.C.	F.C.	Date	Spouse	Religion
1639	Wert, Henri			1795-04-19		
1640	Westbrook, Ricardo	2	4	1797-12-01	m	
1641	Westfall, Abrahaman			1789-04-22		
1642	Wetena, Cirolio			1795-11-20		p
1643	Whelan, John			1797-05-30		
1644	Whilselert, Luis			1793-03-31		p
1645	White, David			1795-02-16		
1646	White, Isaac			1796-07-24		
1647	White, Roberto			1796-07-01		
1648	White, Roberto	2	0	1797-12-01	m	
1649	Whiteside, John			1792-12-04		
1650	Whitock, Lewis			1791-12-19		
1651	Wiles, Roberto	2	0	1796-12-21	m	c
1652	Williams, Jayme			1790-01-27		
1653	Wilson, Andres			1794-05-15		
1654	Wilson, Andres	1	1	1794-12-02	m	p
1655	Wilson, Andres			1795-11-20		p
1656	Wilson, Andres			1796-07-01		
1657	Wilson, Andres			1796-12-21		p
1658	Wilson, George			1794-01-03		
1659	Wilson, George	0	1	1794-12-02	m	p
1660	Wilson, George	0	1	1795-11-20	m	p
1661	Wilson, George			1796-07-01		
1662	Wilson, George	0	1	1796-12-21	m	p
1663	Wilson, George			1797-05-30		
1664	Wilson, George	1	1	1797-12-01	m	
1665	Winsor, Cristopher			1796-07-01		
1666	Winsor, George	2	0	1796-12-21	m	p
1667	Witt, John			1795-02-16		
1668	Wood, Guillermo			1794-12-20		
1669	Wood, Guillermo			1795-11-20	m	p
1670	Wood, John			1792-09-16		
1671	Wood, Maria	0	0	1797-12-01	m	
1672	Wright, Eduardo			1789-04-22		
1673	Wright, Eduardo			1789-04-22		
1674	Wright, Guillermo			1789-04-22		
1675	Wright, Juan			1789-04-22		
1676	Ybernoin, Antonio			1795-11-20	m	c
1677	Ybernois Meloxe, Antonio	0	0	1793-03-31	m	c

	Names	M.C.	F.C.	Date	Spouse	Religion
1678	Ycant, Juan			1795-11-20		p
1679	Yones, Tomas			1793-11-20		c
1680	Yrish, Nathaniel			1790-01-27		
1681	Yspanic, Guillermo	0	0	1793-03-31	m	c

Table 23. New Madrid Militia

	Names	Rank	Date	Comments
1	Adams, Jacobo	milicia	1794-01-08	
2	Adams, Jacobo	milicia	1794-02-08	
3	Adams, Jacobo	milicia	1794-06-15	
4	Aveline, Laurent	milicia	1794-08-07	
5	Aybse, Juan	milicia	1794-01-08	
6	Barsaloux, Juan	milicia	1794-06-15	
7	Barsaloux, Juan Bautista	sargento	1794-01-08	
8	Baudouin, Jose	milicia	1794-01-07	
9	Baudouin, Jose	milicia	1794-02-08	
10	Baudouin, Jose	milicia	1794-08-07	
11	Bernardo, Pedro M.	sargento	1794-08-07	
12	Berthiame, Francisco	milicia	1794-08-07	
13	Besuard, Pedro M.	sargento	1794-01-08	
14	Besuard, Pedro M.	sargento	1794-02-08	
15	Bidle, Daniel	milicia	1794-01-08	
16	Bidle, Daniel	milicia	1794-02-08	
17	Black, Samuel	milicia	1794-06-15	
18	Bodouel, Enico	milicia	1794-08-07	
19	Bodouel, Ynico	milicia	1794-01-08	
20	Bogaud, Jacobo	milicia	1794-06-15	
21	Bonneau, Carlos	milicia	1794-01-08	
22	Bonneau, Carlos	milicia	1794-06-15	
23	Bordeleau, Pedro	milicia	1794-01-08	
24	Boyle, Byron	milicia	1794-08-07	
25	Boyle, Guillermo	milicia	1794-01-08	
26	Boyle, Guillermo	milicia	1794-08-07	
27	Brouillet	milicia	1794-02-08	
28	Brouillet, Luis	milicia	1794-01-07	
29	Brouillet, Luis	milicia	1794-01-08	
30	Brouillet, Luis	milicia	1794-02-08	
31	Brouillet, Luis	milicia	1794-06-15	
32	Brouillette, Luis	milicia	1794-08-07	
33	Brown, Juan	milicia	1794-01-08	
34	Brown, Juan	milicia	1794-02-08	
35	Causieu, Guillermo	milicia	1794-06-15	
36	Charlier, Juan Bautista	milicia	1794-08-07	
37	Chemin, Juan Bautista	milicia	1794-01-08	
38	Chemin, Juan Bautista	milicia	1794-08-07	
39	Chilard, Francisco Michel	cabo 1	1794-01-08	

	Names	Rank	Date	Comments
40	Chilard, Francisco Michel	cabo 1	1794-02-08	
41	Chilard, Francisco Michel	cabo 1	1794-06-15	
42	Chimbers, Guillermo	milicia	1794-01-08	
43	Chimbers, Guillermo	milicia	1794-02-08	
44	Clein, Juan	milicia	1794-01-07	
45	Clein, Juan	milicia	1794-02-08	
46	Clermont, Benjamin	milicia	1794-01-08	
47	Clermont, Benjamin	milicia	1794-01-08	
48	Clermont, Juan	milicia	1794-06-15	
49	Coliere, Bonaventure	milicia	1794-01-08	
50	Cool, Juan	milicia	1794-01-08	
51	Cool, Juan	milicia	1794-02-08	
52	Cool, Juan	milicia	1794-08-07	deserter
53	Cornev, Ephraim	milicia	1794-06-15	
54	Cortner, Juan	milicia	1794-01-08	
55	Cortner, Juan	milicia	1794-02-08	
56	Cortner, Juan	milicia	1794-06-15	
57	Corueu, Ephraim	milicia	1794-02-08	
58	Couieu, Ephraim	milicia	1794-01-08	
59	Courney, Francisco	cabo 2	1794-08-07	
60	Coutu, Jacobo	milicia	1794-01-08	
61	Coutu, Jacobo	milicia	1794-02-08	
62	Cuyol, Francisco	milicia	1794-01-08	
63	Daperou, Jose	milicia	1794-02-08	
64	Davis, Guillermo	milicia	1794-01-08	
65	Davis, Guillermo	milicia	1794-02-08	
66	Davis, Guillermo	milicia	1794-06-15	
67	Davis, Juan	milicia	1794-06-15	
68	Denoyon, Luis	milicia	1794-02-08	
69	Dercoupe, Francisco	milicia	1794-01-08	
70	Deroche, Pedro	capitan	1794-01-08	
71	Deroche, Pedro	capitan	1794-08-07	
72	Deroute, Paulo	milicia	1794-01-08	
73	Dorsey, Samuel	milicia	1794-06-15	
74	Drouilly, Juan Baptista	milicia	1794-01-08	
75	Drouilly, Juan Bautista	milicia	1794-02-08	
76	Drouilly, Juan Bautista	milicia	1794-08-07	
77	Drouin, Etiene	milicia	1794-01-08	
78	Ducombes, Felipe	milicia	1794-01-08	

	Names	Rank	Date	Comments
79	Dumain, Pedro	cabo 2	1794-06-15	
80	Dumais, Pedro	cabo 2	1794-01-08	
81	Dumais, Pedro	milicia	1794-01-08	
82	Dumais, Pedro	milicia	1794-08-07	
83	Dupin, Francisco Riche	cabo 1	1794-01-08	
84	Dupin, Francisco Riche	sargento	1794-08-07	
85	Dupuis, Juan Bautista	milicia	1794-01-08	
86	Dupuis, Juan Bautista	milicia	1794-08-07	
87	Eguins, Pedro	milicia	1794-01-08	
88	Eguins, Pedro	milicia	1794-08-07	
89	Feret, Juan Bautista	milicia	1794-01-07	
90	Ferrey, Juan Bautista	milicia	1794-02-08	
91	Fortiu, Juan	milicia	1794-06-15	
92	Fouchet, Bonaventure	milicia	1794-01-08	
93	Fouchet, Bonaventure	milicia	1794-02-08	
94	Fulham, Juan	cabo 1	1794-01-08	
95	Fulham, Juan	cabo 1	1794-02-08	
96	Fulhoum, Juan	milicia	1794-06-15	
97	Gamelin, Antonio	capitan	1794-01-07	
98	Geoffroy, Pedro	milicia	1794-01-08	
99	Geoffroy, Pedro	milicia	1794-06-15	
100	Goyeau, Antonio	milicia	1794-01-08	
101	Goyeau, Antonio	milicia	1794-02-08	
102	Grandjean, Juan	milicia	1794-06-15	
103	Grandjean, Juan Francisco	milicia	1794-01-08	
104	Grandjean, Juan Francisco	milicia	1794-02-08	
105	Grandjean, Juan Francisco	milicia	1794-08-07	
106	Grimard, Juan Baptista	milicia	1794-02-08	
107	Grimard, Juan Bautista	milicia	1794-01-08	
108	Grimard, Juan Bautista	milicia	1794-08-07	
109	Guerin, Juan Simon	milicia	1794-01-08	
110	Guerin, Juan Simon	milicia	1794-02-08	
111	Guerin, Juan Simon	milicia	1794-06-15	
112	Guilbaud, Carlos	cabo 2	1794-01-08	
113	Guilbaud, Carlos	cabo 2	1794-02-08	
114	Guilbaud, Carlos	cabo 2	1794-06-15	
115	Guilles, Jacobo	milicia	1794-01-08	
116	Guilmore, Juan	milicia	1794-01-08	
117	Guilmore, Juan	milicia	1794-02-08	

	Names	Rank	Date	Comments
118	Guilmore, Juan	milicia	1794-06-15	
119	Guilmore, Juan	milicia	1794-08-07	
120	Hamelin, Laurent	milicia	1794-08-07	
121	Hamer, Juan Maria	cabo 2	1794-01-08	
122	Hamer, Juan Maria	cabo 1	1794-08-07	
123	Hart, Juan	cabo 2	1794-01-08	
124	Hart, Juan	cabo 2	1794-02-08	
125	Hart, Juan	cabo 2	1794-08-07	
126	Hibert, Nicolas	milicia	1794-01-08	
127	Hibert, Nicolas	milicia	1794-08-07	
128	Horsley, Tomas	milicia	1794-01-08	
129	Horsley, Tomas	milicia	1794-02-08	
130	Houde, Juan	milicia	1794-01-08	
131	Hunot, Jose	sargento	1794-01-08	
132	Hunot, Jose	milicia	1794-01-08	
133	Hunot, Jose	sargento	1794-06-15	
134	Hunot, Jose	milicia	1794-08-07	
135	Jackson, Elijah	milicia	1794-01-08	
136	Jackson, Elijah	milicia	1794-06-15	
137	Jackson, Jesse	milicia	1794-01-08	
138	Jackson, Jesse	milicia	1794-06-15	
139	Jacob, Thomas	cabo 1	1794-06-15	
140	Jacob, Tomas	cabo 1	1794-01-08	
141	Jacob, Tomas	cabo 1	1794-02-08	
142	Jourdain, Juan	milicia	1794-08-07	
143	Laderoute, Pablo	milicia	1794-02-08	
144	Laderoute, Paulo	milicia	1794-06-15	
145	Lafleur, Jose	milicia	1794-01-08	
146	Laforge, Pedro Antonio	milicia	1794-01-08	
147	Lafreiou, Jose	cabo 2	1794-06-15	
148	Lambert, Thomas	milicia	1794-01-08	
149	Lambert, Thomas	milicia	1794-06-15	
150	Landoise, Amable	milicia	1794-08-07	
151	Langlois, Francisco	milicia	1794-01-08	
152	Langlois, Francisco	milicia	1794-02-08	
153	Lansford, Moises	cabo 1	1794-01-08	
154	Lansford, Moises	cabo 1	1794-06-15	
155	Laplante, Jose	milicia	1794-06-15	
156	Laplante, Jose	milicia	1794-01-08	

	Names	Rank	Date	Comments
157	Lariviere, Francisco	milicia	1794-01-08	
158	Lariviere, Francisco	milicia	1794-08-07	
159	Lauwureu, Jose	milicia	1794-02-08	
160	Layant, Pedro	milicia	1794-08-07	
161	Lecompte, Pedro	milicia	1794-01-08	
162	Ledoux, Pedro	milicia	1794-08-07	
163	Leduc, Cirillo	cabo 1	1794-01-08	
164	Leduc, Cirillo	cabo 1	1794-06-15	
165	Leduc, Felipe	milicia	1794-01-08	
166	Leduc, Felipe	cabo 2	1794-08-07	
167	Leduc, Jose	milicia	1794-01-08	
168	Leduc, Jose	milicia	1794-08-07	
169	Lefleur, Jose	milicia	1794-06-15	
170	Legrand, Jose	milicia	1794-08-07	
171	Legrand, Juan	milicia	1794-06-15	
172	Leonard, Francisco	milicia	1794-08-07	
173	Lesieur, Francisco	teniente	1794-02-08	
174	Lesieur, Francisco	teniente	1794-06-15	
175	Lesieur, Jose	milicia	1794-01-08	
176	Lesieur, Jose	subt	1794-08-07	
177	Lie, Guillermo	milicia	1794-01-08	
178	Loirier, Paulo	milicia	1794-01-08	
179	Long, James	milicia	1794-08-07	
180	Longue, Felis	milicia	1794-08-07	
181	Maisonville, Jose	milicia	1794-01-08	
182	Maisonville, Jose	milicia	1794-02-08	
183	Maisonville, Juan	milicia	1794-08-07	
184	Maisonville, Juan Bautista	milicia	1794-01-08	
185	Maisonville, Juan Bautista	milicia	1794-08-07	
186	Malbete, Moises	milicia	1794-06-15	
187	Marchand, Didier	milicia	1794-01-08	
188	Marchand, Didier	milicia	1794-08-07	
189	Maurice, Juan Bautista	milicia	1794-01-08	
190	Mayers, Jacobo	sargento	1794-01-08	
191	Mayers, Jacobo	sargento	1794-06-15	
192	McCay, Roberto	subt.	1794-01-08	
193	McChisholm, Hugh	cabo 2	1794-01-08	
194	McChisholm, Hugh	cabo 2	1794-06-15	
195	Mellon, Arthur	milicia	1794-08-07	

	Names	Rank	Date	Comments
196	Meloche, Antonio	milicia	1794-01-08	
197	Meloche, Antonio	milicia	1794-02-08	
198	Meloche, Antonio	milicia	1794-06-15	
199	Mercier, Pedro	milicia	1794-01-08	
200	Mock, Guillermo	milicia	1794-01-08	
201	Mock, Guillermo	milicia	1794-06-15	
202	Noyon, Luis	milicia	1794-01-07	
203	Noyon, Luis	milicia	1794-08-07	
204	Ofman, Frederic	milicia	1794-01-08	
205	Ofman, Frederic	milicia	1794-02-08	
206	Oneille, Jose	milicia	1794-01-08	
207	Oneille, Jose	sargento	1794-02-08	
208	Oneille, Jose	sargento	1794-06-15	
209	Pamard, Romano	cabo 2	1794-01-08	
210	Pamard, Romano	cabo 1	1794-08-07	
211	Paquin, Francisco	milicia	1794-01-08	
212	Paquin, Francisco	milicia	1794-02-08	
213	Paquin, Francisco	milicia	1794-06-15	
214	Peinne, Jacobo	milicia	1794-01-08	
215	Perron, Amable	milicia	1794-01-08	
216	Perron, Amable	milicia	1794-02-08	
217	Perron, Amable	milicia	1794-08-07	
218	Petit, Antonio	milicia	1794-01-08	
219	Petit, Antonio	milicia	1794-02-08	
220	Poirieu, Pedro	milicia	1794-06-15	
221	Pordun, Thomas	milicia	1794-01-08	
222	Pordun, Thomas	milicia	1794-02-08	
223	Pretgel, Juan	milicia	1794-01-08	
224	Pretgel, Juan	milicia	1794-01-08	
225	Pretgel, Juan	milicia	1794-08-07	deserter
226	Pretget, Juan	milicia	1794-06-15	
227	Quirot, Juan	milicia	1794-08-07	
228	Racine, Francisco	milicia	1794-01-08	
229	Racine, Francisco	milicia	1794-06-15	
230	Racine, Juan Baptista	milicia	1794-01-08	
231	Racine, Juan Baptista	milicia	1794-06-15	
232	Rayen, Jacobo	milicia	1794-01-08	
233	Rayen, James	milicia	1794-06-15	
234	Rayley, Michel	milicia	1794-01-08	

	Names	Rank	Date	Comments
235	Rayley, Michel	milicia	1794-02-08	
236	Rayley, Michel	milicia	1794-06-15	
237	Ree, Azov	subt	1794-01-08	
238	Rees, Azon	subt.	1794-02-08	
239	Rees, Azon	subt.	1794-06-15	
240	Robot, Georges	milicia	1794-01-08	
241	Robot, Georges	milicia	1794-06-15	
242	Roch, Augusto	milicia	1794-01-08	
243	Roch, Augusto	milicia	1794-02-08	
244	Roch, Augusto	milicia	1794-06-15	
245	Roubi, Antonio Jose	milicia	1794-01-08	
246	Rouby, Antonio	milicia	1794-06-15	
247	Sabourin, Pedro	milicia	1794-01-08	
248	Sabourin, Pedro	milicia	1794-06-15	
249	Saint Aubin, Luis	milicia	1794-01-08	
250	Saint Aubin, Luis	milicia	1794-02-08	
251	Saint Aubin, Luis	milicia	1794-06-15	
252	Salier, Juan Bautista	milicia	1794-01-07	
253	Salier, Juan Bautista	milicia	1794-02-08	
254	Salier, Juan Bautista	milicia	1794-08-07	
255	Salou, Juan Francisco	cabo 1	1794-02-08	
256	Saloue, Juan Francisco	cabo 1	1794-01-07	
257	Samson, Alexandro	cabo 2	1794-02-08	
258	Samson, Alexandro	cabo 2	1794-06-15	
259	Santa Maria, Estevan	milicia	1794-01-08	
260	Santa Maria, Estevan	milicia	1794-02-08	
261	Santa Maria, Estevan	milicia	1794-06-15	
262	Santa Maria, Francisco	milicia	1794-01-08	
263	Santa Maria, Francisco	cabo 1	1794-06-15	
264	Santa Maria, Jose	sargento	1794-01-08	
265	Santa Maria, Jose	sargento	1794-02-08	
266	Santa Maria, Jose	sargento	1794-06-15	
267	Sasfrai, Pedro	milicia	1794-01-08	
268	Servant, Pedro	milicia	1794-01-08	
269	Sigues, Juan	milicia	1794-06-15	
270	Siuwwieux, Jose	milicia	1794-01-08	
271	Story, Jose	sargento	1794-01-08	
272	Story, Jose	sargento	1794-02-08	
273	Story, Jose	sargento	1794-08-07	

	Names	Rank	Date	Comments
274	Tarteron de Labeaume, Luis	sargento	1794-01-08	
275	Tarteron de labeaume, Luis	sargento	1794-08-07	
276	Teissieu, Nicolas	milicia	1794-02-08	
277	Teusieu, Nicolas	milicia	1794-01-07	
278	Theque, Juan	milicia	1794-06-15	
279	Thompson, Isaac	milicia	1794-02-08	
280	Thompson, Isario	milicia	1794-06-15	
281	Thompson, Isemerio	milicia	1794-01-07	
282	Thorn, Carlos	milicia	1794-01-08	
283	Thorn, Carlos	milicia	1794-02-08	
284	Thorn, Carlos	milicia	1794-06-15	
285	Thorn, Daniel	milicia	1794-06-15	
286	Thorn, Salomon	milicia	1794-01-08	
287	Thorn, Salomon	milicia	1794-08-07	deserter
288	Toulers, Guillermo	milicia	1794-06-15	
289	Trocaubrout, Juan	milicia	1794-01-08	
290	Trocaubrout, Juan	milicia	1794-08-07	
291	Trocaubrout, Juan	milicia	1794-02-08	
292	Tybse, Juan	milicia	1794-02-08	
293	Vachet, Francisco	milicia	1794-01-08	
294	Vachet, Francisco	milicia	1794-02-08	
295	Vadeboncoeur, Pedro	milicia	1794-01-08	
296	Vadeboncoeur, Pedro	milicia	1794-08-07	
297	Waters, Ricardo Juan	teniente	1794-01-08	
298	Waters, Ricardo Juan	capitan	1794-06-15	
299	Welet, Francisco	cabo 2	1794-01-08	
300	Welet, Francisco	cabo 2	1794-02-08	
301	Wilson, Andauve	milicia	1794-06-15	
302	Wilson, George	milicia	1794-06-15	
303	Youet, Rossel	milicia	1794-06-15	

Table 24. New Madrid Origins and Destinations

	Names	M.C.	F.C.	Date	M.S.	Origin/Destination
1	Alley, Juan	2	0	1795-08-08	m	Fort Pitt/
2	Alley, Tomas	1	0	1795-08-08	m	Fort Pitt/
3	Barns, Bernardo	1	0	1795-08-08	m	Fort Pitt/
4	Besmet, Joel			1796-07-01		/Natchez
5	Bogard, Basilio	3	0	1795-08-08	m	Fort Pitt/
6	Boissy, Joseph			1791-04-30		Galiapolis/
7	Born, Juan			1796-07-01		/Illinois
8	Bryan, Adam			1796-07-01		/America
9	Bryane, Andres			1796-07-01		/Natchez
10	Burney, Nicolas			1791-04-30		Fort Pitt/
11	Burns, Miguel	5	4	1795-08-08	m	Fort Pitt/
12	Campbell, woman			1796-07-01		/unknown
13	Clermont, Juan Bta.			1796-07-01		/Puesto Vincinnes
14	Collot, Juan Luis			1791-04-30	m	Galiapolis/
15	Colvet, Julian			1791-04-30		Fort Pitt/
16	Cookes, Andres			1796-07-01		/Illinois
17	Cool, Jacobo			1796-07-01		/left for debts
18	Cory, Yeaeke			1791-04-30		Fort Pitt/
19	Cox, Andres	1	0	1795-08-08	m	Fort Pitt/
20	Crusin, C. Causin			1791-04-30		Galiapolis/
21	Davis, Guillermo			1796-07-01		/Illinois of USA
22	Denoyon, Luis			1796-07-01		/Puesto Vincinnes
23	Dirmont, Juan			1796-07-01		/New Orleans
24	Dode, Luis			1791-04-30		Galiapolis/
25	Douairon, Jose			1796-07-01		/unknown
26	Dugan, Guillermo			1796-07-01		/Canada
27	Farmy, Juan			1796-07-01		/unknown
28	Grimas, Carlos			1796-07-01		/Puesto Vincennes
29	Halley, ...			1796-07-01		/Illinois
30	Halley, Tomas			1796-07-01		/Illinois
31	Harpin, Joseph			1791-04-30		Puesto Vensen/
32	Haus, George			1796-07-01		/Natchez
33	Hilton, Guillermo			1796-07-01		/Natchez
34	Hooper, William			1796-07-01		/Natchez
35	Hooson, Francisco			1796-07-01		/husband left
36	Horten, Antonio			1796-07-01		/Natchez
37	Hubeault, Francisco			1791-04-30		Puesto Vensen/
38	Jonson, Pedro			1796-07-01		/Natchez
39	Kilwell, Elvington	5	3	1795-08-08	w	Fort Pitt/

	Names	M.C.	F.C.	Date	M.S.	Origin/Destination
40	Lafonse, Jayme			1791-04-30		Galiapolis/
41	Legrand, (widow of)			1791-04-30	w	Puesto Vensen/
42	Legrand, Jose			1791-04-30		Puesto Vensen/
43	Legrand, Juan Maria			1791-04-30		Puesto Vensen/
44	Lepes, Nicolas			1796-07-01		/Natchez
45	Liebert, Felipe			1796-07-01		/Natchez
46	Luistes, Juan			1796-07-01		/Natchez
47	Margarita, Claudio			1791-04-30		Galiapolis/
48	McColums, Anselme			1796-07-01		/Natchez
49	McKoy, Guillermo	3	5	1795-08-08	m	Fort Pitt/
50	Miller, Frederick			1796-07-01		/Illinois
51	Moores, Juan			1796-07-01		/Natchez
52	Nany, woman			1796-07-01		/New Orleans
53	Nicolas, Juan			1796-07-01		/Natchez
54	Noel, Ambrosio			1791-04-30		Galiapolis/
55	Parker, Samuel	6	4	1795-08-08	m	Fort Pitt/
56	Philips, Antonio			1796-07-01		/Natchez
57	Rasles, Mathieu			1796-07-01		/Kentucky
58	Rooper, Leonard			1796-07-01		/left for debts
59	Seguin, Jayme			1791-04-30		Puesto Vensen/
60	Selby, David	5	3	1795-08-08	m	Fort Pitt/
61	Shepard, Juan			1796-07-01		/Natchez
62	Simple, David			1796-07-01		/Natchez
63	Smith, Simeon			1796-07-01		/Illinois
64	Smith, Tomas			1796-07-01		/unknown
65	Somes, Juan			1796-07-01		/Sta Genoveva
66	Upham, Roberto			1796-07-01		/Natchez
67	Vachette, Antonio			1796-07-01		/Puesto Vincinnes
68	Villanueva, Carlos			1791-04-30		Puesto Vensen/

Table 25. Other Missouri Names

	Names	Religion	Town	Date	Origin
1	Aime, Charles	c	New Bourbon	1797	Creole
2	Alary, Baptista		St. Louis	1782	
3	Amelen, Lorenzo		St. Louis	1782	
4	Anchí, Agustin		St. Louis	1782	
5	Androzy, Johne	Presbyterian	New Bourbon	1797	America
6	Antaya, Jacobo		St. Louis	1782	
7	Antayá, Miguel		Sta. Genoveva	1787/89	
8	Antaya, Pedro		St. Louis	1782	
9	Barbier, M.	c	New Bourbon	1797	French
10	Bartolome, Pedro		Sta. Genoveva	1787/89	
11	Basó, Maria (widow)		St. Louis	1787/89	
12	Bauvé, Jayme		Sta. Genoveva	1787/89	
13	Bauvin, Vital		Sta. Genoveva	1787/89	
14	Beluar, La Ve.	c	New Bourbon	1797	Creole
15	Bequet, Gabriel		St. Louis	1782	
16	Bequet, Pedro		St. Louis	1782	
17	Bergeron, Antonio		St. Louis	1782	
18	Bernar, Estevan		St. Louis	1782	
19	Bernier, Francisco	c	New Bourbon	1797	Canadian
20	Bernier, La Ve.	c	New Bourbon	1797	Canadian
21	Bienbenu, Jose		St. Louis	1782	
22	Bives, Jean	c	New Bourbon	1797	America
23	Boden, Jose		St. Louis	1782	
24	Boise, Joseph	Methodist	New Bourbon	1797	Irish
25	Bolen, Gabriel	c	New Bourbon	1797	Creole
26	Bolen, Hypotite	c	New Bourbon	1797	Creole
27	Brasó, Maria (widow)		St. Louis	1787/89	
28	Brasot, Luis		St. Louis	1787/89	
29	Brosar, Pedro		St. Louis	1782	
30	Brunet, Baupta.		St. Louis	1782	
31	Buat, Luis		Sta. Genoveva	1787/89	
32	Burget, John	Presbyterian	New Bourbon	1797	America
33	Burie, Barna	c	New Bourbon	1797	America
34	Buris, Luis		St. Louis	1782	
35	Burne, Michel	c	New Bourbon	1797	Irish
36	Buve, Maturen		St. Louis	1787/89	
37	Cadore, Juan Baupta		St. Louis	1782	
38	Caillotdislachance, N.	c	New Bourbon	1797	French
39	Callordia	Anglican	New Bourbon	1797	America

285

	Names	Religion	Town	Date	Origin
40	Cauben, Gulillaume	Anglican	New Bourbon	1797	America
41	Charlevil, Francisco		St. Louis	1787/89	
42	Charteuil, Francisco		St. Louis	1787/89	
43	Chevalier, Pierre	c	New Bourbon	1797	Creole
44	Clark, David	Anabaptist	New Bourbon	1797	America
45	Clark, Francisco	Anglican	New Bourbon	1797	America
46	Clermon, Luis		St. Louis	1782	
47	Cork, Andre	Anabaptist	New Bourbon	1797	America
48	Custard, Frederik	Anglican	New Bourbon	1797	America
49	Dany, Juan Baupta.		St. Louis	1782	
50	Davis, Human	Anglican	New Bourbon	1797	America
51	Dayby, Francisco		St. Louis	1782	
52	Deghire, Paul	c	New Bourbon	1797	Creole
53	Deghize, Andres	c	New Bourbon	1797	Creole
54	Dehault, Pierre Charles	c	New Bourbon	1797	French
55	Delina, Juan Baptista		St. Louis	1787/89	
56	Delisla, Carlos		St. Louis	1787/89	
57	Delisla, Juan Baptista		St. Louis	1787/89	
58	Delisla, Luis		St. Louis	1787/89	
59	Depres, Rene		St. Louis	1782	
60	Detete, Luis		St. Louis	1782	
61	Die, Baupta. de		St. Louis	1782	
62	Dod, Joseph		St. Louis	1787/89	
63	Dodge, John	c	New Bourbon	1797	America
64	Donaou, Joseph	Anglican	New Bourbon	1797	America
65	Donate, Baptista		St. Louis	1787/89	
66	Dorin, Pedro		St. Louis	1782	
67	Dougu, Joseph	Presbyterian	New Bourbon	1797	America
68	Dubaguer, Joseph		St. Louis	1787/89	
69	Dubois, Agustin		St. Louis	1782	
70	Duplesix, Jose		St. Louis	1782	
71	Duval, James	Anglican	New Bourbon	1797	America
72	Duval, John	Anglican	New Bourbon	1797	America
73	Duville, Joaquin		St. Louis	1782	
74	Fenewick, Joseph	p	New Bourbon	1797	America
75	Ferelle, James	Anglican	New Bourbon	1797	America
76	Ferelle, Richard	Anglican	New Bourbon	1797	America
77	Fidechamy, Andre		St. Louis	1782	
78	Fontiny, Jose		St. Louis	1782	

	Names	Religion	Town	Date	Origin
79	Francor, Jose		St. Louis	1782	
80	Gakar, Eliasar	Anglican	New Bourbon	1797	America
81	Gañe, Amable		St. Louis	1787/89	
82	Gensack, M	c	New Bourbon	1797	French
83	Gimes, M. de	c	New Bourbon	1797	America
84	Gonrot, Etienne	c	New Bourbon	1797	Creole
85	Graham, James	Anglican	New Bourbon	1797	America
86	Grenie, Francisco		St. Louis	1782	
87	Griffardo, Alexic	c	New Bourbon	1797	Canadian
88	Haby, M.	c	New Bourbon	1797	America
89	Hales, William	Anglican	New Bourbon	1797	America
90	Haley, William	c	New Bourbon	1797	America
91	Hamilton, Georges	c	New Bourbon	1797	America
92	Hart, Barne	Anglican	New Bourbon	1797	America
93	Hastone, William	Anglican	New Bourbon	1797	America
94	Hayens, James	Anglican	New Bourbon	1797	America
95	Hiwe	Anglican	New Bourbon	1797	America
96	Janis, Nicolas		Sta. Genoveva	1787/89	
97	Japén, Francisco		St. Louis	1787/89	
98	Johnson, Nathan	Anglican	New Bourbon	1797	America
99	Jones	Anglican	New Bourbon	1797	America
100	Jonson, George	Anglican	New Bourbon	1797	America
101	Jonston, Nicolas	Anglican	New Bourbon	1797	America
102	Jordan, Baupta.		St. Louis	1782	
103	Jordan, Noel		St. Louis	1782	
104	La Flama, Jose		St. Louis	1782	
105	La Fortuna, Rene		St. Louis	1782	
106	La Porta, Jose		St. Louis	1782	
107	La Puente, Pedro		St. Louis	1782	
108	Lachance, Antoine	c	New Bourbon	1797	Creole
109	Lachance, François	c	New Bourbon	1797	Creole
110	Lachance, Gabriel	c	New Bourbon	1797	Creole
111	Lachance, Joseph	c	New Bourbon	1797	Creole
112	Lachanchance, Jean B.	c	New Bourbon	1797	Creole
113	Lachanse, Gabriel		Sta. Genoveva	1787/89	
114	Lachanse, Nicholas		Sta. Genoveva	1787/89	
115	Lachanse, Nicholas (jr.)		Sta. Genoveva	1787/89	
116	Lachor, Antonio		St. Louis	1782	
117	Lacombe, Louis	c	New Bourbon	1797	Canadian

	Names	Religion	Town	Date	Origin
118	Lacombe, Nicols	c	New Bourbon	1797	Creole
119	Lacrisp, Francisco	c	New Bourbon	1797	Canadian
120	Lacróa, Juan Baptista		St. Louis	1787/89	
121	Lacutura, Jose		St. Louis	1782	
122	Ladosor, Antonio		St. Louis	1782	
123	Ladosor, Pedro		St. Louis	1782	
124	Lahe, Antonio		St. Louis	1782	
125	Lalivertad, Jose		St. Louis	1782	
126	Lamarcha, Baptista		St. Louis	1787/89	
127	Langloa, Jose		St. Louis	1782	
128	Languy, Pedro		St. Louis	1782	
129	LaRive, Jacobo		St. Louis	1782	
130	Lebo, Pedro		St. Louis	1782	
131	LeConte, Guillermo		St. Louis	1782	
132	Ledu, Luis		St. Louis	1782	
133	LeFebre, Lorenzo		St. Louis	1782	
134	Legran, Jean Marie	c	New Bourbon	1797	Canadian
135	Lelivertou, Baupta.		St. Louis	1782	
136	Lorenzo, Baupta.		St. Louis	1782	
137	Lorimu., Luis		Sta. Genoveva	1787/89	
138	Lorini, Luis		Sta. Genoveva	1787/89	
139	Maddin, Thomas	Anglican	New Bourbon	1797	Irish
140	Magloglin	Anglican	New Bourbon	1797	America
141	Maurice	c	New Bourbon	1797	Canadian
142	Maye, Juan Baupta.		St. Louis	1782	
143	McLeanham	Anglican	New Bourbon	1797	America
144	McLehlil, Alexandro	Anglican	New Bourbon	1797	America
145	McNeal, James	Anglican	New Bourbon	1797	America
146	Meredie, Daniel	Anglican	New Bourbon	1797	America
147	Mersié, Carlos		St. Louis	1787/89	
148	Metic, Jerome	c	New Bourbon	1797	Creole
149	Montgomery, David	p	New Bourbon	1797	America
150	Montmirel, Joseph	c	New Bourbon	1797	Canadian
151	More de Chanp, Jose		St. Louis	1782	
152	Moren, Antonio		St. Louis	1787/89	
153	Moron, Antonio		St. Louis	1787/89	
154	Neivson, James	Anglican	New Bourbon	1797	America
155	Nicole, Gabriel	c	New Bourbon	1797	Creole
156	Pelher	Anglican	New Bourbon	1797	America

	Names	Religion	Town	Date	Origin
157	Perodot, Joseph	c	New Bourbon	1797	Creole
158	Perrolly, Jeremie	Anglican	New Bourbon	1797	America
159	Peyroux, M Henry	c	New Bourbon	1797	French
160	Pino, Jose		St. Louis	1782	
161	Plaine, Daily	Presbyterian	New Bourbon	1797	America
162	Portugais, Francisco	c	New Bourbon	1797	Portugal
163	Richar, Bartolome		St. Louis	1787/89	
164	Richer, Bartolome		St. Louis	1787/89	
165	Richet, Baptiste	c	New Bourbon	1797	Creole
166	Rida, Lorenzo		St. Louis	1782	
167	Roque, Agustin		St. Louis	1787/89	
168	Roy, Andres		St. Louis	1787/89	
169	Roy, Jose		St. Louis	1782	
170	Samoncaud, Fran	c	New Bourbon	1797	Canadian
171	Samuel, M.	Presbyterian	New Bourbon	1797	America
172	San Pedro, Julian		St. Louis	1782	
173	Scott, Joseph	Anglican	New Bourbon	1797	America
174	Selle, Joseph de		Sta. Genoveva	1787/89	
175	Simoneau, Francisco		Sta. Genoveva	1787/89	
176	Sinal, Tomas		Sta. Genoveva	1787/89	
177	Smith, Henry	Anglican	New Bourbon	1797	America
178	Stroder	Presbyterian	New Bourbon	1797	America
179	Sulien, Louis	c	New Bourbon	1797	Canadian
180	Susomo, Rene		St. Louis	1782	
181	Tanis, Nicolas		Sta. Genoveva	1787/89	
182	Tesserot, Joseph	c	New Bourbon	1797	Canadian
183	Tomson, James	Anglican	New Bourbon	1797	America
184	Toroche, Pedro		St. Louis	1787/89	
185	Trichel, Juan Baupta		St. Louis	1782	
186	Troche, Pedro		St. Louis	1787/89	
187	Vivie, Jose		St. Louis	1782	
188	Waiser, Jacob	p	New Bourbon	1797	German
189	Walker, Benjamin	Anglican	New Bourbon	1797	America
190	Wistor, Job	p	New Bourbon	1797	America

References Cited

Anonymous

1959-1963. **Archivo General Militar de Segovia: Indice de Expedientes Personales**. 9 vols. Ediciones Hidalguia: Madrid.

1979. **Archivos del Estado**. Dirección General del Patrimonio Artístico, Archivos y Museos, Subdirección General de Archivos: Madrid.

Bermúdez Plata, Cristóbal
1949. **Catálogo de Documentas de la Sección Novena**. Volume 1. Consejo Superior de Investigaciones Cientificas, Escuela de Estudios Hispano-Americanos de Seville: Seville.

Coker, William S. and G. Douglas Inglis
1980. **The Spanish Censuses of Pensacola, 1784-1820: A Genealogical Guide to Spanish Pensacola**. The Perdido Bay Press: Pensacola, Florida.

Davis, Edwin Adams
1971. **Louisiana, A Narrative History**. Baton Rouge, Louisiana: Claitor's Publishing Division.

Gil Merino, Antonio
1976. **Archivo Historico del Reino de Galicia, Coruna, Guia del Investigador**. Ministerio de Educacion y Ciencia: Madrid.

Gomez Canedo, Lino
1961. **Los Archivos de la Historia de America. Instituto Panamericano de Geografía e Historia**: Mexico, D.F.

Gonzalez Yanes, Emma
1984. **Guía del Archivo Histórico Provincial de Santa Cruz de Tenerife**. Gobierno de Canarias, Consejeria de Cultura y Deportes: Santa Cruz de Tenerife.

Guillén y Tato, Julio
1953. **Indice de los papeles de la Sección Corso y Presas (1784-1837), Archivo General de Marina D. Alvaro de Bazán**. 2 vols. Institutos Francisco de Vitoria e Consejo Superior de Investigaciones Cientificas Ministerio de Marina: Madrid.

Hill, Roscoe P.
1916. **Descriptive Catalogue of the Documents Relating to the History of the United States in the Papeles Procendentes de Cuba Deposited in the Archivo General de indias at Seville**. Washington, D.C.: Carnegie Institution of Washington.

Hoffman, Paul E.
1980. "A Guide to Field Research in Spain for the Family Historian, with Special Reference to Louisiana." **New Orleans Genesis** 19:73:January. Genealogical Research Society of New Orleans, New Orleans, Louisiana.

La Pena y Camara, Jose de, Ernest J. Burrus, Charles Edwards O'Neil, Maria Teresa Garcia Fernandez
1968. **Catalogo de Documentos del Archivo General de Indias, Seccion V, Gobierno, Audiencia de Santo Domingo**. Volume 1. New Orleans: Loyola University.

Lopez Gomez, Pedro, con la colaboracion de Maria de la O Suárez
1988. **Archivo del Reino de Galicia, Catalogo de Instrumentos de Descripcion Documental**. Madrid: Ministerio de Cultura.

Magdaleno, Ricardo
1958. **Secretaria de Guerra (Siglo XVIII)**. Catalogo XXII. Valladolid: Archivo de Simancas.

McDermott, John Francis
1974. "The Myth of the 'Imbecile Governor'-Captain Fernando de Leyba and the Defense of St. Louis in 1780," pp. 314-405. **The Spanish in the Mississippi Valley, 1762-1804**. John Francis McDermott, editor. Urbana, Illinois: University of Illinois Press.

Montero de Pedro, Jose
1979. **Españoles en Nueva Orleans y Luisiana**. Madrid: Ediciones Cultura Hispania del Centro Ibero Americano de Cooperacion.

Morales, Diego
1714. **El Estado de las Poblaciones del Ytza y Peten**. AGI Guatemala 196.

Plaza Bores, Angel de la
1986. **Guia del Investigador, Archivo General de Simancas**.
Madrid: Ministerio de Cultura, Dirección General de Bellas Artes y
Archivos.

Tebeau, Charlton W.
1971. **A History of Florida**. Coral Gables, Florida: University of
Miami Press.

Vaquerito Gil, Manuel, María Blanca Alvarez Pinedo, Agustin Rodriguez
Fernández, Manuel de Arce Vivanco.
1980. **Archivo Historico Provincial de Santander**. Madrid:
Ministerio de Cultura.

Vigón Sánchez, Ana Maria
1985. **Guia del Archivo Museo "D. Alvaro de Bazan", Viso del
Marques**. Madrid: Instituto de Historia y Cultura Naval.

296

Boyds, Alexandre 147
Boyer, Andres 235
Boyer, Francisco 235
Boyer, Francois 235
Boyer, Santos 235
Boyers, Coupaints 235
Boyers, Enrique 167
Boyle, Byron 275
Boyle, Connel 206, 235
Boyle, Guillermo 235, 275
Boyle, John 167
Boyle, Philip 235
Boylon, Aron 235
Boyo, Alexandro 167
Bozeland, John 122
Brabeson, Nicolas 147
Brachelos, Juan 60
Brachflor, C. 167
Braday, John 30
Bradee, Carlos 80
Bradford, Abelard 70
Bradford, David 70, 80
Bradford, E. (son) 71
Bradford, Leonardo 71
Bradford, Nathan 71
Bradley, Henry 30
Bradley, Richard 80
Bradly, John 206
Brady, John 30
Brahan, Santiago 80
Braken, Mary 38
Bramwell 38
Bramwell, Tomas 38
Branan, Jose 206
Branard, Jacobo 235
Brand, John 167
Brand, Jorge 206
Brandon 80
Brandon, Christopher 147
Brandon, Gerard 122, 132, 147, 167

Branle, Federico 206
Branton, Jean 80
Brasbean, B. 103, 167
Brasfield, Joshua 132
Brashars, Tobias 167
Brashcart, Tobias 103, 167
Brashear, Job 167
Brashears, B. 103, 147
Brashier, Jesse 49, 56
Brasó, Maria (widow) 285
Brasot, Luis 285
Brassell, Robert 132
Brasseue, Blse. 80
Bratson, Guillermo 206
Brau, Firmin 80
Braveler, John 80
Brawn, Tomas 167
Brayen, Juan 206
Brazeal, Eliza 30
Breen, Joseph 122
Brenan, James 167
Brenan, Jayme 60
Brenton, John 80
Bresino, Francisco 147
Brest, Juan 206
Brian, Jeremias (wife of) 167
Brian, John 206
Bridis, John 167
Brigate, Adam 80
Briggs, William 38
Brignac, Ve 80
Brinly, John 167
Brislow, J. 38
Briston, John 38
Briton, Jose 206
Bro, Jose 71
Brobston, Nicolas 147
Brocas, W. 103, 122, 167
Brockham, William 167
Brockway, Jesse 167

Broconte, George 167
Brocus, William 132, 147, 167
Brodemigue, Richard 80
Broder, Guillermo 167
Broderick, Guillermo 80, 202
Brody, Juan 122
Brohier, Robert 38
Brohun, G. B. 38
Brokes, David 206
Bronen, Jum 80
Bronnahan, Juan 49, 56
Brooke, Juan 168
Brosar, Pedro 285
Brosard, Francisco 71
Brosard, Pedro 80
Brosset 80
Brosua, Pedro 60
Brotte 71
Brough, Richard 168
Brouillet 275
Brouillet, Juan 25
Brouillet, Louis 235, 275
Brouillet, Luis (father) 235
Brouillet, Luis (son) 235
Brouillette, Luis 235, 275
Brouin, Francisco 235
Broussard, Amt 80
Broussard, Crugin. 80
Broussard, Fr. 80
Broussard, J. B. 80
Broussard, Ls. 80
Broussard, Pre 80
Broussard, Rene 80
Broussard, S. 80
Broussard, Silvn. 80
Broussard, Thre 80
Broussard, Yh 80
Broutin, Naciso 25
Brovim, Jus 206

Brown 80
Brown, David 80
Brown, Ephrain 60
Brown, G. 80, 103, 168
Brown, J. S. 80
Brown, Jacob 103, 132, 147
Brown, James 30, 80, 168, 206
Brown, Jediah 132
Brown, John 30, 80, 132, 168, 235, 275
Brown, Julian 235
Brown, N. 103, 132, 147, 168
Brown, O. 104, 122, 132, 147, 168
Brown, Samuel 206
Brown, Thomas 30, 122, 168
Brown, W. 104, 122, 132, 147, 168, 235
Brownin, Ben 25
Bruce, James 49, 56
Brudhomme 80
Bruiet, Francisco 235
Bruiet, Miguel 235
Bruin, Pedro 104, 168
Bruin, Pedro Brian 147, 168
Brulli, Louis 235
Brumberry, William 80
Brumfield 81
Brunel 81
Brunel, Elias 104, 147
Bruner, Guillermo 30
Bruner, Jorge 30
Bruner, Juan 30
Brunet, Baupta. 285
Brunt, James 147
Bryan, Adam 283
Bryan, Dave 235
Bryan, Jeremiah 104,

122, 132, 147
Bryan, William 202
Bryane, Andres 283
Bste., Ja. 81
Buasfield, Rowlen 202
Buat, Luis 285
Buciere, Miguel 49, 56
Buciguin, Francisco 30
Buck, John 71
Buckholls, Peter 168
Buda, Pablo Dominic 81
Bueralter, George 168
Bugeoz 81
Bugley, Francisco 60
Buinay, John 81
Buker, Anthony 147
Bukly, Adam 147
Bule, Absolum 38
Bull, Absolam 38
Bull, John 168
Bullen, John 104, 122, 147, 168
Bullen, Joseph 168
Bullert, Perminus 168
Bullock, Benjamin 104, 147, 168
Bullock, John 132
Bullock, Jorge 122
Bullol, Etien 206
Bullon, Juan 81
Bun, Jacob 81
Bungo, Jose Pero 60
Bungo, William 168
Buraw, George 235
Burch, Guillermo 104, 168
Burch, Jacques 71
Burch, Jeremias 81
Burch, Juan 168
Burch, Santiago 71
Burd, Sutton 38
Bureau, John 81
Burel, Benjamin 147

Burel, George 147
Burell, Tomas 38
Burgde, William 168
Burget, John 285
Burgis, Engiber 47
Burie, Barna 285
Buriens, Jame 168
Buris, Luis 285
Burk, John 168
Burk, Stephen 206
Burke, Carlos 81
Burke, Mary 38
Burke, Stephen 235
Burke, Tomas 206
Burling, Tomas 104, 168
Burman, Luvlhy 168
Burne, Michel 285
Burner, John 147
Burner, Soloman 132
Burnet, D. 31, 104, 123, 168
Burnet, John 104, 123, 132, 148, 168, 206
Burnet, William 31
Burnett, Benjamin 81
Burnett, D. 81
Burnett, John 168
Burnett, William 31
Burney, Nicolas 283
Burney, Simon 132, 148
Burns 49, 56
Burns, Miguel 235, 283
Burns, Patrick 132
Burns, Samuel 168
Burns, Thomas 168
Burns, William 49, 56
Burrel, Curtis 132
Burrell, Nelly 38
Burry, Nicholas 235
Bursly, James 206
Burton, Jera. 38
Bushnell, Eusebio 60, 168

300

Busk, Reubin 168
Buskirk, Thomas 168
Bussh, Samuel 168
Butayllen, Francisco 234
Buter, Joseph 168
Butin, Samuel 206
Butler, Nataniel 104, 168
Butler, Thomas 168
Butman, Estevan 60
Buve, Maturen 285
Byarad, John 81
Byrne, Michael 236
Cablar, Juan 49
Cable, Jacob 104, 123, 132, 148, 169
Cabral, Matias 49
Cabrera, Baltazar 50
Cabrera, Josefa 50
Cabshar, Jean 81
Cacan Cooper, Enrique 169
Cacaup, Nicolas 25
Cacenhot, Jacob 169
Cacerey, John 169
Cadore, J. Baupta 285
Cafe, Guilliaum 132
Cagel, John 169
Caillotdislachance, N. 285
Cain, Guillermo 60
Caison Cuper, Henry 148
Caldaucle, Ysaac 148
Calder, Maria 50
Calduel, Juan 206
Caldwel, Jayme 236
Cale, Nehemiah 38
Calen, Thomas 206
Calender, A. 104, 133, 148, 169
Caler, Joseph 133
Calhoon, James 169
Callaghan, Daniel 169

Calleghan, Pañ. 81
Calliham, David 202
Calliham, John 202
Callordia 285
Calot, John 104, 148
Calue, Juan Francisco 236
Calvert, Thomas 133
Calvet, the Widow 104, 169
Calvet, William 104, 133, 169
Calvit, F. 104, 123, 132, 148, 169
Calvit, John 123, 132, 148
Calvit, Joseph 104, 123, 132, 148, 169
Calvit, Thomas 104, 123, 132, 148, 169
Calvit, William 104, 123, 132, 148, 169
Cambell, Santiago 206
Came 81
Camel, James 81
Camell, Carlos 236
Cameron, Evan 133
Cammack, Christopher 236
Camotée, De. 81
Campbell, Archibald 38
Campbell, Catalina 236
Campbell, Colin 39
Campbell, Graham 39
Campbell, James 169
Campbell, Jean 71
Campbell, Peter 236
Campbell, R. 104, 123, 133, 169
Campbell, woman 283
Campeat, Joseph 236
Campeau, Joseph 236
Campo 81

Campo, Ypolito 236
Camus, Pedro 104, 123, 169
Cand, Jonathan 39
Canen, Guillermo 236
Cannes, Jon 206
Canney, Juan 207, 220
Canscild, Bewen 207, 220
Cantel, Gui 207, 220
Canue, Guillermo 207, 220
Capo, Antonio 60
Capo, Lorenzo 61
Caratch, J. 81
Carballo, Julian 50
Carbank, Stephen 31
Card, Jack 39
Card, Jonathan 39
Carc, Samuel 148
Carel, B. 104, 148
Carelin, Jacques 81
Carene, Ebenezer 81
Carier, Michel 81
Carjon, Thomas 236
Carlin 81
Carmen R., M. 50, 56
Carnes, Thomas 81
Carney, Thomas 71, 81
Carnly, Thomas 202
Carns, Ricardo 61
Carol, Richard 50, 56
Caron 81
Caron, Juan Bautista 236
Carpenter, Conrad 236
Carpenter, Mary 169
Carpenter, the Widow 104, 169
Carr, John 81, 123, 148
Carr, Joseph
Carradine, P. 104, 123, 133, 148, 169
Carranza, Jose A. 50

Coil, Marcos 105, 170
Cokler, Juan 207, 220
Colbert, John 207, 220
Colbert, Simon 207, 220
Colbert, Thomas 133
Colbertson, the Widow 105, 170
Cole, Guillermo 105, 170
Cole, James 123, 170
Cole, James (father) 105, 149, 170
Cole, James (son) 105, 149, 170
Cole, Mark 105, 123, 149, 170
Cole, Salomon 105, 171
Cole, Stephen 123, 171
Coleco, William 171
Colem, Guillermo 207, 220
Coleman, Ephraim 105, 171
Coleman, Esmaelen 207, 220
Coleman, Henry 171
Coleman, Israel 105, 171
Coleman, Jeremiah 105, 133, 149, 171
Coleman, John 171
Coleman, John R. 202
Coleman, J. Raford 82
Coleman, Nicolas 134
Coleman, Peter 171
Coleman, Toumerk 123
Coleman, William 171
Colems, Tomas 207, 220
Colens, Juan 207, 220
Coles, James 105, 123, 149
Colette 82
Coliben, Samuel 207, 220
Coliere, Bonaventure

276
Colin, Henry 71
Colin, Juan Baptista 25
Colino, Luk 82
Colino, Nicolas 50
Colins filo 82
Colins pere 82
Colins, Guillermo 82
Colins, Honore 25
Colins, Josua 149
Colins, William 149
Colle, Marcos 123
Collell, Francisco 134
Collender, A. 105, 171
Collerman, G. 105, 171
Collier, Thomas 61
Collignood 82
Collin, Tomas V. 207, 220
Colline, Luc (father) 82
Collingrood, Robert 82
Collins, Carlos 105, 171
Collins, Denis 105, 171
Collins, Guillaume 82
Collins, James 171
Collins, Jean 134
Collins, Jno. 202
Collins, John 149
Collins, Jose 207, 220
Collins, Josua 105, 171
Collins, Luc (son) 82
Collins, Theophilus 82
Collins, William 31, 105, 123, 171, 202
Collot, Juan Luis 238, 283
Collu, Jacobo 238
Colman, Ephraim 149
Colman, John 134, 149
Colman, Richard 25
Colo, James 238
Colomb, Joseph 25
Colomin, Antonio 50

Cols, James 149
Cols, Salomon 149
Cols, Steven 149
Colvet, Julian 283
Colwel, Diego 207, 220
Comau, Chs. 82
Comeau, Simon 82
Comens, Juan 208, 221
Comes, Ygnacio 208, 221
Comins, Thomas 50, 149
Comon 82
Comor, Miguel 208, 221
Comos, Juan Baptista 71
Compagnot, Francisco 238
Compagnot, Pedro 238
Compagnot, Pierre 238
Companoy, Ma. (widow) 238
Comparg, Francisco 123
Compin, Claudio Gabriel 238
Compugnol, Francois 238
Coneau, Chs. 82
Conely, Redman 105, 171
Coner, Guillermo 208, 221
Connal, Carlos 208, 221
Conneghan, Thomas 171
Connel, Daniel 171
Connells, Robert 171
Conner, Juan 105, 171
Conneway, Carlos 25
Connor, Bryan 61
Connor, Ephraim 238
Connor, Peter 171
Connors, Juan 238
Conoby, Jacobo 208, 221
Conoly, Patrick 171
Conrad, John 238
Constant, Jacobo 50
Constonck, William 171
Conticle 134

304

Cook, George 61, 149, 171
Cook, Guillermo 61
Cook, Jacobo 238
Cookes, Andres 283
Cool, Jacobo 238, 283
Cool, Juan 276
Cooper, Henry 25, 105, 123, 149, 171
Cooper, Henry (father) 149
Cooper, Henry (son) 105, 149
Cooper, Jack 31
Cooper, Jacobo 208, 221
Cooper, Jaime 106, 171
Cooper, James 31, 238
Cooper, Jesse, 171
Cooper, Juan 61, 71
Cooper, S. 31, 106, 124, 134, 149, 171
Cooper, W. 25, 50, 56, 106, 124, 149, 171
Coots, Jacobo 171
Copengen, John 25
Coplan, Jonatas 61
Coppingens, Jean 25
Cora, James (father) 134
Cora, John 134
Cordery, Thomas (f.) 82
Cordrey 31
Core, Job 149
Core, Richard 149
Corek, Richard 31
Coreles, John 149
Corey, James 238
Corifario, Pedro 61
Coris, Juan 208, 221
Cork, Andre 286
Cormatek, Thomas 238
Cormier, Jn. Bte. 82
Corner, Juan 171
Cornev, Ephraim 276

Corona, Vicent 50, 56
Corprel, Gabriel M. 82
Correl, Juan 106, 171
Corriere, Francisco 26
Corry, Jeremiah 106, 171
Corry, Job 106, 124, 134, 149, 171
Corte, Marcos 171
Cortes, Dimas 61
Cortner, Juan 238, 276
Corueu, Ephraim 276
Coruna, Jose Antonio 50
Coruna, Josefa 50, 56
Cory, Jacobo 283
Cory, Job 172
Cory, Ricardo 106, 172
Cory, Yeaeke 283
Coskain, Antoine 82
Costa, Benito 61
Costen, Isaac 39
Costero, George 238
Coter 82
Cott, Daniel 172
Cott, Estevan 106, 172
Cott, Juan 106, 172
Cotta, Jacobo 238
Couguenil, Francisco 238
Coujlon, Robert M. 82
Couke, Andres 238
Coulo, Santiago 239
Counnien, Pasgual 239
Courege, Juan 26
Courent, Guillermo 239
Cournai, Juan 239
Courney, Francisco 276
Courtney, John 106, 124, 134, 149, 172
Cousley, Francisco 239
Couteley, Francisco 239
Couteux, Diego 239
Coutrie, Jacquet 239
Coutu, Jacobo 276

Cowan 31
Cowan, John 172
Cowan, William 239
Cowel, Juan 106, 172
Cowen, R. 31, 61, 82
Cox, Andres 239, 283
Coyl, John 172
Coyleman, Jacobo 106, 172
Coyles, Hugh 106, 149, 172
Crabin, Carlos 239
Crafford, William 172
Crafts, Nicolas 39
Craig, Guillermo 61
Craig, Silas (father) 134
Craig, Thomas 31, 239
Crain, Silas 134
Crambert, Agustin 61
Crane, Hibon 149
Crane, Mrs. 106, 149
Crane, Waterman 106, 124, 149, 172
Crave, Josiah 208, 221
Cravin, John 106, 134, 149, 172
Craw, James 202
Crawford, Andres 208, 221
Crawford, George 39
Crawford, Joseph 172
Crawford, Tomas 208, 221
Crayton, Roberto 106, 172
Creay, John 31
Creighthon, A. 61
Creigy, Guillermo 82
Creswell, Simeon 61
Crichine 83
Crider, Michael 134
Crispin, Tomas
Cristian, Nicolas 25

Cristianem, Juan 239
Crock, Edouard 239
Crofts, William 39
Crook, Yas 83
Crosbi, Miguel 61
Croso, David 134
Crow, David 134
Crow, Jacobo 239
Crozer, Mary 50, 56
Cruely, Bennet 134
Cruik, Faquin 239
Crumhott, Jacobo 106, 172
Crump, William 172
Crusin, C. Causin 283
Crutheirs, Juan 106, 172
Cruthus, Thomas 172
Cruz, Jacobo 208, 221
Cruz, Waterman 172
Cruzert, William 106, 150
Cuarse, Enrique 61
Cueteau, Jacobo 239
Cuetue, Jacobo 239
Cuetue, Santiago 239
Culbert, John 239
Culbert, William 239
Culbertson, Samuel 106, 124, 150
Culp, G. 83
Cumingham, Thomas 172
Cummins, Thomas 106, 172
Cumstick, David 172
Cuningham, A. 39
Cunningham, A. 39
Cunningham, James 39
Cunninghams, Juan 239
Cunninghan, C. 106, 172
Cuntow, Roque 239
Cuny, Ve 83
Currau, Guillermo 208, 221

Curry, John 39
Curtin, Thomas 71
Curtis, B. 106, 124, 134, 150, 172
Curtis, John 134
Curtis, Jonathan 124, 150
Curtis, M. 106, 172
Curtis, Richard 106, 134, 150, 172
Curtis, Richard (son) 134
Curtis, W. 106, 124, 134, 150, 172
Cury, Andres 239
Custard, Frederik 286
Cuts, John 83
Cuus, Tomas 208, 221
Cuwy, William 208, 221
Cuyol, Francisco 276
Daigle, Alexandro 83
Daigle, Luis 83
Daigre, Baptista 83
Daigre, Francisco 83
Daigre, Pablo 83
Dairmont, Juan 239
Dalphen, Francois 83
Daltesse 83
Dalton, Honera 39
Dalton, Thomas 71
Danah, Tomas 106, 172
Dandley, James 26
Danes, Luisa 50, 56
Daniel, Patrick M. 71
Daniel, Robert 134
Daniel, W. 61, 106, 124, 150
Daniels, Thomas 106, 172
Danise, Juan 239
Dany, Juan Baupta. 286
Daperou, Jose 239, 276

Darby 83
Darby, St. Marc 83
Darix, John 150
Darlington, Joseph 172
Darron, Thomas 172
Daugherty, Antonio 106, 172
Daughtel, Jose 208, 221
Daure, Jean 239
Davenport, Jaime 106, 172
Davenport, John 172
Daves, Thomas 83
Davidson, Thomas 239
Davion, Juan 208, 221
Davies, Francisco 172
Davies, Samuel 239
Davis, (widow of) 239, 240
Davis, Benjamin 240
Davis, Berij 240
Davis, Daniel 71, 134
Davis, David 39
Davis, Elisha 172
Davis, Guillermo 106, 172, 240, 276, 283
Davis, Human 286
Davis, John 26, 61, 124, 173, 240, 276
Davis, Juan, (widow of) 240
Davis, Landard Hugh 173
Davis, Landon 124
Davis, Marie 71
Davis, S. 61, 106, 124, 134, 150, 173, 240
Davis, Thomas 39, 150, 240
Davison, James 71
Davison, William 240
Dawney, Guillermo 134
Dawson, John 31, 134
Dawson, Nicholas 39

Day, Aaron 240
Day, Benjamin 134
Day, Nayor 134
Daybread, Andres 240
Daybread, Juan 240
Dayby, Francisco 286
Days, James 173
Dayton, E. 106, 124, 150,173
De Brady, Juan 106, 173
de Frontenac 240
De Populas 83
Deaderick, Juan 173
Deaivonge, Jose 208, 221
Deajon, Clem 134
Dean, John 39
Dean, Patricio 61
Dearmits, Alexandro 240
Decker, Lucas 240
Declouez, Cher. 83
Decuir, Fois 83
Decuir, J. Pre 83
Dée, Le 83
Deetz, Henry 150
Deforge 31
Deforge, John 31
Deforge, Peter 31
Degan, Jose 240
Degano, Joseph 240
Deghire, Paul 286
Deghize, Andres 286
Degle, Francisco 83
Degle, Francisco A. 83
Degle, Juan Baptista 83
Degle, Luis 83
Degle, Pablo 83
Degle, Simon 83
Degle, Simon Pedro 83
Dehault, Pierre Charles 286
Dejoy, Jacque 124
Deken, Jorpe 208, 221
Delaina, John 134

Delainé, Mathieu 83
Delamorandier 83
Delany, Juan G. 61
Delate, Claudio 71
Delbe, Stephen 134
Delfin, Francisco 50
Delgado, Jn. 83
Delhodmme 83
Delin, Juan 208, 221
Delina, J. Baptista 286
Delisla, Carlos 286
Delisla, J. Baptista 286
Delisla, Luis 286
Delisle, Carlos 240
Delislo, Charles 240
Deloignon 83
Delon, Federico 208, 221
Demanch, Nicolas 134
Demarets, Ve 83
Demaus, George 134
Denham, R. 107, 150
Denisse, Juan 240
Denoyom, Silvestre 240
Denoyon, Luis 240, 276, 283
Denuelle, Francisco 208, 221
Denuy, Carlos 26
Deny, Juan 240
Depres, Rene 286
Derbanne, J. B. 83
Dercoupe, Francisco 276
Derçon, Guillaume 83
Derison, Abraham 39
Derlac, Girardo 240
Derlac, Juan 240, 241
Derlacqus, Jean 241
Dermett, Bryan M. 83
Deroche, Pedro 241, 276
Derovien 83
Derrous, Francis 241
Derrouse, Francisco 241
Deruin, Estevan 208,

221
Derusver, Francisco 241
Dervin, Elizabet 107, 173
Desalles, Pedro 71
Desbigny, Pedro 241
Descautel, Antonio 71
Desholels, Nas. 83
Despeintreux, Lucas 241
Desroussee, Francisco 241
Desrousserd, Francisco 241
Detaillis, Fr. 241
Detallie, Joseph 241
Detete, Luis 286
Deuimtes, Benjamin 241
Deuset, Francisco 71
Devall, R. 72, 107, 124, 134, 150
Devalt 39
Deverneys, Antonio 83
Devidrine 84
Devis, Leiua 208, 221
Devis, Pedro 208, 221
Devis, Richard 72
Devoir, Samuel 208, 221
Devores, Nicolas 241
Dial, John 84
Diane, Cornelius 202
Diaz Bernix, Pedro 61
Diaz, Rafael 61
Dicks, Nathan 173
Dickson, Lewis 134
Dickson, Roger 173
Dicouel 84
Die, Baupta. de 286
Diekles, Carlos 208, 221
Dilbig, Thomas 72
Dill, James 150
Dions, Cornelius 202
Dirhussen, Juan 173
Dirmont, Juan 283

307

Dugas, Chs. 84
Dugas, Jn. 84
Dugas, Jucin 72
Dugas, Pre 84
Duggard, Guillermo 242
Duglese, Jean 26
Duhon, B. 84
Duhon, Ch. 84
Duhon, Claude 84
Duiett, Luis 26
Duinre, Ambrosio 242
Duit, William 135
Duitt, Ezekiel 173
Dulendue, Solas 39
Dulisne 84
Duls, Henry 150
Dumain, Pedro 277
Dumais, Pedro 242. 277
Dumais, Pierre 242
Dumay 242
Dumay, Ambrosio 242
Dumayo, Ambrosio 242
Dumbar, Guillermo 107
Dumon, George 150
Dun, George 135
Dun, James 135
Dun, Richard 107, 124,
    135
Dunahow, James 208,
    221
Dunavan, Daniel 173
Dunavan, John 107, 150
Dunbar, Guillaume 72
Dunbar, Robert 107,
    124, 135, 173
Dunbarr, Robert 135,
    173
Dunbarr, William 173
Duncan, Benjamin 173
Duncan, George 174
Duncan, Joseph 107,
    150, 174
Duncan, Santiago 61

Duncan, William 50, 56
Dunesson, John 135
Dunlap, John 174
Dunman, John 84
Dunman, R. 84, 107, 174
Dunn, Jayme 242
Dunn, John 135, 174
Dunn, Michael 242
Dunnam, Ruben 124
Dupin, F. Riche 242,
    243, 277
Duplantier, A. 72, 84
Duplesix, Jose 286
Duprat, Alexandro 61
Dupuia, Charle 84
Dupuid, Ambroin 84
Dupuig, Juan 243
Dupuis, Isidoro 243
Dupuis, J. Bautista 243,
    277
Dupuiy, Isidro 243
Dupuy, Carlos 84
Duralde 84
Duran, Bartolome 50
Durang, John 174
Durbin, Joseph 84
Durcan, Joseph 150
Durch, Guillermo 107,
    174
Dureght 135
Durond, Rogero 174
Durr, Sebastian 174
Dutaville, Francisco 243
Duting, Juan 208, 221
Dutreueble, J. Bautista
    243
Dutrubler, Juan 243
Dutrumbles, J. Bautista
    243
Duval, James 286
Duval, Jean 84
Duval, John 286
Duvall, Richard 135,

150
Duvé, Mariana (widow)
    243
Duver, Josefa (widow)
    243
Duville, Joaquin 286
Duwitt, William 174
Dviny, Hugh 174
Dwet, Israel 150
Dwet, Jese 107, 174
Dwight, Sixins 135
Dyer, John 31
Dyon, William 150
Dyson 135
Dyson, C. 107, 124, 150,
    174
Dyson, Elimon 135
Dyson, John 150, 174
Dyson, Joseph 107, 135,
    150, 174
Dyson, Leonard 31
Dyson, Thomas 107, 135,
    150, 174
Earheart, Jacobo 107, 174
Eason, Charles 135, 174
Eastman, Abel 107, 150,
    174
Easton, Guillermo 61
Eddy, Samuel 208, 221
Edmonds, Timothy 174
Edward, Jaime 107, 174
Edwards, Juan 61
Egaim, Petu 243
Eguins, Pedro 243, 277
Eichard, Vern 243
Eldergill, J. 107, 135, 150
Eleaver, James 174
Eleson 84
Elherington, John 150
Elioten, Juan 243
Elliot, Guillermo 107,
    174, 243
Elliot, James 107, 124,

309

151, 174
Elliot, William 243
Elliott, Thomas 84
Ellis, Abraham 107, 174
Ellis, Abram 124, 151
Ellis, Carlos 26
Ellis, Harde 174
Ellis, Hardi 84
Ellis, Jacob 174
Ellis, John 124, 135, 151, 174
Ellis, John (father) 107, 135, 151, 174
Ellis, John (son) 107, 135, 174
Ellis, Mateo 61
Ellis, Richard 107, 108, 124, 135, 151, 174
Ellis, Richard (son) 151
Ellsworth, John 174
Elmore, Juan 108, 174
Elsworth, Guillermo 62
Empel, Juan 208, 221
Empfil 243
Emphill, Jones 243
Emphris, Justus 151
Endergil, Juan 72
Eneson Carenton, J. 84
Eneyohton, Roberto 151
Engelard, Felipe 85
Engele, Philip 243
Engelhurt, Philip 72
English, John 31
English, Robert, 39
Enrusty, John 174
Ensor, George 243
Entzalgo, Juan A. 62
Erdelgil, John 151
Erls, Richard 85
Ernest, Catherine 40
Errick, Juan 72
Ervehen, John 72
Ervin, James 108, 151,

174
Ervin, Juan 108, 151, 174
Erving, Roberto 174
Erwall, James 135
Erwin, John
Erwin, William 108, 124, 135, 175,
Escott, Anne 72
Escouffié 85
Esgr, Jonatan 208, 221
Eskildsen, Pedro 85
Eslignan, Madama 209, 222
Esllins, Taushn 124
Esmael, Guillermo 209, 222
Espinar, Domingo 72
Espino, Ana 50
Espino, Rosalia 50
Essex, Thomas 175
Estan, Juan 209, 243
Estan, Ranzon 209, 222
Estello, William 175
Estidier, Jose 209, 222
Estimal, Madama 209, 222
Estod, Samiel 209, 222
Estuard, Guillermo 209, 222
Eubanks, Stephen 85
Eudems, Nicolas 243
Buing, Carlos 175
Buing, Samuel 175
Buins, David 40
Evans, David 40
Evans, John 31
Evans, Lewis 175
Evans, Luis 175
Evans, Thomas 135
Eveille, L' 85
Evens, William 243
Ever, Thomas 175

Evin, John 135
Ewiner, Jean 135
Ewing, Adam 62
Fabuel, Samuel 209, 222
Facio, Francisco F. 62
Fage, Juan 124
Fageson, Samuel 222
Faghy, John 209, 222
Fague, Michel 151
Fairbanks, W. 108, 124, 135, 151, 175
Fairlie, James 50, 56
Faith, Jose 243
Fak, John 151
Falcon, Jose 50
Falconer, Francisco 243
Falconer, Guillermo 108, 175
Falconer, John 50, 56
Falknen, John 209
Fallan, James 243
Fample, Margarita 85
Fanna, (dead) 72
Faoullar, Jobile 85
Far, Estevan 209, 222
Fardif, Constancio 50
Farel, Thomas 151
Farell, Benjamin 40
Farell, Jose 72
Farley, John 31
Farmar, Robert 31
Farmer, Mrs 50, 56
Farmer, William 175
Farmy, Juan 283
Farney, Antonio 243
Farnis, Guillermo 175
Faro, Alexandre 151
Farquhar, J. 108, 135, 151
Farra, Alexander 135
Farrell, Thomas 135
Farroco, Alexandro 108, 175

311

Fontenau, Tomas 85
Fontenau, Y.Ls 85
Fontenau, Yas. 85
Fonteneau, Simon 85
Fontener, William 152
Fonteneu, Jacques 85
Fontenu, Henri 85
Fontiny, Jose 286
Fonton, Juan 85
Fontune, Miguel 62
Fool, Nancy 244
Fooy, Benjamin 31, 108, 152, 176
Foozeman, George 152
Forc, Jn 85
Ford, John 108, 152, 176
Ford, Joseph 136, 152, 176
Ford, Robert 125, 136, 152, 176
Fordais, James 152
Fordice, James 31
Fordler, John 176
Fore, Simon 85
Forester, Joseph 136, 152
Forget, Peter de 85
Foriet, Florentin 85
Forman, Ed. 85
Forman, Ezekiel 108, 176
Forman, Ismy 108, 176
Forman, Jorge 108, 176
Forman, Samuel S. 176
Formosa, William 244
Forneret, Luis 51
Forster, James 108, 176, 222
Forster, Juan 209
Forsyth, James 176
Forthize, Roberto 209, 222
Fortiu, Juan 277

Fosite, Robero 85
Foster, James 85, 108, 136, 152, 176
Foster, John 108, 125, 136, 152, 176
Foster, Mary 108, 136, 152, 176
Foster, Sarah 136
Foster, T. 108, 125, 136, 152, 176
Foster, W. 108, 125, 136, 152, 176
Fouchet, Bonaventure 277
Fouchet, Ventura 244
Fouedsey, B. 244
Fouliniount, Richard 244
Foultis, Estevan 72
Fourdain, Jevis 244
Fourman, Edouard 85
Fourone, Alexandre 176
Foutchec 85
Fowler, Alexandre 176
Fowler, John 176
Fowler, Jose 108, 176
Fowler, Sarah 40
Foy, Pedro 209, 222
Foye, Benjamin 176
Frahan, Juan Bta. 86
Frahan, Remon 86
Frahise, George 176
Frail, Eduardo 108, 176
Frances, J. Gordon 209, 222
Francor, Jose 287
Frank, French 136
Frannel, Augusto 86
Frannin, Jayme 209, 222
Frasery, Alex 26
Fraye, Jose 209, 222
Frederie 86
Freed, John 136
Freeman, Thomas 136,

152, 176
Fremont, Agustin Ch. 244
French, Henry 176
Fridge, Alexander 72
Fridge, Catherine 72
Fridge, John 72
Frines 86
Frison, Juan 244
Frons, Juan 209, 222
Frost, Yese 62
Frugé, Pu. 86
Fruge, Ve. 86
Fruland, Isaac 86
Fry, Than. 86
Fuelier, widow 72
Fuente, Rosalia de la 51
Fuentes, Ramon 62
Fulds, Daniel 176
Fulds, Felipe 176
Fulds, John 176
Fulford, G. Gibson 86
Fulham, John 244, 277
Fulhoum, Juan 277
Fuller, Mortacea 86
Fullet, Mordicai 32
Fulley, Yrael 176
Fullie, Isidoro 86
Fullie, Juan Carlos 86
Fulsom, Israel 32, 136
Fulson, Ebinezer 32
Fulton, Alex. 86
Fulton, Alexandro 209, 222
Fulton, Alexis 176
Fulton, David 136
Funlison, Richard 244
Fur, John 176
Furman, John 177
Furney, Matias 244
Furny, George 152
Gabeant, Pedro 244
Gabourel, Joshua 40

312

Gaeyce, Miguel 177
Gaillard, Ann 108, 152
Gaillard, I. 108, 125,
152, 177
Gaille, Jean 86
Gains, Ambrosio 177
Gairy, Jorge 72
Gakar, Eliasar 287
Galan, Rita 51, 57
Galbeau, Carlos 244
Gale, John 72
Gale, Matias 40
Galguera, Juan 209, 222
Gallaghen, Carlos 209,
222
Gallagher, William 177
Gallcher, John 177
Gallegos, Juan 51
Gallehan, Patrick 32
Gallehon, Patrick 86
Gallican, William 177
Gallien, Ve 86
Gallimore, D. 109, 136,
177
Gallup, Paleg 62
Gally, Juan 72
Gamble, William 152
Gamelin, (widow of) 244
Gamelin, Antoine 244
Gamelin, Antonio 244,
277
Gamelin, Margarita 244
Gañe, Amable 287
Gane, Luis 51
Garad, Juan 177
Garan, Pedro 244
Garau, Pierre 244
Garbutt, John 40
Garcia, Francisco 51
Garcia, Juan 72
Garden, William 51, 57
Gardener, Henry 177
Gardnhart, Michal 86,

202
Gardor, Roberto 177
Garet, Juan 109, 177
Gargaret, Maria 26
Garill, Nicolas 244
Garkind, Juan 109, 177
Garlan, William 177
Garlia, Maria 244
Garner, John 32, 86
Garnet, Ben 40
Garnet, Juan 209, 222
Garnett, Benjamin 40
Garnhart, Enrique 72
Garnhart, Jorge 72
Garon, Uriak 177
Garques, Juan 244
Garrette 86
Garrino, Thomas 136
Gartles, John W. 86
Garvan, David 62
Garzon, Antonio 51
Gascon, Juan 177
Gaskin, John 152
Gasland, James 152
Gati, Juan 209, 222
Gauld, George 51, 57
Gaulin, Louis 244
Gaultien, Louis 244
Gautier, Ed. 40
Gavenir, Pedro 244
Gawen, Jesse 209, 222
Gayo, Antonio 245
Gazoiche, Juim... 245
Geaphert, Jacob 177
Geddis, Molly 40
Geigor, Juan 62
Gelesbie, William 152
Gelmour, Simeon 40
Geneocux, Jose 245
Geniez, Santiago 26
Genis, Robert M. 152
Gensack, M 287
Geoffroy, Pedro 245,

277
Geomit, Patrick 177
Geonel, Patrick 177
Georgius, Philip 32
German, Juan 245
Geroult, Andres 245
Gervair, J. Bautista 245
Geuouix, Jose 245
Gibault, Pedro 245
Gibault, Pedro (priest)
245
Gibson, David 152
Gibson, Gabriel 177
Gibson, Gibion 136, 152
Gibson, Gil 109, 152, 177
Gibson, John 177
Gibson, Randolf 152
Gibson, Reuben 109,
125, 136, 152, 177
Gibson, Robert 109, 152
Gibson, S. 109, 125, 136,
152, 177
Gienin, Juan Simon 245
Gigante, Miguel 62
Gil, Miguel 51
Gilbert, Cristi 152
Gilbert, Cristobal 109,
177
Gilbert, John 152, 177
Gilbert, Robert (son) 62
Gilbert, William 109,
125, 152, 177
Gilchrisl 86
Gilchrist, John 32
Gilcrist, Jesse 32
Gilehart, Nimrod 32
Gilekust, Guillermo 209,
222
Gilks, Bukins 86
Gillaird, Mistress 177
Gillard, Tacitus 136
Gillaspie, Guillermo 109,
177

Green, Guillermo 246
Green, Henry 109, 125, 178, 246
Green, John 87, 109, 153, 178, 246
Green, Joseph 109, 136, 153, 178
Green, Nathan 109, 178
Green, Pedro Wilkes 62
Green, Rodolph 136
Green, Rodolphus 40
Green, Samuel 62
Green, Thomas 136, 153, 178
Green, T. Masten 109, 125, 153, 178
Greenfield, Jesse 109, 178
Greenhill, Josiah 40
Greenleaf, David 109, 178
Greepy, Thomas 153
Greffin, Juan 109, 125, 178
Gregor, Benjamin 223
Greham, Thomas 178
Grelol, Pre 87
Grenie, Francisco 287
Gretion, John 32
Grévenbesiz, J. B. 87
Grevenbesiz, Ls. 87
Grevenbeu, Barmy 87
Grevenbeu, Fois 87
Grews, Richard 87
Grey, Buflin 109, 178
Grey, James 32, 178
Grey, Robert 32
Grey, Ruffin 178
Griest, James 51, 57
Griffardo, Alexic 287
Griffin, Absalom 202
Griffin, Christobal 62
Griffin, Daniel 178

Griffin, Gabriel 109, 125, 136, 153, 178
Griffin, James 202
Griffin, John 109, 137, 153, 178
Griffin, T. 109, 137, 153
Griffith, Llewellyn C. 73
Griffith, Llwellyn 87
Grifin, Francis 178
Grigson, James 137
Griman, Juan 246
Grimard, J. Bautista 246, 277
Grimare, Pierre 246
Grimaret, Pedro 246
Grimas, Carlos 283
Grimes, Hattvi 137
Grims, Ricardo 109, 178
Grinud, Maria 51, 57
Gris, Michel 153
Griswelle, Stephen 178
Grmitenan, Guillermo 223
Gromt, Andres 246
Grotim, John 32
Grub, Nicholas 178
Grubb, Benj 87
Grubb, Benjamin 179
Grubb, Nicolas 179
Grubson, Grubion 125
Gruel, Benjamin 179
Grufin, John 153
Gruiden, Benjamin 246
Grun, Joseph 137
Grunwell, Jeremiah 202
Guadarrama, Matheo 62
Gualbaud, Francisco 246
Guarlia, Maria 246
Guellet, Francisco 246
Guenard 87
Guenard, Jean 87
Guenne, Ambroise 87
Guere, Pedro 246

Guerin, Juan Simon 246, 247, 277
Guerir, Maria Ignacia 51
Guerra, Salvador 51
Guff, Nic 179
Guff, Tomas 179
Guiday, Ana (widow) 87
Guiday, Joseph 87
Guiday, Juan 87
Guiday, Pedro 87
Guidony, Pedro 223
Guidrie, Jh 87
Guidrie, Pre 87
Guidry, Francisco 87
Guidry, Jose 87
Guidry, Malau 87
Guidry, Pedro (1st) 87
Guidry, Pedro (2nd) 87
Guidry, Pedro (2nd) 87
Guidry, Soulier 87
Guierin, Pedro 247
Guierrier, Pedro 247
Guilbaud, Carlos 247, 277
Guilford, Jeremiah 179
Guill, Jacobo 247
Guill, Nicolas 247
Guill, Suzana 247
Guilland, Rene 62
Guillaume 87
Guillaume, Guillaume 87
Guillebeau, Chs 87
Guillebeau, F 87
Guillebeau, Yn. 87
Guillermo 247
Guilles, Jacobo 277
Guillet, Miguel 62
Guillory, Cde 87
Guillory, Jh. 87
Guillory, Thomas 87
Guilmore, John 247, 277, 278

315

316

Harrel, Jacob 32
Harrie, Jose 223
Harrigal, D. 110, 153, 179
Harris, Lewis 40
Harris, Nathan 248
Harrison 137
Harrison, Benjamin 248
Harrison, John 179
Harrison, Joseph 110, 125, 153, 179
Harrison, Nicolas 248
Harrison, Peter 32
Harrison, Richard 110, 125, 137, 153, 179
Harrison, Samuel 63
Harshaw, Archibald 88
Hart, Barne 287
Hart, George 202
Hart, Juan 248, 278
Hartin, John 137
Hartley, Jacob 110, 179
Hartley, John 125, 137, 153, 179
Harton, Abraam 153
Harvard, C. 110, 179
Harvey, J. 248
Harvison, Thomas 179
Haskinson, Ezekiel 153
Hastone, William 287
Hat, Benllun 32
Hathorn, William 179
Hatten, Robert 153
Hatton, Demy 223
Haubert, Nicolas 248
Haukins, Peter 153
Haunot, Gabriel 248
Haus, George 283
Hauser, Gasper 179
Haut, Juan 248
Havve, William 179
Hawers, John 153
Hawid, C. 125, 153

Hawkins, P. 110, 125, 137, 153
Hawley, Daniel 180
Hay, Archibal 154
Hay, John 223
Haybraker, John 110, 154
Hayeesard, Joshua 154
Hayens, James 287
Hayes, James 110, 125, 154, 180
Hayes, Malachy 40
Haylock, Elenor 40
Hayluck, Francis 40
Hays, Bosman 88
Hays, David 180
Hays, James 180
Hays, John 88
Hays, William 88
Haysse 88
Hayward, Charles 137
Hayward, Stephen 154
Hayward, Toucha 154
Heady, Samuel 110, 137, 154, 180
Headycorn, Simon 180
Heardford, Maria 51, 57
Heartley, John 180
Heasly, Juan 248
Hebe, Alesey 88
Hebe, Belony 88
Hebe, Juan Carlos 88
Heber, Carlos 88
Heber, Francisco 73
Heber, Juan Baptista 88
Heber, Juan Pedro 88
Hebers, J. 88
Hebers, Jh. 88
Hebers, Jn 88
Hebers, Min 88
Hebert, Bautista 73
Hebert, Belony 73
Hebert, Carlos 73

Hebert, Francisco 73
Hebeu, Pierre 88
Hecky, Francis 40
Hekey, Francis 40
Helchen, Benjamin 154
Helen, James 110, 154
Hellbrand, David 110, 180
Helveson, Godefroy 26
Hemell, Carlos 110, 180
Hemming, Nancy 40
Hempill, Jones 248
Hencock, Alexandro 180
Henderson, A. 110, 180
Henderson, Henrique 180
Henderson, J. 88, 125, 180
Henderson, W. 110, 125, 137, 154, 180
Hening, Sorge 63
Henning, Guillermo 223
Henricks, Ysaac 63
Henry, Juan Baptista 73
Henry, Juan Lazaro 63
Henry, Mairi milicano 73
Henry, Mitchel 180
Henry, Peter 40
Henson, Widow 88
Herdy, Samuel 125
Here, Andres 88, 110, 180
Hergeroder 88
Herhart, Jacob 154
Herickland, Dan 154
Herling, Alexan 88
Herman, Jacob 88
Herman, Jb. 88
Hernandez, Catalina 51
Hernandez, Gaspar 63
Hernandez, Manuel 51
Hernandez, Martin 63
Hernois, Joseph 180

317

Hernon, Eduard 41
Herovin, James 154
Herowins, William 154
Herr, Luisa 51, 57
Herrsan, Guilermo 180
Herwin, James 125
Hesse, James 154
Hetty, Ps. 88
Heu, Samuel 73
Heuall, John 73
Heur, George 248
Heury, Pierre 88
Hewitt, Kufsell 248
Hewlete, Daniel 41
Hewlett, George 41
Hewm, James 41
Heword, Jaime 180
Hibberson, Jose 63
Hibbs, John 223
Hibernois, Antonio 248
Hibert, Nicolas 278
Hichison, Stewart 180
Hickly, David 73
Hickman, John 32
Hicky, Daniel 73, 88
Hicky, Philip 73
Hidalgo, Isabel 51
Hids, John 137
Higdon, Jepthah 110, 180
Higdon, Jesse (Jepthah) 125, 137, 154
Higdon, Mary 180
Higgins, Barney 73, 110, 180
Higgins, Jose 223
Higgins, Pedro 248
Higginson, Stuart 110, 180
Highebottom, James 32
Higinbottom, Samuel 32
Higui, Daniel 88
Hikey, Michal 248

Hill, E. F. 41
Hill, Edward Felix 41
Hill, Jeremiah 137
Hill, Pedro 110, 180
Hill, Samuel 248
Hill, William 180
Hiller, Margarita 110, 180
Hilliams, Jayme 248
Hilling, Helene 73
Hilling, Jaques 73
Hilo, Jaquin 248
Hilonds, Jaime 110, 180
Hilot, Ricardo 180
Hilton, William 248, 283
Hinds, Guillermo 223
Hinkson, Juan 248
Hinkson, Roberto 248
Hins, James 73
History, Ephraim 110, 180
Hiteliliny, John 26
Hitleel, John 154
Hiton, John 223
Hitton, William 248
Hivens, Thomas 154
Hiwe 287
Hjollies 88
Hoard, Joseph 110, 154
Hoard, Robert 110, 154
Hoare, Richard 41
Hobbard, Tomas 110, 180
Hoben, John 223
Hocktit, Josua 154
Hodel, David 125
Hodge, David 51, 57
Hodge, Eleanor M. 41
Hodskinson, Robert 41
Hodson, Fes. 248
Hogan, John 180
Hogan, Ruben 63
Hogarty, Peter 88

Hogdon, Daniel 154
Hogg 73
Hoggatt, James 32
Hoirn, Samuel 180
Holand, John 154
Holden, Joseph 137
Holden, Thomas 89
Holderpok, Jorge 63
Holftur, King 89
Holladay, Juan 110, 125, 180
Holland, Jeremias 180
Holland, John 110, 154
Holland, Jorge 110, 180
Hollaway, John 89
Hollinger, Adam 26
Hollingsworth, Juan 223
Holloway, George 137
Holloway, John 137
Holly, John 180
Holly, Rolan 180
Holmes Smith, John 41
Holmes, B. 110, 125, 137, 180
Holmes, Frank 41
Holmes, Jaime M. 63
Holmes, Joseph 89, 126, 137, 181
Holmes, Sarah 110, 137, 154, 181
Holmes, Simon 126, 137
Holmes, Thomas 33
Holms, Lubis 181
Holoom, Nataniel 181
Hols, David 154
Holsce, Juan 223
Holsten, G. 154, 210
Holsten, Stephen 138, 154
Holsten, Stephen (father) 138
Holston, John 138
Holston, King 154

Holt, David 111, 154, 181
Holt, Debdall 154
Holt, Debral 138
Holt, Dibdal 111, 181
Holt, Dibial 154
Holt, Elizabeth 111, 154
Holt, John 111, 126, 154, 181
Holy, John 181
Homes, B. 126, 154
Homes, Joseph 154
Homes, Simson 154
Homes, Thomas 154
Hones, Enry 41
Hood, Walter 33
Hood, wife of 248
Hooens, Benjamin 154
Hookus, Henry 155
Hoopen, Juan 63
Hooper, Absalom 33
Hooper, William 283
Hooson, Francisco 283
Hooten, Phillip 89
Hoover, Jacob 41
Hopkins, Ebenezer 89
Hopkins, Gideon 181
Hoplitto, Boston 248
Hoplon, Abner 33
Hord, wife of 248
Horeless, Edouard 155
Horflein, George 155
Horine, S. 181, 210
Horlen, Antonio 248
Horne, Benjamin 33
Horner, Juan 248, 249
Horris, Groves 181
Horsley, T. Young 249
Horsley, Tomas 249, 278
Horten, Antonio 283
Horten, Estevan 126
Hortin, A. 89, 111, 138, 181

Hortley, John 111, 155
Horton, Antonio 249
Hoskins, Joseph 155
Hoskinson, Ezechiel 181
Hosnur, Youngs 63
Houde, Juan 278
Hough, Benjamin 223
Housdan, William 138
House, Casper 181, 210
Houssaye, La 89
Houvam, Jacques 181
Houvre 89
Hovent, Bolen 223
Hover, Jacob 181, 210
Hovington, John 138
Hovington, Peter 138
Hovington, Peter (father) 138
Howard, C. 111, 155
Howard, J. 111, 155, 181
Howard, Philipe 89
Howe, William 111, 181
Howland, Guillaium 138
Howpock, Michel 89
Hoyt, Moses 63
Hubart, Stephen 89
Hubauset, Pablo 73
Hubbard, Ephrain 181, 210
Hubbard, Stephen 33
Hubbard, Thomas 181
Hubbell, John 181
Hubbert, William 138
Hubeault, Francisco 283
Hublard, Tonatas 223
Hudsalt, Jemima 111, 155
Hudsel, Gemema 138
Hudsell, William 181
Hudson, Francis 249
Hudson, Thomas 26
Huestas, Antonio 63

Huet, Gregorio Jose 63
Huet, Roxel 223
Hufman, Jacobo 111, 181
Huggs, Tomas 111, 181
Hughes 73
Hughes, Ediward 41
Hughs, Samuel 138
Hughs, Thomas 181, 210
Huittler, Daniel 111, 181
Hukison, Steward 181, 210
Hulain, L. 89
Hulbert, Tomas 126
Hulbert, William 111, 138, 155
Hulbost, William 138
Huling, Jonatas 223
Hulings, Juan 249
Hull, Abiather 63
Hull, Ambrocio 63
Hull, Daniel 33
Hull, Dow 89
Hull, John 89
Hult, James 126
Hume, James 41
Humphrey, Ana 111, 181
Humphrey, Jorge 111, 181
Humphrey, Ostrip 138
Humphreys, Eustice 111, 126, 138, 155, 181
Humphreys, Jorge G. 181
Humphreys, Ralph 181, 210
Humphries, Liv 41
Humpreys, Garnet 41
Hunney, Jean 26
Hunot, Jose 249, 278
Hunot, Jose (father) 249
Hunot, Jose (son) 249

322

Lucker, Juan 255
Lucque, Jochin 47
Luech, Levi 255
Luemnes, Guillermo 255
Luenue, William 255
Luigron, Carlos 255
Luintiman, Tomas 256
Luis, Albert 184
Luis, John 184
Luistes, Juan 284
Lulalford, Thomas 91
Lum, John 91, 113, 126, 140, 156, 184
Lum, William 184
Luneford, Moise 256
Lusk, James 185
Lusk, John 113, 126, 156, 185
Lusser, Luis 27
Lusy, Samuel 185
Luting, James 140
Lutz, Johan A. 203
Luzer, Solomon 185, 211

Lyaton, Jaime 113, 185
Lyix, Jaquin 256
Lyman, Captain 140
Lyman, Jean 140
Lynch, Miguel 64
Lyon, Matheu 185, 211
Lyons, Jermas 113, 185
Lyson, Jean 91
Lytle, Nathan 91
Lyy, John 185
Macario, Maria 52, 57
Mack, Guillermo 256
Mackey, Michael 256
Mackin, James 140
Macormek, Jones 256
Macqueen, Juan 64
Macullagh, Alex 52, 57
Madars, Manuel 156
Madden, Manuel

(Emaniel) 113, 126, 140, 156,185
Maddin, Thomas 288
Madier, Alexander 33
Madonel, Gines 256
Madres, Jose 224
Maffret, Juan 74
Magee, Malcom 27
Maggot, Daniel 113, 126,140, 156
Maggot, Roswell (Rosel) 113, 126, 140, 156
Magloglin 288
Magoune, Hugh 156
Maguibinne 256
Mahier, Miguel 74
Mahiou, Francoia 91
Mahon, Robert M. 256
Maiale, Patrice 91
Maileng, Alexandro 224
Maille, Andre 92
Main, Jacobo 64
Main, Juan 74
Mais, Jose 256
Maisonville 256
Maisonville, Francisco 256
Maisonville, Jose (son) 256
Maisonville, Joseph 256, 279
Maisonville, Juan 256, 279
Maisonville, J. Bautista 256, 279
Makefaik, Roger 156
Makolei, Pak. 92
Malbete, J. Moises 256
Malbete, Moises 256, 279
Malet, Juan Baptista 74
Malet, widow 74
Malgros, Benjamin 92

Malgros, William 92
Mallet, Antonio 256
Mallet, Jose 256
Mallon, Arturo 256
Mallvents, Luis 256
Malrot 92
Malvol 92
Man, Frederick 113, 185, 211
Man, George 33
Man, Samuel 185
Manachie, Hugo 185
Manadace, Henry 185
Manadiac, Henry 140, 211
Manadne, Enrrique 113, 185
Manadne, Enrrique (jr.) 113, 185
Manadue, Henry 92, 203
Manchan, Francisco 224
Mancien, Pedro 256
Mancier, Antonio 64
Mandall, Samuel 185
Mandeler, Guillermo 225
Mañe, Juan 64
Manedeau, H. 113, 127, 140, 156
Manie, Andas 185, 211
Manier, William 140
Manily, Jayme 225
Manne 92
Mans, Larans 225
Mansco, Federico 113, 185
Manuel, Pre 92
Marbal, Ezra 156, 211
Marbel, Abner 156, 211
Marbel, Earl 113, 185
Marbles, Ezra 185
Marcantel 92
Marcantel, De. 92

Marcelas, Peter 33
Marcelin, Maria 27
Marchal, Guillermo 225
Marchal, Juan 185, 211
Marchall 92
Marchand, Didier 279
Marchard, Didier 256, 257
Marcos, Frederick 185
Marcos, S. Menden 64
Marcus, Frederick 211
Margarita, Claudio 284
Marguet, (widow of) 257
Marguet, Madame de 257
Marianne, John 92
Marie, Andre 92
Marie, Anne 74
Marin, Gabriel 52
Marion, Luis 74
Markalls, Henry 42
Marn, Martin 140, 211
Marney, John 156, 211
Marquet, Bernardin 257
Marquet, Louis 257
Marreno, Julian 52
Marseles, Peter 33
Marshall, George 64
Marshall, John 185
Marshall, W. 52, 57, 74
Marten, Genere 225
Marten, Guillermo 225
Marter, Hugo Ricardo 185
Martimon, Daniel 225
Martin, Abner 185
Martin, Alexandro 225
Martin, Allen 52, 57
Martin, Andres 92
Martin, Claude 92
Martin, Domingo 52
Martin, E. Burill 64

Martin, Gabriel 92
Martin, Jacque 140
Martin, James 140
Martin, John 113, 127, 140, 156
Martin, Juan Bapta. 185, 211
Martin, Juana 52
Martin, N. 140, 156
Martin, Pierre 257
Martin, Samuel 185
Martin, Thomas 113, 185
Martin, William 185, 211
Martin, Yh. 92
Martin, Zacie 92
Martinez, Josefa 52, 57
Martinez, Martin 64
Martini, Ant 92
Marton, Abner 42, 185, 211
Marty, Femous 225
Marvill, Abner 113, 185
Maskall, Henry 42
Mason, Joseph 257
Massen, Edmund 42
Masters, Jonathan 113, 185
Matair, Luis 64
Matanza, Antonio 64
Mathe, Madam 92
Mather, Alexander 33
Mather, Guillermo 113, 185
Mather, Jaime 113, 185
Mathews, Andrew 33
Mathews, Daniel 257
Mathews, Guillermo 257
Mathews, Hugh 185
Mathews, John 33
Mathews, Vm. 257
Mathieu, John A. 156

Mathis, Daniel 257
Mathus, Isariel 140
Matteair, Ezehel 33
Matunin Bernard, P. 257
Matus, Hugh 185, 211
Mau, Ve 92
Maudsley, Pedro 64
Mauger, George 42
Maurace, Pedro 127
Mauran, Juan R. 64
Maureau, Ve 92
Maurice 288
Maurice, J. Bautista 257, 279
Maurice, Ve 92
Mauriceau 92
Mauricio, Antonio 51
Mavor, Christopher 140
Max, George 186, 211
Maxey, Roberto 64
May, Humphrey 186, 211
May, Nielis 186
Maye, Juan Baupta. 288
Mayer, L. 42
Mayers, Jacobo 257, 279
Mayers, Richard 140
Mayes, Abraham 33
Mayes, Stephen 92, 203
Mays, Abraham 113, 127, 140, 156, 186
Mays, Antonio 186
Mays, Stephen 113, 127, 140, 157, 186
Mayses, Richard 157
Mayson, Richard 113, 157
Maza, Fernando de la 64
Mazaes, John 186
Maze, John 92
Mazurier, Ma. 27
Mc. Jeannis 92
Mc. Moleo, Pacolo 257

327

McAuley Bartlet, N. 42
McBey, Silas 186
McBilland, Thomas 186, 211
McBluce, Thomas 186, 211
McBride, John 186, 211
McCabe, Edward 113, 186
McCable, Edouard 157.
McCaland, David 140
McCanza, William 257
McCartney, John 186, 211
McCay, Robert 257, 279
McChisholm, Hugh 257, 278
McClachlan, Patricio 225
McCleery, Juan 64
McCleland, Jacobo 257
McCleland, Juan 258
McClelland, John 258
McClendon, Joel 34
McClentiek, William 186, 211
McClor, James 186
McCluer, Walter 27
McClur, Jose 225
McCoklmeck, Johen 258
McColler, David 74
McCollock, James 186, 211
McColums, Anselme 284
McComas, Tomas 225
McCome, Juan 225
McComohy, Anthony 186
McCormack, John 186
McCormick, David 64
McCormick, Mathias 258
McCormier 92
McCourtney, Jose 258
McCoy, Donald 27, 113,

186
McCullock, Jacobo 258
McCullock, James 258
McCullock, Mateo 114, 186
McCully, Jorge 258
McCurtin, Cornelius 34
McDanel 92
McDaniel, John 92
McDermot, Patricio 114, 186
McDermot, Thomas 186, 211
McDewal, Azon 225
McDonal, James 225
McDonald 258
McDonel, Jayme 258
McDonell, Alexandro 258
McDougle, G. 114, 186
McDouyel, Alexander 186, 212
McDowell, Donald 64
McDuffey, Arch 114, 140,186
McDugall, William 157, 212
McElhanny, William 42
McElroy, James 186, 212
McEnery, Jayme 64
McEnery, Juan 64
Mceter, John 186
McFagin, John 186, 212
McFarlan, Samuel 225
McFarland, David 114, 186
McFarland, James 140
McFarland, John 140, 157
McFarlan, Jacobo 258
McFarley, Jacob 258
McFarten, John 92
McFee, Constancia 64

McFee, Juan 114, 186
McGaney, Hugh 186, 212
McGerg, Hugh 186
McGilivray, Fendly 34
McGill, Daniel 114, 186
McGill, James 140, 186, 212
McGill, Thomas 140, 212
McGillivray, Fineley 34
McGillivray, James 34
McGlaccon, Edmond 34
McGlaccon, James 34
McGlaughlin, John 34
McGovebick, Rubin 157, 212
McGreen, Thomas 186
McGrew, James 27
McGrew, John 27, 34
McGuore, Hugh 157, 212
Mchan, Moses 140
McHandy, Robert 64
McHanlos, G. 127
McHatin, John 186, 212
McHeath, Patricio 114, 186
McIntire, John 34
McIntoche, William 114, 157, 186
McIntosh, Eunice 114, 140, 157, 186
McIntosh, James 74, 140
McIntosh, Jaques 74
McIntosh, John 34
McIntosh, Juan II. 64
McIntosh, Samuel 127
McIntosh, William 187, 212
McIntyre, James 114, 127, 187
McIntyre, John 187, 212
McIntyre, Peter 34
McKan, Moses 140

328

McKay, Pedro 258
McKensie, Frederick 42
McKentoche, Abner 258
McKenzey, James 187, 212
McKey, Daniel 187
McKinney, James 258
McKnight, Jorge 187
McKoy, Guillermo 258, 284
McLan, A 42
McLane, Malcolm 203
McLanen, Js. 92
McLaughlin, Batt 258
McLaughlin, Henry 187, 212
McLean, James 258
McLean, Juan 64
McLeanham 288
McLeary, Hugo 225
McLehlil, Alexandro 288
McLen, Juan 225
McMean, Patrick 140
McMillan, James 258
McMollen, Jacobo 258
McMulen, Jayme 225
McMullen, James 34, 140
McMullin, Jayme 140
McMurray, John 140
McNamie, Pedro 27
McNanuer, Peter 27
McNeal, James 288
McNeil, Orniel 64
Mconohy, Anthony 187, 212
Mcor, Samuel 127
McPin, Miguel 225
McPin, Roveut 225
McPurg, Alexandro 225
McQueen, Santiago 64
McRuite, Juan 225
MCullogh, John 34

McVoy, E. 187, 212
McYnfere, George 187, 212
Meace, James 258
Meaces, Jacobo 258
Meares, Jacobo 258
Mecanty, Juan 225
Mecleman, Jayme 225
Meco, Juan 92
Meders, Edward 92
Medows, Edward 34
Meek Falam, Juan 225
Meers, Samuel 64
Megochan, John 34
Meighan, Edmund 42
Meighan, Edward 42
Meighan, Laurence 42
Meigs, Daniel 64
Melançon, Bto 92
Melançon, Jh 92
Melayes, Luis 258
Meley, Tomas 258
Melivies, Miguel 258
Melln, William 187
Mellon, Arthur 258, 259, 278
Meloche, Antonio 259, 280
Melone, John 93
Meloni, Patricio 225
Melos, Ysabel 51, 57
Mendez, F. 51, 57
Menjiez, Archibald 187, 212
Menzies, Archibald 140
Meolloh, Guillaume 93
Mercer 42
Mercer, Heyland 64
Mercer, Pedro 280
Meredie, Daniel 288
Merel, Johon 225
Merient, Juan Francisco 225

Merier, Thomas 187, 212
Merrey, Francisco 27
Merrey, Samuel 27
Mersié, Carlos 288
Mersten, John 93
Mertuin, Jacobo 259
Mesa, Gabriel 52
Mescen, William 225
Mesias, Maria 52
Metic, Jerome 288
Metivi, Luis 259
Mettez, Joseph 259
Mettord, Jacob 187, 212
Meuice, George 259
Meullion 93
Meyer, Levis 42
Mgillivray, James 34
Mgillivray, Lachlin 34
Mgillivray, Laughlin 34
Mguay, Samuel 187
Mice, Juan 225
Michel, Alexandro 187
Michel, David 157
Michel, Francisco 259
Michel, Jose 259
Michel, Ma. 27
Migal, Daniel 64, 140, 187
Migal, Jose 64
Migrot, Roswell 187
Migue, Jean 93
Miguel, Andres 225
Miguel, David 127
Miguel, Francisco 225
Milan, Pb.e 93
Milburn, Enrrique 114, 187
Milchez, Lawrence 187, 212
Miler, Arch. 187
Miler, Jacob 74
Miles, Samuel 64

329

331

332

142, 158, 190
Pipi, Guillermo 227
Pips, Abner 116, 190
Pips, G. Nesey 190
Pirrie, James 75
Pitipier, Jorge 94
Pitipier, Joseph 94
Pitipier, Juan 94
Pitre 94
Pitt, Charles 43
Pitt, William 43
Pittman, Boner 190, 213
Pittman, Bukner 116, 190
Pittman, Noah 142, 213
Plaine, Daily 289
Plannet, Charliy 142
Platner, Henry 116, 142, 158, 190
Plesent, Nara 227
Plyapper, G. 43
Podras, Julian 75
Pointe, Pae La 94
Poirel, Flin 94
Poirez, Ches 94
Poirier, Pedro 263, 280
Pok, Alexandro 227
Poldevin, Roberto 263
Pollock, Jorge 94
Pollock, Thomas 142, 203
Polter, Ebenezer 190
Polter, Juan 191
Pomry, Tomas 227
Ponce de Leon, Jose 65
Ponell, Antonio 65
Pons, Ana 65
Pons, Mathias 65
Pontbent, Francisco 263
Pontell, Tomas 263
Poor, Patrick 34
Poplin, James 35
Porborn, Jacob 142

Porcer, Hugo 227
Pordun, Thomas 280
Poret, Jeau 75
Pornel, Manke 95
Porter 53, 58
Porter, Andrew 191, 213
Porter, Samuel 116, 191
Portugais, Francisco 289
Potten, Guilliano 142
Potter, Ebenezer 116, 191
Potter, Obadiah 65
Potts, John 43
Potts, Thomas 43
Pouneuf, Pablo 263
Pountney, William 116, 158
Poupan, Rene 65
Pourchous, Antonio 116, 191
Poussett, Francis 75
Povus, Daniel (son) 127
Powel, Marke 127
Power, Enrique 227
Power, Samuel 263
Power, Tomas 263
Powers, James 35
Pradier 95
Pradon, Alexandre 142
Prater, William 95
Prather, Ricardo 227
Pratt, Juan 65
Prejean, Chs. 95
Prejean, Marin 95
Presler, Pedro 191
Presley, Pedro 116, 191
Pressete, Juan 263
Preston, Guillermo 116, 191
Preta, Ysabel 53, 58
Pretchet, Juan 263
Pretgel, Juan 280

Prethon, Juan 263
Prevol, Ve 95
Price, Leonardo 116, 191
Price, Lurvilling 191, 213
Price, Samuel 43

Prichard, Roberto 66
Pride, Jaime 263
Prince, Yh. 95
Principe, Francisco 227
Principe, Ynico 227
Pringle, James 191
Prisman, Than 95
Pritchard, Juan 263
Pritchards, Job 116, 191
Prock, Mathias 142
Proctor, Reuben 116, 158, 191
Proffitt, George 75
Profit, (dead) 75
Profit, Carlos 75, 227
Progene, Jose 227
Prosper, Juan 95
Prospero, Juan 95
Protzman, Enry 191
Prouet, Besley 28
Provange, Daniel 95
Provem, Samuel 263
Provoit, Poisely 158
Prowell, William 28
Prudome, Tomas 263
Pruett, Beezely 191
Pruit, Beesley 116, 127, 159, 191
Publico, Jose 53
Puente, Pedro de la 53
Pughs, David 191, 213
Puller, Nataniel 191, 213
Pulson, Captain 142
Pupu, F. Maria 263
Purcell, Joseph 53, 58

Purdon, Guillermo 227
Purnell, William 43
Pusly, Abil 227
Putman, Buckey 191
Pyatte, Jacobo 116, 191
Pyburn, Jacob 28
Queburne, Jones 263
Quenez, Antonio 263
Quenez, Pedro 263
Querkil 95
Quibau, Carls 263
Quin, Juan 227
Quin, Patrick 191, 213
Quin, William 227
Quinelty 95
Quinisime 95
Quinlin, Jayme 227
Quintana, Miguel 53
Quirk, Edmond 127, 142, 159
Quirk, William 127
Quirot, Juan 263, 280
Quithe, Benjamin 35
Rab, Nicolas 127
Rab, Nicolas (father) 142
Rab, Nicolas (son) 142
Raby, Cader 116, 128, 159, 191
Racine, Francisco 263, 264, 280
Racine, J. Bautista 264, 280
Ragan, Thomas 227
Rahos, William 142, 213
Railli, Miguel 264
Raily, George 142
Rain, Jose 227
Rain, Roberto 227
Raines, Samuel 128
Rainsford, Captain 53, 58
Raitre, Me. 95
Rajer, Alexandro 264
Raley, Cader 191

Rallis, Juan 128
Ramard, Rd. 95
Ramer, Miguel 116, 191
Ramos, Melchora 53
Ramsey 53, 58
Ramsey, Geoffroy 264
Randal, Samuel 264
Randell, Tensa 116, 191
Randolf, Henry 159
Random, Andrew 142
Randon, John 28
Rane, Cornellius 28
Rangez, Pedro 264
Ranmeson, Martin 191, 213
Ranner, Samuel 116, 191
Ransford, John 95
Rap, Nicolas 142
Rapali, Garred 75
Rapalie, Garza 75
Rapalise, Juana 116, 191
Rapalye, Garet 191
Rapalye, Isaac 116, 191
Rapalye, Santiago 116, 191
Rasles, Mathieu 284
Rasmus, Daniel 191, 213
Ratcliffe (Rattef), W. 127, 142, 159
Ratcliffe, John 116, 159, 191
Ratleff, William 35, 116, 191
Ratler, Juan 227
Ratliff, D. 95
Raunsford, John 35
Ravas, Samuel 191
Ray, Archibel 142, 213
Rayan, Daniel 227
Rayburn, George 43
Rayen, Jacobo 264, 280
Rayen, Jacoby 264

Rayen, James 264, 280
Rayley, Michel 280, 281
Rayner, Daniel 159
Raysals, Thomas 159
Read, Hardy 35
Read, Jose 227
Reagan, George 264
Reagan, George N. 264
Reah, Frances 35
Reaid, Juan 191
Real, William 142
Reburn, John 264
Redick, Samuel 191
Ree, Azov 281
Rees, Azov 281
Reed 95
Reed, Ezra 66
Reed, Juan 264
Reed, Lebbeus 66
Reed, Thomas 116, 159, 191
Rees, (widow of) 264
Rees, Arturo 264
Rees, Azon 264
Rees, Huberd 35
Reese 35
Reflen, Carlos 227
Regger, Juan 66
Regh, Morris 264
Reide, William 95
Reilley, Mathias 264
Reilly, Tomas 116, 191
Relyn, Juan 95
Remington, Thomas 43
Remington, Tomas A. 43
Renato, Jesse 227
Rendeau, Joachin 264
Rendeau, Jose 264, 265
Rendon, Juana 53, 58
Renekin, Enrrique 227
Rennalls, Mr. 43
Reston, Thomas 35
Reyan, George 265

336

337

338

339

Shey, Joseph 194, 214
Shilling, Bolser 194
Shilling, Jacob 117, 194
Shilling, Palser 117, 128, 159, 194
Shilling, Polsen 159
Shirky, Patrick 194
Shoals, Christopher 143, 214
Sholar, Levi 75
Shonaner, Juan 117, 194
Short, John 159
Short, William 159, 194, 214
Shote, John 143
Show, Hugh 194
Shrank, Thomas 228
Shreeve, Ysrael 268
Shunk, John, 128, 143, 159, 194
Shvoly, John 194, 214
Sibbald, Jorge 66
Sibley, Joseph 96
Siebert, Philip 268
Sieur, Noel Antoine 268
Sigues, Juan 281
Silch, Waling 268
Silc, Abner 160
Siliven, Tomas 194
Silkezag, William 160
Silkreg, Guillermo 117, 143, 194
Silvestre, Yh 96
Simes, Jean 96
Simmons, Charles 118, 128, 143, 160, 194
Simmons, James 143, 160
Simms, Eduardo 228
Simon, Gilbert 35
Simoneau, Francisco 289
Simple, David 268, 284
Simpson, Henry 160

Simpson, John 54, 58, 160
Simpson, Walter 66
Sims, Mathew 203
Sinal, Tomas 289
Sinclair, Gaspar 194
Sinclair, G. Mitchel 118, 143, 160, 194
Sincops, Josepha 268
Single, Adam 96
Singleton, Jayne 194
Sinson, Tomas 228
Siuwwieux, Jose 281
Sivesay, David 118, 194
Sivezay, Gabriel 118, 194
Siwasey, Emanuel 43
Six, Adams 228
Skerelles, Jacobo 268
Skerettes, Jacobo 268
Skerrett, Isidore 268
Skipper, Michel 28
Slater, Hugh 118, 194
Slater, Joseph 118, 143, 194
Slats, Antony 194, 214
Slaughter, John 194, 214
Slites, Juan 268
Sloan, A. 118, 143, 194, 214
Sloan, James 194
Sloan, Patrick 194
Slockhowe, Anos 228
Slone, Arthur 194, 214
Slone, Joseph 194, 215
Slory, Sprint 194, 215
Slusher, John Jacob 43
Sluter, Juan 118, 194
Small, Joseph 194
Small, Juan 228
Smides, Juan 228
Smiley, Thomas 118, 143, 194

Smily, Juan (son) 195
Smily, Thomas 128, 160
Smis, Juan 75
Smit, Benjamin 195
Smit, Guillermo 54, 58
Smit, Jorge 228
Smit, Juan 228
Smit, Maria 54, 58
Smit, Tomas 228
Smith, Adolphus F. 118, 203
Smith, B. 75, 128
Smith, Calvin 118, 195
Smith, Carlos 195
Smith, Catalina 118, 195
Smith, Christopher 195, 215
Smith, Clarisa 43
Smith, David 118, 128, 143, 160, 195
Smith, Dury 43
Smith, Ebenezer 118, 128, 160, 195
Smith, Eduardo 195, 215
Smith, Eleaezer 195
Smith, Elias 118, 195
Smith, Elisha 195, 215
Smith, Esequias 66
Smith, George 28, 128
Smith, Godfrey 195, 215
Smith, Henry 289
Smith, Hugh 195
Smith, Israel 128, 143, 203
Smith, J. A. 43
Smith, Jacques 75
Smith, James 75, 118, 128, 143, 160, 195, 215
Smith, John 35, 118, 128, 143, 160, 195, 215
Smith, John H. 44

340

Smith, John Moses 118, 203
Smith, Joseph 160, 195, 215
Smith, Lucins 118, 195
Smith, Lucius 160
Smith, Luis 195
Smith, Lutheo 96
Smith, Madama 75
Smith, Martin 118, 160
Smith, Mathew 268
Smith, Peter 118, 128, 160, 195
Smith, Phel. 195
Smith, Philander 118, 128, 143, 160, 195
Smith, Philetus 118, 160
Smith, Philinu 118, 195
Smith, Philitus 118, 195
Smith, Phitalus 160
Smith, Randolph 143
Smith, Reuben 195, 215
Smith, Richard 143, 215
Smith, Robert 195, 215
Smith, Samuel 128, 143
Smith, Simeon 284
Smith, Tere 118, 195
Smith, the Widow 118, 195
Smith, T. 35, 44, 96, 118, 160, 195, 215, 268, 284
Smith, William 97, 118, 128, 143, 160, 195, 203, 228, 268
Smith, William B. 143, 160
Smith, Zacarias 195
Smith, Zacarias (son) 195
Smith, Zachariah 118, 143, 160
Smith, Zachariah (father)

118, 203
Smith, Zachariah (son) 118, 203
Smiz, Jacobo 268
Sneer, Tomas 160
Snell, Christian 97
Snell, Christopher 35
Snell, Henrique 28
Snelling, Richard 44
Snikler, Gaspar 160
Snoddy, Andres 228
Snoddy, William 28
Snody, Andy 195, 215
Snow, Isaac 97
Snow, Isaiah 97
Soasen, Joseph 268
Soileau, Aug. 97
Soileau, J. B. 97
Soileau, Noel 97
Sola, Jose 54
Soldener, Francisco 268
Soles, Moses 268
Solidet, Samuel 128
Solivan, William 160
Solivester 118, 195
Sollin, A. Auguste 268
Solomon, Hyam 35
Soloven, Daniel 195
Somes, Juan 284
Sommers, Juan 268
Sorel 97
Soto, Don M. de 97
Soto, Maria Josefa 54
Souderis 97
Soudre, Carlos 228
Soues, Juan 268
Soulie, Juan Luis 97
Southerland, William 44
Spaekman, Juan 195, 215
Spain, Francis 118, 128, 160, 196
Spain, Jaime 118, 196

Spalden, James 196
Spalding, James 169, 215
Speirs, William 35
Spericot, Mathieu 97
Spicer, Cristopher 66
Spins, Juan 196
Spires, Juan 119, 128, 160, 196
Splun, Tomas 119, 196
Springel, Jacob 196
St Louis 97
St. Jean, Luis 268
St. Martin, Madama 268
Sta Maria, Pedro 196, 215
Stachey, Joshua 97
Stacy, Joshua 35
Staiter, Joseph 160
Stampley, G. 119, 128, 143, 160, 196
Stampley, H. 119, 128, 143, 160
Stampley, Jacob 119, 143, 196
Stampley, John 119, 128, 143, 160, 196
Stampley, M. 119, 196
Stampley, Peter 143
Stan, Steven 44
Standley, Benjamin 144
Standley, Joseph 144
Stanley, Robert 97
Stark, Robert 97, 119, 196
Starkey, Jayme 268
Staybraker, John 196
Ste Mair, Joseph 268
Steddam, Moyse 28
Steel, John 35, 119, 144, 160
Steen, Samuel 75
Stefen, Jacob 196

Sutton Baulis, Richard 161
Suzget, Carlos 129
Swafford, Thomas 28
Swanson, Peter 55, 58
Swasey, Elija 119, 129, 144, 161
Swayze, David 197
Swayze, Stephen 97, 204
Swazey, Elija 161
Swazey, Gabriel 119, 144, 161, 197
Swazey, John 119, 129, 161
Swazey, N. 119, 129, 144, 161, 197
Swazey, R. 119, 129, 144, 161, 197
Swazey, Samuel 119, 129, 144, 161, 197
Swazey, Sarah 144
Sweezey, Samuel 144
Sweyze, Evan 197
Swillevant, Patrick 28
Tabor, I. 97, 119, 129, 161, 197
Tabor, W. 119, 129, 144, 161, 197
Tacheu, Jonas 228
Tait, Robert 55, 58
Taitt, Guillermo 197, 215
Take, Juan 119, 197
Take, Miguel 119, 197
Talbert, Juan 269
Talet, William 197
Talkiner, Enrique 228
Tambleston, Vath N. 197
Tampson, George 44
Tamus 97
Taner, Jose 269
Tang, Joseph Chas 28

Tanis, Nicolas 289
Tanner, David 119, 129, 161
Tardiveau, Bartholome 228, 269
Tarinton, Tomas 120, 197
Tarteron Labeaume, L. 269, 284
Tasaid, Samuel 228
Tastelly, Antonio 269
Tate, Eduard 66
Tate, John 197, 215
Tats, John 161
Tavely, James 120, 161
Tavis, Joseph 35
Taylor, Abraham 144, 161
Taylor, Grace 44
Taylor, Isaac 120, 161, 197, 215
Taylor, Joe 44
Taylor, Jorge 66
Taylor, Juan 228
Taylor, Peter 97, 197, 215
Taylor, Roberto 269
Taylor, Thomas 35, 36
Taylor, William 98, 269
Teahan, Memon 98
Teal 97
Teasdale, Isaac 66
Tebbs, James 269
Teeling, Luve 44
Teflo, Mathias 28
Teissieu, Nicolas 282
Telar, Nicolas 228
Tell, Stephen 144, 215
Tellet, William 44
Temer, Robert 98
Temple, Guillermo 228
Templete, Juan 98
Teneron, Patricio 228

Tengleton, Joseph
Tening, Pedro 66
Tenio, widow 76
Tennan, Daniel 197, 215
Tepedor, Andres 228
Tepeltylas, Daniel 197, 215
Terbonnes, Ve 98
Terbonnesairy 98
Terio, Eusebio 76
Terney, George 144
Terrioz, Paul 98
Terry, Jaime 120, 197
Terry, John 120, 144, 161, 197
Tervin, Richard 28

Tesien, Nicolas 269
Tesserot, Joseph 289
Tesson 98
Testa, Pedro de 98
Tete, Jayme 228
Tetro, J. Bautista 269
Tetroic, J. Bautista 269
Teusieu, Nicolas 282
Texada, M. 120, 129, 161
Texton, Askin 28
Thechelet, Levi 269
Theque, Juan 282
Theriau, Marie 98
Theuy 98
Thibaudol, Pre 98
Thibaudoz, Ans. 98
Thibaudoz, Ant. 98
Thibaudoz, Ofr. 98
Thibaudoz, There 98
Thilluerp, Robert 98
Thiriet, C. 269, 270
Thiriot, Juan 270
Thockmorton, M. 197
Thomas, Enrique 76
Thomas, Enrriche 98

343

Trahan, Yn. 98
Trahan, Yoh 98
Trapp, Jean 44
Trasher, Juan 120, 198
Trasuer, Federico 67
Travellion, Richard 198
Travers, Guillermo 67
Travers, Thomas 67
Travis, James 55, 58
Tremble, J. Bautista Du 270
Trenor, Patricio 67
Trenthan, Martin 161, 216
Treplot, George 161
Tresgel, Jose 55
Trevilion, Temple S. 198
Trevillon, R. 120, 144, 161
Tribeaut, Nicolas 270
Trichel, Juan B. 289
Trijo, Charles 144
Trimble, Jacob 198
Triste, Widow 99
Trocaubrout, Andres 270, 271
Troucaubrout, Juan 282
Troche, Pedro 289
Trockmorton, Mordica 120, 198
Troclebroad, Juan 271
Troop, Jorge 120, 198
Trouittes, Pedro 28
Troup, George 36
Troy, Mrs. 44
Trudey, Baptista 129
Truely, Benet 120, 129, 161, 198
Truely, J. 120, 129, 144, 161, 198
Truman, Tomas 129
Trunbull, Juan 67
Truvins, John 198, 216

Tsenhood, B. 129, 144
Tucanbrote, Julian (hijo) 269
Tucker, Betty 44
Tucker, Charles 36
Tucker, William 44
Tuertiment, Tomas 271
Tule, Juan 229
Tullie, Jean Charles 76
Tullier, Juan 99
Tullier, Ysidoro 99
Tulter, Charles 99
Tuluje, Noel 229
Tuncote, Jose 271
Tunlof, Presting 198
Tunnay, Francisco 271
Turboys, Juan 271
Turdue, Guillermo 67
Turent, Jose 271
Turfey, Patricio 129
Turnbull, John 36, 76
Turnbull, Walter 36
Turner, Matheo 161
Turner, Roberto 198
Turney, George 144
Turney, Mathew 198
Turpin, P. Pleasant 120, 129, 144, 161, 198
Tustiman, Tomas 271
Tuuceret, Antorire 271
Tuvey, John 129, 144
Tuvis, Juan 198
Tux, John 198
Tuy, Nataniel 129
Twely, Nataniel 120, 198
Twins, Tomas 120, 198
Tybse, Juan 282
Tyler, Elisha 44
Ublesilde, Enrique 229
Ulmen, Guillermo 67
Underwood, Jehu 67
Underwood, T. 55, 58

Uph, Jacob 198, 216
Upham, Roberto 271, 284
Urchy, Juan 229
Ury, Roberto 129
Usher, Joseph 144
Usher, William 44
Ussé, Pedro 99
Utley, Elisha 67
Vachard, Antonio 271
Vachet, Francisco 271, 282
Vachette, Antonio 271, 284
Vadeboncoeur 271
Vadeboncoeur, Pedro 271, 282
Vadeboncon, Pedro 271
Vahan, John 161
Valbenda, Antonio 271
Valentine, Jas. 44
Valete, Francisco 271
Vallancurt, Francisco 271
Vallepet, Luis 198
Valois, Luis 271
Valrelimant, Ketez 271
Van Hooke, Samuel 271
Vancheret, Jose 120, 129, 198
Vancheret, Juan 120
Vandenbemden 271
Vandenbemden, Jose 271
Vandenbemden, Julian 271
Vandenbemden, Luis 271
Vandenlenden, Jose 272
Vandernaiy, Pedro 272
Vanderstines, Pedro 272
Vandevoas, John 199,

345

347